AFTER JUTLAND

D1572389

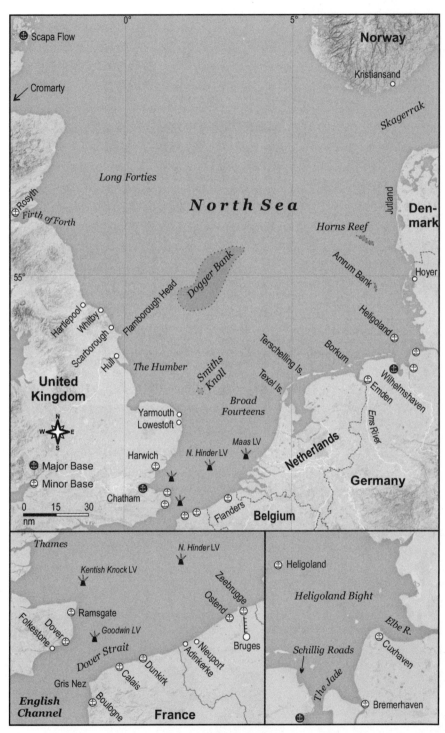

Map 1.1 **The North Sea**

AFTER JUTLAND

The Naval War in Northern European Waters, June 1916–November 1918

James Goldrick

Naval Institute Press
Annapolis, Maryland

This book was made possible through the dedication
of the U.S. Naval Academy Class of 1945.

Naval Institute Press
291 Wood Road
Annapolis, MD 21402

Library of Congress Cataloging-in-Publication Data is available.
978-1-68247-327-6 (hardcover)
978-1-68247-328-3 (eBook)

♾ Print editions meet the requirements of ANSI/NISO z39.48-1992
(Permanence of Paper).
Printed in the United States of America

26 25 24 23 22 21 20 19 18   9 8 7 6 5 4 3 2 1
First printing

All maps in this book are courtesy Vincent P. O'Hara.

Contents

Illustrations

Maps

Acknowledgments

I REMAIN VERY GRATEFUL TO David Stevens for his constant friendship and help, including the benefit of his own extensive research into the Great War navies. I want to recognize a continuing debt to Vice Admiral Peter Jones, Professor Jon Sumida, and Dr. Nicholas Lambert. I am also grateful to my friends of the Sea Power Centre–Australia and the splendid staff of the library of the Australian Defence Force Academy. Similar thanks go to Steve Prince and the equally splendid staff of the Royal Navy's Historical Branch at Portsmouth, as well as the staffs of Churchill College Archives, the Royal Naval Museum Library, the Liddell Hart Centre, the UK National Archives, the National Maritime Museum, the Liddle Collection, the Imperial War Museum, and the United States Naval War College Historical Collection.

Vince O'Hara very generously drew the maps for this book, for which I am particularly grateful, and provided me with much good advice. I should note that Vince's help has been typical of the kindness and support I have had from other historians. Stephen McLaughlin and Toby Erwin have both been extremely helpful with material about the Russian navy, while Stephen put me in touch with Sergei Vinogradov, who very kindly provided photographs of Russian ships and people. Dr. Michael Epkenhans assisted me with my inquiries about certain aspects of German operations and very kindly consented to my use of quotations from some of his own scholarly— and extremely important—work on the Imperial German Navy. Brigadier General Michael Clemmesen was equally helpful in relation to his own work on the Great War. I am grateful to Simon Harley, not only for letting me have a copy of his draft work on the diary of Admiral Duff, but for the efforts that he and others have done to put material on line in The Dreadnought Project. Dr. Jann Witt made available photographs from Archive of the German Naval Association, Laboe, for which I am also very thankful, as I am to Michael Pocock of Maritime Quest for his generous assistance.

Grateful acknowledgment is made for permissions to quote the works cited herein. For those whose literary heirs and original publishers I have been unable to trace, may I here record my acknowledgments. In addition to the literary executors of the estates concerned, I am grateful to the master and fellows of Churchill College for access to the papers of Admiral Sir Reginald Plunkett-Ernle-Erle-Drax and Vice Admiral Leslie Ashmore. I am grateful to the Trustees of the National Maritime Museum for access to the papers of Admiral of the Fleet Earl Beatty and Admiral of the Fleet Sir Henry Oliver and Admiral Sir Barry Domvile, Admiral Sir Alexander Duff, Admiral Sir Louis Hamilton, Admiral Sir Herbert Richmond, and Admiral Sir William Tennant; to the trustees of the Imperial War Museum for the papers of Admiral Sir William Goodenough, Admiral Sir Trevylyan Napier, Admiral Sir Richard Phillimore, Vice Admiral Lord Ashbourne, Vice Admiral Sir Cecil Talbot, Captain Sir Philip Bowyer-Smyth, Captain Oswald Halifax, Captain the Honorable P. G. E. Acheson, Commander C. H. Drage, and Commander J. H. Bowen; to the University of Leeds for the papers of Admiral Sir Harold Burrough, Admiral Sir Matthew Best, Admiral Sir Morgan Singer, Captain A. W. Clarke, Captain R. W. Blacklock, and Captain R. F. Nichols; to the Liddell Hart Centre at King's College London for the papers of Captain J. M. Howson. My particular thanks go to the editor of *The Naval Review,* Vice Admiral Sir Jeremy Blackham, for the permission to cite articles from *The Naval Review.*

Notwithstanding my debt to so many, I emphasize that the judgments and interpretations in the text are mine alone, as is the responsibility for any errors.

Abbreviations

CMB	coastal motor boat
DSO	Companion of the Distinguished Service Order
DNI	Director of Naval Intelligence
HMAS	His Majesty's Australian Ship
HMS	His Majesty's Ship
NID	Naval Intelligence Division
NNW	north-northwest
RAN	Royal Australian Navy
RFC	Royal Flying Corps
RM	Royal Marines
RN	Royal Navy
RNAS	Royal Naval Air Service
RNR	Royal Naval Reserve
RNVR	Royal Naval Volunteer Reserve
SNIS	Service of Observation and Communications (Russian navy)
SSE	south-southeast
SSW	south-southwest
USN	United States Navy
VC	Victoria Cross

Table of Equivalents

Guns

Metric	British
75-mm	3-inch
88-mm	3.4-inch
105-mm	4.1-inch
150-mm	5.9-inch
21-cm	8.2-inch
28-cm	11-inch
30.5-cm	12-inch
38-cm	15-inch

Torpedoes

Metric	British
45-cm	17.7-inch
45.7-cm	18-inch
50-cm	19.7-inch
53.3-cm	21-inch

Distances

All distances in this book are given in nautical miles giving the old Admiralty mile as the reference for the nautical mile. This is one minute of arc subtended along a great circle. It is some 4 feet or 1.248 meters longer than the current nautical mile.

1 nautical mile = 1,853.2 meters = 6,080 feet

1 knot = 1 nautical mile per hour

Compass

360 degrees in a circle

32 points in a circle

1 point = 11¼ degrees

8 points = 90 degrees

16 points = 180 degrees (reversal of course)

AFTER JUTLAND

Introduction

AFTER JUTLAND EXAMINES THE NAVAL CONFLICT in northern European waters for the last two-and-a-half years of the Great War. The principal subject of this book, as in *Before Jutland*, is the Royal Navy, but the analysis extends to the Imperial German Navy and the Imperial Russian Navy, as well as to the United States Navy after April 1917. Furthermore, although its operations on France's northern coasts were on a much smaller scale than its allies or its protagonists, attention is given to the ships of the French Navy that operated alongside the Dover Patrol.

This book's precursor, *Before Jutland*, assessed the responses in 1914–15 to the challenges created by new technologies; it sought to explain how the protagonists coped with the mass of unexpected problems they encountered, resulting in forms of naval warfare unlike anything ever before experienced. *After Jutland* takes up the story when two years of war and a succession of major engagements as well as a multitude of small-scale encounters had created a body of hard-won experience in each navy, while many of the new technologies had achieved a level of capability unthinkable before 1914. Although the present volume strives to work within an understanding of the external factors at play, most notably the evolution of national strategies as nations sought to bring the conflict to a successful conclusion, its focus is not so much naval high command as naval operations. Space does not permit a narrative of every encounter but using select examples, I have tried to provide a more complete understanding of what happened at sea in the years between the Battle of Jutland and the passage of the German High Sea Fleet to internment on 21 November 1918. The naval conflict in this period involved much more sustained effort and attrition than the popular image of Grand Fleet battleships idle in Scapa Flow and High Sea Fleet squadrons moribund in their anchorages allows.

This book does not describe every aspect of the war against the U-boats; that subject has been addressed by other authorities. Rather, although it examines the challenges of detecting and attacking U-boats (because these problems bear upon so many aspects of naval operations in the First World War) its principal concern with the campaign is how U-boat suppression affected the main fleets. Arguably, the subject of *After Jutland* is the war behind the U-boat war and the war behind the Allied blockade of the Central Powers. The main fleets of each nation protected their own campaigns of economic warfare while also seeking to achieve decisive effects against their opposition. In this they failed, although in failing they created an apparent stalemate that both permitted and intensified the U-boat campaign and the Allied blockade. Both sides could provide the cover of their main fleets necessary for these endeavors, but they found it impossible to undermine the protection provided to the elements that were doing so much damage to them elsewhere. It was a situation in which there was not one predominant naval power but a dispersion of fleets in being, which by their very existence limited the options of their enemies but could not prevent their opponents from conducting what can best be termed the "war of supply."

After Jutland tries to elucidate why, despite extraordinary advances in material and techniques since 1914, operations apparently succeeded in nothing more substantial than maintaining the status quo. Our principal questions are these: first, whether the navies of this study achieved all that they might have between 1916 and 1918, given both the capabilities and the limitations of the ships and weapons they had to hand; and second, if the navies did not succeed, why was this so?

After Jutland is more forthright in many of its judgments than its predecessor, *Before Jutland*. This is first the result of critical demand from readers; some felt that more could have been said about the subject. But I may also be more confident in my analysis and alert to the lessons of naval warfare that should reasonably have been learned by 1916, even if the personnel of 1914 can be excused their ignorance. Nevertheless, I have tried to preserve a measure of charity, based on my own experience and mistakes at sea. The words of one of the most attractive personalities of the war, who died when his flagship *Invincible* exploded on 31 May 1916, were quoted in the concluding paragraph of *Before Jutland* and they remain relevant. When observing the failures of another officer at sea, Rear Admiral the Honorable H. L. A. Hood observed, "There but for the grace of God goes Horace Hood."[1] While researching, analyzing, and describing events at sea between 1916 and 1918 and coming to understand just what the seagoing personnel of every navy went through, your author often had cause to think, "There but for the grace of God go I . . ."

June 1916—
The War at Sea

1

A FTER NEARLY TWO YEARS OF WAR, on 31 May 1916, the main fleets had met off the coast of Jutland in the approaches to the Skagerrak. The Battle of Jutland had been fought and come to its apparently inconclusive end. The British had already named the encounter for the land and the Germans the sea, yet both protagonists were hard put to understand the implications of the battle. The British lost fourteen ships and more than 6,700 men killed; the Germans eleven with just over 3,000 dead. The British suffered the shocks of devastating explosions in their battle cruisers and armored cruisers. The Germans lost an old pre-dreadnought the same way, but most of their sinkings came only after much battering by British heavy guns. The British thought they had cut the High Sea Fleet off from its bases, but the Germans succeeded in breaking through the British rear overnight. When dawn came on 1 June, the Grand Fleet was presented with a sea empty of its enemy, but the High Sea Fleet had been hit so hard it would take months to return to full strength. Everything had changed, but nothing had changed. For all the protagonists at sea, the question was, what next?

The naval war had become three dimensional well before the middle of 1916, taking a toll not only of warships but of the merchant ships that in previous conflicts were subject to capture but not destruction without warning. Losses from the Allied transport fleets and among the neutral shipping that contributed so much to the movement of Allied material and men were of increasing concern, even if the Germans had stepped back from their first unrestricted submarine campaign. The Germans, largely cut off from the globe's resources, were faced with the possibility that U-boats might represent their only tool for breaking a stalemate at sea that paralleled the one that had developed on land.

The new capabilities represented by the submarine were obviously key to this evolution of maritime warfare, but there was more to it. Despite their limitations, both heavier- and lighter-than-air craft had begun to play important roles in both the North Sea and the Baltic, while the greatest single influence on naval operations was the mine, used both offensively and defensively. All four combatants (as well as some of the neutrals) had been forced to expand their minesweeping forces a hundredfold and continuous effort was devoted to keeping swept channels open to both naval forces and merchant shipping. For the British and French, these cleared passages ranged along their coasts and out from their major ports, as well as across the English Channel, while the Germans worked to maintain access to the Heligoland Bight and the shipping passages north to the Danish coast and southwest to the Netherlands. The most important users of the channels in the Bight were the U-boats and it would not be many months before their clearance and protecting the sweepers became the highest priority task of the High Sea Fleet. For their part, the mine defenses of the Gulfs of Finland and Riga remained central to Russian strategy and their protection and renewal in the spring among the principal missions of the Baltic Fleet.

The submarine and mine threats made the naval war increasingly one of small ships, often working in sight of friendly land but in arduous conditions. They were themselves vulnerable to mines, the single greatest cause of losses of small surface ships and submarines during the war. Yet the impost on the flotillas had not diminished the importance of the major fleets, since the patrol forces' safety depended on the protection the heavy ships provided, whether directly or indirectly. Naval staffs were acutely aware that their light craft, many of which were slow and poorly armed conversions of fishing vessels, were extremely vulnerable to surface and even submarine attack. This was most true for the British, who not only had the long and exposed coasts of the British Isles to consider, as well as traffic north and south, but the merchant shipping that moved between the continent and England in the south and crossed to Scandinavia farther north. The Battle of Jutland confirmed the Grand Fleet as the dominant force in northern waters but showed the difficulty of achieving a decisive victory against the High Sea Fleet. It also highlighted material and tactical deficiencies that brought into question the Grand Fleet's superiority over its opponent. The British had long understood that German coastal waters and the Heligoland Bight were too well defended to allow the forward deployment of their battle squadrons, but they were confident an open sea encounter with the High Sea Fleet would achieve decisive results. The reality proved otherwise and to the old problem of how to bring the enemy to action new uncertainties had been added.

The British and the French

The ace in hand for the British had been the increasingly sophisticated signals intelligence organization centered on Room 40 in the Admiralty Old Building. This could never guarantee forewarning of a German sortie, but the British maintained a picture of German dispositions, which meant that they had a good idea which battle squadrons were in the North Sea anchorages and which were operating in the Baltic. It extended to formations such as the torpedo boat flotillas, on which the British kept a close watch for any forward deployment to the Belgian ports. As a result, the British had not only been able to make dispositions to deal directly with predicted German offensive activity but could also manage their own training and refit schedules with some confidence. This was particularly important for the Grand Fleet, since its ability to respond immediately to any major German operation was always least at the time its units, particularly the short-legged destroyers, required refuelling, as was inevitable after a fleet exercise. The ace was still held, but the events of Jutland revealed that it was not enough to win the game while the possibility that the Germans would realize their vulnerability loomed.

Overall control of Britain's naval war rested with the Admiralty in Whitehall. The primary naval member of the Board of Admiralty that supervised the Royal Navy was the First Sea Lord, Admiral Sir Henry Jackson, who had been in office since early 1915. His political chief, the First Lord, was a former prime minister, Arthur Balfour. Jackson's most important assistant for operations was the Chief of the War Staff, Acting Vice Admiral Sir Henry Oliver. The seagoing leadership of British forces in home waters had changed little since the start of the war. Admiral Sir John Jellicoe was appointed commander-in-chief (C-in-C) of the Grand Fleet (and thus of the "Home Fleets" in British waters as a whole) in August 1914. Most of his staff had been with him since that time. The Battle Cruiser Fleet remained under the command of Vice Admiral Sir David Beatty, while the Harwich Force was led by Commodore Reginald Tyrwhitt. Both Beatty and Tyrwhitt had been in these roles since the outbreak of war. Subordinate squadron, division, and capital ship commands were subject to routine rotation, but still had significant continuity. Many captains had been in their ships since the prewar start of a commission. Rear Admiral William Goodenough had been commanding a light cruiser squadron from the cruiser *Southampton* since 1913 and would remain in post a few months yet.

Photo 1.1   **Admiral Jellicoe**   *Sea Power Centre, Australia*

The Royal Navy's major formations were distributed along the British east coast. The battle squadrons that were the core of the Grand Fleet remained at Scapa Flow and Cromarty Firth in the north of Scotland, while the battle cruisers operated out of Rosyth. Each of these forces had assigned cruisers and destroyers. The days of capital ships operating with only a handful of scouting craft had long passed. Another formation, the Third Battle Squadron, consisting of the battleship *Dreadnought* and *King Edward VII*–class pre-dreadnoughts, served as an anchor in the south, based at the Swin anchorage near the mouth of the Thames River. A powerful group of light cruisers and destroyers named after the port of Harwich (where the ships were located) was intended to support the main forces from both north and south, depending upon the contingency. The Eighth Submarine Flotilla, also at Harwich, provided most of the submarines that patrolled the approaches to the Heligoland Bight. While monitoring the blockade in the south presented relatively few challenges, performing that duty in the north required constant patrols by the auxiliary cruisers of the Tenth Cruiser Squadron, which sought to ensure no merchant ship passed without examination.

The historical concern Britain always had for the control of the low countries seemed well justified by the difficulties which German occupation of the Belgian coast represented for British strategy, particularly one focused on maintaining a huge army in France and the material support of an even greater French effort on land, as well as substantial commitments in the Mediterranean and other theaters of war. Possession of the northernmost Channel ports gave the Germans direct access to the English Channel and additional defense in depth of the Heligoland Bight. The operations of the British units stationed in the south were inevitably constrained by the presence of significant German forces on the Flanders coast, even with the assistance the French could provide from their Channel bases. To protect the Channel and to maintain pressure on the Germans on the Flanders coast, a large force of monitors, destroyers, and patrol craft operated as the Dover Patrol under Vice Admiral Sir Reginald Bacon. The British, however, could never be sure whether a German sally from the Heligoland Bight was aimed at the east coast, or would be directed south. It was for this reason the older, but still powerful battleships of the Third Battle Squadron were based in the south and why the Admiralty was loath to send the Harwich Force north unless it was certain what the Germans intended. In practice, the Harwich Force had few opportunities to combine with the Grand Fleet.

Each of the major British and French ports had substantial local forces, including older destroyers, while there were submarines and light craft distributed at Britain's smaller east coast ports, partly as the last-ditch defense against surface bombardment or even a raid ashore, but increasingly to contribute to the antisubmarine patrols maintained along the major shipping lanes and across the U-boat transit routes. Minesweepers were present around the coast in growing numbers, pursuing their unremitting campaign to ensure that port approaches and the all-important war channels for shipping along the coast remained clear. The proliferation of U-boat minelayers made this ever more challenging, since

Photo 1.2

Admiral Wemyss and Admiral Beatty

Sea Power Centre, Australia

there could be little surety that even an area swept a day before remained free of mines.

The difficulties the British faced in closing off the German occupied ports of Ostend and Zeebrugge were additional reason for the Germans to base submarines and light craft there, since they were so much closer to their potential targets. Further, although they had been extraordinarily successful in protecting cross-Channel traffic, British efforts to close the Dover Strait by mines, nets, and patrols were largely ineffective. For all these reasons, the Belgian coast loomed ever larger in British thinking and the recapture or neutralization of both Ostend and Zeebrugge became increasingly important elements in the debates over policy both at sea and on land. In the meantime, the Dover Patrol continued a campaign that was a mix of efforts to block the strait against U-boats and operations against the German forces on the Flanders coast. In this, the British were supported by the much smaller, but hardworking local French naval forces under Vice Admiral Pierre Ronarc'h. If their combined efforts were less successful than they thought, the Anglo-French forces at least complicated the situation for the Germans, whose growing fear of an attack on the Flanders coast was demonstrated by the energy they put into building more heavily armed fortifications.

The Germans

Despite the High Sea Fleet's achievements in what the Germans called the Battle of the Skagerrak, all was not well in the Imperial German Navy. Underlying everything was an increasing sense that the navy was failing the nation, an understanding, admitted or not, that extended to all ranks. Popular dissatisfaction related both to the argument that the naval arms race had made an unnecessary enemy of Britain, as well as the more immediate view that the battle fleet was providing practically no strategic return for the resources invested in it. The disparity between the sacrifices of the army and those of the navy was stark. Jutland moderated the discontent, both national and naval, but its effect was only temporary when it became clear the direct strategic results of the "victory" of the Skaggerak were practically nil. Although many shortages of food, coal, and other materials were due more to poor planning and coordination within Germany than the still incomplete economic blockade, the popular perception was that they resulted from the Royal Navy's control of the seaways and, by association, the inability of the Imperial German Navy to fulfil its promises to the state. What had been a great national project seemed to be a failure. All this meant the potential of the U-boats to change the paradigm was significant for the navy's sense of its own worth, as well as the military and strategic effects the submarines were expected to achieve.[1]

The Imperial German Navy remained hamstrung by a divided system of control theoretically subordinate to the erratic Kaiser Wilhelm II. The Admiralty Staff (the German Admiralstab will be used to avoid confusion) was under the supervision of Admiral Henning von Holtzendorff, but had only limited operational authority, which could be overridden by the kaiser and sometimes ignored by the fleet commander. Other officials, such as the head of the Naval Cabinet, Admiral Georg von Müller, and the state secretary of the Imperial Naval Office (Reichs-Marine-Amt), Admiral Eduard von Capelle, also had direct access to the kaiser and independent supervision of important elements of the service, including personnel and procurement policy. The growing authority of the army's Great General Staff was also influencing naval decision making as the army's controls extended further into the German economy. The navy's ability to secure the resources it needed was increasingly under threat.

The major operational command of the German navy was the High Sea Fleet under Admiral Reinhard Scheer. His authority covered the battle squadrons, scouting groups, and torpedo boat flotillas, as well as the attached U-boat flotillas. Scheer's key subordinate commander was the newly ennobled Franz von Hipper, commander of the scouting groups and principally responsible for the defense of the Heligoland Bight. While his interest was normally the North Sea, Scheer would act as operational commander in the Baltic should the situation demand his presence there. Up to this time, the threat in the eastern sea theater was not such as to require the C-in-C's presence. Overall operational

Photo 1.3
Admiral Scheer
German Naval Association Archive

command of the Baltic continued to be exercised by Grand Admiral Prince Heinrich, the kaiser's younger brother. In both the North Sea and Baltic there were local commands with immediate responsibility for port defenses, but the Heligoland Bight was the responsibility of the High Sea Fleet, while Prince Heinrich had subordinate flag officers assigned to the defense of the passages from the Kattegat and offensive operations against the Russians in the eastern Baltic. The occupied Belgian territories on the Flanders coast had their own naval commander in Admiral Ludwig von Schröder, with authority over the coast defenses and the light forces and U-boats operating from Ostend and Zeebrugge.

The Grand Fleet remained the principal focus of the High Sea Fleet, but this was increasingly in question. The Germans had yet to decide whether the engagement of 31 May to 1 June spelled the end of their hopes for achieving superiority over the enemy force, or whether there were still opportunities to reduce British strength far enough to achieve victory. In the meantime, the Germans' three-front problem continued to nag at them. They faced the British in the North Sea and the Russians in the Baltic, but the potential for a British thrust through the Kattegat and the Baltic passages, possibly in combination with a British amphibious landing and attacks in the Bight and from the Russian fleet, remained a deep concern. The Germans had no strategic depth in this region. The entrance to Kiel Fjord, inside which was their major naval base, was little more than twenty nautical miles from the southern entrance to the Little Belt, the western passage from the Kattegat. The most recent scare of a British attack was as recent as April 1916. It was a fear of which the German commanders had never rid themselves. Admiral Scheer confirmed after

Photo 1.4
Vice Admiral von Hipper
German Naval Association Archive

the war that he always thought a British "Baltic Project" had real potential, if the Royal Navy could have concentrated sufficient force.[2]

A Baltic Project, however, was regarded as unfeasible by most in the Admiralty. The first problem was that any attempt to penetrate the Baltic passages would almost inevitably bring conflict with Denmark and Sweden. The Danes were conscious that the Germans might well preempt a British advance by occupying the country. Anxious to maintain their neutrality, the Danes thus made a point of their intention to prevent the transit of combatant forces, a policy aimed more at the British than their neighbor to the south. Although there were elements in the German navy that regretted the soft approach of leaving Denmark be, the Germans were more concerned that the straits be closed to the Royal Navy than they themselves could utilize the passages at will. In fact, the German navy used the Baltic passages when it needed to. In maintaining their own defensive measures, the Germans enjoyed the tacit cooperation of Denmark's naval commander, Vice Admiral Otto Koefed-Hansen, who had disposed his forces to resist any British attempt to pass the Danish straits and was backed in this by Denmark's foreign minister. Danish naval support had extended to mining the Öresund in what was effectively a three-way arrangement with Sweden, aimed particularly at preventing the passage of British submarines, as well as positioning—and training—their own submarines to dispute any approach by British surface forces.[3]

The British were also acutely aware of the operational challenges inherent in any attempt to break into the Baltic. The possibility of such an attack was the subject of recurrent debate in the Admiralty and within the Grand Fleet, as well as being cherished by a number now outside the tent, such as Lord Fisher, who regretted the diversion of Britain's army to France and the resulting lack of troops to support a descent on the straits. Its practicality had been repeatedly denied by both the War Staff and Jellicoe, although there was recognition the Germans should be put under pressure by operations into the Kattegat, which could at least keep the enemy guessing. Jutland itself had interrupted such a British operation. By 1916 even an attempt by submarines to penetrate the Baltic was considered impossible, given the patrols and minefields. The Germans did not, however, take everything on trust and had supplemented minefields originally laid in the Little Belt with fields south of the other two passages. Neither the Öresund nor the Great Belt could be completely closed, given the need for merchant shipping to move, but the exits from the three passages were constantly watched by

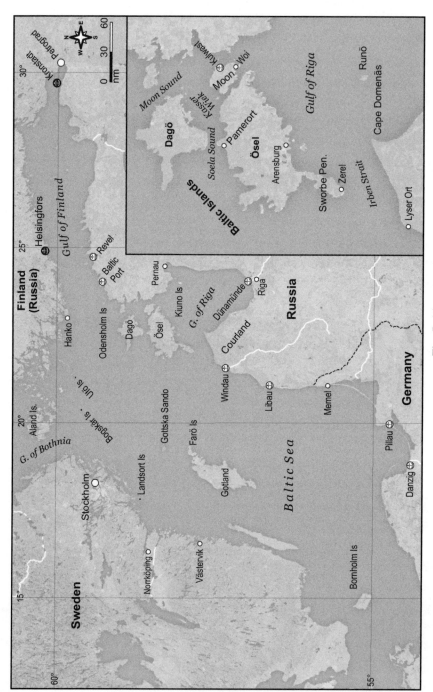

Map 1.2 The Baltic

airships and aircraft, as well as light forces, the latter supported by at least one pre-dreadnought stationed within the protection of nets as a guard ship. This duty was important enough to keep one of the old battleships, *Hannover*, in commission in 1917 when the Second Squadron was withdrawn from operational service.

The Russians

In the Russian view, their own key weakness was the Gulf of Riga. The most straightforward threat was a renewed German land offensive sweeping around the southern coast of the gulf, but if the Germans were to secure control of the islands outside the Gulf of Riga, the effects would be immediate and profound. The seaward flank of the Russian army protecting Riga would become vulnerable to bombardment from the sea, while the Germans could use Ösel (now Saaremaa) and Dago (now Huiimaa) islands as forward operating bases, threatening the naval defenses of the Gulf of Finland and effectively neutralizing the offensive capabilities of at least the surface units of the Baltic Fleet. A German attack in 1915 temporarily penetrated the Gulf of Riga, but at some cost. The Germans claimed a moral victory that helped cement Russian defensive attitudes, but what had become clear was that a successful assault would require a combined operation to capture and occupy the islands outside the Gulf. This could not be mounted without cover from the High Sea Fleet and the full cooperation of the army. In June 1916, the attention of the High Sea Fleet's command and the Great General Staff were elsewhere. The German army had, in any case, no troops to spare, with major fighting at Verdun and in southeastern Russia and with the Allied offensive on the Somme about to start.

Russia had a secondary theater in the Arctic Sea. The ports of Archangel and Murmansk were important, if seasonal, links to the Allies. Although constantly overloaded, with inadequate facilities, they were nevertheless vital in maintaining the flow of supplies. The Germans were therefore sending U-boats to attack the shipping between Russia and Britain. There was always the danger of a single German raider, but submarines and mines were the threats that the Russians had to manage, something for which the British had to provide increasing help.

The Russian Baltic Fleet was more powerful in 1916 than it had been at the start of the war. Four dreadnoughts were operational, while the first quartet of new fast destroyers based on the *Novik* design had at last emerged from the shipyards and additional units would be commissioned by the end of the year, but the Russians had yet to take advantage of these accessions of strength. The Russians' defensive approach also constrained the employment of the very effective British submarine flotilla that had been operating in the sea since late 1914, causing angst for the Royal Navy.[4] This was partly due to Vice Admiral V. A. Kanin, C-in-C of the "Active Fleet," who was not a strong personality. The seagoing forces had suffered a devastating blow with the death of the charismatic Admiral N. O. von Essen in 1915.[5] Kanin had few of the qualities of an operational commander but may have been selected instead of von Essen's nominee, Admiral L. B. Koerber, his chief of staff, only because Koerber had a Germanic surname and Kanin did not. Kanin's future was in doubt as the chief of naval staff in the Stavka and the navy minister had both come to believe his weak leadership was contributing to the fleet's problems. The tsar himself described Kanin as being "more like a Professor than an Admiral."[6] Nevertheless, Kanin was not alone in his passive approach. The memory of the naval disasters of the Russo-Japanese War also affected the judgment of the tsar and the military high command. The combination of the Stavka's defensive fixations with the dominant position of the army and the tsar's obsession with preserving the dreadnoughts meant the C-in-C's room for operational initiatives was limited. Matters did not improve greatly even when in 1916 operational control of the Baltic Fleet was transferred from the Sixth Army to the new Naval General Staff.[7]

Russia's offensive mining campaign of late 1914 had not been properly followed up, in part because of the fear of losing the handful of fast cruisers and destroyers available to send to the western Baltic, but more because of the mistaken idea that Russian strength should be husbanded against a German assault. In 1915 the Russian navy played an important role in supporting the Russian army and harassing the advancing Germans from the sea in the Gulf of Riga, but this success loomed too large in the mind of the C-in-C, who declared in 1916, "The fundamental, strategic picture is clear. The Baltic Fleet is a continuation of the extreme flank of the army; the task of the Fleet is, as far as possible, to support the movements of the army, protecting it against envelopment by the German fleet."[8] Even more significant was Kanin's public response to German claims of mastery of the Baltic, "Let them come to the Gulf of Finland."[9]

There were more active commanders in the Baltic Fleet. Rear Admiral A. I. Nepenin, the dynamic head of the fleet's reconnaissance and intelligence organization was one. He had set up an extremely effective signals intelligence system, which was combined with a network of shore-based observers. Nepenin had also sponsored naval aviation's development in both surveillance and attack. Another was Captain (soon to be Rear Admiral) A. V. Kolchak, chief of the Mine Division, effectively the senior officer of the light forces that operated from the advanced bases established around the Gulf of Riga. But, although they could undertake covert minelaying raids, Kolchak's ships were not powerful enough to risk venturing to the south and west for extended periods without heavy support. Further, Kolchak's promotion to vice admiral and transfer to the Black Sea fleet as its C-in-C were already under consideration. He would leave the Baltic at the beginning of July 1916.

All this meant the Germans were not challenged in the western Baltic, with which they were well content. This allowed them to consider their exercise areas around Kiel reasonably safe. This was important, because the Baltic was a much better training area than the North Sea, both for major units and for light craft and submarines—the entire U-boat training force was Baltic based. Furthermore, the ability to keep only minimal surface forces in theater was itself a vital component of Scheer's strategy of wearing down the Grand Fleet, since he could focus the High Sea Fleet on the North Sea, without the need to make substantial detachments. This considerably simplified planning. Had the Russians mounted a sustained surface campaign against the convoys to and from Sweden, which were instituted largely as an antisubmarine measure, the Germans would have been hard-pressed to protect them with the limited forces assigned to the Baltic. The new ships entering service with the Russians in 1916 would have had to have been met by first-line units from the High Sea Fleet.

Photo 1.5
Rear Admiral Nepenin
Sergei Vinogradov

The Russian failure to go onto the offensive in the western Baltic was critical in another way. The shipping lanes from Scandinavia were more of a lifeline than the Germans liked to admit. While Swedish iron ore and other metals were essential for German industry, so were the horses and food supplies sourced from Sweden, Denmark, and Norway, as well as the semi-illicit trade from which American (and some British) interests continued to profit. To be fair, the Russians feared that Swedish sympathy for the Germans would spill over into a declaration of war and an assault on the Aland Islands, endangering the Gulf of Finland and Petrograd. They believed the Swedes, at ease in archipelagic conditions, would prove impossible to dislodge, particularly if they acted in consort with the Germans. Admiral Kanin had therefore sought and received approval for a preemptive attack on the predicted Swedish forward bases in the approaches to Stockholm if hostilities threatened.[10] The potential threat from Sweden was another excuse for the Russians to fixate on defending the Gulf of Finland. In addition to the renewal of the mine fields that was started every year as soon as the thaw allowed, more work went into fortifications on both sides of the Gulf of Finland, as well as islands to seaward of the gulf. Along with a multitude of lighter weapons already distributed more widely on the coast, 30.5-cm guns of the same type as mounted in the dreadnoughts were being installed on the Finnish coast and the island of Örö. Similar efforts were being made on the islands outside the Gulf of Riga.

The Neutrals

The Swedes were walking their own tightrope. They were ready enough to protect their own shipping against Allied depredations and to give German merchant vessels the sanctuary of their waters, but they had also allowed some of the Allied merchant ships trapped in the Baltic at the start of the war to break out via Swedish waters. This extended on occasion to physically preventing German warships from interfering with the passage of British and French merchant ships. While German indignation eventually proved too much, forcing the Swedes to lay additional minefields and formally restrict passage through the Öresund, many Allied vessels had nevertheless got clear and away. Both the Norwegians and the Dutch faced similar problems in maintaining neutrality. The Germans benefited from the shelter that their territorial waters provided for the passage of U-boats, surface forces, and the occasional blockade runner, but not to the extent the British sometimes claimed. Both nations did their best to protect their waters and generally succeeded in maintaining a balanced approach. The Royal Navy often chafed over the restrictions on its freedom of action close to the coasts of Norway and the Netherlands, but Britain could not afford the breach with these countries, or the effect on American public opinion, that deliberately ignoring them would create.

In June 1916, the future of the naval war in both the North Sea and the Baltic was only to be seen through a glass darkly. Both the British and the Germans had yet to digest the results of the encounter between their main fleets and the coming months would be marked by intense debates within their leadership over the way ahead. The hopes of the protagonists for a decisive result were fading, while the prospect that the maritime conflict would be one of attrition grew apace. It was a prospect that was already reality for those at sea.

The Navies 2

The Royal Navy

T HERE WERE MANY DIFFERENCES in the management of British ships from that of their German and Russian counterparts. Those differences were much greater in major units than in the light forces and submarine arms, but for the crews of the capital ships who lived out so much of the war in fleet anchorages, some were critical. The most important was recognition that morale had to be maintained, and this was the responsibility of the fleet's leaders. The Royal Navy had suffered many unexpected setbacks, but its admirals were determined to maintain the spirit of the service. In 1918, when an American officer joining the Grand Fleet remarked on its "splendid morale" within the hearing of the C-in-C, Beatty turned and said, "The big problem here is morale. Now morale is my problem."[1] This is not a remark likely to have been made by his German equivalent.

The Grand Fleet's disposition in remote harbors kept both officers and men on board and helped create a feeling of community. One of the objections more thoughtful commanders had to the battle squadrons' possible transfer to Rosyth was that at Scapa "men can't envy the officers their greater freedom in the way of visits and leave ashore."[2] Significantly, where other navies' ships were in similar remote situations—the solo deployment of the Russian *Slava* to the Gulf of Riga being one example—there was a similar sense of community. This was demonstrated in *Slava* by the cold reception given the Bolshevik delegates who visited the ship in mid-1917.[3] Had the British fleet been operating from its home ports in the south things might have been different, and from 1917 onward the Admiralty's increasing fears of subversion would have been more justified. Despite strenuous efforts, the various naval barracks were nearly overwhelmed by numbers they had not been designed to manage. An Australian sailor commented in June 1918 that he and his compatriots were so appalled by the quality of barracks food that they were "compelled to buy our own meals when ashore. . . . How these poor unfortunate British sailors survive is a queerie."[4]

Without the distractions of family and shore life available at Wilhelmshaven and Helsingfors, Grand Fleet officers also had time to organize "lectures, singsongs and diversions of various sorts, all of them of the simple and popular variety."[5] That officers initiated many activities seems, despite the divisions of class in the Royal Navy, to have been a key difference from both the Germans and Russians. The cinema played an increasingly important role, although finding space to show films was sometimes difficult. The battleship *Emperor of India* used her central engine room. By 1918, the "kinema" was being shown every night in the big ships, with officers getting their turn on Saturdays.[6] One light cruiser was running three Charlie Chaplin showings a week in harbor, which the captain noted that his crew revelled in.[7] Amateur dramatics were particularly popular, recognized by the refrigerated meat ship *Ghourko*'s modification to provide a fully equipped stage, which ships used for their productions.[8] These provided an additional outlet, giving ships' companies license for satire against rival units and their own officers.[9] Audiences on board *Ghourko* sometimes suffered from being located immediately above the refrigerated spaces, but the ship was in "constant demand."[10]

Another factor was sport. The British interest in (if not obsession with) games, across all classes and regions, meant it was a much more natural activity than for the Russians or Germans and was considered recreation, not training. The Royal Navy had established a physical training branch in 1912 and junior officer development included instruction in soccer, more the game of the lower deck than rugby. Boxing also became an important sport in the Grand Fleet. The Admiralty entered four expert coaches into the Royal Naval Volunteer Reserve (RNVR) as chief petty officers and dispatched them north in 1917.[11] This was a shrewd move. Boredom often manifested itself in brawls on the lower deck.[12] Aggressive junior ratings could be encouraged into boxing competitions to dissipate accumulated testosterone, while bouts provided an opportunity for officers and ratings to meet on an equal basis. The success of the newly arrived graduates of the Royal Australian Naval College in the Grand Fleet boxing competitions was an important contribution to their high reputation.[13] Admiral Beatty claimed there were 18,000 spectators at the Grand Fleet's boxing carnival in July 1917.[14] Another activity in the warmer months was the fleet regatta, which involved both ratings and officers—the C-in-C was co-opted to act as stroke oar in the veterans' boat of HMS *Queen Elizabeth*.[15] Betting on these events was run on a grand scale with careful assessments of the odds, even if the rowing and sailing skills of some personnel meant regattas bore a "resemblance to Saturday aquatics on the Serpentine."[16] There were officers and many ratings who "never went ashore" and did not participate in these collective activities,[17] but in the Royal Navy this was from choice, not compulsion, and those who were least active were by no means least content.

It was not a perfect system. The weather in Scapa Flow was often so bad that personnel could not be landed for exercise at all, while the shortage of playing fields was another argument for a move to Rosyth.[18] There were abiding concerns that the relative idleness of the big ships encouraged homosexual behavior; one battleship captain described the Flow as "that hotbed of buggery."[19] The much harder working destroyers did not always receive the required support from their depot ships and their operating cycles meant opportunities for organized activity ashore were even more limited, while there was little to do on board. A new arrival to the Grand Fleet flotillas in February 1918 found them "in a state of staleness."[20]

The next factor supporting high morale was the Royal Navy's organization of sailors into their messes, comprising on average a dozen or more ratings under the supervision of a leading hand. While this was mirrored in the other navies, the sailors' autonomy in certain aspects of their existence was much greater. Each mess was responsible for preparing its own food. Staples were provided as rations and the mess also received a daily allowance per man to purchase additional items. This required careful management, particularly as prices rose during the war and mess members had their pay docked if the collective overindulged in extras. Nevertheless, it gave the lowest ranks control over a vital aspect of their life on board. It is likely that well-run junior ratings' messes in the British service fed the men better than the midshipmen and sometimes, within the limits of the cuisine, better than the wardrooms. Those of the senior ratings almost certainly did. The very junior officers were often subject to fraud in their victualing, which they lacked the sophistication to identify.

The British system for the provision of food was also extremely effective, even if it came under strain as the war progressed. This forced reductions in the basic ration although these were carefully applied, explained in detail, and monitored anxiously.[21] Rationing was also extended to officers and even to the commander-in-chief's mess, in the expectation that "officers could conform generally to the allowances of bread, sugar, meat and potatoes."[22]

The regime was not particularly stringent and brought the admission from the Grand Fleet's Russian naval observer that he "had a feeling of better general health than before."[23] Admiral Beatty's own mess's rationing was policed by his flag lieutenant. An associated initiative from 1917 was a recycling program. The total of fats collected came to nearly five tons a month, while empty tins exceeded that weight, as did used clothing.[24] It was no surprise to other units that flagships produced the most wastepaper.[25] The sufferers were the pigs being raised ashore for meat, and the seagulls of Scapa Flow and Rosyth, who had done very well since August 1914.

The Grand Fleet did not rely on official sources alone and there were important benevolent and commercial mechanisms to improve the quality of life. An industrial-scale charity came into being with the "Vegetable Products Committee," which supplied "thousands of tons of fruit and vegetables."[26] A highlight in 1916 was the supply of 5,000 sacks of new potatoes by the farmers of Jersey. There was no problem finding volunteers to assist with their unloading.[27] At the beginning of 1917, the New York branch of the committee donated 600 pounds sterling for apples and oranges. The C-in-C urged ships to send thank-you letters to America—at a suggested rate of four per ship—with the clear recognition that gratitude is the lively expectation of favors to come.[28] Canteens continued to provide "luxury" items. Although these became more expensive as the war continued, they were available in sufficient scale to satisfy most needs. Jellicoe himself was the moving spirit behind other initiatives, including the Grand Fleet Fund, which consolidated donations sent from around the world to assist "Petty Officers and Men wounded and incapacitated during the war."[29] A "Newspaper Fund" was another innovation, run on a cost recovery basis. Banking arrangements on board were improved to ensure junior ratings did not hold large amounts of cash, always an inducement to gambling.[30]

The next key difference was the rum ration. An eighth of an imperial pint of rum diluted with three parts of water was available to every adult rating every day. Petty officers received their ration undiluted, which meant it did not spoil. The distribution was a high point of the day—one the supposedly alcohol-free lower decks of the German and Russian navies could not enjoy. Officers, by comparison, had access to a much wider range of drinks and for much longer hours. While this was the source of some resentment, several factors kept complaints within bounds. First, the officers paid for their alcohol; second, there were some illicit transfers to the mess decks, while an invitation to receive a quiet drink in the privacy of the wardroom or gunroom pantry was a common reward to a well-performing rating (or an entire boat's crew). This could operate on a mass scale. After the Dogger Bank action in 1915, Commodore Goodenough of the cruiser *Southampton* thanked a volunteer party sent from the battleship *Orion* to assist with coaling and then "whacked out drinks all round" in his day cabin.[31] Finally, although dilution of the rum into "grog" was carefully supervised, means were often found to obtain the alcohol before it was watered down. Rum served as an internal currency, and ratings exchanged their "tot" for work or favors. While there were real problems with alcohol in the Royal Navy—arguably much greater in the wardroom and warrant messes than among the ratings—it represented an important contribution to the quality of life. The arrival of the U.S. Navy, which had been "dry" on board since 1914, provided food for thought to many who were concerned by the level of drinking, although some American officers availed themselves enthusiastically of British hospitality. This caused one young British officer to comment, "The U.S. Navy may be dry, but gee. . . ."[32]

The midshipman system was a source of strength for the relationship between wardroom and lower deck in the Royal Navy. Ratings perceived the midshipmen were subject to an even more arbitrary regime than their own, inherent to their passage to commissioned rank, and they were willing to give the young officers both advice and intimate information. While British midshipmen could abuse their command status, in general they displayed more tact than their nearest equivalents in the German ships. Their situation was often such that they had to. There were failings. Many midshipmen were very young, since their accelerated graduation sent them to sea at sixteen. They spent too much time under instruction and were employed, apart from the key experience of boat handling, on too many make-work activities. Furthermore, the quality of their immediate supervision varied widely. Many sub lieutenants in the capital ships were on probation because of inadequate performance or poor behavior, while the best junior officers had left for destroyers or submarines.[33] Bullying was frequent, although it rarely reached the point it did in one unit in which junior midshipmen were "forced to strip and behave indecently," an episode that drew the wrath of the commander-in-chief and Admiralty.[34]

Coaling was a strength. This was much more an "all hands" evolution in the Royal Navy than in either the German or Russian service and usually happened more often. By 1917, after many years of practice, "coal ship" had reached a peak of efficiency and the record sustained hourly rate was over

400 tons;[35] it had been 289 tons a decade earlier.[36] Only the commanding officer and a handful of others—usually the duty cooks and the band (if the executive officer liked music)—were excused from the backbreaking work of transferring coal from the collier's holds and distributing it around the ship's bunkers. A temporary freemasonry existed while coaling. Officers and men worked side by side and spoke and sometimes shouted to each other with a disregard for rank that applied at no other time.[37] Personnel being allowed to wear what they liked for the dirty work involved, coaling was also an excuse for fancy dress as, to be fair, it was in the German navy, but there was a serious element. Coaling was a key indication of a ship's efficiency. A moment's inattention could result in death or injury. An observer noted, "slow coaling is, perhaps, the commonest form of 'silent protest' on the part of a dissatisfied crew, and a ship which maintains a steadily depressing 'curve of coaling' is generally credited with being due for a general shake-up of personnel."[38] For this reason, total times and hourly averages were publicized throughout the Grand Fleet. Esprit de corps and earlier readiness for sea were not the only motivations. The earlier the work was finished the sooner a ship's company could clean their ship and themselves and get some rest. The ability of the oil-burning ships to fuel by simply pumping the liquid from a tanker was deeply envied.

There were problems: pay was one. The war caused significant price inflation; and wages in civilian industry, notably munitions workers, rose steeply. A separation allowance for the navy was not enough and some families, particularly those of junior ratings, suffered real hardship. It probably helped that officers maintaining families on their pay alone experienced their own form of genteel poverty. Other problems afloat are more apparent from individual officers' accounts than from the discipline statistics. Although 1917 represented the peak of many offenses during the war, the recorded numbers were moderate in relation to the size of the navy, and the nature of the charges did not indicate endemic problems, except with alcohol.[39] On the other hand, diaries from 1917 and 1918 suggest there were more collective disturbances than are recorded in the Admiralty archives, even when the incident concerned was formally reported.[40]

There was resentment when crews were pushed too hard and this could result in displays of mass disobedience. Competitive general drills, which bore little or no relation to potential contingencies in action, were widely viewed as simply a way of keeping personnel occupied.[41] In early 1917, the executive officer of Inflexible was alarmed when his new commanding officer insisted on the ship's company working in the afternoon after coaling from the early hours following return to harbor, commenting, "we shall be a nice discontented crowd."[42] When *Inflexible* went into dock, but at such short notice for sea that leave could not be allowed, forty-eight sailors broke out of the ship. The executive officer had expected close to a hundred to go.[43] In September 1917, twelve sailors broke out from the destroyer *Maenad* alongside in Lerwick. They were recovered, but soon broke their confinement. Their revolt included firing the ship's forward gun (fortunately with a blank charge) and rifling the wardroom wine store before they were subdued. In this, as in other incidents, the official response was to remove the officers who had allowed such a situation to develop, as well as to punish the men.[44] Disparity in living conditions was another problem, particularly in destroyers where the officers' ready access to hot water was bitterly resented.[45] Submarines by comparison, were a fully shared misery at sea. Their officers and ratings could, however, be highly critical of the accommodation available in their depot ships. Given some of the vessels selected for the role, a medical officer was being tactful in 1919 when he wrote "the choice [of these ships] has not always been a happy one,"[46] but submariners were prepared to forgive a great deal—provided there was "plenty of hot water."[47]

The Imperial German Navy

By comparison, the German navy never broke away from its home-port mentality, something probably inevitable given its very restricted operations before August 1914 and the strategic situation after that date. The navy was ill equipped to meet the challenges of war. The gulf between the officers and sailors was too wide to allow the fleet to manage the increasing stresses that it experienced as the war went on. Had the battle fleet been more active, it is likely that its problems would not have helped to trigger unrest, mutiny, and eventually revolution. In the circumstances in which the High Sea Fleet found itself after Jutland, they formed a fatal combination. Little official effort was made to improve conditions on board. Too much reliance was placed on facilities supposedly available ashore, which were more than adequate for the officers, but practically nonexistent for ratings, the more so as prices for food and alcohol rose. Kiel was better off in this regard and a deployment to the Baltic always welcome, but Wilhelmshaven "offered only a Sailor's Home, some films and a number of bars, which were not nearly enough."[48]

British and American observers after the war noticed that the German ships had not experienced the same moderation as those in the Royal Navy of the early efforts to strip out flammable materials, while they did not have the high-quality paints of American units. In consequence, they appeared unwelcoming and uncomfortable. The truth was that growing shortages of paint, soap, and cleaning materials had limited what could be done. Ships became increasingly shabby, something which struck Vice Admiral Souchon in 1917, fresh from detached command in Turkey. He was shocked by the internal condition of the battleship *Prinzregent Luitpold*, commenting to his wife that "these iron holes . . . [are] . . . bound to have a depressing effect on morale."[49]

Recreational activities were initiated by the sailors themselves, without the same degree of external support the Grand Fleet enjoyed. That many officers, including bachelors, had apartments ashore (something practically unheard-of for single men in the Royal Navy) where they could enjoy time with their families increased their distance from the lower deck still more. Sailors could only sleep ashore with special—exceptional—permission, and long leave was dependent upon the ship being in dockyard hands. For short leave, unlike the British ports, there were not enough sailors' hostels in Wilhelmshaven to provide cheap and comfortable accommodation.[50] The mental and physical separation between officers and ratings meant later efforts to improve morale often misfired. As the events that transpired in 1918 clearly demonstrated, officers had little real idea of lower deck sentiment. Lecture programs were instituted, but these were specifically for propaganda purposes rather than for general interest and were poorly received. When competitive sports were introduced, the reaction was that this was simply physical training in disguise.

Victualing and alcohol consumption helped further poison the relationship between officers and men in the big ships. The quality of the food served to the sailors in the capital ships, never particularly high, steadily deteriorated, as did the quantity. Officers bought their food separately and had the funds to exploit the black market; thus they continued to eat well at a time when the sailors were being given "a soup mixture which was so thin and weak and so poorly prepared that I always felt hungrier after the meal than before it."[51] Later in the war there were accusations that officers were taking food ashore for their families. Drinking parties were regular events in wardrooms, while the lower deck was allowed alcohol on board only for major holidays such as Christmas. Other shortages nagged because sailors felt that their officers were not subject to the same privations. Soap became a burning topic, particularly among stokers unable to clean themselves after a stint in a filthy bunker or stokehold.[52] Again, the issue was made more serious by the perception that officers were hoarding soap for themselves—and by the fact, unlike the Royal Navy, that not all the officers got their hands dirty working alongside their sailors to coal ship.

Manpower was a constant problem for the German navy. Finding competent junior officers and reliable ratings for the expanding U-boat force was a challenge in itself. Minesweeping also drained manpower, particularly as the work required skilled seamen, with little room for the inexperienced and untrained. The merchant reserve was one source of personnel, but by the end of 1916 the idea of an all-volunteer submarine force was abandoned and the High Sea Fleet subjected to a series of appeals and increasingly strident directions that major units release junior officers for U-boat service.[53] This not only reduced experience levels in the surface fleet, it accentuated the existing difficulty: the best junior officers and those who were probably most at ease with the lower deck were steadily leached out of the big ships, as were some of the most technically adept sailors. Their replacements were often not of the same quality, let alone experience. Newly trained junior officers were thrust immediately into supervisory roles; their preparation in schools and training ships had gone unseen by the sailors and thus had nothing of the transparency of the rites of passage undergone by Royal Navy midshipmen. Often lacking tact and sympathy, they were deeply resented.

Engineers continued to be treated as second-class officers and reacted accordingly. The High Sea Fleet suffered grave shortages of specialist engineers and these were getting worse by 1916. The continuing refusal of the leadership of the navy to give them the military status that they claimed—the rank of captain had only just been opened up—meant the engineers were also increasingly alienated from the executive branch. Consequently, they concealed many emerging morale and discipline problems within their departments from their commanders. It is also likely the shortage of experienced officers contributed to some of the engineering defects that plagued the big ships.

The warrant officers (Deckoffiziere), who provided an important bridge between the command and the ship's company were similarly resentful of attempts to reduce their status and group them with petty officers. Von Tirpitz himself admitted that the Deckoffiziere, nearly three thousand strong at the start of the war, were the "backbone of the Navy."[54] The engineers among them certainly provided expertise that had to substitute for the shortage of commissioned engineers. Nevertheless, even as they were employed in more responsible posts to make up for the lack of officers in other branches, their claims to recognition were repeatedly rejected. Arrangements for progression in the lower deck were similarly ramshackle. Inflexible regulations that confined promotion to petty officer to those who had joined as volunteers prevented the promotion of long-serving conscripts. This was steadily becoming a more serious issue in 1916 as the "classes" that should have completed their compulsory service in 1914 or 1915 accumulated additional years to the point at which they would have been eligible for promotion had they been volunteers.

As with the Royal Navy, the numbers of small craft steadily increased, creating what in some ways were completely different organizations to the main fleet. In torpedo craft and submarines, life at close quarters and active programs combined in most cases to prevent the problems accumulating in the capital ships. Distinctions customary in battleships largely disappeared on board a torpedo boat at sea. They were practically nonexistent in a U-boat or within the hardworking minesweeping force. Leave arrangements in the minor vessels were more flexible than in the capital ships and victualing done on a whole unit basis, avoiding one of the greatest sources of resentment. Some units even allowed their people to take food with them when they went home on leave, something unthinkable in the big ships (at least for the sailors).[55] The small ships also adopted unofficial methods for getting more food—and shared the benefits fairly. There is certainly this implication in then-Lieutenant Frederic Ruge's lunching on a goose "honestly bought in Libau" before his destroyer sailed for Operation Albion in October 1917.[56]

The Imperial Russian Navy

It is difficult to develop a fair picture of the Imperial Russian Navy in 1916. This is not only because of the limited material available in other than the Russian language, but also because so many narratives are colored by the experiences of the revolution and the special pleading in later years of both Reds and Whites. The Baltic also differed from the North Sea in one important respect that most affected the Russians. From November until at least March, and in some areas—after a particularly severe winter—until May, the sea became icebound. This included much of the Gulf of Finland. Most ports could only be kept open with icebreakers, if at all. Russian naval operations effectively ceased for at least four months until the spring thaw; air operations were not so constrained, particularly as the days lengthened in the spring. The impossibility of conducting naval operations over the winter had important practical and psychological effects. Training and readiness inevitably declined, while the attention of personnel turned away from professional to personal—and sometimes political—matters.

The peculiar nature of the Baltic campaign and the distribution of the operational and support elements of the Russian navy created significant problems, exacerbated by the national government's incapacity to deal with the challenges of the war and the increasing war weariness of the population. Inflation and food shortages not only created difficulties in keeping the navy's people fed, but since some two thirds of the sailors came from urban communities, the growing problems in the cities had a much greater effect on the navy's morale and outlook than they did on the army with its much greater proportion of peasants.

The Baltic freeze created another dynamic. The various squadrons were effectively isolated from each other. Some training could be achieved and there is little doubt the fleet's leaders should have been more imaginative, but cold, darkness, and shortages of fuel limited what could be done. The dreadnoughts and older battleships at Helsingfors, already restricted in their operations over the summer months, probably suffered the most from ennui. Their large crews, essential for steaming and fighting the ships at sea, were the most difficult to find useful employment for. There had already been a mutiny on board *Gangut* in October 1915, which the ship's captain ascribed in part to the "lack of combat action."[57] Although sailors were allowed a monthly leave of absence during the winter months,[58] this was little recompense, while the breakdown of civil society ashore did not help morale and certainly exposed junior personnel to external political influence. Matters were not helped, as in the High Sea Fleet, when officers had much more generous leave and the money to enjoy life ashore, as well as better food and access to alcohol. There were also anomalies in pay and conditions that created resentments between personnel retained beyond their initial enlistments and those who had been reenlisted.[59]

In another parallel with the Germans, the Russians made little effort to organize recreation for their sailors until a change in the C-in-C of the Baltic Fleet in late 1916. Cinema performances were regular events (Britain's Rear Admiral Phillimore was shocked by the risqué nature of some of the films, describing them as "very *French* & we should say 'improper,' but in this country it is not thought so"[60]), but even playing cards was forbidden in the mess decks, probably through a well-meant desire to prevent gambling. Religion was a solace, particularly as it had a substantial musical element, with singing part of the twice daily prayer services in the big ships.[61] Music was central to the Russian sailors' existence. One British observer noted, "The only relaxations that the Russian sailor could enjoy were his music, singing and dancing. At the slightest encouragement the balalaikas or harmonicas would be brought out and soon the glorious sound of Russian male voices in perfect harmony and the wild exhilaration of Russian dancing would bring an air of gaiety and sentiment to a community that had been, a moment before, languishing in the depths of a deadly depression."[62] Despite a deliberate emphasis on education and training, particularly in the winter months, there was strong sense among the sailors in the big ships that much of their daily routine was simply designed to keep them occupied.

The separation between the wardroom and the lower deck was even greater than that in either the British or the German navies. There were ethnic divisions as well as those of class and education. A substantial proportion of the officer corps derived from the Baltic states or from Finland. Both groups had strong Germanic elements. The former were nicknamed "barons" in the Russian navy, but the label lost any undertone of affection as the reverses of the war had their effect. Although the barons had a reputation for professionalism, they were often even more remote from their sailors than their Great Russian equivalents, insisting on very formal modes of address from their subordinates, when the Russians, particularly in small ships, were content with the Christian name and patronymic.[63] All concerned were harsh in their application of discipline, something which repeatedly horrified British observers in the Baltic submarine flotilla.[64]

The training schools and maintenance areas at Kronstadt presented other problems. Shortages of capable personnel meant there was little dynamic leadership available for the recruits and specialist trainees who were concentrated on the island. Its proximity to Petrograd and its remoteness from operations meant that Kronstadt was particularly susceptible to subversion by revolutionary elements in the capital. The local commander's answer was the enforcement of an even stricter disciplinary regime than in the active fleet.[65] As 1917 was to demonstrate, however, this only helped sow the dragon's teeth. Political awareness seems to have been greater among shore-based personnel than in the fleet and greater in big ships than in the light forces. While the 1905 mutiny in *Potemkin* in the Black Sea and that on board *Pamiat Azova* in the Baltic in 1906 were memories the Russian navy could not shake off, political agitation within any unit varied considerably, depending upon a few key individuals.

The officer corps was divided within itself in both professional and political outlook. The Russian government's poor performance was progressively undermining the officers' natural loyalty to the system and, although the evidence is difficult to judge in hindsight, a number in key positions were beginning to consider what would be needed to replace the Tsarist autocracy and position themselves and like-minded colleagues to respond to political change. Junior officers, particularly those still under training in Kronstadt and Petrograd, were suffering a crisis of confidence in the monarchy. This accentuated a generation gap of technological expertise and enterprise also apparent in the British and German navies. Although the ideological divisions were not just based on age and seniority, older officers were not only ill at ease in an increasingly technological service, but their natural conservatism also made them unwilling to contemplate the changes that would inevitably flow from an alteration in government, while corruption continued to dog the navy at many levels. There were also divisions of outlook between shore and seagoing personnel. Again, these were present in the navies of the other combatants, but the strategic situation, the largely defensive role of the Russian navy, and the geography and climate meant the bases and ships were more closely bound together, while at the same time, they were more divided from each other than the Germans, let alone the British. As a result, shore-based senior personnel could exert great influence on individual ships and formations, as well as on the fleet as a whole—and that influence was deeply resented.

Operational Challenges

3

T HE PROTAGONISTS HAD COPED with many of the challenges encountered in 1914 but had still to adjust to many more to exploit the new technologies. There were, of course, perennials. Climate profoundly affected the campaigns in both North Sea and Baltic. There were seasonal windows for operations, especially offensive ones, and lunar monthly windows in which the combinations of tides, currents, and nighttime visibility were favorable. Even in ideal circumstances, the chance to strike at the enemy could effectively be restricted to a few days in an entire year; these windows were opened or closed by the actual weather. Many of the emergent technologies with the greatest potential, particularly against an enemy on the defensive, required benevolent combinations of sea state, wind, and visibility all too rare in northern European waters. The offensive efforts of all the protagonists, subject as they were to other factors of unit readiness, may thus seem curiously intermittent to the present-day observer. Many opportunities were missed for many reasons, some wholly avoidable, but the assertion of a novelist of a later war that there was an enemy other than the human opponent was just as true between 1914 and 1918.[1] The sea can be very cruel.

Navigation

Navigation remained a key problem, particularly for the British with their greater scale of operations, but professional skills had deepened in all navies. Small ship mariners developed their own personal sense of locality, akin to that of fishermen. The Royal Navy came to understand tales of the southern Dogger Bank being identified by the smell of gas were true, and equivalent insights developed for the German forces in the Heligoland Bight, as well as the more wide-ranging U-boats, leavened as all crews increasingly were by reservists who had been fishermen or small ship sailors. The forces of all nations working in the Channel developed an acute understanding of its tides, currents, and shifting shallows. For their part, Russian light forces acquired the familiarity with the complex Finland skerries to operate among the islands at speeds and in conditions of low visibility unthinkable before 1914, "with the precision of a racing car driver."[2]

Equipment was still primitive, although the importance of knowing water depth was reflected in the increasing installation of depth sounders. The fit of gyroscopic compasses, although general in British battleships and the newer submarines, was only extended to light cruisers starting in 1916. Destroyers and other small craft still depended on magnetic units, but this was not the disadvantage it might seem. The Germans were further advanced, but also experienced problems. Until modifications were made to gyrocompasses after the war, they were "of very little use during rough weather."[3] British submarines navigated on the surface with a magnetic unit. Nevertheless, much closer attention was paid than before the war to determining compass errors, whether gyroscopic or magnetic, as well as accurately recording courses and distances run.[4] Even for a short passage to dock in the Tyne following emergency repairs in the Humber after Jutland, the battleship *Marlborough* swung ship to check how her damage had affected deviation.[5] Thus, while the expected navigational error of five nautical miles after eight hours remained, the radius of uncertainty did not increase much further over time, unless visibility was poor for several days.[6] It was this that put the Second Battle Squadron twenty miles out in its reckoning in March 1918.[7] Making a landfall in such circumstances was a challenge, although the steep coast of Scotland made this easier for the British ships in the north than in the southern North Sea. Individual ships or small formations could reverse course and wait for the visibility to improve, but this was a much more difficult proposition for the whole Grand Fleet.

What made the navigational uncertainty even more problematic was the proliferation of minefields, which might have been laid with a less than certain knowledge of their position. Even in an area as confined as the Gulf of Riga, mistakes were made that could have serious consequences for friendly forces. Minelayers themselves had adopted new systems for precise navigation. A British innovation was the taut-wire measuring system, adapted from use by hydrographers, by which wire paid out under strain recorded distance run.[8] This could be very effective—in 1918 an American minelayer managed a run of 122 miles without a wire break.[9] All combatants had long since accepted that an enemy minefield only required sweeping if it interfered with the freedom of operation of friendly forces. Once a field's position was known with reasonable certainty, it could be buoyed, or simply plotted and declared. Priority for buoyage was given to the British war channels and the French, German, and Russian equivalents that ran along the coasts and into ports and harbors. These channels, along which friendly and neutral shipping passed, were regularly swept for mines and patrolled by antisubmarine units. Promulgation of mine danger areas and maintaining an up-to-date picture became one of the most unremitting tasks for headquarters and individual units. The mine threat was also a restraint on offensive operations. Apart from the potential inaccuracy of friendly fields, the first indication of an enemy field could be the explosion of a mine. Mines themselves became one of the key interests of signals intelligence, since the report of a mine could indicate whether a field had been discovered and interception of a signal declaring a mine danger area in enemy waters could be an important indicator to that enemy that a new field had been laid.

Fog was frequent in the southern North Sea and the Channel, affecting both operations in the open sea and around harbors and anchorages. Matters were not much better in the Baltic. Low visibility operations were commonplace and the techniques to manage them became progressively more sophisticated. Repeated collisions demonstrated the need for clear understanding, not only about maneuvering rules, but whether zigzags should continue in fog. After the collision of the battlecruisers *Australia* and *New Zealand* in April 1916, the British confirmed that any alteration of course had to be by signal rather than at a previously planned time. Commanders learned not to execute complex course changes in such situations, realizing that destroyers were sluggish at very slow speeds and a reduction did not necessarily result in safer conditions. However, as the second division of the Fourth Battle Squadron demonstrated through the use of siren signals to order a sharp turn, the risk of maneuvering was sometimes preferable to the alternative. In this case the formation had no alternative, as the ships found themselves dangerously close to the rock-bound Norwegian coast in thick fog.[10] A searchlight directed aft was added to the fog buoys streamed astern, since "the luminous blur could be seen at a far greater distance through fog than the hull of a ship."[11] Anchoring in place was another technique employed if caught by fog; the Russians sometimes did this well out into the Baltic, although it was usually ordered by the British and Germans only in the immediate vicinity of harbor.

As to navigational aids, early ideas of removing light ships and even of placing decoys in the wrong position had given way to their selective retention and coordination of lighting times with the movements of ships and formations, while lights in areas with constant traffic shone at reduced power to give as little help as possible to enemy submarines and minelayers.[12] Lightships on the Dogger Bank were used as points of reference by both sides. Depth soundings were also exploited to the full. The Royal Navy's Harwich Force developed techniques such as running in line abreast over the distinctive north-south Brown Ridge in the southern North Sea, giving a line of longitude accurate to within one mile. In sunny weather, this could be combined with a sun-sight to give a reasonable fix. Not surprisingly, the ridge was used as a muster point for the Harwich Force, particularly when supporting a Grand Fleet operation. A line of latitude could also be found by running over the twenty-fathom line north of Terschelling.[13]

Not yet in place in Britain was a systematic approach to sharing such expertise around the navy—after Commodore Reginald Tyrwhitt ["Commodore (T)"] distributed his "Navigational Notes," the Third Cruiser Squadron's commander admitted "the information is quite new to me."[14] This reflected a wider British tendency, partly driven by the fear of compromise, to restrict vital information to formation and even fleet commanders.[15] The Admiralty was so concerned to protect its mastery of the German codes that not even the C-in-C of the Grand Fleet was provided with systematic access to the decrypts. This extended to restricted circulation of critical information such as the location of newly laid mines. A failure to encourage flag and command level discussions did not help. Even as late as July 1917, one admiral noted, "squadrons are inclined to be in watertight compartments and probably discussions seldom go beyond the Gunnery questions of the moment."[16]

Plotting and reporting the position of the enemy was a vital problem associated with navigation. The Battle of Jutland confirmed that much still needed to be done. If units were out of contact for an extended period or never in contact with the flagship at all, it was easy for the combined relative error to be greater than the visibility. This was the cause at Jutland of the twelve-mile mismatch between *Iron Duke* and *Lion* that made Jellicoe's deployment such a difficult decision. The key requirement at sea was therefore that the relative positions of the flagship and the reporting units be understood. To this end, flagships began to issue a "Reference Position" at regular intervals, used as the basis for all future reporting. It had the added advantage of providing a time check. The deficiency was that an update was only possible for units in sight of their flagship—or at the most in sight of a unit at one or two removes from the flag. There was also a requirement for skilled personnel to manage plotting and reporting in good time. Rear Admiral Napier summed up the difficulties during a 1917 debate over the relative advantages of reporting hostile forces in true or magnetic bearing, "light cruiser Officers have to STEER—PLOT—THINK—TAKE BEARINGS— and ESTIMATE ENEMY'S COURSE—all in 'Magnetic'—and to think very quickly in making enemy reports . . . to convert all these to 'True' would be very complicated and confusing."[17] What was not argued was the need for more precision than the "within two points" margins of existing emergency contact reports. To reduce the Grand Fleet flagship's own errors, *Iron Duke* was fitted with an Anschutz Patent Dead Reckoning Instrument, an automated system with inputs from the log and gyrocompass, which meant that her track was continually shown on the plot, greatly simplifying the work of plotting.[18] Even when the system worked, the cumulative problems of accurate reporting forced Beatty's own plotting officer to admit after the war's end that there was a great deal of art (in other words, guesswork) in maintaining the "strategic plot" and forming a coherent estimate of the enemy fleet's position, disposition and course—the last being particularly hard to estimate correctly by a shipborne observer.[19] Aware of the difficulty of creating an accurate picture, one of the most experienced British scouting commanders, William Goodenough, later commented, "Commanders must be prepared to meet with these errors. If they trust implicitly to an absolutely correct position, instead of being so prepared, they will find that their minds and movements become rigid and not elastic." [20]

Another lesson had been learned from Jutland: the need to maintain a duplicate chart and position record, well away from the primary conning station.[21] This was particularly important for light cruisers, which were useless as scouts or as formation commanders if they lost their reckoning through action damage. Destroyers, which had practically no ability to maintain an accurate reckoning under action conditions, just had to hope someone would tell them where they were, even if the problem was simple in the North Sea—for the British a westward course was a homeward one, for the Germans, it was southeastward. One junior officer described trying to work out the location of *Obdurate* on the night of the Battle of Jutland as "making bricks without straw," a problem solved only by his captain's sensible insistence on simply "following father."[22]

There were inevitable casualties from just being at sea. Lionel Dawson, a British destroyer captain with hard-won prewar experience, found wartime conditions even more challenging. Already bearing the scars of multiple prewar incidents, during thirty months in three ships, Dawson suffered four collisions—three serious enough to require dockyard repair—and two groundings, as well as fouling two buoys and losing a topmast. All the collisions were in poor visibility and two were with submarines that Dawson's *Lurcher* was escorting. At least three incidents were not reported to higher authority.[23] Dawson's experience was not exceptional and his professional competence unquestioned; he would be promoted commander in 1920. The British lost eight destroyers wrecked during the war, the Germans three torpedo boats. Many more were sunk or damaged in collision—the French lost five destroyers this way. The Harwich Force statistics—of the incidents actually reported—confirm the challenging conditions. In 1916, there were twenty-two collisions, six groundings, and six major berthing incidents, compared with twenty-one collisions, seven groundings, and eleven berthing incidents in 1917 and twenty, five, and five in those categories in 1918.[24] The danger of collision, particularly at night, was one reason why convoys were viewed with so little favor among the small ships; and the experience of 1917 and 1918, with many such accidents, confirmed they had a point. Matters in the Channel were complicated by the fact that British and French units could and did collide with each other, questions of cause and blame having to be managed with great tact. With this experience, when the Americans arrived in European waters, arrangements were quickly made to conduct joint inquiries but take separate national action after an accident.

Senior commanders and the Admiralty repeatedly issued admonitions to reduce speed in low visibility and in confined waters, but operational conditions meant accidents did happen. Arguably this was well recognized, erring captains who admitted their mistakes often being simply adjured to "be more careful in future."[25] Four such warnings were issued to Dover Patrol captains on one day in March 1918 for striking submerged objects, grounding, or hitting a buoy in the previous two months.[26] The French official history made the point that "excessive severity" only stifled initiative.[27] A failed attempt to conceal an incident often aroused the wrath of senior command rather than the incident itself, although Commodore Tyrwhitt gently explained to the Admiralty that an unreported collision of July 1915 of which the light cruiser *Carysfort* had been accused was caused by a trawler of the same name.[28] As in Dawson's case, however, this did not stop captains keeping an incident to themselves if they thought they could get away with it.

Unit Efficiency

The efficiency of individual units varied widely in all four navies and was largely dependent on a combination of time in commission and operational employment. Excessive haste in returning refitted ships to operations certainly affected safe navigation. HMS *Dublin* ran over antisubmarine nets outside Larne Harbor in April 1916 because only the notices "of the most urgent character" had been checked in the limited time available before the ship sailed from Belfast.[29] The need for capital ships to work up and practice gunnery was, however, well understood. This was why Jellicoe did not take the powerful but brand-new *Royal Sovereign* to Jutland. She had only arrived in Scapa on 25 May.[30] German methods were similar. The battleship *Bayern* was completed in mid-March 1916 but did not join the High Sea Fleet as an operational unit until mid-July.[31] The battle cruiser *Hindenburg* commissioned on 10 May 1917 and was occupied with trials and training until 25 October.[32]

Less attention was given to smaller ships. Cruisers attached to the Grand Fleet or the Battle Cruiser Fleet did best, being given two weeks to work up at Scapa Flow in what was popularly termed the "Awkward Squad,"[33] but this was not universal in the Royal Navy. Units were employed operationally by the Harwich Force before they were worked up, despite the dismal example of the brand-new *Arethusa* at the Battle of the Heligoland Bight in August 1914. The destroyer *Skate*, accepted into naval service in the Clyde on 19 February 1917, arrived in Harwich on the afternoon of the 22nd and sailed at midnight to escort a convoy, which her first lieutenant rightly described as "a bit 'ard" for a brand-new and untrained ship.[34] After Jutland the captain of the light cruiser *Chester* reproached himself bitterly for accepting too many boys and new hostilities-only junior ratings when his ship commissioned in May 1916.[35] Discipline broke down among the young and inexperienced upper deck personnel of *Chester* when the ship was swept by German gunfire and many sought shelter rather than remaining at their positions. The award of the Victoria Cross to Boy Jack Cornwell for staying at his post may have provided a salutary example, while drawing attention away from the poor behavior of others.

British destroyers were in such short supply it is doubtful whether any received sufficient training, even though the crews in new ships were extremely inexperienced. Lieutenant Commander Taprell Dorling sailed for the first time in *Telemachus*, "in weather which could only be described as delightful . . . [and] . . . found at least 25% of the men prostrated by sea-sickness."[36] Commander A. B. Cunningham discovered in 1918 how "wretched" was the shooting of his new command, the flotilla leader *Termagant*, which he believed was because "Dover destroyers were so desperately hard-worked that they had no time for firing practices or exercises."[37] German boats got more time for training while maintenance was conducted on a flotilla basis, rather than the British practice of withdrawing of individual units for boiler cleaning and repairs. The Russians did as much maintenance as they could during the icebound months, which allowed substantial repairs to be made with confidence that there was sufficient time. Major items of machinery from the battleship *Slava*, icebound in the Gulf of Riga, were refurbished in Reval dockyard over the winter of 1915–16.[38] Smaller ships similarly trapped did much work on board, with the assistance of personnel sent from Helsingfors and Kronstadt. The downside was that inactivity created the need for an extensive workup every spring before the crews were again efficient. This was a period of vulnerability for the Russians because the Germans, based in largely ice-free areas of the Baltic, could start preparing for operations much earlier.

Training additional personnel became an important task for the big ships, one that loomed larger as the war continued. Providing manpower for the multitude of smaller craft needed was the main reason for decommissioning many of the oldest major units. But such measures were not enough for the British to man their antisubmarine craft, or the Germans their U-boats and minesweepers. As the pressure to man an ever-larger antisubmarine force increased, the British set targets for trained personnel from the major units of the Grand Fleet. The Germans were somewhat less systematic, but their battleships, too, were functioning as nurseries of the new arms by late 1916. When the Americans entered the war, they soon found their home-based battleships had to devote much time to training gun crews for merchant ships and naval transports.

Gunnery

Gunnery systems and procedures became increasingly sophisticated in the capital ships; and the associated developments, particularly director control, were being extended to cruisers in the Royal Navy. Destroyers and other light craft remained much more basic up to 1916, with guns being individually laid and trained. German small ship shooting seems to have been generally better than the British. Commodore Tyrwhitt admitted in May 1916, "our destroyers merely waste ammunition at the longer range, that is over 6,000 yards."[39] By 1917 German torpedo boats had limited centralized control with indicators on each gun that provided range (to the nearest hundred meters) and thus elevation, the deflection required, and the orders to fire.[40] As this followed on a program of replacing 88-mm weapons with the much more powerful 105-mm, German craft were very much more effective than they had been in 1914.[41] British efforts to fit improved fire control systems lagged somewhat, starting systematically in 1916. By the end of the war all destroyer leaders and some of the newest destroyers had full director control, while simpler systems had been installed in older ships.[42] Russian fire control practices were relatively sophisticated, in many ways comparable to the best elements of both British and German systems. A program was under way in 1916 to rearm cruisers with improved 6-inch and 13-cm weapons. The new 4-inch destroyer gun was already proving a success, while new mountings were being fitted that would markedly increase its range.[43] Work was also in hand to increase the elevation of the main armament guns of the older battleships. Both developments would give the Germans some unpleasant surprises.

Engineering

Engineering presented many problems. All the protagonists were aware by this time that operational availability depended upon proper maintenance schedules, whether the ships went into dock in individual rotations or as part of an entire squadron. A welcome realization by the British was that hull growth diminished in northern waters, extending the docking interval for major units to twelve months from six.[44] This reduced the strain on the floating docks in the north and increased battleship availability. Propulsion technology had yet to mature. Barely a decade after the first turbines had entered naval service the early units were aging fast and presenting unexpected difficulties. Machinery inspections of the first generation of British dreadnoughts in 1917 revealed corrosion and debris inside the turbine casings.[45] By late 1916 the Grand Fleet had to allow both reciprocating engine units and "the older turbine ships" additional time for essential maintenance.[46] American officers in the Grand Fleet in 1918 believed the operational speeds of the oldest British dreadnoughts had dropped to no more than seventeen to eighteen knots.[47] When *Dreadnought* herself rejoined the Grand Fleet in March 1918 she could not keep up, being able to sustain barely seventeen knots. A major breakdown in July 1918 provided the excuse to pay the ship off completely.[48] The battleship *Superb* was another source of concern.[49] The High Sea Fleet was no better off. The first German capital ship with turbines, the battle cruiser *Von der Tann*, suffered repeated turbine defects in 1916 and 1917.[50] Although regimes of inspection and cleaning were introduced in both navies, the problem may well have contributed to more than one ship stripping its turbine blades. British destroyers frequently suffered this defect from liquid water remaining in the steam when it hit the blades.[51] There were also problems with quality control in the turbines manufactured for new construction. The Russians were hindered by their ability to produce modern propulsion machinery. A factory established just before the war in Petrograd was turning out turbines, but the lack of national diesel manufacturing capacity meant real difficulties for the ambitious submarine program. Although four of the new *Bars* class had been commissioned by April 1916 and there were eighteen more under construction for both the Baltic and Black Sea fleets, German diesels originally intended for the class were unavailable. The Russians substituted engines from their river monitors; these were much less powerful and proved unreliable. There were great hopes for the new *AG* (Russian initials for "American Holland") class, the first batch of which were built in Canada, shipped to Russia in sections, and reassembled at the Baltic Works in Petrograd. These five boats started to enter service late in 1916.[52]

Condensers and boilers gave problems in all the navies, more so in German service than the British. Engineering problems multiplied for the Germans as metals such as copper, tin, and zinc became scarce. By 1918 condenser tube failures were frequent in the torpedo boats,[53] although war-built British destroyers had their own problems from poor quality control.[54] *Seydlitz* suffered repeated condenser defects in 1918,[55] while the Germans were dogged by poor quality coal, which particularly limited the operational speeds of their battle cruisers. Although they embarked on a wide program of fitting supplementary oil firing in 1915, this created its own difficulties, *Von der Tann*'s system failing outright during the Jutland battle.[56] Engineering expertise remained a problem for the Germans, who suffered from a 30 percent or greater shortfall in their commissioned engineer officers. While impressed by German damage control procedures, for example, there was serious postwar British criticism of engineering practices in *Seydlitz* at Jutland, particularly in allowing boilers to be contaminated with salt water through unrecognized damage to a condenser.[57]

Coal firing created challenges for ship cleanliness. One veteran executive officer (admittedly of the oil-fired battleship *Revenge*) later commented that "coal-burning ships were . . . never really clean during the war."[58] American naval observers in 1916 were even more forthright. British ships were "very dirty; coal dust ground in and salt water everywhere. Rust all over; mess decks kept as well as possible and fairly clean . . . under conditions of practically continuous coaling and going to sea in bad weather with no chance to clean up."[59] Oil had its problems as well. Rushing ships to completion created the deficiencies of tank sealing and resulting leaks in war-built units that had been experienced by the very first oil-burners; this was only cured by much-improved quality control.

Operational endurance was still a "nagging tooth," particularly for destroyers and torpedo craft.[60] The pervasive submarine threat and the need to screen the big ships meant destroyers were required to sustain relatively high speeds for much longer than prewar designers had envisaged. The changed operational requirement was clear in the latest wartime German torpedo boat designs; some had nearly double the range of their predecessors. With higher speeds required during the day than in the relative safety of darkness, summer was worse than winter. The additional hours of daylight in the North Sea in high summer made a marked difference in the time destroyers could remain at sea. Even allowing escorts to maintain a steady base course while their big ship consorts zigzagged was not enough, while efforts to fuel at sea were frequently stymied by the challenges high sea states created when bringing ships into close proximity.[61] The availability of oil became a worry for the British as U-boats hit the tankers coming from the overseas fields, but fuel supply was a key concern for the Russians as well. Although the trials speed of their new dreadnoughts was a very encouraging twenty-three knots, this depended upon the availability of British "Admiralty" coal from south Wales, which had to come via Archangel. The British did their best, but the Arctic port was only open in the warmer months, while Russia's inland transport system was under great strain, creating problems of supplying the admittedly inferior Russian coal. The Russians had to husband their stocks, giving another pretext to justify the overly cautious employment of their big ships.

Jutland gave a considerable fillip to damage control and individual personnel protection in both the British and the German navies, while the American navy was an early beneficiary of British experience through its attachés' extensive reporting. The latter were clearly using privileged information, sometimes with direct access to British documents. Improved portable pumps, breathing apparatus, firefighting clothing, and anti-flash gear were among the innovations. There was a renewed drive, albeit more rational than the over-enthusiastic efforts of 1914, to remove wooden fittings and other combustibles. Bulkhead integrity had proved a weakness, and work was done to reduce the number of penetrations, better seal the remainder, and confirm the watertightness of compartments through air pressure tests.[62] The British and Americans were impressed in postwar inspections that each German major unit carried a damage control model of the ship concerned (although one was recovered from the cruiser *Emden* in 1914, its significance does not seem to have been appreciated).[63] This allowed a much more sophisticated approach to managing stability and buoyancy if the hull were breached.

There were occasional unexpected structural issues. A critical (and embarrassing) problem for British big gun monitors was that the shock of firing their main armament shattered the porcelain lavatory pans in the sailors' heads. A first direction to disconnect the lavatories from the fixed water pipes when going into action was eventually replaced by a shockproof mounting for the pans devised on board *Sir Thomas Picton*. Urgent necessity had clearly been the mother of invention.[64] Top weight was another factor. The problem was particularly severe in destroyers when fitted with additional antisubmarine weapons. By 1917 the Admiralty's urgent review brought reductions in spare gear and even the amount of food embarked.[65] Both Germans and Russians had to take similar steps, particularly in units that received heavier gun armament. Bigger ships took less drastic measures to compensate for new equipment and, in the case of the Royal Navy, for the additional deck armor that the experience of Jutland seemed to demand. The British had already dispensed with their heavy, largely useless torpedo nets; the experiences of *Derfflinger* at Jutland forced the Germans to appreciate that damaged nets could foul propellers. After June 1916 their removal was a priority.

Signals Intelligence

Communications warfare continued to evolve. The British signals intelligence system had matured considerably, although structural problems remained. The cryptographic organization in Room 40 remained separate from the Intelligence Division and under the control of the Chief of the War Staff, who, along with the Director of the Operations Division, was prone to make assessments of raw data without sufficient regard for context, or for the understanding of German naval operations the civilian cryptographers had developed. Captain Herbert Hope did remarkable work, but the scale on which analysis operated remained inadequate until changes were made in 1917. A shortage of staff had other effects. While a relatively close relationship with the Russians was maintained, limitations on the ability to decrypt material meant Room 40 did not examine signals originating in the Baltic until August 1916.[66] These would have helped considerably with understanding the complete pattern of German operations, notably the readiness of units in the training areas. Even more critically, it was later discovered that analysis of Baltic material would have provided easier access to new German cypher keys and simplified working out the structure of revised codes.[67]

The British had made progress in other ways. Fourteen direction-finding stations had been established around the coast and there were more under construction in 1916. This received impetus because the zeppelins had found accurate navigation during their raids on England practically impossible without positional updates based on triangulation of their radio transmissions by German direction-finding stations. The British could monitor and fix the zeppelins' signals, providing vital early warning. Because they had a broader base for triangulation, the British fix on a zeppelin's position was often more accurate than German stations could achieve. U-boats also made liberal use of wireless and this became an increasingly important source of intelligence. While the "time late" nature of any fix meant that the likelihood of a submarine being detected and engaged was negligible, it provided indication of the general locality of the U-boats. The necessary linkages were only slowly created in the Admiralty, but this could be key in determining the operating patterns of the enemy submarine force.

As the British realized, signals intelligence was becoming increasingly important for the Germans, although the Imperial Navy remained oblivious to its cyphers' vulnerability. The German navy's cryptographic bureau was based at Neumünster. It was established in 1915, ironically after operations on the western front had alerted the Germans to the potential of intercepting British naval communications. Neumünster's principal error was its eagerness to pass on decryptions to the fleet in time to be of tactical value. This alerted the British to their own vulnerability, although their response was initially incomplete, focusing on radio silence at sea rather than developing cyphers that would be more difficult to break. Nevertheless, the Admiralty had some idea of the threat. Later countermeasures included sending dummy messages. Aircraft-equipped formations operating in the North Sea would receive both real and dummy alerts to the presence of zeppelins, preventing the Germans from making a connection between their enemy's signal traffic and his knowledge of their operations.[68] Operational instructions based on intelligence were formally endorsed "NOTBYWIT" to indicate that they were not to be passed by radio. Breaches were the subject of immediate censure.[69]

Senior German commanders remained confident of the security of their signal texts, even though they now understood, at least for the surface fleet, the importance of radio silence at sea, driven largely by the fear of direction finding. New measures had been introduced to improve the security of cyphers, but they were incomplete and the fleet itself received a new signal book in 1916 with little enthusiasm, due to its complexity. Given Prince Heinrich's concern in 1914 over the fate of material from the grounded German cruiser *Magdeburg* and some appreciation of the Russian organization's quality, it is surprising signals were routinely transmitted in the Baltic that would not have been sent in the North Sea.[70] This may, however, have been unavoidable, given the separation between Prince Heinrich's headquarters in Kiel and his advanced force commander in Libau.

The Imperial Russian Navy, a leader in signals intelligence before 1914, continued to capitalize on an extensive prewar effort and the windfall from *Magdeburg*. This extended to continuing cooperation with the British. A sophisticated organization covered not only interception and decryption, but traffic analysis and efforts to estimate the location of transmissions. This included interception and direction-finding stations around the Russian coast, while shipborne direction-finding equipment was ordered in December 1915. Installation began in April 1916 with the first sets going to the destroyer *Novik* and two of her new sisters.[71] Other units already had signals intelligence staff embarked, while the analysis organization ashore provided both pre-sailing briefs and support for units at sea with the rapid decryption and turnaround of intercepts. The Service of Observation and Communications (Russian acronym SNIS)[72] benefited from the personal direction of Nepenin, perhaps the most dynamic officer in the fleet, who also commanded the increasingly capable aviation force.

Antisubmarine Warfare

The antisubmarine problem continued to defy solution. Working out how to detect submarines was perhaps the greatest technological challenge of the war at sea. Although understanding of submersibles' capabilities and limitations deepened steadily, something reflected in the antisubmarine patrol and search plans developed by the British,[73] most submarines could dive within a minute—reduced to thirty seconds in some boats—while the fastest surface unit could only cover a thousand yards in the same time. British prewar experiments made it clear that destroyers and other small vessels did not have sufficient draft to strike the hull of a boat even when it was at periscope depth. Aside from the small chance of hitting the periscope, ramming tactics only worked if the submarine were caught trying to dive or had lost trim. Big ships had generally been the victor in the relatively few rammings of an already submerged boat that resulted in a kill. It was also slowly being appreciated that the distance a submarine could move underwater, combined with its ability to remain submerged for many hours, meant waiting for it to surface did not have a high probability of success, particularly if nightfall was approaching. Extensive experiments were being undertaken into acoustic detection by 1916. Most promising were passive hydrophones that listened for machinery noise. There were, however, serious limitations. Their detection range was short, albeit increasing, while they generally required the listening unit to be stopped or moving very slowly. Towed systems were evolving, but there was a long way to go before they would be effective when antisubmarine units were escorting merchant vessels or big warships.

Until methods of underwater detection and tracking could be developed, the "time late" conundrum meant the submarine, once fully submerged and trimmed, was close to invulnerable. This remained true even after underwater weapons began to enter service. Submarines also benefited considerably from darkness. A trimmed-down submarine on the surface was not easy to see at night and, once submerged, practically impossible to relocate. Furthermore, submarines were much more difficult to sink or disable than had been expected. Headquarters knew by 1916 they had to discount the great majority of claims a submarine had been destroyed. Direct gunfire was not always effective against a curved pressure hull, and depth charges, which started to enter service in 1916, had a lethal range of only a few feet rather than the tens, or even hundreds, of feet kill radii envisaged. The same over-optimism extended to the net barrages and minefields laid in the English Channel and in other focal areas. Greater flexibility was at least shown in some ways. Contrary to service custom in the Royal Navy, the first unit on scene was directed to take charge when prosecuting a submarine, with the senior officer required to wait until an appropriate moment before taking over.[74] However, the fixation on hunting submarines rather than providing direct protection to their targets still dominated thinking in the Royal Navy in particular.

Submarine Warfare

Submarines themselves had come a very long way from their infancy of 1914,[75] but many aspects of their use were still being worked out. Direct comparisons between the British and Germans are difficult. The British had the advantage of starting with a bigger submarine force than the Germans and expanding relatively less, which meant there was a greater base of experience. They had also lost fewer boats up to the middle of 1916–18 to the Germans' thirty-two.[76] Manpower would, however, be strained with the introduction of the steam-driven *K* class. The British had far fewer targets to attack than the Germans, although their focus on patrolling the enemy's coast meant their experience was otherwise comparable. Significantly, no British dreadnought was ever successfully torpedoed by a U-boat, despite several attacks, although three German battleships were hit, as was the battle cruiser *Moltke* on two occasions. That none were sunk contributed to the concern that the 18-inch torpedo was not up to the job,[77] something particularly apparent after *E38*'s hit failed to sink the elderly light cruiser *München* in October 1916. Later versions of the new *L* and *K* classes would carry 21-inch weapons. As for the Russians, the consistently critical attitude

Photo 3.1   HMS *K12* with seaplane   *Royal Navy Historical Branch*

of the British submariners in the Baltic was not wholly unfair.[78] They were, however, crippled by inadequate machinery, as well as the Russian high command's fixation on defensive operations. The Baltic itself was a difficult theater for submarines, with salinity variations affecting depth control and clarity of water that made submerged units visible from the air. Russian torpedoes were also often unsatisfactory. This may have been the result of problems with torpedo design, as well as deficiencies in local manufacture, but the Russian policy of mounting the weapons on external "collars" outside the hull exposed them to corrosion and salt water ingress.[79] Effectiveness was not helped by their usually running shallow, with easily detectable wakes, allowing ships time to maneuver clear. British torpedoes were also criticized for broaching and alerting their target when fired at long range.[80]

The basic problems of submerged attack had been solved, notably maintaining depth as torpedoes were discharged. The British took up a prewar idea in 1915 to produce an early form of simulation in the "Attack Teacher," which combined a periscope and scale models to replicate attacks. Calculation of the firing solution remained essentially in a submarine captain's head, but Commander Martin Nasmith developed a handheld slide rule, which evolved into the "IsWas," that helped solve the problem,[81] particularly the difficult estimation of the "angle on the bow" of the target ship.[82] The Germans developed an equivalent instrument by the end of the war. In 1917 the British recognized that new submarine captains needed better preparation and instituted the "Commanding Officers' Qualifying Course," also known as the "Periscope Course" (nicknamed the "Perisher"— partly in recognition of its failure rate, historically around 20 percent). It focused on conducting attacks at close quarters on fast-moving surface ships; a successful officer had to maintain a tactical picture in his head from brief looks through a periscope. The Germans believed that working up each new boat in the Baltic provided sufficient preparation for novice captains. This served well enough, but later increases in numbers, combined with attrition, meant experience was increasingly diluted in the U-boat service, which affected performance.

Despite increased offshore navigation expertise—merchant mariner reservists filled many submarine navigator billets in every navy— submarines liked to confirm their location by sighting a prominent headland. This was standard U-boat procedure, encouraged by the fact that their targets were often coasting merchant vessels employing the same navigational technique. British submarines, returning to an often fogbound coast, bottomed at intervals to establish the depth of water and thus their distance from shore. The problems for submarines in relation to other friendly forces were already well known. Surface units tended to regard any submarine as hostile and attack without waiting to confirm identity. Matters were not helped by the inconsistent distribution of information about the movements of friendly submarines—*Birmingham* could well have attacked *G6* in July 1916, thinking she was hostile.[83] A veteran of service in *J2* commented, "From the danger point of view I voice the opinion of most [British] submarine men when I say that the British Navy was our biggest enemy."[84] A submarine attacked by its own side usually did not stick around to argue out the matter, but dived and conducted the same evasive measures as in the presence of enemy forces. This was by far the most prudent course, but when both submarine and ship were mistaken, the results could be tragic. In heavy weather in the Norwegian Sea on 16 September 1917, the submarine *G9* mistook the destroyer *Pasley* for a U-boat and fired two torpedoes. One struck but did not explode. *Pasley* turned to ram. Although both submarine and ship realized the error at the last moment, it was too late for *Pasley* to avoid hitting *G9* aft of the conning tower. The submarine sank, leaving only one survivor.

Later assessments by both British and American experts (the latter with no reason for special pleading) suggested any German submarine design advantage derived largely from the greater efficiency of their diesels, which generated three times the horsepower with much greater reliability than British models. German submariners regarded the British *E*-class diesels as

Photo 3.2   **German UB II-type U-boat**   *German Naval Association Archive*

a "cheap blacksmith's job,"[85] although when a survivor of *U45* saw that *D7*'s starboard engine "was in such a bad way that the supports were lashed to the hull with wires and ropes wherever possible, and every pipe-joint had tomato and tobacco tins hanging under them to catch the leaks. The Hun stoker looked up . . . with a smile and said, 'All same us!' "[86] Both sides judged if a submarine running on the surface was enemy by whether she was emitting smoke—German diesels did not.[87] In other respects, even if their main and auxiliary machinery was not as conceptually advanced, the Royal Navy's designs were better, as was much equipment, with the exception of optics.[88] In May 1919, the very experienced Commander Cecil Talbot commented of a surrendered boat, "Out in *U86*, diving in Whitsand Bay . . . she is a dreadful boat for diving, and took up very unpleasant inclinations several times, somewhere about 30 degrees; apparently the Germans had to rush the crew forward & aft to control her." He later wrote, "The boat gets under well but is a brute to handle at slow speed submerged . . . unless drastic steps are taken at once, she slowly & deliberately takes up very steep angles; her trim varies constantly at different depths."[89] British submarines admittedly also had problems of depth control and several submarines were saved only because the North Sea's bottom was closer to the surface than their hulls' crush depth.[90] Although this was understood by most captains,[91] it took a postwar loss in the deeper Atlantic for the necessary design changes to be made. The generally shallow waters of northern Europe were thus an unadvertised benefit, as was the muddy sea floor in so many areas, which allowed a "soft landing" when bottoming. Even so, by 1916 submarines were going well below what were previously considered unsafe depths, two hundred feet being not unknown for a British boat. This took time to filter through to the antisubmarine community. The first depth charges' maximum actuation depth was eighty feet.[92]

Aviation

Aviation had yet to fulfil its maritime potential. This was due to a combination of immature technology, competing strategic and operational demands, and confusion over employment. Systems as vital as reliable compasses were still under development. Both main fleet commanders were convinced of the value of airships for scouting, although the German effort was hamstrung by the priority given the strategic bombing campaign against Britain. Arguably, increasing interest among senior elements of the Royal Naval Air Service in strategic bombing was also a diversion from their main effort.[93]

In the meantime, the British knew they lacked the technology to produce a rigid airship as capable as the latest zeppelins, but, prodded by Admiral Jellicoe, production of a more capable semirigid model (the North Sea type) was in hand, while exercises were undertaken to determine how far from the British coast the existing types could support the fleet. The zeppelins proved their worth over the Heligoland Bight. Two or three airships conducted daily patrols when the weather permitted. Three were required to achieve a full survey of the Bight, but two were normally thought sufficient. Facing little threat (so far) from hostile aircraft, the zeppelins could operate at low level. This allowed the airship to spot mines from overhead. The zeppelins even deployed buoys to mark newly located fields.[94] However, these local operations were much less demanding than long-range reconnaissance over the northern and western North Sea and many techniques of over-the-water navigation and reporting remained immature.

The potential of aircraft and airships for antisubmarine work was becoming apparent and all sides were establishing new coastal bases and developing new types. The number of machines suitable for the long endurance operations required remained relatively limited in 1916, a combination of the fact that sufficiently powerful engines were only just coming to maturity and the competing demands being made on aircraft production capacity. In mid-1916 seaplanes were limited in range and carrying capacity. Sea state and wind (or lack of it) could very easily make deployment impossible from a mother ship in the open sea, which contributed to Admiral Jellicoe's interest in airships. Seaplanes operating from coastal bases had similar problems. Nevertheless, these restrictions had not stopped aviators developing improved methods of attack. The Germans planned to deploy twin engine torpedo carrying seaplanes to the Baltic and Flanders in 1916. The aircraft were as light as possible to carry their specially designed lightweight torpedo. As soon became clear, they were working at the limits of practicality and structural strength and required "extraordinarily skilled pilots" to operate them.[95]

Embarking landplanes in ships had just been adopted by the British as a work-around, although these aircraft could not be recovered at sea. Launched from a flying-off platform over the bows, they had a "one shot" capability. The concern was not the loss of an aircraft after each sortie, but the risk of killing its pilot when ditching. The launch arrangements also confined the type to light fighter aircraft, useful enough against zeppelins, but not against enemy ships. The scheme confirmed that aviation ships at sea needed high speed, both to keep up with the fleet and generate the minimum wind to launch their machines. This would be a feature, at least for the British, of all the units brought into service in the later years of the war. The Germans did not have the same priority for ship-launched aircraft, principally because the zeppelin did so much work, but also because the geography of the Baltic meant the defense of Kiel and offensive operations against Russia could be carried out from shore bases. This equally applied to the Flanders coast and to the Heligoland Bight. The combination of their geographical situation and their own defensive focus saw the Russians in the Baltic take much the same approach, even though a substantial force of seaplane carriers was assembled in the Black Sea.

New Developments in Warfare

Other avenues were being pursued. Both the British and the Germans were working on fast motor boats. The projects shared the aim of creating an offensive capability that could pass unscathed over minefields. The British priority was the High Sea Fleet's anchorages, the German the waters of the Gulf of Riga in which the Russians operated largely unchecked, although they saw uses for the new type off the Flanders coast as well. The Germans developed remote-controlled units carrying an explosive charge, detonated on contact with the target. A shore controller steered the boat by a cable that unreeled as the boat went, the controller receiving instructions by radio from an escorting aircraft. This was inherently an inshore weapon, given the limited length of cable that could be deployed, but had considerable potential. The British solution was a 40-foot manned fast boat, designated a coastal motor boat (CMB) carrying a torpedo, small enough to be carried on a light cruiser's davits, although a 60-foot type too big for such use was soon under development. The concept was for the CMBs to be launched when in range of their targets and recovered after their attack. Their speed, it was hoped, was such that the Germans would not have time to mount an effective pursuit.

The British struggled to produce an effective mine. All the existing types suffered defects that the navy was slow to recognize, and slower to remedy. Only when the Admiralty and trials authorities finally admitted the superiority of the German models with their activating "horns" was the design and production initiated of units that were practically copies of captured German units. The H2 mine became the mainstay of the British mining effort but was not available in large numbers before the end of 1917.

The Germans did not have the same problems of design, but their mine production had to compete for increasingly scarce materials. This meant that the navy had sufficient mines for vital defensive and offensive work, notably by minelaying submarines, but never the vast stockpiles that the British had imagined were in German inventories before the war. Mines received high priority in Russia and mine manufacture continued apace, despite the increasing problems of Russian industry. Its prewar types had proved reliable in service, while a new, more powerful deepwater weapon (the M1916 type) was under development. Sustained production was essential, since the defensive fields protecting the Gulfs of Finland and Riga could lose up to 50 percent of their mines over the winter. Submarine minelaying had been the subject of interest before the war and, the first two *Bars*-class craft in the Baltic were modified to carry external mines over the winter of 1915–16, while two additional units were being more extensively altered during build.[96]

Much had been learned since 1914, but much about integrating the emerging technology had yet to be understood. The remaining years of the war would see further radical change, the opening of some new avenues and, as the fate of the zeppelins would demonstrate, the closing of others. Above all, the environment still dictated in large measure what could happen and when. None of the seagoing or airborne elements were entirely masters of their own fate.

The Shadow of Jutland

4

THE BRITISH RETURN FROM JUTLAND was a dispiriting experience. Inevitable post-combat reactions combined with lack of sleep and the strain of coaling and ammunitioning to depress spirits. Above all, the "sad disappointment"[1] of the empty horizon on 1 June that confirmed the successful escape of the High Sea Fleet lay heavy. While no one was sure how severe German losses were, the Grand Fleet's were all too obvious. The reception of the ships in port added to the misery. Those returning to Rosyth "were baffled when workers on the Forth Bridge shouted at us as we passed under the great arch . . . we were being subjected to unmistakable abuse."[2] This obloquy was caused by a dismal statement issued by the Admiralty, which created public dismay. The Grand Fleet understood immediately that it gave the impression the Germans had won a victory. *Marlborough*'s captain wrote: "Having smashed up half the German fleet, sent a good many to the bottom, and driven the remainder into harbour, it was a bit of a shock when we read the papers' comments."[3] For the Harwich Force, which missed the battle, it was even worse: "That deplorable phrasing . . . made us feel like so many whipped dogs . . . we felt that the Harwich folk were looking very sideways at us."[4] They were right, failure to achieve decisive victory hit hard on a population that had expected much of its navy. What hit the Grand Fleet and its families hard were the losses, with few rays of light as the stragglers came home. Nearly twelve hours behind the battle cruisers, the belated arrival in Rosyth of *Southampton*, battered flagship of the Second Light Cruiser Squadron, was greeted with "much relief." The "depressing gaps" in the battle cruiser lines had given little cause for optimism about *Southampton*'s possible fate.[5]

The British decision not to conceal their losses paid dividends when German claims of victory lost credibility as news of other sinkings, notably the battle cruiser *Lützow*, leaked out, forcing an official admission a week after the battle—one urged, to his credit, by the kaiser. Nevertheless, British information management left much to be desired. There is justice in the claim the Royal Navy never again enjoyed the domestic or global prestige it had commanded since Trafalgar. This had implications for how both allies and neutrals regarded Britain. The tsar pointed out to his British naval liaison officer that the first news he received was from the Russian front line, when each sector reported that German trenches "were displaying boards bearing the inscription, 'We have sunk the British fleet.'"[6] The tsar remarked that this had a very depressing effect on the Russian soldiers, suggesting even a continental nation's army may have some comprehension of sea power.

Jutland and the High Sea Fleet

The Germans were elated by their achievement, but relieved by their escape. *Derfflinger*'s gunnery officer admitted that "a load fell from my heart"[7] when dawn broke on 1 June. That the fleet had been in battle and survived was itself an enormous, if temporary, morale booster, and June 1916 saw a peak in the High Sea Fleet's fighting spirit.[8] As the Austro-Hungarian naval attaché reported from Wilhelmshaven, "the fleet is absolutely *enthusiastic and intoxicated with victory.*"[9] Yet the extensive damage suffered by so many major units, as well as the loss of the brand-new *Lützow*, made it clear the Grand Fleet remained a much more powerful fighting force than its opponent. Admiral Reinhard Scheer had the most food for thought. His handling of the fleet was essentially opportunistic. Much critical attention has been devoted to Jellicoe's incomplete tactical understanding, but Scheer's comprehension had been even more limited.[10] His aggressive second approach to the Grand Fleet might have paid dividends in other circumstances, but Scheer had trusted to fortune in the absence of a clear tactical picture and was nearly caught. "The thing just happened—as the virgin said when she got the baby."[11] Fundamental questions about Scheer and his staff's understanding of the battle space do not seem to have been directly addressed, let alone resolved on board *Friedrich der Grosse*. Nevertheless, the confusion of 31 May and 1 June 1916 highlighted to Scheer the need for more effective long-range reconnaissance if his weaker fleet were to succeed in isolating a component of the British forces without again being brought to action by their main body.

At the same time, the battle reinforced Scheer's view that the best way to attack the British would be a renewed campaign of unrestricted attacks on merchant shipping. This was a key point in his report to the kaiser.

Nevertheless, the admiral was willing to try an all-arms effort again. He had not abandoned hope of achieving further successes against the Grand Fleet and intended U-boats play a vital role. In part, Scheer's continued focus on their potential military employment came from recognition that achieving consensus on unrestricted submarine warfare would take time, given the objections of the chancellor and significant elements in the political leadership and civil service. The navy itself was divided on the question and von Holtzendorff and the Admiralstab favored at least prosecuting a campaign of prize warfare while the matter was settled. Scheer was loath to "campaign in [this] milder form"[12] and felt the U-boats should work with the fleet until a favorable decision. He also had in mind that the restored morale of the High Sea Fleet would remain high if it remained active.

Scheer's aim was still to draw the British fleet out and reduce its strength by a series of U-boat attacks, but the submarines' contribution to the Jutland action was disappointing. The submariners themselves were unenthusiastic about the dispositions before the battle, given the difficulties of intercepting heavily escorted formations as they came out and returned to port.[13] Investment of the main British bases could not achieve the necessary cumulative effect because the U-boats had to be widely dispersed to keep clear of each other. The U-boats had not intercepted any British units on departure, while there were no successes against crippled units struggling home. *U51* fired a single torpedo at *Warspite* and *U46* attacked *Marlborough* with another weapon, but neither hit. *U63* was fortunate to avoid being rammed after the U-boat misread the surface picture while positioning to attack another ship (probably one of *Warspite*'s newly joined escort), only to find the battleship bearing down on her. Her emergency dive resulted in *U63* hitting the bottom and then returning uncontrolled to periscope depth. She was lucky not to be sighted and attacked. More U-boats were dispatched to the British coast in early June to intercept units moving between bases for repairs, but still had no success. While British formations were encountered, their high speed and evasive steering prevented the U-boats getting into attack positions. In any case, operations close to shore suited the small UB and UC types much more than the slower diving large U-boats. New tactics were needed, as was more training in attacking fast-moving and heavily escorted targets. Scheer at least had time to experiment. Damage to his capital ships was so extensive that even a reduced force could not be mustered before mid-August. The British had problems finding enough large docks for their cripples, but the Germans also had limited refit capacity. *Moltke* had to be repaired in the commercial Blohm and Voss yard at Hamburg, a turret from the battleship *Rheinland* was cannibalized to permit timely completion of *Von der Tann*'s work, while *Seydlitz* emerged with a concrete patch over the hole in her *Bertha* turret.[14]

The difficulty was coordinating the submarines with the operations of the main fleet. Once submerged, the U-boats were not just slow, but effectively immobile. This put a premium on communications to ensure they were in the right spot before they needed to dive as a prelude to immediate action. Consequently, the fleet's submarine force commander was transferred to the battleship *Prinzregent Luitpold*, which had a better fit of radios than a light cruiser and would be close to the flagship, making it easier to coordinate U-boat operations with the C-in-C. The submarine commander was not embarked in *Friedrich der Grosse* because of a shortage of working space and the limited number of radios in the fleet flagship. During June and July 1916 new dispositions were subjected to trial. These included a North Sea deployment in July with U-boats disposed in a large circular formation, expected to give the most opportunities for repeated attacks on an advancing enemy force. Fourteen boats conducted the operation over ten days, sinking or capturing several merchant ships and trawlers and badly damaging the sloop *Rosemary*, but there were only fleeting contacts with major units, their escorts and zigzags preventing any attacks.[15] These contacts were with cruisers and destroyers operating off the Norwegian coast to intercept the expected departure of a raider of the *Möwe* type. Despite the efforts of "no less than 13 armed merchant ships, 14 cruisers and 18 destroyers" over four days, the British found nothing.[16] The trigger had been an agent's report, rather than signals intelligence, but there was other evidence of German activity in the Kattegat. The British were aware that the German efforts against merchant shipping had reduced significantly but had no idea of what the U-boats were attempting. Their picture was confused even further by *U48*'s capture of the merchant ship *Pendennis*, which escaped from the Baltic only to fall foul of the mass submarine sortie. The British could not be sure who or what had taken her prize.

By late July, the High Sea Fleet staff decided that offshore U-boat barriers placed across the expected British approach would be the best tactic. The northern lines would be manned by High Sea Fleet U-boats, those in the south by boats from Flanders. They could be positioned to catch the Grand Fleet during both its advance and withdrawal, particularly if zeppelins made timely sightings. Scheer insisted that the airships were fundamental to any fleet deployment. The zeppelins would be available as scouts for any new sortie into the North Sea. The fleet had the benefit of the first of the "super-zeppelins" with their greater lift and range. *L30* was accepted into service on 30 May and conducted her first scouting mission on 5 July. *L31* would follow on 14 July, with more units every month.[17] Scheer's greatest challenge was keeping the zeppelins focused. Although the airships were conducting North Sea patrols one day in four,[18] their commander, Peter Strasser, was obsessed with resuming attacks on England. He proposed increasing the force to provide for the full requirements of the fleet, estimated at twelve units in the air, with six more on standby,[19] as well as the strategic bombing campaign. In reality, raids on England would inevitably suck resources from the naval role. The larger the force, the greater the temptation to increase the numbers dispatched on bombing raids. Perhaps even more critical, the skills required for bombing were not the same as those for reconnaissance. The Germans suffered from divided aims. Zeppelin attacks on the United Kingdom were resumed at the end of July with the new moon and lengthening nights. Whatever the propaganda and military benefits of this campaign, sufficient time did not remain for the training in over-water scouting and warship identification vital in producing accurate reports.

Reforms in the Grand Fleet

For his part, Admiral Jellicoe was not idle after Jutland. He was bitterly disappointed by the results of the battle, and the Russian naval observer in the Grand Fleet was not alone in observing the admiral appeared "rather depressed."[20] This may have been as much the effect of two years in command of the fleet—the C-in-C himself admitted that "the job is more than most people over 55 [he was 56] can tackle for very long."[21] Nevertheless, Jellicoe's determination to learn and apply the lessons of the battle, even if some ran contrary to his existing policies, must stand as an important contribution to the Royal Navy. The approach to reform was carefully controlled, with committees formed to examine the problems that had arisen during the battle, but it was also (largely) unhesitating. Many changes followed. Perhaps most urgent was reimposition of the proper precautions for handling ammunition and propellant. Examination of the Jutland wrecks has confirmed that obsession with achieving a high rate of fire resulted in neglect of the regulations.[22] Interlocks and doors had been left open or even removed, while bare charges were stacked in handling rooms and working chambers. Given that turret armor could be penetrated, this made catastrophic explosions practically inevitable. The Admiralty quickly identified the key issue. Although the battle cruisers and armored cruisers had suffered in battle, the problem also involved the battleships, and the fleet rapidly improved its procedures. In the Grand Fleet itself, much more emphasis was given to the need to increase deck armor, something probably worthwhile, but not as significant as the officers of the fleet asserted.[23]

Gunnery received new attention. One aspect was raising the standards of the battle cruisers. A concern before the battle, their performance on 31 May raised serious questions, despite attempts by Beatty and his staff to talk up their achievements. A second, more ambitious aspect was the development of techniques to concentrate the firing of two or more ships on a single target. This required not only new short-range radios and procedures to share fire control information and spotting corrections in real time but also improved close range maneuvering. Bringing all the components of this system together was a big task that came fully to fruition only in 1918, but it greatly increased the lethal power of the battleships and was progressively extended to cruisers before the end of the war. Another innovation came through "throw-off" practices, in which ships fired at each other with an artificial offset inserted in the aim. This allowed much more realistic shooting at much higher speeds than against a towed target.[24] When the Americans arrived in the Grand Fleet at the end of 1917, they were deeply impressed by the progress the British had made.

Jellicoe was also sure there needed to be changes in the fleet's operational dispositions and tactics. Central to the new approach was the composition of the force. With a long-term plan to move the bulk of the Grand Fleet to Rosyth, the immediate permanent basing of the Fifth Battle Squadron in the Firth of Forth reflected a compromise between the Admiralty's desire to improve the Royal Navy's ability to intercept a German raid on the east coast, Beatty's eagerness to have the powerful new battleships under his direct command, and Jellicoe's determination his subordinate not be given a force so powerful that he would risk becoming entangled with the High Sea Fleet.[25] The C-in-C would not again allow the Battle Cruiser Fleet (a title he regarded as creating a misapprehension as to Beatty's proper subordinate role as a scouting commander) to stray far from the Grand Fleet.

The battle squadrons' organization changed in other ways that reflected plans already in train but confirmed by the experience of battle.[26] With the exception of the relatively fast and heavily gunned *Agincourt*, the 12-inch gun battleships were shifted into the Fourth Battle Squadron, with the

First and Second taking the 13.5-inch gun units, the new 15-inch gun *R*-class *Agincourt,* and the 14-inch gun and equally fast *Canada.* This, when all five *R*-class vessels were complete, would create a group of nineteen super-dreadnoughts—twenty-four, when the Fifth Battle Squadron was included. Although some would always be absent in refit, this was a very powerful force, more than strong enough to overwhelm a German fleet that would, at best, have only a handful of new 38-cm gunned ships to supplement its 30.5-cm and 28-cm units. Given Jellicoe's new views of the difficulty of managing more than sixteen ships in line,[27] as well as the fact that the Fourth Battle Squadron units were relatively slow (and getting steadily slower as their machinery aged), this added strength to accepting that the older ships could be based separately and might not join in time to form part of the fleet in action. Such a separation was inevitable with the move to Rosyth, since the Fourth Battle Squadron could not be fitted inside the anchorage when the rest of the fleet was there and would have to remain farther north at Cromarty.[28] In the coming months, as the U-boat threat increased and the need for destroyers elsewhere in British waters grew, this would also be a factor in Jellicoe's willingness to immobilize a battle squadron if it became essential to divert the Grand Fleet's destroyers to other duties. There was another element, a personal one. Jellicoe did not trust the Fourth's commander, Doveton Sturdee.[29] The latter had a much more independent approach than Jellicoe liked and was the subordinate admiral whom the C-in-C would trust least with these new, more flexible arrangements. The Fourth would almost inevitably be the rearmost unit in the line and thus less likely to permit unwelcome displays of initiative.

With all but a few major ships back in service in early July, Jellicoe planned new fleet exercises. These were delayed by a report of the sailing of the High Sea Fleet. This was soon identified as false, but fog further retarded the Grand Fleet's departure until the 17th. Two days were spent on "P.Z.s" (the designation given to the fleet's tactical exercises) near the Shetlands. The harsh experience of Jutland meant that the improvement of reporting procedures was the C-in-C's first priority and the exercises included new experiments with aircraft. Although they were usually unsure of their own position, units in the air could assess the enemy's course much more accurately than surface vessels. This was key information for making sense of the tactical picture and Jellicoe was very encouraged by the results. There were, however, few aviation ships available to support the Grand Fleet, which had to make do with the elderly and unreliable *Campania* and the small

Engadine. Kite balloons extended ships' horizons to a limited extent, but not sufficiently to provide the C-in-C with information early enough to make a real difference.

The exercises also experimented with more flexible control of the battle squadrons, particularly in response to massed torpedo attacks. Jellicoe now accepted that the differing levels of risk to the various sections of the line justified it being "broken" and passing out of his control in some circumstances. He focused on a much more aggressive use of the van while the center and the rear—geometrically the most vulnerable to torpedoes—maneuvered to get clear of the enemy attack. Later exercises, notably those of 21 September, took these ideas further, including simultaneous reversals of course by the entire line, a battle maneuver not considered practicable by the British before Jutland. Even past advocates of divided tactics were dubious about the early results of "the C-in-C's wholesale conversion to independence of Squadrons," but such growing pains were inevitable with such a significant change in doctrine.[30] Experience gained in experimental mass torpedo attack exercises by light forces in the "inland sea" of Scapa Flow was used to practice more aggressive tactics by the destroyer flotillas.

Operations in the South

If operations in the northern areas in June and July 1916 reflected an inevitable lull following the main fleet action, southern waters were much more lively. A few days after Jutland, Scheer approved a plan agreed earlier with the Flanders coast commander, Admiral von Schröder, to deploy to Zeebrugge the Second Flotilla, which included some of the fleet's largest and most modern destroyers. The repairs of so many major units meant the flotilla could readily be spared. One British measure was of great concern to the Flanders Command. The Belgian ports had been the most active U-boat bases before their withdrawal from the campaign against merchant shipping in late April. U-boat successes in the Channel earlier in 1916 resulted in Dover Command's attempt the same month to place mines and nets parallel to the German-occupied coast at twelve miles distance, out of range of the coastal batteries. Deciding the location was helped by information provided by the French from the wreck of the recently destroyed *UB26*.[31] In theory, given shallows to the east off the Dutch coast and the north-south running minefields that closed the deeper channels to seaward of the ports still in Allied hands, this arrangement would enclose the Flanders U-boats. The "Flanders Barrage" suffered the same problems with poor mines and

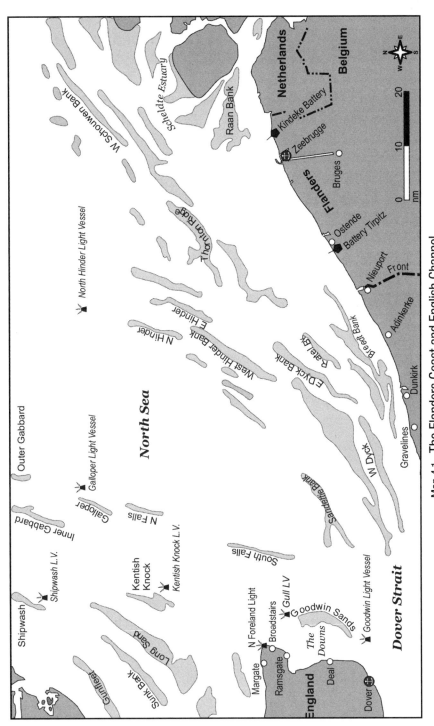

Map 4.1 The Flanders Coast and English Channel

hard-to-manage nets as earlier attempts at barriers in the Channel. It had some effect, however, although just how much was not clear for many years. *UB13* was sunk soon after the nets were laid on 24 April, and *UC3* was lost on 27 May. The final victim was *UC7* on 3 July.[32] *UB10* was caught for eight hours in the newly laid explosive nets on 24 April and got back into Ostend with the remains of a net entangled in her propeller, but no other boats were lost.

The British found it difficult to assess the barrage's effectiveness, particularly because of the temporary end of the U-boats' commerce campaign. Admiral Bacon mistook lack of interference with cross-Channel traffic for the German submarines' inability to penetrate the strait, but this was not an opinion universally held. There was another element. It was usually hard to be sure when a boat had been destroyed. If submerged, detonating a mine meant the loss of the entire crew. Failure to make an expected radio report or the failure of a boat to return to its home port were generally the only indications of a sinking. It would take years before submarine losses were properly attributed and in 2018 many wrecks remain lost. The Germans had no high opinion of the quality of British mines, but the barrage—despite its defects—was still a dangerous obstacle. Over the following months, the British and French conducted surface patrols and maintenance on the nets and their markers by day, with submarines taking up the watch at night. The Germans responded with surface sorties, but more often harassed the ships on the barrage with air attacks and occasional long-range shots from their shore batteries.

The destroyers of the Second Flotilla sailed from Germany on 7 June and were first detected by British the next day. The Admiralty was already aware of the movement, which created new problems for the vital cross-Channel transport route. Commodore Tyrwhitt conducted a sweep toward Terschelling with the entire Harwich Force of six light cruisers and thirty destroyers but did not find anything. The Germans had already got through to Zeebrugge. The prospect of a greatly increased German ability to raid the Channel forced the detachment of two cruisers and a half-flotilla from Harwich to Dover. Tyrwhitt was less than happy with this reduction in his striking force. Although the Dover Patrol possessed only a single light cruiser, he thought the big gun and smaller monitors, together with the twenty-four destroyers based there were more than enough to deal with the Second Flotilla and the Flanders torpedo boats, at least in daylight. This proved the case as early as 8 June when an exchange of fire between the Dover forces and units of the Second Flotilla and the Flanders Second Half-Flotilla resulted in the Germans being forced to cover with a smoke screen the withdrawal of *V67*, hit and badly damaged by the monitor *Lord Clive*. What would be a more difficult problem for the British, as both sides came to realize, was the prospect of raids during the long darkness of the winter months.

Tyrwhitt had other reservations about the detachments. While he kept his own force at high readiness, he was increasingly uneasy about Bacon's employment of his ships. Dover Harbor was extremely exposed in heavy weather and the vice admiral did not help by insisting on unrealistic notice for sea that bore heavily on men and machinery. Their deteriorating relationship was indicated by Tyrwhitt's irritated letter of 30 July 1916 to Bacon complaining about the latter's insistence the detached units would only be released from Dover when their reliefs arrived, something that Commodore (T) considered made it impossible to meet the competing demands on his ships.[33] At this stage, Bacon enjoyed the support of the Admiralty and of Jellicoe, but confidence in his ability was diminishing among other commanders and his juniors.

In the meantime, the important shipping route between the Netherlands and England became the new center of attention. On 23 June the mail packet *Brussels* was intercepted and taken into Zeebrugge. Her captain, Charles Fryatt, was tried by court-martial on the grounds of resisting U-boat attacks in his earlier commands, notably by attempting to ram a surfaced boat, which the Germans argued was illegal by a civilian of the merchant navy. Found guilty, he was executed on 27 July 1916. Intended as a deterrent for other merchant ship captains, this proved yet another miscue by the Germans, handing the Allies a martyr, one particularly attractive to Americans infuriated by the deaths of their own nationals at sea. Fryatt's apotheosis was not confined to print. Within a year he was the subject of a silent movie.[34]

Protection of the other cross-Channel ferries and imports from the Netherlands consumed much of the Harwich Force's energy in the following months. Ironically labelled the "Beef trip," in memory of the time before refrigeration when ships' boats were sent inshore to collect the day's fresh meat, operations at first focused on defending the passage from the Sunk to the Maas, with light cruisers and divisions of destroyers allocated to different areas. Given the speed at which events could move when an enemy force approached, it rapidly became clear that close escort was required. This created immediate complications. Dutch national vessels had to be left out of the first efforts at escorting the traffic, in order not to endanger their neutral status, while single destroyers were assigned to each Allied ship. By late July it was apparent better arrangements were needed, and a convoy system was instituted. Up to nine merchant ships departed from each side of the Channel every two to three days, under the escort of a light cruiser and four destroyers. A force of equal strength was deployed to cover the approaches to Zeebrugge. There were a few habitual stragglers, but despite most of the passage being at night, the formations generally held. The "Beef trip" was heartily disliked by the Harwich Force, but it was an extremely effective defensive measure and indication the overall approach to protecting merchant shipping needed to change. One of its destroyer captains later pointed out that the casualty list among the escorts between 1916 and 1918 was longer than that of the merchant ships.[35]

Before returning to Germany, the Second Flotilla sailed on 22 July to conduct a final sortie against the Anglo-Dutch trade. *B111* was designated to lay a mine field off the North Hinder Light Vessel, accompanied by seven other units. The latter were to protect the minelayer and intercept any merchant vessels they encountered. The Harwich Force was out in strength that night, Tyrwhitt's *Carysfort* and a destroyer division patrolling near the North Hinder, with a second cruiser, *Canterbury,* and four more destroyers working near the Maas Light Vessel. The British had no specific intelligence of the German operation, although they must have been on alert. At 0015 *Carysfort* sighted the German flotilla three miles ahead and went in chase. The Germans immediately turned easterly for home. The combination

Photo 4.1   **German Second Flotilla at Zeebrugge**   *German Naval Association Archive*

of maneuvering to avoid a possible torpedo attack, a rain squall and the Germans' very effective use of smoke made Tyrwhitt lose contact after less than half an hour. He had, however, ordered *Canterbury* and her division to intercept the Germans' likely escape route.

A further encounter followed at 0145, but the British did not handle this well. The destroyer *Melpomene*'s report of six destroyers was not taken at face value by *Canterbury*, whose captain was unsure whether this was Tyrwhitt's group. The four destroyers did not share these doubts but separated into two groups when the lame duck *Matchless* fell astern, suffering the effects of a badly aligned stern rebuilt after her 1915 mining. *Milne* remained with *Matchless*, leaving *Melpomene* and *Morris* to go on ahead. The latter two had only a fleeting engagement with the Second Flotilla. In difficult conditions, German gunnery proved a little better than the British, with *Melpomene* suffering some damage before the proximity of minefields caused *Canterbury* to recall *Melpomene* and *Morris*. Once again, the German smoke screens proved very effective.[36] When the Second Flotilla sailed for home on 31 July, it could be sure it had caused the British considerable anxiety, even if the material results were limited (the minefield laid by *B111* claimed two merchant vessels, but no warships).

Tyrwhitt found himself under considerable pressure to act against the zeppelin raids. The destruction of an airship at sea in 1915 had shown there were possibilities for surface forces, although the zeppelins became increasingly cautious about approaching warships. Stationing cruisers and destroyers offshore forced the zeppelins to make their approach to the coast in the dark. It soon became clear, however, that aircraft were the only effective means of shooting down a zeppelin. The Harwich Force had only one seaplane carrier, *Vindex*, but timely reporting of the arrival of the zeppelins over England would allow her being stationed underneath their likely flight path home. In fact, reports from light ships and scouts at sea of the airships' approach proved useful by alerting the inland defenses, particularly in clear weather, while the Germans' liberal use of radio meant that direction finding was also rapidly becoming a vital source of queueing.

Vindex included some innovations. In addition to a handful of seaplanes, she carried two Bristol Scout landplanes. Unencumbered by floats, these had the performance necessary against the high-flying airships. *Vindex* herself was faster than any earlier aviation ship. At twenty-three knots, she could generate enough wind to launch a Scout even in a flat calm. The first encounter came on 2 August when units of the Harwich Force met three of the six zeppelins that had lifted that evening. While the cruiser *Conquest* engaged one airship, *Vindex* launched a Scout, which attacked *L17*. After getting overhead, the pilot dropped canisters of Ranken Darts, each containing a pound of high explosive, but succeeded in causing only light damage. It would take the new incendiary bullets to provide an effective countermeasure to the huge airships. The Scout ditched at the end of its endurance, and the pilot spent an anxious few hours clinging to the slowly sinking machine before he was rescued by the Belgian merchant ship *Anvers*. This was the start of what could become a more effective campaign against the zeppelins. But the Harwich Force soon suffered blows that made the reduction in the surface threat after the Second Flotilla's departure of little comfort. The cruiser *Cleopatra* was mined on 4 August while operating with the Dover Command. It was almost certainly a British mine, and her absence for two months' repair was a bitter pill to swallow. On 13 August, while escorting a "Beef trip," the destroyer *Lassoo* was torpedoed and sunk by the submarine *UB10*. Although only five men were killed, *Lassoo* broke in two shortly after being struck and there was no hope of salvage. Hit by these losses and forced to detach substantial parts of his command to other parts of the coast, Commodore (T) must have wondered, as the Naval Staff Monograph notes, "why his famous flotillas were called the Harwich Force."[37] In the meantime, the High Sea Fleet was on the move again.

The Torpedoes of August

5

BY MID-AUGUST SCHEER WAS READY for another try. His new target: Sunderland. The primary aim was not its bombardment but forcing action with the British under favorable circumstances. The success of the scheme was dependent, as Scheer knew, on the zeppelins and U-boats fulfilling their potential. The High Sea Fleet was not at full strength when it sailed on 18 August. *Seydlitz* and *Derfflinger* were still under repair and the two remaining battle cruisers of the First Scouting Group had to be supplemented by the newly completed 38-cm gunned *Bayern*, *Grosser Kurfürst*, and *Markgraf*. This was a powerful force to place against Beatty's depleted Battle Cruiser Fleet, but only the First and Third Squadrons with fourteen battleships followed them out. The Second Squadron remained behind; there would be no pre-dreadnoughts in the deployed High Sea Fleet. Scheer's determination to keep the scouting forces closer to the main body mirrored that of Jellicoe; the First Scouting Group was only twenty miles ahead of the battle squadrons. The weather was initially as good as 31 May and Scheer had high hopes for the scouting powers of the eight zeppelins aloft. However, as 19 August wore on, increasing cloud and thunderstorms combined to limit the airships' effectiveness, dependent as they were (like the surface forces) on good visibility to understand what was going on.

The British knew the Germans were moving, thanks to a Room 40 intercept at 0919 on 18 August, almost twelve hours before the High Sea Fleet emerged. The Grand Fleet sailed later that day to concentrate east of Aberdeen. Jellicoe was on leave near Edinburgh, with Burney deputizing for him, but arrangements were in place for the C-in-C to rejoin at short notice. Jellicoe sailed from Dundee in the light cruiser *Royalist* and transferred to *Iron Duke* after dusk. The evolution proved dangerous. With the flagship detached from the main body for the transfer, one of *Iron Duke*'s destroyer escort was unsuccessfully attacked by *UB27*. The Battle Cruiser Fleet left

Rosyth on the evening of the 18th, having been directed to take station thirty miles in the van of the battle fleet. The Harwich Force was ordered out to the Brown Ridge, well to the east of Yarmouth, while the Third Battle Squadron was kept ready in the Swin. The Dover Force patrols were concentrated in case of a German move against the cross-Channel transports.

The Admiralty's scheme of response was essentially defensive, and most of the available submarines were stationed off the most likely target areas on the east coast. *E23*, the only submarine to encounter the High Sea Fleet, had initially been deployed to attack U-boats on passage. The dispositions still suffered from the lack of coordination apparent at Jutland. Perhaps because of the inherently restricted transmission of its telegrams, the Admiralty once more failed to distribute sufficient information around the dispersed formations before they sailed. The latter did not help by not passing on their own intentions to other commands, which could have been managed by further telegrams before departure. Thus, Tyrwhitt sailed with the Harwich Force uncertain whether the Grand Fleet would be out as well. Even when it became clear—as he expected—that it was, he would not have "the slightest idea" of the location of the Grand Fleet until late afternoon on the 19th.[1] The defensive dispositions also stemmed from the Admiralty's understandable preoccupation with protecting the Channel. The Second Flotilla's recent deployment to the Flanders coast renewed concerns the Germans might attack the south while staging a diversion farther north. The Admiralty feared that concentrating the Harwich Force and the Grand Fleet could leave the Channel open. If the Third Battle Squadron were required to face a force of enemy capital ships it would be in desperate need of the modern light cruisers and destroyers only Tyrwhitt could provide.

The main body of the Grand Fleet and the battle cruisers were in position by dawn on 19 August, just as *Iron Duke* rejoined and Jellicoe resumed command. By 0540 the battleships were on a southerly course at the now customary antisubmarine speed of eighteen knots. Although Beatty had carefully taken his directed station only thirty miles ahead, Jellicoe shortly afterward ordered him to close within visual range. An encounter had already taken place. The light cruiser screen ahead of the Battle Cruiser Fleet ran into the first line of U-boats and at 0557 *Nottingham* was hit by two torpedoes from *U52*. One blew the bottom out of a boiler room. All power was quickly lost. *Nottingham* made a visual report to her sister ship, *Dublin*, and eventually rigged an emergency aerial, but *U52* shortly afterward finished the job with a third torpedo amidships. This hit made the

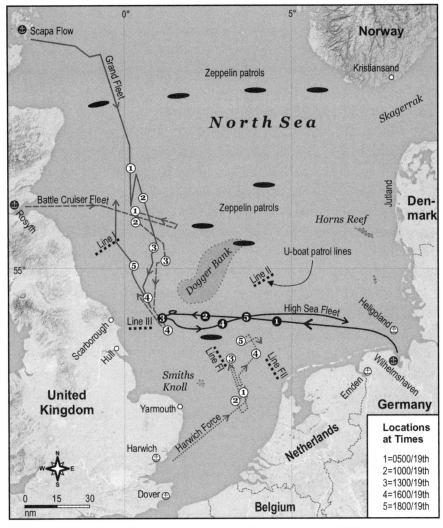

Map 5.1 The High Sea Fleet Sortie of 19 August 1916

cruiser's captain accept that "my old friend was really done in."[2] *Nottingham* listed increasingly to port, going under bows first at 0710. Time allowed for an orderly evacuation, although there were not enough boats and rafts. The captain and four officers were the last to leave and walked into the water like a "bathing picnic," as one described it, ending up clutching a spar, "looking like swallows on a telegraph wire."[3] The group kept up its morale by sharing the contents of the navigator's hipflask. Many ratings were loath to enter the water, and nineteen drowned or succumbed to exposure before rescue, two more dying later. Destroyers were soon on the scene, but their rescue efforts were hindered by repeated submarine sightings. At least two ratings were dragged into the propellers of a destroyer getting suddenly under way as she responded to the report of a periscope. The sinking hit *Nottingham*'s squadron consorts hard, "like losing one of the family."[4] Just as concerning, the light cruiser's destruction confirmed such ships were vulnerable to submarine attack. The high speed and evasive maneuvering customary since just after the outbreak of war were no longer enough.

Nottingham's initial emergency signal indicated she had been hit by a mine, but Goodenough, her squadron commander, was less certain and suggested that it had been a torpedo, something confirmed by *Dublin*'s repeated reports. This placed Jellicoe in a quandary when he finally received *Nottingham*'s original signal at 0650, nearly an hour after the event. Because the Battle Cruiser Fleet had been making ground to the north during this time, Jellicoe's advanced forces were clear of whatever lay to the south, but he decided to turn the whole force north until the situation was clarified. Jellicoe intended this only as a temporary move because he did not change the relative position of his scouting units, which were now astern. Jellicoe's assessments lay in the shadow of the increasing restrictions that he faced on his fleet's movements in the southern North Sea. Submarines were bad enough, but the proliferation of minefields had forced the British to clear two major swept channels that ran southeast (L Channel) and southsoutheast (M Channel) from outside the Firth of Forth. These were effectively the only safe water for the Grand Fleet to approach the likely battleground with the High Sea Fleet. If the L Channel were mined, and the C-in-C suspected the Germans knew enough about the two channels to take such a step, there would be very limited room to maneuver.

Jellicoe had good reason to keep his options open. The Admiralty had just informed him that direction finding confirmed the High Sea Fleet was well out into the North Sea. At 0800 came further critical information. This was a report a submarine had torpedoed a German battleship outside the Heligoland Bight earlier that morning. *E23* was able to follow this up with her own signal to the ships at sea at 0916, "Enemy's battleships enemy's battle cruisers enemy's light cruisers steering west. 54° 20′ N, 5° E 4 a.m. [0500 GMT] claim one enemy battleship hit."[5] That *E23* expected to transmit this message to the other side of the North Sea was significant. She carried a high-power Poulsen unit, whose fit was being extended to all the overseas boats. For the first time, British submarines could operate as advanced reconnaissance units, although setting up to transmit was no small task, *E23*'s long-range aerial having to be deployed under a kite. Sent on D wave, the signal suffered extensive interference from Commodore (T)'s units. This meant the Harwich Force did not take in the critical "4 a.m." element of *E23*'s report and formed the impression the High Sea Fleet was four hours steaming to the east of its actual position. This was to make Tyrwhitt's job of assessing his situation even more difficult. Further confirmation the Germans were out came when *L13* was sighted by the Harwich Force. It was a reasonable assumption that an airship would be scouting so far west only in support of a major operation.

Scheer had his own problems. *E23* hit *Westfalen* with a single torpedo on the starboard side at 0505. The German battleship suffered extensive damage, taking in eight hundred tons of water before the flooding was controlled. *Westfalen* attempted to remain with the fleet, but the strain was too much for her bulkheads and she was detached at 0630 with an escort of torpedo boats. *E23* had another go at the returning *Westfalen* with two torpedoes from a range of 1,500 yards at 0721. Both missed and *E23* was forced to go deep. She surfaced at 0845 and her report was dispatched at 0916. The incident must have worried Scheer. He was uncertain whether *Westfalen* had been struck by a mine or torpedo until the report of *E23*'s second attack reached him.

Attrition could work in both directions and the two most recent sorties by the High Sea Fleet had seen a capital ship damaged in the approaches to the Heligoland Bight. The hurt to the ship was bad enough, but Scheer was justifiably irritated by *Westfalen* reporting the incident by high-power wireless. He feared that British direction-finding stations would triangulate the signal. The Germans still did not know the extent to which the British had penetrated their cyphers (although their communications "hygiene," while at sea had improved significantly since 1914, they were still too free with radio in harbor), but the wavelength of the transmission and the type of cypher would be additional indications that major units were in the North Sea. Scheer was right. Room 40 had experienced problems with changes in the German cypher key on 18 August but passed a report of the attack and its position to the Grand Fleet at 0730.

Despite the setback, Scheer remained confident he could continue. His appreciation of the situation over the next few hours would be shaped by his assumption the *Westfalen* incident would have been the trigger for any British response. This belief was reinforced by the succession of assessments from Neumünster which reported, among other things, that British surface forces had sailed from the Firth of Forth on the morning of the 19th. More confirmation came in signals from *U53*, which spoke of three capital ships and four light cruisers steering north more than a hundred miles northwest of the High Sea Fleet. *L31* had sighted only light cruisers in the same area, but eventually followed up with a signal reporting enemy heavy forces. Her information was necessarily incomplete as the detection was made in rain and cloud at low level and at sufficiently close range (six thousand yards) for the British to commence what Mathy, *L31*'s experienced captain, described as "rapidly improving" gunfire.[6] The zeppelin's reports also suffered from increasing positional errors. The surface units were able to make reasonable sense of them, but when *L31* compared her position with *Moltke*'s later in the day it became apparent there was a fifty-mile discrepancy.

Scheer's confidence survived another submarine sighting, to avoid which the High Sea Fleet ran southwest for an hour, but his situation became more complex with another zeppelin report of enemy forces. *L13* sighted the Harwich Force at 0630. Her initial report was reasonably accurate, putting the British strength at a cruiser squadron accompanied by two destroyer flotillas, steering southwest. This estimate of the British course was revised to north in a later report and then, in a third signal received at 1223, to the less precise northerly. By this point, *L13*'s captain, Prolss, was convinced he was shadowing capital ships and he confirmed this in a further signal that Scheer received at 1230. His task was not an easy one. Visibility was deteriorating, with increasing low-level cloud and developing storm cells, something the zeppelins particularly feared. For the remainder of the daylight hours of 19 August, visibility was consistently better at sea level than from a thousand feet or more overhead. Prolss' observations were therefore intermittent, and after 1250 *L13* lost contact outright. He would be severely criticized in the aftermath of the operation for his errors in identification, ostensibly due to his background as a non-seagoing reservist. Ship recognition from the air was a specialized skill, however, and the zeppelin force never sufficiently trained in it. Visibility around the High Sea Fleet itself was also much better than closer to the English coast, giving Scheer further cause for false confidence in the effectiveness of his airship screen.

The German C-in-C had already decided to abandon the planned bombardment and seize the opportunity to isolate and destroy an important British force. The geometry of an engagement with forces coming from the southwest was more favorable for the High Sea Fleet than from the north, since there was much less chance that the British could get between the Germans and the Heligoland Bight. This made a sally south the more attractive option. For half an hour the High Sea Fleet retraced its ground, while Scheer waited for the First Scouting Group and his advanced light forces to reposition themselves to the south. At 1300 he began his advance to intercept the British force in that direction. On board *Moltke*, Hipper was less sanguine about the prospects and more concerned than his C-in-C about the British forces to the northwest. He directed *L11* to scout in that quadrant.

Fearing submarines across his most likely axis of approach to the Germans, Jellicoe eventually decided to make for the southern M channel and turned the fleet farther west at 1234 to approach the northwestern entrance of M. The Fourth Destroyer Flotilla from the Tyne was ordered to rendezvous with the battle fleet at 1500, when Jellicoe expected to turn southeast. Half an hour after this decision, *Iron Duke* took in a signal from the Admiralty reporting that directionals had placed the German flagship at 54° 32′ N, 1° 42′ E at 1233.[7] The Grand Fleet had just altered temporarily to the east to avoid a U-boat sighted by *Minotaur*. The Admiralty report placed the main body of the High Sea Fleet only forty miles south of the British battle cruisers. This made action appear imminent and *Iron Duke* brought the fleet to immediate readiness. The sighting of zeppelins appeared to confirm that the High Sea Fleet must lie to the south. At 1415 Jellicoe even signaled, "The High Sea Fleet may be met at any moment. I look with entire confidence to the result." This produced "a roar of delight" in at least one ship.[8] However, neither the seaplane launched by *Engadine* against a zeppelin, nor the observers in the kite balloon deployed by *Hercules*—a first for the battle fleet and precursor of many more—saw any enemy ships.

In the meantime, Tyrwhitt was attempting to work out the location of the High Sea Fleet. He initially believed that the Germans were to his south and turned his force south-southwest at 1250. Had he maintained his previous northerly track, the commodore would have encountered the High Sea Fleet little more than an hour later. The first intimation his assessment might be wrong was the position of Jellicoe's rendezvous with the destroyers from the Tyne. This was confirmed when the Admiralty's report of the 1233 position of *Friedrich der Grosse* was passed to *Carysfort* by the frequency guard ship, *Undaunted*, at 1350. Tyrwhitt turned north again at 1412, but his renewed approach was cut short, this time by Jellicoe himself. The C-in-C decided the best use for the Harwich Force would be to block the inevitable German withdrawal and at 1435 he ordered Commodore (T) to station himself north of Terschelling, ready to conduct a night attack on the retreating German fleet. Tyrwhitt turned northeast at 1504. The effect of all these course changes, unknown to the commodore, was to destroy any chance that he could place the Harwich Force across the High Sea Fleet's line of retreat. Since attacking from ahead was practically essential for a successful massed surface torpedo attack, this would prove critical a few hours later. The second, ironically, was that the cruisers and destroyers sidestepped the two lines of U-boats deployed from Flanders to the northwest of Terschelling.

Meanwhile, Scheer was facing a situation of growing complexity. *L13* was unable to regain contact with the force that she had reported. Scheer was aware through the reports from *U53* and *L31* that there were British formations to the northwest, but he assessed that these were scattered groups conducting an operation in that area. He was conscious that *Westfalen*'s indiscretion could have alerted the British to his presence, even if the attacking submarine had made no report. The danger that the British could concentrate against him, slight at this point, increased as time went on and the High Sea Fleet remained so far west. Bombardment of Sunderland was no longer a practicable option, and it was becoming apparent the contact expected with *L13*'s reported force was not taking place. At this point a further report from *U53* confirmed the presence of British heavy forces to the north. The significance was that they were steering southward, while *U53*'s next signal spoke of ten enemy capital ships. If accurate, this was a larger force than a single British battle squadron or the Battle Cruiser Fleet and strongly suggested the entire Grand Fleet was at sea.

Scheer's thinking at this point is not clear from the official records or even his own memoir.[9] The latter must be taken with a grain of salt, while it remains uncertain just how much the Germans understood what had really happened until, in 1928 and the year of Scheer's death, the fourth volume of the British official history became available. Certainly, the admiral did not intend to risk another main fleet engagement. Day was drawing on. The thrust south had produced no results, while there was no longer any serious possibility of attacking Sunderland. The picture in the north remained confused, but it was now obvious there was a substantial force of capital ships in the area, as well as light forces. The German history chronicling these events claims that Scheer considered making a move north with the idea of setting his torpedo craft on any British force he found, but was constrained by the heavy fuel consumption of the short-legged boats of the Seventh Flotilla, while those of the Fifth were in not much better state.[10] The endurance of its older units was a key limitation on the German fleet's capability, but the truth was remaining so far west meant that the risks of the High Sea Fleet being attacked steadily rose. Scheer had to factor in the forces reported by *L31*, and he risked being caught between two fires, while the location of known minefields was another constraint. Furthermore, the High Sea Fleet was itself open to submarine attack. There had been sightings throughout the morning and although all were false, *Westfalen*'s example must have loomed large in his mind. Additionally, if attrition of the Grand Fleet by submarine was the fundamental intent of the operation, the multiple lines of U-boats had to be allowed a chance. *U53*'s reports indicated that she was maintaining intermittent contact with British forces, while at least two of the lines already deployed had prospects of interaction. Orders had earlier gone out from *Prinzregent Luitpold* for Line III, stationed off Flamborough Head, to reposition farther east on the basis of *U53*'s report of ten battleships. It remains uncertain just how many of the five submarines received that direction, but at least one (*U66*) was well to the northeast of her original position when she came into contact with the British. Scheer therefore decided to turn for home at 1435.

Jellicoe was not slow to deduce that his protagonist had refused to become entangled. Although the Grand Fleet turned southeast to proceed down M Channel at 1522, Jellicoe had already indicated to Beatty that at 1600, if nothing had been seen, the British scouting forces were to turn back. On this occasion, Jellicoe's fears that his forces were being led into a submarine trap were realized. Beatty's light cruisers made multiple sightings to their south, which were the surfaced U-boats of Line III, while further sightings of zeppelins were made as well. The British turn northwest—Jellicoe at 1557 and Beatty at 1603—kept the battle squadrons clear of the U-boats but the Battle Cruiser Fleet was closer to Line III and would soon pay the price. *Falmouth* made herself more vulnerable by turning back to drive off *L21*. *U66* was watching the British advance and her captain, von Bothmer, had already attempted two attacks on the battle cruisers at relatively long range, firing two torpedoes in the first and a single weapon in the second. All had missed, undetected by the British ships, but *Falmouth* proved a better target.

The cruiser had just turned north at twenty-four knots when two torpedo tracks were sighted on the starboard bow. *Falmouth* believed the first weapon passed close ahead, while a second hit well forward, an observer reporting that he "saw her disappear behind an enormous column of water."[11] A third, unseen, struck aft and did the most damage, destroying the low-power propellers and steering gear and breaching the tiller flat. In fact, *U66* only fired two torpedoes—the one which missed was imaginary.

Falmouth temporarily lost power and radio, but her consort *Chester* closed her to keep the U-boat down. Destroyers from the Thirteenth Flotilla also came to assist. *U66* made another attack with a single weapon. This failed, but von Bothmer still had one torpedo left and was determined to use it. While the destroyer *Pasley* and the trawler *Cooksin* attempted to set up for a tow, *U66* repositioned and fired her last weapon, which passed underneath *Falmouth*; sighting the U-boat's periscope, *Pasley* immediately cast off and made for *U66*'s diving position. A single depth charge was enough to put out *U66*'s internal lighting and partly dislodge a hatch cover, bringing in a great deal of water before the submarine's crew could dog the cover down. Not surprisingly, *U66* "preferred the deeper regions of the North Sea and dived to a depth of 100 feet," where she remained for six hours.[12] *U66*'s inability to conduct another attack gave *Falmouth* a reprieve. The cruiser was forced to move under her own power because the damage to bow and stern made her unmanageable under tow. Although two propellers and her machinery were still serviceable, the best *Falmouth* could manage was a little over two knots as she made for the Humber and safety. By late evening, seven destroyers made up her screen.

As the battle cruisers and their light forces headed north, matters were complicated by the deployment of five British submarines at three-mile intervals in a north-south line across what proved to be the track of Beatty's force. These not only became mixed up with the German units that remained in the vicinity but, when Beatty's ships came in sight, were initially unsure as to their nationality. *E30* sighted and chased a U-boat apparently bent on attacking the submarine flotilla's destroyer, *Trident*, while *G10*, farther north, initially set up for an approach on what proved to be *Lion*. Just after Lieutenant Commander Bernard Acworth broke off his attack, through his own periscope he watched another periscope scrape past his submerged bow. On his reporting the sighting to *Trident*, the latter thought it was *E30*, but subsequent analysis left Acworth in little doubt it had been hostile.

U65 found herself well positioned when Lieutenant Commander von Fischel sighted elements of the Battle Cruiser Fleet. He closed at high speed on the surface and dived at 1851 to set up for an attack. In the increasing haze, von Fischel had underestimated the range to his target: there was nothing to be seen through the periscope. Undaunted, von Fischel brought the boat partly to the surface, keeping *U65* trimmed down as he closed. Finally, at 1948 he fired four torpedoes at the nearest heavy ship at a range of some 2,700 yards. This was *Australia*, but von Fischel's intent was better than his eye. Two weapons were spotted by the destroyer *Lapwing* and passed between *New Zealand* and *Inflexible*, following *Australia*, while the alerted *Inflexible* put her helm over and was able to let the third and fourth torpedoes pass clear astern, the last by "just a few feet."[13] Von Fischel was convinced that he, his executive officer, and his navigator all witnessed a hit on a battleship, and saw "flame and after the explosion the ship's masts were gone and part of the 'upper superstructure' was also carried away."[14] *U63*'s report was enough to convince Scheer a British capital ship had been severely damaged, an important counterbalance to *Westfalen*'s hit.

Falmouth's struggle to the coast continued overnight. Two tugs and two more destroyers joined from the Tyne after daybreak. The tugs had more luck taking charge of the crippled cruiser, but they were not up to the job. The port's most powerful salvage tugs were committed to transporting small submarines to the White Sea to join the flotilla in the Baltic. Despite continuous patrolling by the destroyers, *Falmouth* presented an inviting target when she was detected by *U63* later in the morning. Lieutenant Commander von Schultze chose his moment well and got between two of the destroyers to fire two torpedoes at *Falmouth*. Both struck, one on the already damaged stern and the second amidships. *U63* was sighted by the destroyer *Porpoise*, which turned to run down the periscope. Von Schultze immediately attempted to take *U63* deep, but *Porpoise* clipped the submarine's hull astern, the U-boat's captain later declaring "had he been rammed two centimetres abaft the place struck, the rudder would have been damaged and the submarine lost."[15] While depth charges did not hurt the submarine further, von Schultze judged it wise to withdraw. *Falmouth* took on a heavy list to starboard and her captain ordered the ship abandoned. Given the hits *Falmouth* had taken, this was understandable, but mistaken. The cruiser did not capsize and was even kept under tow, the speed of which was eventually increased with the assistance of a third and eventually a fourth tug; but not until late afternoon did a team of volunteers under the ship's executive officer re-embark to search for wounded and examine the ship's watertight integrity. Their limited efforts were not enough, but *Falmouth* remained afloat until 0810 the next day, when she finally capsized and sank, barely twenty-five miles from port. There was a final attempt to beach the ship, but this was too late and *Falmouth* went down south of Flamborough Head in eleven fathoms. While *Falmouth*'s captain observed that more powerful tugs could have got the ship into harbor in time, more active damage control, even with the relatively primitive techniques of the day, might have helped.[16]

The zeppelins did not make their withdrawal entirely unscathed. Cruising in cloud at two thousand feet, *L30* passed over a trawler, which she mistook for a harmless neutral. It was a Q ship, *Sea King* disguised and renamed *Remexo*, whose disguise proved as effective against the airship as it was intended to be for U-boats. The alert trawler got several rounds away with its 6-pounder before a shocked *L30* was able to drop weight and gain the shelter of cloud. *Remexo*'s crew thought they had scored at least two hits on the gondola, but only managed near misses. The zeppelin's crew, who had experienced the smoke of shell bursts entering the control station, had to admit themselves frightened, even if their airship was unscathed.

With the battle fleets drawing apart, there remained only the Harwich Force and the British submarines in the Heligoland Bight with any chance of intercepting the High Sea Fleet. While Tyrwhitt continued to head for Terschelling, Jellicoe canceled his order since neither he nor Beatty could support the Harwich Force. Shortly after receiving this message, Tyrwhitt was provided updates by the Admiralty and Jellicoe, which together made it clear the High Sea Fleet was likely to be fifty miles northwest of the Harwich Force and heading for home. At 1606 Tyrwhitt turned to intercept and by 1800 the Germans were in clear sight to the north. What gave Tyrwhitt pause was that the German fleet had zeppelins in company, which meant Scheer would be well informed of the Harwich Force's strength and movements, at least while daylight remained. Tyrwhitt opened to the south

Photo 5.1   **HMS *Falmouth* sinking**   *Sea Power Centre, Australia*

before paralleling the High Sea Fleet's eastward course to ensure he could not be cut off. Meanwhile, he considered the situation. He could use the dark hours to work around in front of the Germans for a night torpedo attack, but the High Sea Fleet would be thoroughly alert to this possibility. Scheer was already preparing to dispose his light forces in the van against just such an attempt. Jellicoe soon confirmed that he could provide no support. Matters were made even worse by the fact the weather was clearer to the east and that a half-moon would rise shortly after sunset. The confusions of earlier in the day, when Tyrwhitt, as he later admitted, was "groping in the dark" had put the Harwich Force in a poor position.[17] At 1900, Tyrwhitt turned for home, not much consoled by an Admiralty order to that effect which he received a quarter of an hour later.

The six other British submarines allocated to the Heligoland Bight in addition to E23 did not enjoy her luck. H5 and E38 both saw something of the High Sea Fleet as it moved east but could not get close enough to attack. E38 observed the smoke of the returning fleet in the moonlight, but the difficulty that the submarines had in making detections at night and the timing of the High Sea Fleet's return meant the Germans got clear without further incident. The British suffered a heavy loss in the form of E16 and her entire crew. Her disappearance remained unexplained until the wreck was found west off Heligoland by German divers in 2001, with clear evidence (a large hole in the hull) that she had struck a mine.[18] The sinking by E54 of the Flanders minelayer UC10 off the Schouwen Bank on 21 August was only partial recompense.

Strategic and Operational Consequences

The operations of 19 and 20 August had profound results. The British naval staff history put the irony in a nutshell, "it is typical of the vagaries of naval war that while the Battle of Jutland, whose name is a household word, had no immediate effect on fleet strategy, August 19, a day when not a shot was fired by either side [sic] marks a definite turning point in the war at sea."[19] The British were frightened by the newly demonstrated lethality of the U-boats against fast-moving light cruisers, although some had "long expected [a] German policy of Bait + Zeppelins + Submarines" to be utilized against "our Main Fighting Force."[20] Jellicoe was inclined to fault Beatty for not using his large number of destroyers to screen his light cruiser force, as well as the battle cruisers themselves,[21] but their vulnerability came as an unpleasant surprise to the light cruisers. Both Nottingham and Falmouth had been steaming at well over twenty knots and conducting evasive steering when they received their initial hits. They were thus not "soft targets." While there was clear evidence there had been some failed attacks as well, Jellicoe believed he could no longer deploy even light cruisers without their own screening destroyers. This dismal judgment was confirmed in exercises at the end of August. Submarines *J1* and *J3* were successful in attacks on screened cruisers proceeding at twenty-three knots and zigzagging. Despite ideal conditions of wind and sea, the submarine periscopes were not always detected, while the torpedo tracks also often went unseen. When an attack on a disabled cruiser was exercised, on the model of *Falmouth*'s experience, the results were equally bad, even in the presence of multiple destroyers, until a smoke screen was laid down around the target. Much more encouraging, and clear indication of where the priority for development should go, was that the airship *SS41* reported she could see the submarines at periscope depth from a height of eight hundred feet.[22]

The problem was the Grand Fleet simply did not have sufficient destroyers to cover capital ships and cruisers at the same time. The Admiralty did what it could, but there were not enough destroyers to meet Jellicoe's demands as well as those for operations elsewhere in home waters and in the Mediterranean. There the commerce war was taking a heavy toll in a theater in which the U-boats felt free to operate with little restraint in the general absence of American-flagged vessels. As Jackson, the First Sea Lord, remarked to a seagoing captain, "one can't get a destroyer for love or money now."[23] Moving the main fleet to Rosyth would reduce the demand on destroyers and help increase their effective endurance for operations in the areas of greatest threat, but Jellicoe now believed the Grand Fleet could not be deployed into the southern North Sea unless the situation was exceptionally favorable. In this he was supported by Beatty and by most expert opinion within the fleet. This collective judgment was not reached without argument, however. There was a lively debate among Beatty's staff as to the balance between defense and offense. The fear remained that the navy was not pursuing a sufficiently aggressive strategy. The problem was thrashed out at a conference on board *Iron Duke* on 13 September and the policy agreed there endorsed by the Admiralty ten days later. This accepted that the main fleet should not normally proceed south of a latitude in line with the Farn Islands to the west and Horns Reef to the east (55° 30′ N) or east of longitude 4° E. The exceptional circumstances that would justify deployment were when a properly screened and prepared fleet could bring the Germans to action in daylight. Even though the need for greatly improved night fighting procedures had been recognized after Jutland, the Grand Fleet did not "propose to fight a fleet action at night. Therefore it is no use placing the fleet so as to intercept the High Sea Fleet at or shortly before night."[24] The Admiralty was forced to accept the possibility the Germans could raid the east coast and escape. It had already warned the government, since this policy contradicted assurances given to east coast towns at the beginning of the war and carried significant political risks, particularly when there was agitation over the apparent invulnerability of the zeppelins—and slowly growing popular concern over the accumulating losses of merchant vessels. Transfer of the main fleet to Rosyth was considered a partial remedy. The benefits of the new base were not only the shorter distances involved, but for the destroyers in particular, avoidance of the often appalling conditions around the northern coast of Scotland and the Orkneys. The sea state during the German raid on Lowestoft in April 1916 was so bad Jellicoe had been forced to leave the flotillas behind and come south with the battle squadrons escorted only by cruisers. The danger in this situation was that conditions in the south might be good enough to allow the German light forces to remain at sea, making the Grand Fleet extremely vulnerable to a massed torpedo attack without the benefit of much of its usual screen. It would, however, be many months before the move to Rosyth was finally achieved.

Both Grand Fleet and the Admiralty were aware that the High Sea Fleet could not be allowed to develop the idea it could strike at the United Kingdom without accepting existential risk. Apart from reinforcement of the east coast defenses and minefields, this placed a premium on strengthening submarine patrols off the German coast—as well as the ability to deploy them in good time across the German lines of advance and withdrawal. The offensive use of mines also needed new priority, although the limited number of effective mines in the British inventory and differences of opinion as to where in the Bight new fields should be laid meant the campaign could not be mounted in any sustained manner for several months.

The dates of 19 and 20 August carried further lessons for fleet and ship organization. Damage control needed more attention. While the captain of *Nottingham* believed his ship could have been saved if she had not been hit by the third torpedo, the devastation of the boiler rooms caused by the first hits had not only disabled the light cruiser but also unnerved some of her key engineering staff and other personnel. Many simply milled about the upper deck without systematic efforts to set them to work.[25] *Falmouth* appears to have been even more of a missed opportunity, given the time she took to sink after her final torpedo hit. *Nottingham*'s sinking and the fate of her people in the water also showed the need for more life rafts and other life-saving gear. Neither ships' boats, which were often damaged or incapable of being launched in time, nor equipment such as boat booms and wooden fittings were enough to provide adequate support in the water for a crew of any size. One small ship, conscious of this problem, carried wooden dog kennels on the upper deck! The need for good damage control was sharply reinforced on the night of 24 August when *Valiant* gored *Warspite* inside Scapa Flow. *Valiant* had been moving to follow her sister ship on the subcaliber range for a night firing exercise. On a dark night, with no navigation lights, the two were slow to see each other. Only the rapid action of *Valiant*'s navigator prevented the collision from being even more disastrous. As it was, both ships required extensive repairs. The incident was successfully kept secret, although both captains were court-martialed and severely reprimanded.[26]

The contest between the signals intelligence organizations had reached new levels of sophistication, although there remained much to learn. The British were conscious of the extent to which their early warning of German fleet movements relied upon the High Sea Fleet using radio for the passage of preparatory orders. British direction finding and decryption of the Germans' transmissions while at sea worked well, but German circuit discipline had improved in light of their own experience at Jutland. Furthermore, the Grand Fleet had to be appropriately positioned to take advantage of such information. If such interceptions were the first indication the High Sea Fleet was already at sea, it was already too late for the British to catch their adversary. Of even greater concern was evidence the Germans were not only systematically monitoring British transmissions through their Neumünster organization, but had succeeded in breaking the cypher—to an extent that allowed them to provide the type of tactical information that had proved so important for the British. This weakness was also significant because the British had to be even more careful in their own use of German signals lest the latter finally realize their harbor transmissions were a major British source of information. The British were thus conscious they needed to develop new methods of achieving early warning. This meant an additional role for the submarines deployed around the Bight, made possible by the progressive fit of the more powerful Poulsen 3-kilowatt radios to the *E*-, *G*-, and new *J*-class boats. These installations gave the submarines the ability to send a signal to the other side of the North Sea with confidence. By the beginning of 1917, reporting the enemy fleet would be their priority task, ahead of immediately attempting an attack.[27] This constraint on their ability to attack enemy ships was not well received by submariners, who considered the new radios taking up some of their already cramped accommodation only added insult to injury.[28]

Jellicoe's view that aviation represented a key weakness for the British was confirmed by the apparent ubiquity of the zeppelins. His priority remained rigid airships of a capability equivalent to the German units, but British rigid designs remained problematic at best. The lead unit of the new orders, airship No. 9, would prove so limited in lift and endurance when completed later in the year the Admiralty initially refused to accept her into service. More encouraging was the steady arrival of non-rigid airships to work from bases springing up along the coast of Britain. The first of the new coastal airships had deployed to Pembroke in June. By the end of the year there would be fourteen units available for North Sea operations. Their endurance confined them to little more than a hundred miles from the coast, but they began to cooperate systematically with the fleet. Jellicoe considered the non-rigid airships only a stopgap, but exercises and trials were carried out to develop search patterns and reporting techniques and the C-in-C himself went up.[29] Efforts were made to improve endurance, and in September the light cruiser *Canterbury* succeeded in taking airship *C1* under tow at high speed, as well as refueling her and even conducting a crew change. Further trials were less successful, with one airship being ripped and deflated. Seaplanes, now fitted with wireless, also began to play a more active role from the shore bases, which involved fewer challenges for takeoff and landing than from ships in the open sea. Seaplanes had much the same restrictions in range as the non-rigid airships, but in combination they promised much more effective coverage of coastal areas.

Consequences for the High Sea Fleet

As for the High Sea Fleet, Scheer had reason to be encouraged by the results of the operation. The Germans eventually had to accept that no British capital ships had been damaged (British honesty after Jutland had restored credibility lost by refusing to admit to the sinking of the battleship *Audacious* in 1914), but the destruction of two light cruisers showed what the U-boats were capable of by this stage of the war. Scheer planned further ventures. The training and maintenance cycles of the battle squadrons and scouting groups, still recovering from Jutland, meant he could stage operations at approximately monthly intervals, at least until winter and the difficulties which its weather and extended darkness brought for his scouts and light forces. The lesson of not delaying maintenance had been well learned in 1915, when Admiral von Pohl was forced to cancel an operation because of the accumulation of unaddressed defects. The C-in-C had a window of about ten days in each month before the training and maintenance programs needed to resume.

Scheer's good intentions were flawed, as confirmed by his faulty understanding of events, because the High Sea Fleet could not generate a comprehensive tactical picture from which the fleet and its supporting elements over and underwater could be directed.[30] Another obstacle was the employment of the two elements key to his weaker fleet gaining the initiative—zeppelins and submarines. Scheer's relationship with the charismatic Strasser, commander of the zeppelin force, suffered from the fact that the conflict was indeed the "lieutenant and lieutenant commanders war."[31] Strasser had expertise in airship work, which Scheer did not—and which the admiral could not obtain from alternative sources. He was also in a very strong political position. Scheer himself was attracted to the claims that the zeppelins could achieve victory through the effects of their bombing on the British population, but he was also under pressure from a German people increasingly dispirited by the standoffs on land and sea. Strasser, continuing to urge strategic bombing's primacy, capitalized on this and avoided hard questions about his aviators' operational competence. Much was made of the fact that L13's commander was a reservist and his mistaken assessment of the composition of the Harwich Force attributed to a lack of seagoing expertise. Urged on by Strasser, Scheer made a plea to the Reichs-Marine-Amt that "only the very best young officers in the Navy must be selected for Zeppelin commanders."[32]

The problem with the submarines was the continuing debate over the conduct of the war against shipping. Scheer continued to set his face against anything less than full, unrestricted warfare, but there was increasing pressure from elsewhere in the navy for a resumption of systematic attacks using the prize rules. This created two concerns for Scheer. First, he did not believe a constrained anti-shipping campaign would be sufficiently effective; second, he felt that diverting U-boats to this work removed a key component of his construct to wear down the Grand Fleet. His submarine commanders remained unenthusiastic about their part in Scheer's concept of attrition—which was yet another complication. Despite the satisfaction of sinking the

British light cruisers, the U-boat captains felt they received relatively little return from their efforts against the Grand Fleet and hankered for the freedom of independent operations against commerce. In the meantime, however, the High Sea Fleet's submariners would do what their commander-in-chief told them. Analysis of the events of 19–20 August suggested that the widely dispersed single lines should be replaced by a series of at least three lines, set across the expected path of the Grand Fleet, each U-boat positioned between the gap in the line ahead. This arrangement was intended to work much the same way as a minefield and recognized the very limited ability to move and restricted periscope visibility of a submerged unit. It certainly required careful coordination. The boats of the forward line had to ensure they were not detected by the advancing enemy and refrained from attacking until the latter became engaged with both the central and the rearmost formations.

The first brick to be removed from Scheer's construct was the Flanders submarine force. Despite the High Sea Fleet commander's views, the Admiralstab directed the Flanders U-boats to resume commerce warfare according to prize rules, while the minelayers were reallocated to focal areas of merchant traffic. The initiative for this step came from the local submarine commander, rather than the Admiralstab itself—further evidence the new forms of naval warfare were changing relationships of command and rank in the German navy.[33] The Flanders U-boats were not under Scheer's authority, so the C-in-C could do little more than protest. Since the British forces in the southern bases were not his primary targets, Scheer could manage with the flotillas based in Germany, but these represented the minimum for his concept to remain workable. He was prepared to release a handful of the German-based boats for operations against commerce while the main fleet was in its maintenance and training cycle, but this was his limit. The Flanders boats began their new tasking with enthusiasm. By mid-September it was clear the campaign against shipping was moving to a new level in the waters of the English Channel and the southern North Sea.

The zeppelins also took up their strategic bombing campaign again, with a thirteen-ship raid on 24 August. Forewarned, elements of the Harwich Force sailed to take station under the zeppelins' likely flight path. There were multiple encounters between the airships and the surface forces, six zeppelins reporting they had interacted with warships. The zeppelins were severely hampered by strong westerly winds, which made it very difficult to get clear of the cruisers and destroyers pursuing them. British gunfire was not particularly accurate, but *Conquest* damaged two of *L13*'s gas cells with a round of 3-inch, forcing the zeppelin to jettison her bombs and head for home. A week later, naval and army airships combined to mount a sixteen-ship raid, the biggest of the war. The Harwich Force was once more on outpost duty and its units engaged but did not hit *L11*. Heavy winds again made things difficult for the Germans. Units ended up all over southeast England and the Midlands, often with little idea where they were, but some succeeded in reaching London's outskirts. The new army airship *SL11* was shot down by a fighter aircraft using the new incendiary bullets, crashing with the loss of all its crew. This incident, harrowing enough for the airship crews who witnessed *SL11*'s fiery end, was not only an important boost to British morale, but clear indication that the zeppelin's days were numbered. This was a reality the German naval air arm had yet to grasp.

The Baltic in Summer

6

W HEN THE BALTIC SEA'S FIGHTING SEASON opened in 1916, the Gulf of Riga remained the focus of Russian activity. Dredging Moon Sound continued to give the pre-dreadnoughts another access than the Irben Strait, while additional coast defense artillery was installed on the islands outside the gulf. Naval warfare's changing nature was demonstrated by a successful air attack on *Slava* on 12 April. Although the three bombs that hit did only superficial damage, they left seven dead. The Russians needed to improve their antiaircraft defenses and their readiness since ice coverage was no longer the sole determinant of the maritime fighting season. The year 1916 would be marked by an air campaign waged by both sides against each other's ships and bases, as well as extensive air surveillance around the Gulf of Riga. Each side largely relied on shore bases, but both had a single seaplane carrier, the Germans, *Santa Elena*, which usually operated out of Libau, and the Russians, *Orlitza*, which normally worked in the northern gulf.[1] Air-to-air combat became increasingly intense, although neither side achieved sustained superiority. The air war remained a learning process, epitomized by one Russian destroyer officer's commenting, "the planes flew quite low and their bombs were very small, while our anti-aircraft guns were not very efficient. Only a few German planes were shot down that summer, but with one exception they scored no hits on our destroyers."[2]

Although there were occasional airship raids, the dynamics of their North Sea employment and the strategic bombing of Britain meant the best zeppelins were not usually employed in the Baltic, with the inferior Schutte-Lanz and Parseval types used instead. While they had an important early-warning role patrolling the entrances to the Baltic, the airships could have performed useful work in the eastern areas. Prince Heinrich urged that Germany's strategic bombing campaign be extended to Petrograd, but this would have diverted more units from the North Sea and the campaign against Britain than either Strasser or Scheer was prepared to allow in the summer of 1916.

Slava and her consorts continued 1915's support of the Russian army from seaward by conducting harassing bombardments, which were a considerable irritation for the German army. A vital element of the spring renewal of Russia's defensive minefields was to ensure the Irben Strait remained closed to German surface craft and submarines, since *Slava*'s freedom of movement—indeed the battleship's survival—depended on the Gulf of Riga remaining clear of the enemy. Thus, in addition to more than four thousand mines being laid in the Central Position and the Advanced Position in and outside the Gulf of Finland, mines were placed in the strait, with further laying taking place in the following months. The pace of operations picked up elsewhere in May as the weather warmed, but the situation was very different to 1915 for the British and Russian submarines. The Germans were evolving a much more sophisticated approach to antisubmarine operations, which included adopting convoy for cross-Baltic movements, combined with using Swedish territorial waters as a refuge for merchant ships. Airships were employed in the approaches to Kiel, but it was heavier-than-air craft that proved particularly effective against submarines. The German bases on the eastern side of the Baltic allowed aircraft to patrol off Libau and Windau. Water clarity was often such that even a deeply submerged boat could be seen from overhead and this helped change the game.

The first major Allied submarine operation was encouraging: the Russian *Volk* under Lieutenant Ivan Messer sank three German merchant ships on 17 May. But her British consorts at sea, *E9* and *E19*, were ordered to attack only major warships. By this point, the Germans had no intention of providing any targets from their few surface units in the Baltic. *E19* under Commander Francis Cromie spent the time conducting a careful evaluation of the entrances to Libau, which the Germans used as a base for the light cruisers and torpedo boats of their advanced force. Cromie's intent was to establish the best position outside the minefields from which a submarine could attack ships emerging from the port. Although he preferred a more offensive strategy, Cromie believed that if the British submarines were to be effective within the Russian defensive obsession with the Gulf of Riga and the Gulf of Finland, they had to be deployed forward in this way. He reported accordingly at the end of May. Admiral Kanin allowed further sorties by both Russian and British submarines, but they did not go well. *Gepard* attacked an iron ore convoy off the Swedish coast and fell afoul of a disguised decoy, Ship *K* (whose original name was *Kronprinz Wilhelm*). Ship *K* rammed *Gepard*, forcing her down. The Germans were convinced they had sunk the Russian boat, but *Gepard* suffered only a glancing blow that damaged her superstructure and a deck gun; she got home to Reval. A second Russian boat, *Bars*, attacked another convoy on the surface on 28 May and was also jumped by Ship *K*. The latter's gunnery was more enthusiastic than accurate, but *Bars* was lucky to get clear without damage.

E18 did not return from patrol at all. On 26 May, outside Libau, her captain, Robert Halahan, blew the bows off the destroyer *V100* with a single torpedo. Despite a dozen men dead and more wounded, calm conditions and good damage control meant that the destroyer was successfully brought in for repair. *E18* conducted an unsuccessful attack on three torpedo boats the next day and continued on patrol until the end of the month. She then started for home, but never made it. Her wreck was discovered in 2009 off Hiiumaa. Examination suggested that *E18* detonated a mine amidships while on the surface, probably on 2 June, given the wreck's location.[3] There were no survivors. The British hoped *E18* was simply delayed, but eventually had to accept her loss. The lack of German public claims and, perhaps more significant, no interception of associated German radio traffic suggested strongly even then that *E18* had been sunk by a mine, rather than antisubmarine craft.

To the loss of *E18* and the damage to *Gepard* were added *E1*'s experiences. On 28 May she unsuccessfully attacked a merchant ship, using for the first time two modified Russian external torpedo launchers to fire a salvo of three torpedoes in all. However, the Russian weapons ran close to the surface and were seen early enough for their target to take evasive action. Surfacing to charge her batteries later that day, *E1* was forced under and bombed by an airplane. When the submarine came to the surface again, there was another aircraft waiting for her. *E1* did not escape until darkness fell. In the absence of any obvious oil leaks, it was apparent the aviators must have been tracking the boat even when she was well below periscope depth. The lesson was reinforced the following week when *E9* and *E19* deployed off Libau to cover a Russian surface sortie against the German convoys. *E19* had a particularly uncomfortable time, being repeatedly bombed on 10 June and again two days later. The sustained harassment again suggested the aircraft knew the submerged boat's position and were handing the contact over to successive reliefs. Cromie fought back on the surface with *E19*'s obsolete deck gun, but it was not up to the task.

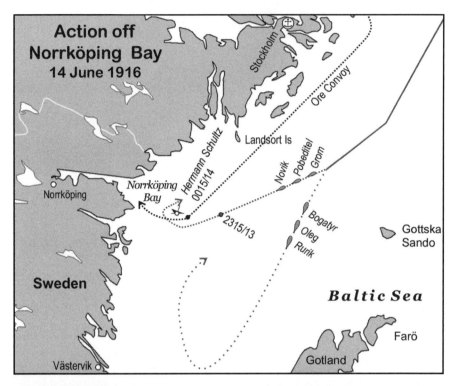

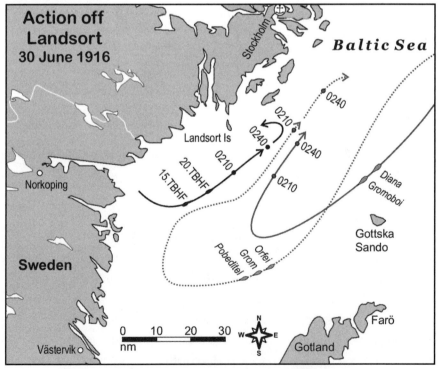

Map 6.1   Baltic Convoy Attacks, 1916

The Russian operation that the British submarines were supporting was only a limited success. The armored cruiser *Rurik* and the cruisers *Bogatyr* and *Oleg* were to deploy with destroyers and torpedo boats to attack an iron ore convoy off the Swedish coast. Information about German movements was based on intelligence gleaned by the British naval intelligence network working from the embassy at Stockholm and the consulates in the main Swedish ports, combined with interceptions of the SNIS. The Russians were aware that timing was critical. This forced cancellation of the first attempt when the cruisers were caught by fog south of the Finnish skerries and forced to anchor. The second try a few days later got further. The force's real offensive strength was the trio of large destroyers led by the newly promoted Rear Admiral Kolchak in *Novik*. These ships were detached to close the Swedish coast on the evening of 13 June, while the cruisers and remaining light forces stayed on the eastern side of the strait between Gotland and Sweden. At midnight *Novik* and her consorts encountered a southbound convoy escorted by the auxiliary cruiser *Hermann Schultz* and three smaller units. The merchant ships were showing navigation lights and the Russians were unsure whether the assembly ahead of them was hostile, or a neutral Swedish formation. Not unreasonably, but critically, Kolchak prevaricated. He eventually fired a shot across the bows of the nearest unit to test the reaction. It was sufficiently dramatic to confirm the convoy was indeed German. The merchant ships immediately made for Swedish territorial waters while *Hermann Schultz* turned to engage and the smaller escorts began to lay smoke. Kolchak thought his adversary was a cruiser, rather than an auxiliary, and kept his range. The German auxiliary had no chance against the Russian destroyers and was eventually sunk by a torpedo from *Grom*, but her defense bought enough time for the other ships to reach safety.[4] The Russians initially believed they had destroyed at least three ships, an estimate revised upwards to five as intelligence came in, but *Hermann Schultz* had done her job too well and the convoy escaped, bar damage to two of the escorting trawlers.[5] The Russian official history suggests that *Novik*'s group should have interposed themselves to the west between the lit-up convoy and the Swedish mainland before engaging, while the cruiser/destroyer formation could have attacked from the east.[6] This would have meant that the merchant ships had nowhere to run, with their escape routes to the mainland and to Gotland cut off. Given that the location of the encounter could have been predicted from the intelligence that the target was a convoy bound for Germany, Admiral Pavlovich had a good point, but Kolchak's prevarication was probably just as significant.

Events on land brought a new interest in the Baltic on the part of the German General Staff. The Russian offensive masterminded by General Brusilov had begun and was putting great pressure on the Austrians. With the Verdun campaign in progress on the western front and obvious preparations in hand for a British offensive, German options to help were limited. General von Falkenhayn was particularly concerned that the Russians would shift troops from the north to reinforce the main effort against Austria. On 19 June he inquired whether the navy could undertake operations in the Baltic on a scale that would convince the Russians the next thrust would be against the northern front. While the Imperial German Navy had renewed prestige following the Jutland action, this was a bad moment to ask. The High Sea Fleet could deploy only ten serviceable dreadnought battleships. Not one of the battle cruisers would be operational until August and the light cruisers were in no better state. It was true the Second Squadron of pre-dreadnoughts was available, even though it had suffered the loss of *Pommern*, but neither Admiralstab nor Fleet Command were prepared to accept the likely risk even to these old ships. As a sop to the General Staff, the navy agreed to keep the Second Squadron in the Baltic and advertise its presence, hoping this would make the Russians worry about possible moves against the Gulfs of Riga and Finland.

In the meantime, the apparent success of the raid of 13–14 June served as a fillip to Russian morale and added to Kolchak's growing reputation as the most aggressive of the Imperial Navy's seagoing commanders. A protégé of the late Admiral von Essen, with a prewar reputation as an Arctic explorer who had also emerged with credit from the Russo-Japanese conflict, he was already under consideration to replace the commander-in-chief of the Black Sea Fleet. This was an extraordinary step for an officer who had been a rear admiral only since May, but the Russian government needed to make best use of the few public heroes it had in senior command and the Black Sea Fleet was under a cloud due to its continuing failure to catch the battle cruiser *Yavuz Sultan Selim* (the former *Goeben*). Also, as a member of the reformist naval "study groups" set up in 1906, Kolchak had later led in arguing the case with the Duma for the Russian navy's reconstruction. He was respected in political and administrative circles in Moscow and had the confidence of the minister for the navy, Vice Admiral Grigorovich.[7] At forty-two, Kolchak's youth seems to have convinced even Britain's Vice

Admiral Beatty (nearly four years older) that he had been beaten at his own game of being the youngest admiral around when the new C-in-C Black Sea Fleet's appointment was announced.[8]

Given the sortie's encouraging results, the Russian fleet command was prepared to repeat the effort. Intelligence on 28 June suggested that the Germans, who had suspended the iron ore convoys, would resume their passage the following day. Vice Admiral Kurosh, commanding a cruiser division, was placed in charge of a force consisting of the armored cruiser *Gromoboi*, the cruiser *Diana*, and eight destroyers. Notably, none of the commanders had been involved in the previous sortie. While it was understandable the C-in-C wanted to share opportunities around the fleet, the limited experience of commanders would work against their ability to seize what opportunities offered. Furthermore, given the Russian belief that the Germans were including cruisers in their escort force, the ships allocated for the advanced unit were inadequate. The C-in-C did at least designate the battleships *Imperator Pavel I* and *Andrei Pervozannyi*—neither of which, significantly, was a dreadnought—as a covering force, but both were kept at anchor off the island of Lyum (Lom) in the Finnish skerries. Even at immediate notice for sea, it was unlikely they could intervene if the advanced units encountered superior forces.

Kurosh's force sailed from Lyum on the afternoon of 29 June. Just after, they were advised that fog on the Swedish coast had delayed the German convoy by at least a day. Kurosh nevertheless decided to continue south. Once again, the three fast destroyers were dispatched ahead of the main body to close the Swedish coast. Although there were only a few hours of darkness that night, fog extended well offshore. Late in the evening, the destroyers sighted and stopped a Swedish freighter, which they sent on its way. After closing the coast to confirm their position in the very difficult navigational conditions, the destroyers turned north. Russian intelligence that the Germans had strengthened their covering forces was partially correct. Two half-flotillas, the Twentieth and the Fifteenth, under Lieutenant Commander Count von Roder were on patrol off Landsort. The eight boats included three destroyers of the newest German design in the Twentieth Half-Flotilla, equivalent to the *Noviks*. The Russian commander saw no value in becoming entangled with such a force and immediately withdrew, reporting the German's location to Kurosh. Von Roder followed, but did not close the distance, possibly because he did not want the faster units of the Twentieth Half-Flotilla to become separated from their consorts. He attempted a torpedo attack, but the seven weapons the Germans fired had little chance of hitting, given the speed at which the Russians were clearing the area.

Admiral Kurosh was uncertain about the situation. When torpedo craft were sighted by *Gromoboi* and her consorts to their west, Kurosh at first feared that they might be his own fast destroyers (whose silhouettes were practically identical to the new German boats) and delayed opening fire while he confirmed the location of the First Division. Although Kurosh ascertained within about twenty minutes that the Russian destroyers were well to the northeast, he was fortunate von Roder proved equally cautious. The latter was concerned the Russian firepower might overwhelm his ships, despite the restricted visibility even after dawn broke at 0210. Von Roder eventually worked into an attack position at a range of five thousand yards, when his units fired twelve torpedoes at the Russian cruisers. The latter had little trouble in avoiding them and began to drop increasingly accurate fire around the German boats. The latter then withdrew, laying down smoke and artificial fog as they departed to confuse the Russian fire. This proved successful, particularly as the Russians were too cautious to begin a general chase. Kurosh broke off the action when the Germans passed out of range and began his own withdrawal. The general lack of enterprise has been commented upon by both Russian and German observers.[9] Why the commander

Photo 6.1   Russian destroyer *Novik*   *Sergei Vinogradov*

of the First Division did not rejoin Kurosh is one question; another is why von Roder did not take greater risks in engaging the unenterprising Russian cruisers, even if the latter were accompanied by their own light forces. The combination of natural mist, artificial fog, and smoke screens might well have confused the Russian tactical picture sufficiently to allow a successful torpedo attack at close range, particularly as the Germans did not think the Russian cruisers were well handled.

The Russian forces all got safely home, but there was diminishing enthusiasm for renewed surface attacks on convoys. This was partly due to Kolchak's transfer to the Black Sea, but the danger of entanglement with the Swedes was worrying the Foreign Ministry. Relations were not improved by the submarine *Vepr* sinking a German merchant ship without warning in the Gulf of Bothnia on 16 July. The Swedes argued that *Syria* had been inside their territorial waters and, as a Swedish warship rescued the survivors, they had reasonable evidence for their claim. Matters were not improved when the following day two German merchant ships were captured by Russian surface forces, also in the Gulf of Bothnia. The evidence is less certain as to their location, although one had a Swedish pilot embarked. The combined diplomatic effect of these incidents was to bring anti-shipping operations to a practical halt.

Operations in the Gulf of Riga

At least *Slava* was doing good work in the Gulf of Riga. At the beginning of July, the need to prepare for a new Russian offensive drew urgent requests from the Twelfth Army for naval gunfire support. The old battleship conducted several bombardments, during which she was struck on her armor belt by a 21-cm shell from a shore battery, an impact that caused little damage. *Slava* also successfully beat off several air attacks. Further help was given when the offensive began on 16 July. Although Twelfth Army failed to make any significant gains, the Russian warships were once more a serious annoyance to the German Eighth Army. The Russians became aware from signals intelligence the German army had put the navy under pressure to do more to help. Thus, the start of German minesweeping operations in the Irben Strait on 9 July came as little surprise.

There had been further exchanges between Prince Heinrich, Scheer, the Admiralstab, and General von Falkenhayn on the question of an amphibious assault on the offshore islands. The prince directed his advanced force commander, Rear Admiral Langemak, to review earlier proposals for a combined attack. Langemak had devised a plan that required minimum reinforcement (two battleships) from the main fleet, but Scheer, intent on his campaign of attrition in the North Sea, was unenthusiastic. As the Admiralstab pointed out, the army was in no position to provide the necessary troops.[10] In the meantime, a limited, purely naval effort to open the Irben Strait would have to do. Initial efforts were encouraging, although the Germans remained cautious. Fearing a surprise attack by the Russians, Prince Heinrich ordered that sweeping only take place in clear weather. Poor conditions meant that operations stopped after a few days and did not resume until the end of July. Despite the cover of shore defenses and precautions against surface attack, the German minesweepers were exposed to the air and the Russians began their own series of harassing air raids.

The area to seaward of the strait remained very dangerous from the mine threat alone. The Germans knew the position of their own old fields, and cleared one laid in June 1915, but had little idea what mines the Russians had laid. This was brought home on 15 August when two torpedo boats engaged on escort work went to investigate smoke on the horizon and found themselves in a minefield north of Windau. V162 struck two mines in succession and sank quickly; S168 hit a mine amidships, which flooded her boiler rooms and left her disabled. Hard work kept the badly damaged torpedo boat afloat for a tow home. Six days later the Russians suffered the loss of the small destroyer Dobrovolec to one of their own mines in the Irben Strait. By the end of August, the Germans believed they had made enough progress in opening access to the gulf to set a trap for the Russians. Rear Admiral Langemak intended to use the new remote-controlled boats carrying explosives and torpedo-carrying aircraft. His concept was to lure the Russian surface forces toward the Irben Strait, where they would face a combined attack by submarines and aircraft. The motor boats would be employed inshore against gunboats, particularly Khrabryj, which were also proving a thorn in the German army's flesh.

Despite the efforts of the newly formed Bootskommando Kurland, the motor boats were not yet operational when Langemak set his plan in motion on 11 September, so the venture's target was Slava. The bait was a minesweeping force pushed well into the Irben Strait and supported by the cruisers Augsburg, Strassburg, and Kolberg. Three small submarines, UB30, UB31, and UB33, were stationed inside the Gulf of Riga, ready to intercept any Russian surface units. An augury for the future, twelve bomb- or torpedo-armed seaplanes were also a significant part of the plan. By 12 September it was clear to the Russians a major German attempt to penetrate the gulf was under-way. *Khrabryj* exchanged fire at long range with *Strassburg* but did not risk closing with such a powerful adversary. The main Russian response came in the form of the cruiser *Diana* with three *Noviks* and four smaller destroyers; *Slava* brought up the rear. The Russians were already reinforcing the Gulf of Riga. *Slava*'s near-sister, *Tsesarevich* was in transit through Moon Sound, with armored cruiser *Admiral Makarov* due in a few days. At 1730, *UB31* managed with difficulty to get into an attack position on *Diana*. Dead calm conditions made showing a periscope very risky and the U-boat was nearly run down by one of the cruiser's escorts before she got a single torpedo away. It missed unseen, although the Russians were acutely aware of the German submarines' presence, with repeated (largely imaginary) sightings of periscopes. Shortly afterward, *Slava* joined the formation, which took up position south of the island of Abro (now Abruka).

Their demonstration achieved, the German cruisers were withdrawing when, just after 1800, the planned air attack was mounted on the Russians. Initially eight bombers arrived on scene. They made no hits but used flares and rockets to create a diversion. The main attack came in the form of four seaplanes under Lieutenant Edler. Despite the efforts of the other aircraft, their approach was detected and Edler claimed later that the Russians "opened up with all calibres" including *Slava*'s 30.5-cm.[11] Although no aircraft was hit by anything more than splinters, Edler reported the vast columns of water thrown up by shell fire made flying very difficult. At least one torpedo failed on drop, but two were seen to run straight. Their wakes were also observed by *Slava* and one of her escorts. Both missed, although the Germans thought they hit a destroyer. The torpedo drops may have been premature at ranges of twelve hundred and thirteen hundred meters, but, for a first attempt, the operation was remarkably well conducted. *Slava*'s report of the airborne torpedo attacks was initially not believed in Baltic Fleet headquarters. It would take further attacks by Edler's seaplanes on Russian merchant ships to convince the staff ashore a new era had dawned.[12] The Germans themselves felt they had much to get right. Despite extensive preparations for the mission, the disappointing results confirmed that both material improvements and more training were required before an effort on the same scale could be restaged. The aircrew thought they had been operating at the limits of the aircraft and the weapons they carried, while the defensive response was more formidable than they had expected.[13]

Weather took a hand on the evening of 12 September with a southwesterly gale that disrupted the German minesweeping effort and effectively halted any offensive activities. The Germans suffered another setback when *Augsburg* ran aground. She floated clear but suffered hull damage sufficient to require her withdrawal. When the German sweeps resumed, the conflict became one of small ships. While the Germans continued their efforts to clear a channel in Irben Strait, the Russians deployed light craft by night to lay mines behind the German advance. Given the threat of the U-boats, which the Russians believed were operating from a forward base within the Gulf of Riga, the four major units remained in Moon Sound, where shallow water, defensive nets, and mine fields protected them from underwater attack. Although the Germans had hoped for more, *Slava* and her consorts became much more circumspect about conducting operations along the German-held coast of the gulf.

Submarine Operations

A period of intense frustration began for Cromie, the British submarine flotilla commander. Kanin's limited nerve had not been strengthened by the loss of a submarine and the close shaves of May and June. Any enthusiasm for offensive deployments rapidly diminished. Matters were not helped by an equally obstructive Russian commodore of submarines, N. L. Podgursky, whom Kanin used to shield himself from the outspoken British commander. Cromie admitted that he "got positively rude" about Kanin's refusal to employ the British boats more offensively.[14] Rear Admiral Nepenin did what he could to support Cromie, but Kanin proved immovable. Russian boats were still allowed out to attack commerce, but the British patrols were restricted to targeting German major warships and were largely contingent on the need to cover Russian surface deployments into the central Baltic against sorties from Libau or Steinort. Since the C-in-C took concern about Sweden as an effective veto on surface operations south of the Gulf of Finland, this meant the *E*-class boats could not fulfil their true potential.

The pending arrival of four *C*-class submarines should have been a real fillip for the British submarine force. After submarine penetration of the Kattegat became impossible in early 1916, the Admiralty had cast around for alternative ways to reinforce the Baltic flotilla. Provided they were not too large, submarines could be moved from Archangel to the Baltic through the Russian internal canal and river system. The older, but still serviceable *C*-class boats were the biggest that could make the passage successfully.

They were in no way ideal, but capable enough as local defense units to free the *E*-class boats for offensive work. Curiously, Cromie was not advised of the plan until the four boats' passage to Russia had started. The quartet were given a hasty refit at Chatham and began their tow north on 3 August, arriving in Archangel after many travails on the 21st. In an even more remarkable effort, they were immediately placed on barges and sent south, arriving in Petrograd on 9 September. Taken to Kronstadt to be prepared for Baltic service, all seemed well until it was discovered their batteries, transported separately, had been badly packed, and additional 18-inch torpedoes had gone astray. Even after some imaginative improvisation by Cromie's engineers and their Russian counterparts, the first boat was not ready before late October. With shakedowns required, none of the *C*-class boats would be properly operational during the 1916 fighting season.[15] In the meantime, the Baltic submariners took their own measures against air attack. The boats' vulnerability to observation from the air was confirmed by trials at sea, and it was clear the external paint scheme needed change to make the submarines less visible. To the submariners' surprise, the color of the bottom half of the hull also made a difference in detectability, and boot topping and red anti-fouling paint were replaced as soon as possible. Local fits of antiaircraft weapons were also planned, although these would have to wait until the extended maintenance period in winter.

Changes in the Russian Command

Kanin at least consented to a resumption of offensive mining, albeit in the most limited way. Since the key iron ore ports were in the Gulf of Bothnia, the German convoys' passage could be made more difficult if the strait between Sweden and the Aland Islands were mined outside Swedish territorial waters. Provided existence of the field was declared, Sweden could have no grounds to object. The operation was carried out without interference on 30 August, and 821 mines were deployed on a north-south line over fourteen miles. This was something, but clearly not enough.

Just where the pressure for a change of command in the Baltic came from is uncertain. Admiral Kanin temporarily broke out of his defensive mindset with a proposal for an amphibious assault on the coast of Courland, to outflank the Germans and eject them from Libau and Windau. The idea was rejected by the army, however, and with it died Kanin's ideas for offensive use of the fleet.[16] It is likely, being no longer Kanin's subordinate, that Kolchak gave his views freely during his briefings at the Stavka, which included a long interview with the tsar. The British liaison officer at Stavka, Rear Admiral Phillimore, was also aware of Cromie's frustrations, while Rear Admiral Nepenin's growing reputation would have given real authority to any concerns that he expressed. Finally, in early September, the C-in-C's unsatisfactory performance forced Admiral Rusin, chief of the Naval General Staff, to approach the tsar and seek Kanin's relief. Rusin was particularly critical of Kanin's failure to exploit the opportunities offered while Germany was short of operational units in the weeks after Jutland.[17] In public, Kanin's relief was on the grounds of ill health, but even the Stavka accepted that the Baltic Fleet had become "slack." Rusin's view was that Kanin's continuation in command risked "the extinction of the fighting spirit of the personnel."[18] Rear Admiral Nepenin was the obvious choice in the absence of Kolchak. The tsar considered Nepenin to be as "strong willed and able" as Kolchak and immediately approved the change.[19]

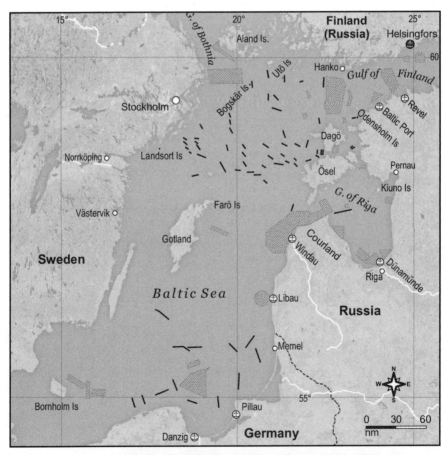

Map 6.2 Baltic Sea Minefields and Mined Areas, 1914–1917

Photo 6.2   Russian battleship *Sevastopol*   *Sergei Vinogradov*

A junior officer later claimed the news was "received with great joy and hope by all in the fleet, especially in the Destroyer Force, which being all the time in the van, appreciated the former activity of the Admiral."[20] The reality was more complex. Nepenin did not enjoy the support of all his senior officers. While he could make some changes, including the submarine force commander, others remained who had their own agendas, and there were criticisms of Nepenin's selection, as an individual and for his alleged lack of recent sea service. These were motivated largely by personal animus. Nepenin had not achieved flag rank through the conventional path of big ship command, but came to the post of C-in-C from years providing intelligence and reconnaissance for the fleet, as well as developing its air force. Furthermore, he had commanded torpedo craft at Port Arthur during the Russo-Japanese War and spent several years in command of light forces in the Baltic from 1907. Nepenin's focus was therefore as operational as any seagoing officer and his understanding of the overall situation very much more sophisticated.[21]

The newly promoted vice admiral made his presence felt by an immediate visit to the ships in the Gulf of Riga and the western bases as well as to Reval. Nepenin's offensive intent, however, was largely stymied by the continuing reluctance of the Supreme War Council to endorse operations that might create problems with the Swedes. He received no new directive and thus formally had no greater scope than his processor.[22] Nepenin's order to his submarines to conduct unrestricted warfare was immediately vetoed by the council. He had no more luck with attempts to employ the four dreadnoughts more actively. *Sevastopol*'s grounding in the skerries in September did not help, particularly as she proved difficult to refloat and was not operational again until late November. Despite higher authority's reluctance, Nepenin at least had some freedom of action with the remainder of the fleet, whose real offensive capability still rested in *Novik* and her sisters. Nepenin therefore determined on a resumption of the offensive mining campaign in the southern Baltic, focused on the German coast. On 17 October, *Novik* and four sister ships each embarked forty mines and sailed for Steinort. Deployment of the two hundred mines was somewhat disjointed due to inexperience and confusion in signals. The Russians nevertheless completed the lay undetected over the night of 18–19 October, although they sighted German units. The field claimed a merchant ship and a minesweeper before the Germans could clear it.

German Offensive Operations

The Germans made use of the remainder of the fighting season, despite the High Sea Fleet's focus on the North Sea and the Baltic C-in-C's reluctance to risk his modern cruisers. Until the resumption of unrestricted warfare, the Baltic force had the services of several new minelaying submarines. Accepting the threat posed by Russian minefields, missions were mounted inside the Gulf of Finland. During September and October, the small and handy submarines set fields along the Finnish coast, off Reval, and even in the approaches to Kronstadt. The mines went undetected until the middle of October when they began to claim some important victims. One destroyer was sunk and a second, *Letun*, one of the new *Novik* type, had her stern blown off and was never repaired.

The successful submarine operations had another effect. Rear Admiral Langemak was increasingly of the view that the mine fields in the Russian Advanced Position were ineffective and the Germans should conduct offensive operations in the approaches to and perhaps within the Gulf of Finland itself. Largely on his own initiative, he organized an operation for 26 October with the cruisers *Strassburg* and *Kolberg* and several torpedo boats. Four seaplanes were embarked in *Kolberg* and three of the torpedo boats, with the intent of deploying them once the force was close enough to Russian positions. Langemak's formation immediately ran into a severe gale that whipped up the sea to the extent that the smaller craft rolled heavily enough to snap masts and wash two of the seaplanes over the side. When the torpedo boats sought the lee of Gotland, the admiral was forced to call off the operation. The withdrawal was greeted with relief by Prince Heinrich, who had not been fully informed of Langemak's scheme and did not believe it justified the risks. Over the following days a lively debate ensued between the Baltic C-in-C and his advanced forces commander. Langemak eventually persuaded Prince Heinrich that attacks by light forces were worthwhile and the Baltic forces should apply the same pressure on the Russians the Flanders units were exerting on the British and French in the Channel. Dealing with the Libau-based commander from Kiel, the grand admiral was not wholly convinced, although Langemak was sensitive enough to his concerns to confine the next attempt to torpedo boats rather than the valuable (and scarce) cruisers, with *Kolberg* (wearing Langemak's flag) and *Strassburg* kept as distant cover to the southwest. Langemak's credibility now rested directly upon his estimate of the state of the Russian mine defenses, on which the whole venture depended. In both this judgment and his assessment of the targets likely to be found by his torpedo boats, Langemak was sadly mistaken.

On the evening of 10 November, eleven boats of the Tenth Flotilla were approaching the Gulf of Finland when they experienced their first setback. At 2030, *V75* struck a mine and was disabled, her boiler rooms flooded. By 2200 it was apparent she could not be saved and *S57* went alongside to take off the crew. Just as *S57* completed this tricky evolution, a second mine detonated beneath *V75* and tore her into three pieces. *S57* could not get clear in time and was badly damaged before herself detonating a mine. Matters were not helped by a report of a submarine, but the flotilla eventually sorted itself out. *S57*, her bows blown off, was dispatched with a torpedo after her crew and that of *V75* had been transferred to *G89*. The latter was detached to find *Kolberg* and *Strassburg*. The flotilla commander, Lieutenant Commander Wieting, kept his nerve. Initially fearing he would have to detach additional boats to support *G89*, the fact the one boat had all the survivors on board and had reported she was in deep water and thus outside the danger area meant he could continue with the plan, although his reduced numbers meant he could not detach any units to sweep south. There was, however, no Russian shipping at sea, nor any Russian patrols in the area. In the absence of targets, three torpedo boats were sent in to attack Baltic Port, but it too was empty of shipping. The trio had to content themselves with bombarding the dock area and the port signal station from close range. They caused some damage, but 88-mm caliber naval guns were far from ideal.

Wieting decided to withdraw, taking a dogleg north to clear the mine danger area. The flotilla was in line ahead when *V7*, the seventh in sequence, struck a mine astern. *V72* thought she had been hit by a submarine torpedo and opened fire to scare her supposed attacker away. Fatally, the gunfire brought *V72*'s consorts back to support her. In the darkness, Wieting believed it signaled that Russian surface ships had caught up with them. Shortly afterward, *G90*'s stern was blown off by yet another mine. Both units were crippled and could not, given the proximity of the Russians, be saved. The survivors abandoned ship, after which the two boats were sunk by gunfire and torpedoes. Misfortunes continued. *S58* struck a mine at 0400 and sank by the stern. The remaining units focused on picking up survivors. The work had just been completed when *S59* detonated a mine that blew off one propeller. Wieting's nerve still held, despite feeling that he and his ships were trapped in "the devil's boiler."[23] *S59* had most of the survivors of *S58* and *G90* on board. Time was running out, since the Russians had been alerted by the attack on Baltic Port and the danger was that the fast *Noviks* would be sent in pursuit. If the survivors were to be rescued, the job had to be done quickly. Despite the continuing mine threat, Wieting's flag captain, Krech, took *S56* alongside *S59* and got every man off before sinking the crippled torpedo boat with a torpedo.

The flotilla suffered a final blow at 0611 when *V76* struck a mine. As with most of the other boats, she was hit in her stern and thus disabled, but quite capable of floating. Again, Wieting had to reject the idea of taking her in tow. The risk of mines to the few remaining undamaged units was too great and the threat of Russian attack growing. *V76* was scuttled and the remaining trio headed for the rendezvous with the covering force. Even after deep water was reached, the flotilla's travails continued. Wieting's *S56* suffered a loss of feed water, which brought her to a halt. While *S56*'s engineers repaired the broken pipe, her consorts had to go alongside to transfer fresh water, a difficult evolution at the best of times. It was with great relief that Wieting finally met the forces waiting to the southwest.

The Russian destroyers raised steam as soon as the news of the attack on Baltic Port came through, but, although *Novik* and her consorts sailed at 0400, they were recalled by signal. Intensely frustrated, they remained at anchor in the approaches to their base. Nepenin's reasoning is uncertain. The Germans had maintained radio silence until the first mine strike, but the traffic that ensued must have given SNIS an idea of what was going on— its reconstruction of events immediately afterward was accurate enough about the early German losses. However, the discoveries of mines within the Gulf of Finland may have given the C-in-C pause. Only at 0900, when intercepted messages suggested there was at least one German cripple still in the vicinity, were the Russian destroyers released. Dispatched to the last reported position of the damaged German, they found nothing, and ideas of following the enemy south were abandoned when a thick fog came down.

Further signals analysis by the Russians revealed the extent of the German disaster. The latter were engaged in inevitable recriminations. Prince Heinrich felt his guidance had been ignored by Langemak, although the physical separation between Kiel and Libau had played its part in creating confusion as to plans and intentions. Both Admiralstab and the Fleet Command were critical of the operation, which they did not believe had potential benefits compatible with the risks that were run. Just as significant was the disdain expressed by junior but operationally experienced officers in key staff positions about the inability of the older generation to cope with the new challenges, resulting in their subordinates suffering the consequences. The disaster became known as "The Massacre of the Innocents" although the one comfort was that the casualties had been surprisingly light, with only sixteen dead and twenty wounded, despite each boat having a crew of over eighty. [24] That the younger officers did not hesitate to make their views known was another manifestation of the changing dynamics brought about by the increasingly high technology/small unit nature of the war.[25] Given this, and the fact that Prince Heinrich had lost confidence in his forward commander, Langemak's position was untenable. He was sent to command the defenses of Heligoland. His successor was the shrewd Albert Hopman, who had been serving in the Admiralstab. Already a veteran of the Baltic, Hopman was considered a safe pair of hands, but this did not stop him regarding the prospect of such an independent command with relish. Arguably, Hopman was in a strong position, since the affair did little for Prince Heinrich's credibility as C-in-C. The Germans initially attempted to conceal the loss of so many ships but were trumped by the Russians who announced the sinkings in a bulletin that was uncomfortably accurate.

A last offensive effort for 1916 also came to grief. Prince Heinrich finally succeeded in securing two new zeppelins for a raid on Petrograd, despite being so late in the year. The season would not allow a sortie so far east, but on 28 December a venture against the ports in the western Gulf of Finland seemed possible. Bad weather and the effects of low temperature on machinery meant that her crew lost control of *L38*. They were lucky to be able to make a forced landing, but the airship was wrecked in the process. The kaiser, who had moments of good sense, was justifiably critical of attempting a zeppelin raid in winter.[26] It was a poor end to the season for the Germans and something for the Russians to balance against their own recent losses.

The Start of Winter

The Russians needed the solace. On passage with the battleship *Andrei Pervozannyi* and the cruiser *Bajan* to refit at Kronstadt, the armored cruiser *Rurik* was badly damaged by a U-boat laid mine on 19 November off Gogland (Hogland), an area in the Gulf of Finland that had been considered safe. Although her repairs could be completed over the following few months, this incident was a psychological blow, given the ship's importance and war record and the gulf's having been safe until then. Although the Russians did not believe that many mines could have been laid, the effect was to limit the passage of major units to swept channels, maintenance of which represented yet another load on the already hard-pressed sweepers. The very small number of mines involved contributed to the unhelpful idea they had been laid from fishing vessels by Finns who were covert supporters of the Germans.[27] That this could be seriously suggested was another indication of the deteriorating situation in the Russian empire.

Most of the other winter dispositions were already made. *Slava*, lightened for her passage through the newly dredged Moon Sound, withdrew from

Photo 6.3   **Battleships in the ice—Helsingfors**   *Sergei Vinogradov*

the Gulf of Riga, leaving *Tsesarevich* and *Admiral Makarov* to remain on station during the freeze. *Slava* proceeded to refit first in Kronstadt, then in Helsingfors, where her ship's company experienced the jealousy of the crews of the marginalized pre-dreadnoughts *Imperator Pavel I* and *Andrei Pervozannyi*. While this rancor has been described as having underlying revolutionary sentiments,[28] it more likely reflected the inactive sailors' natural resentment of *Slava*'s operational record and her popular reputation as the only unit of their squadron that had seen action, a syndrome mirrored with less intensity but on a greater scale between the battle squadrons of the Grand Fleet and the battle cruisers.

Nepenin concluded the year with visits to all the major formations and to bases in both the Gulfs of Finland and Riga. With work continuing on the defensive fortifications, as well as newly constructed destroyers and submarines expected to join the fleet in the following twelve months, Nepenin had reason to feel confident about prospects in 1917, particularly because he might well have secured greater operational autonomy than his predecessors. In the meantime, although the ships' companies were using their stand-down to "amuse themselves ceaselessly,"[29] the new C-in-C did his best to raise standards and at the same time provide more support to the lower deck. This included sporting competitions, particularly for football. Nepenin "even began to plan a Sailors Club in Helsingfors. In the winter of 1916–17 however this was too little and too late."[30] The C-in-C's insistence on enforcing marks of respect ashore was not well received and the pressure that he placed on many of his less capable subordinate commanders unappreciated. Whether later accusations as to his lack of tact are fair is difficult to judge. Given the effects of Kanin's inactivity, it is likely that Nepenin had few alternatives.

As for the Germans, the increasing likelihood of unrestricted submarine warfare, soon translated into reality, meant new opportunities for action in the Baltic. While the High Sea Fleet had to maintain sufficient strength in the North Sea to protect the minesweepers keeping the passages clear for the U-boats, substantial detachments would be possible in a way that was not when the battle squadrons had to maintain a cycle of readiness for deployment into the North Sea. 1917 would be a very different year in the Baltic.

Little Ships, Submarines, and Aircraft

7

S CHEER INTENDED A NEW PLAN of submarine traps in September, but the weather was so bad he was forced to cancel the venture on the 19th, when the fleet's window of availability closed. This released the zeppelins for a raid on England on the night of 23–24 September, while the Second and Sixth Torpedo Boat Flotillas were dispatched to attack merchant shipping off the Dutch coast. Although a battle squadron went to the Baltic for training, Scheer sent out elements of the High Sea Fleet on 25 September to see the torpedo craft home. The British got warning, but in accordance with the new policy the Grand Fleet did not sail. With no indication that the entire High Sea Fleet was involved there was no reason to move. To ensure the security of the southern ports and shipping, the Harwich Force was ordered to rendezvous west of the North Hinder, while the Third Battle Squadron was brought to short notice and additional submarines were stationed off the coast. The First Scouting Group and the First Squadron deployed, however, only to the west of Heligoland to cover the flotillas as they returned from their largely fruitless sortie. A single encounter occurred as dusk was falling on 26 September, when *E53* sighted the returning German units but was driven deep by torpedo boats without being able to attack. The German capital ships were at sea for less than a day and saw nothing of the enemy. This type of short-range mission, combined with guard duty in the Bight, would be the main operational employment of the big ships in the future. It was not a stimulating prospect for their crews.

The zeppelin raid was a disaster for the Germans. The four newest airships attacked London, while eight older units made for the Midlands. Already damaged by antiaircraft fire from the ground, the brand-new *L33* was crippled by machine-gun fire from an RFC airplane. The airship did not catch fire but came down in marshland where the crew was captured. *L32* suffered a similar succession of hits from ground-based fire and was then machine-gunned by an RFC BE2. It crashed in flames, killing all on board. The British, to their delight, received an intelligence windfall from the wreck, including the latest signal book. *L33* proved a windfall of another sort since the wreck could be examined in detail. Its clear superiority over contemporary British rigid airships, with ten times the usable "lift," was such that the Admiralty substituted two copies of *L33* for an existing order. It was a curious throwback to the days of sail, when captured French warships became design models for the Royal Navy's new construction—for similar reasons.

Despite this setback, the Germans tried again on 25 September. *L31* under its experienced and aggressive commander, Heinrich Mathy, got as far as Portsmouth, where the local defenses proved effective enough to prevent the zeppelin from bombing the naval dockyard. The airships suffered no casualties on this air raid, but a venture on 1 October brought a loss. *L31* was shot down with no survivors over Potter's Bar. Incendiary bullets from a fighter aircraft did the job again, notably despite the zeppelin's efforts to gain height, a technique in which the airships usually had the advantage. This was a loss Strasser and his seniors could not ignore, but the full story was worse still. In the bad weather that night, the surviving airships had either been forced to turn back or "wandered" over southern England desperately searching for recognizable targets.[1] New, higher-climbing machines would be needed, together with new tactics and more careful use of weather to achieve anything like the results that Strasser promised.

Prospects of renewed main fleet operations promised some relief from the zeppelins' problems. However, Scheer's plans to attack Sunderland were brought to a halt by the Admiralstab's decision on 6 October to order a full resumption of prize warfare. The U-boats' unavailability to support the fleet prevented long-range sorties into the North Sea. As the High Sea Fleet staff pointed out, the successes of 19 August had awakened "the greatest hopes," and submarines were essential to continuing the work.[2] It is true that the "venomous" memorandum produced by Scheer's chief of staff with its bitter criticism of the Admiralstab was as much a political as an operational document.[3] A key element was Scheer's and his senior advisors' view that the only valid form of *Handelskrieg* (trade war) was unrestricted, and they were desperate to convince the government this was the correct strategy. It was nevertheless still true that the U-boats also remained, as they probably always were, the best instrument for reducing the strength of the Grand Fleet. Without them, the High Sea Fleet ran the risk of being overwhelmed by a force that had overcome many of its weaknesses and whose superiority continued to grow. Scheer still hoped to isolate a substantial British force and cast about for different solutions. He believed that at Jutland the Battle Cruiser Fleet was much farther away from Jellicoe's battle squadrons than it should have been and that the British could well continue with this policy. Notwithstanding later German comments about the Royal Navy's unwillingness to run risks, Beatty was considered an aggressive commander, overly ready to put his force to the hazard with ships that were clearly vulnerable. Lack of U-boats meant the Germans had to be circumspect when they deployed, but a comprehensive zeppelin screen could provide the High Sea Fleet with the superior understanding to locate and destroy a detached British formation without becoming entangled with the Grand Fleet.

Scheer's new concept involved sending the flotillas out to intercept North Sea shipping with the battle squadrons acting as their cover. His venture in October may have been the first of what Scheer intended as a series, with the British (Beatty) assessed as likely to take the bait on a second or third occasion. The autumn weather turned foul, preventing the zeppelins from forming the screen outside the Bight critical to Scheer's plan. Only on 18 October—just before another window of fleet availability was due to shut—did the weather moderate sufficiently to set the operation in train. Scheer's radio orders were intercepted by Room 40 a few hours before the High Sea Fleet sailed in the early hours of the following day. The now-customary dispositions were made in the south, while the formations in the north were brought to short notice for sea but did not immediately sail. Submarines were dispatched from Harwich with others sent out from northern bases to take up defensive positions. Jellicoe feared the operation might cover the deployment of disguised commerce raiders into the Atlantic and therefore sent preparatory orders for a strong force of cruisers to patrol between Scotland and Norway.

Seven British submarines were already disposed around the likely exit routes from the Heligoland Bight. *E38*, operating north of Terschelling, spotted the First Scouting Group at dawn on 19 October. The submarine could not get close enough to either the battle cruisers or the battle squadrons that followed them, and an attack on a light cruiser failed when *E38* lost depth control. She had more luck when another light cruiser operating in the rear of the fleet came in sight; this was the elderly *München*. At 0843, *E38* fired two torpedoes, one of which hit, causing substantial flooding and damage to *München*'s condensers, which contaminated her feed water.

The crippled cruiser was taken in tow, first by a torpedo boat and then by the cruiser *Berlin*, although not before the latter avoided another torpedo fired by *E38*. This was the submarine's last effort, as her battery was almost exhausted. Her captain, Jessop, could console himself with one success amidst his repeated setbacks.[4]

Scheer was now subject to the same fears as Jellicoe. The cruiser *Stettin* was convinced that she had also only just avoided submarine attack. There was thus the possibility that the fleet was facing the type of submarine trap that Scheer had set for the British in previous sorties. The C-in-C turned to the east-northeast at 1030 to make for the Horns Reef passage. Scheer's assessment that the operation should be curtailed was confirmed by reports from Neumünster, which indicated British submarines were taking up special dispositions, something that suggested the British knew the High Sea Fleet was at sea. This judgment was supported by *L14*, which reported sighting the Harwich Force to the southwest. Well over a hundred miles away and with the weather deteriorating, this was no sort of quarry for Scheer to risk remaining at sea to engage. The conditions were increasingly unsuitable for his light forces and the zeppelins, so Scheer ordered a general withdrawal. The final approach to the Horns Reef passage was made after dark and of the three British submarines in the area, only *G3* had a brief encounter with screening torpedo craft, which forced her deep. By midnight, the High Sea Fleet was in safe waters. Scheer's order to the zeppelins to return home was intercepted by Room 40, confirming the brief sortie was being wound up. The Admiralty then recalled the Harwich Force and canceled the cruiser operation in the north. The British were irritated at the continuing inability of their torpedoes to sink major German warships, and fitting 21-inch tubes in new submarine designs received further impetus. As Jellicoe commented, "They are very difficult to sink, or else our torpedoes don't hit hard enough."[5] This was not entirely true. Despite the High Sea Fleet's shortage of light cruisers, whose losses since 1914 had yet to be made up, *München* was not considered worth a full repair. Patched up, she became an accommodation ship.

This was the last sortie by the entire fleet for eighteen months. Circumstances and his own judgment made further operations less attractive for the German commander. Scheer did not give up hope entirely, but caution permeated every aspect of the attempts that followed. The onset of winter reduced the opportunities for both torpedo boats and zeppelins but there were other factors at work. The absence of his own submarines and the presence of the enemy's in such numbers created the prospect the Germans would suffer attrition rather than the Grand Fleet. Mines were another consideration, despite the minesweepers' work keeping the passages out of the Heligoland Bight clear. Had Scheer known of the Grand Fleet's determination to avoid night action, the short days of winter might have provided him with opportunities for harassing actions involving only part of the High Sea Fleet, with relatively little risk of interception. In the meantime, Scheer intended to reinforce the Flanders Command with the Third and the Ninth Flotillas in late October. While the Third Squadron went to the Baltic for training, the First Squadron and the Scouting Groups remained available to cover the dispatch of the flotillas from the edge of the Bight, and plans were under way for the torpedo craft to leave on 22 October. The movement, however, was subject to an unexpected interruption.

Operations against the High Sea Fleet

Whatever its disappointment at yet another aborted encounter with the High Sea Fleet, the Harwich Force was occupied with its own offensive plans. The long awaited Coastal Motor Boats had achieved operational status. Tyrwhitt's intention to use them for an attack on the Schillig Roads was delayed by the High Sea Fleet's sortic of 19 August and then by a combination of weather and short notice operations. What was essential for a CMB raid was surety of targets before the boats were dispatched and confirmation the anchorages were not protected by surface booms that could rip their bottoms out. This required air reconnaissance of the German estuaries. What followed showed the difficulties of both aircraft and light naval craft operations in the North Sea. Either the wind and sea state were such that the seaplanes and CMBs could not be launched, even if they had not already been damaged in their stowages, or calm conditions brought the almost inevitable fog. Heavy weather curtailed a first attempt at reconnaissance on 29 September. This resulted in the seaplane, launched from a coastal base, being called back. Attempts to refuel and then tow the aircraft resulted in its damage and eventual sinking. That an England-based machine had been considered capable of this task was a sign of increasing capability, but the experience suggested its employment was premature. Seaplanes brought much closer to their target by a carrier remained the more practical option. A further attempt on 22 October with two machines launched from *Vindex* fared better, but fog in the Bight was so thick that both were forced to return. Only No. 9760, with Lieutenant Erskine Childers (of *The Riddle of the Sands* fame) embarked as the observer, saw anything of the enemy in the form of a half-flotilla of torpedo boats—and two seaplanes launched from Heligoland in pursuit. Stymied by low-lying cloud, her crew even brought No. 9760 down on the sea to get a better view, but still saw little of value.

The Germans were thoroughly alerted to the possibility of a British surface raid, believing that any seaplanes operating so far east had been launched from a ship. The flotillas' departure for Zeebrugge was placed on hold to screen the fleet. The routine zeppelin patrols were supplemented by an order for every available airship to launch and the First Scouting Group and the First Squadron with their supporting units began to move into the Bight. These orders were intercepted by Room 40, causing concern in the Admiralty that the unsupported Harwich Force might be cut off. Just after his ships sighted zeppelin *L17*, Tyrwhitt was ordered to withdraw. *L17* did not attack but maintained contact for more than two hours before losing sight of the British force. One of the limitations of the zeppelins was forcibly demonstrated. So strong was the southeasterly crosswind the airship could not keep up with the twenty-two knots of the surface ships. Even the more powerful *L34* was unable to join in time to take over the pursuit. Significantly, heavier-than-air machines not only gave chase to the British aircraft, but seaplane No. 722 bombed the British ships—an observer commenting, "He must have done a good flight as we were a good 80 miles from Borkum at the time."[6] No. 722's attack was ineffective, but the increasing capabilities of heavier-than-air craft were beginning to change the priorities of German naval aviation.

Operations in the English Channel

Events conspired to delay a CMB attack indefinitely. By freeing up the flotillas, the restrictions on the High Sea Fleet allowed the Germans to increase their pressure on the British ports and shipping routes in the south. Deployment of the Third and Ninth Flotillas to Flanders strengthened the German forces threatening the Channel. This put the Harwich Force back on the defensive. The Admiralty became aware of planned movements by the High Sea Fleet late in the morning of 23 October. The nature of the sortie was not apparent and the Grand Fleet was once more brought to short notice for sea. Commodore (T) was ordered to a position off North Hinder and was on station before dawn on the 24th. By this time, further radio intercepts indicated at least one German flotilla had gone south. In the darkness, the light forces of the two sides did not make contact and, after further intercepts confirmed the Germans were already well clear, Tyrwhitt headed home. The transfer clearly presaged an attack on the Channel, and on 26 October the Admiralty ordered Commodore (T) to dispatch a light cruiser and four destroyers to Dunkirk as a reinforcement for the Dover Patrol. This was too little, too late. Commodore Michelsen, commanding the High Sea Fleet flotillas, had gone ahead of his ships to Zeebrugge to prepare for a raid. Even as the additional Harwich units made their way south, the German force was leaving harbor.

The Allies' defensive problem in the Channel had been simplified by Admiral Bacon's admission of defeat over the Flanders Barrage, not only through enemy action, but bad weather as well. The underpowered monitors with the firepower to keep German light forces at bay were practically unmanageable in the southwesterly gales that were increasingly frequent (and sudden) as autumn drew on, while the nets needed calm weather for any repairs. The Germans were also strengthening their shore batteries and had plans to install 38-cm guns in the new "Deutschland" battery, with a range of more than 50,000 yards. *General Wolfe* had already been straddled by the 28-cm "Tirpitz" battery at 32,000 yards and *Prince Rupert* at 34,000. As Bacon noted, "there was no help for it but to discontinue the patrol."[7] Unfortunately, although the barrage claimed more U-boats than initial postwar analysis suggested, Bacon remained overly sanguine as to its effects and attributed increases in German activity in the western Channel to the barrage's reduced effectiveness, rather than the Germans' own changes in their operations. This attitude would not help him in 1917. In any event, the Germans removed substantial components of the net lines and the deep minefields, despite facing their own difficulties from the weather of autumn and winter. The work was assigned to the old torpedo craft that the German navy (not having the same requirement to protect shipping as the British) used as minesweepers in preference to converted fishing vessels.

Fearing a night attack, Admiral Bacon later asserted he took one precaution that proved vital, the nighttime passage of loaded troopships was suspended and there were only a few empty transports at sea. He may have been strictly correct about troop carriers, but there were fifty-seven supply ships in the Channel that night. As so often happened in night warfare, however, darkness shielded all but one from the German raiders. Despite Bacon's precautions, the Dover Patrol was neither well organized nor mentally prepared for the attack. Bacon later argued cogently in his memoir of the impossibility of maintaining surveillance of the Channel at night with the forces available.[8] He wrote to the Admiralty, "It is as easy to stop a raid of express engines with all lights out at night . . . as to stop a raid of 33-not [sic] destroyers on a night as black as Erebus."[9] However, there were three closely associated problems that affected the British response on this and later occasions. The first was Bacon's inability to delegate and keep his subordinates informed. His chief of staff later in 1917 commented that Bacon "planned and did many things with which I was quite unacquainted."[10] Second was the lack of arrangements that allowed a sighting unit to be immediately sure whether another ship was friend or foe. Deficient recognition systems were only a part of this problem. More critical was the need for the movement of all units to be organized such that there was no risk of any ship being in the wrong place. The Channel's navigational challenges made this extremely difficult, but more could have been done, particularly through the rigid demarcation of operating areas. This would have made a great difference to the tendency, understandable in units patrolling night after night, conscious of dozens of other Allied craft in the area, to assume an unexpected sighting was of a friendly unit. Too many British—and French—ships were frightened to fire first, lest they hit the wrong target. A wider anxiety to avoid accidents in a crowded seaway may have contributed to at least one British destroyer operating with navigation lights on, helpful to an errant drifter wanting to keep out of her path, but very dangerous in the presence of enemy surface forces.

The Germans allocated twenty-four torpedo boats to their raid. The plan was for the two half-flotillas of the Ninth Flotilla to proceed southwest down the Channel to attack the main shipping route between Folkestone and Boulogne. An hour behind them, two half-flotillas of the Third Flotilla would attempt to "roll up" the drifters and other small craft tending the antisubmarine net barrage. In addition to the separation in time between the two full flotillas, each half-flotilla was well removed by distance from its partner, in the hope of avoiding confusion. The first wave began its approach to the British patrol areas just after 2000. The Germans passed through the barrage, sighting the destroyers of the newly arrived Harwich Force division on their way to Dunkirk—but not being sighted in turn—and a lone Dover Patrol destroyer, *Flirt*. The latter saw the Germans but was confused by *V30* immediately flashing back the same recognition code that *Flirt* had signaled. The Germans rapidly passed out of sight and an uncertain *Flirt* decided that they were from the Harwich Force. She did not report the encounter. This meant the vital knowledge that there were already German forces south of the barrage was not available to Bacon or the ships of the Dover Patrol. Much of the later confusion can be ascribed to this information gap.

As the Ninth Flotilla searched for Allied transports, the Third Flotilla began its approach. At 2210 the drifter *Waveney* came under attack. *Flirt*, alerted by the gunfire, made her way north and found the sinking *Waveney*. The old destroyer's priority was to rescue the drifter's survivors. This was another critical error; on the testimony of the few survivors of *Flirt*, there were destroyers in sight when she stopped to conduct the rescue, but *Flirt*'s captain thought they were French. The armed yacht *Ombra*'s assessment at 2220 was more accurate. The Germans were finding it difficult to locate any targets and began to use their searchlights. *Ombra*'s experienced captain immediately radioed "Enemy's warships 20 miles east of Dover" and set about getting the drifters away from the barrage. At this point, the last half-flotilla of German torpedo craft arrived and sighted the hapless *Flirt*. The elderly destroyer was blown out of the water, with the loss of all on board. Only the boat's crew dispatched earlier to help *Waveney* survived. *Ombra*'s signal alerted Bacon, who immediately ordered out the destroyers from the western side of the Channel and directed the additional Harwich Force division to leave its anchorage off Dunkirk. The cruiser *Carysfort* was also ordered out, but—at two hours' notice for sea—she would not sail in time. The other Harwich Force division, led by *Lawford*, did not move from the Downs because of a mistake in interpreting *Ombra*'s signal—"warships" was read as "airships."

The Third Flotilla sank only six drifters during an hour spent near the barrage. The darkness that cloaked their approach and contributed to the defenders' confusion made it very difficult to detect the small vessels. In the southwest, the Ninth Flotilla also had only limited success. They were seen by the hospital ships *Jan Brydel* and *St Denis*. The first recognized the Germans for what they were, the second did not. In any case, neither could report a sighting because of their noncombatant status. The sole victim was the transport *Queen*, on passage showing her navigation lights and oblivious to a tail of five enemy torpedo craft until she was challenged, stopped, and boarded. Her crew took to the boats before the Germans attempted to sink the ship. *Queen* was still afloat when the torpedo boats withdrew and did not actually founder until about 0500. The Eighteenth Half-Flotilla encountered two French patrol vessels. The trawlers *Montaigne* and *Albatros II* had heard firing but thought a zeppelin raid was in progress. One of *Albatros II*'s gunners did his best to convince his commander that "the enemy is in sight," but both ships assumed the contacts were friendly. *Montaigne* was sunk and *Albatros II* damaged. The latter managed to make off in the darkness with four dead and many wounded, getting into Boulogne the next morning.[11]

By 2330 the Third Flotilla was withdrawing from the barrage and the Ninth Flotilla had also turned for home. Shortly afterward, the patrol vessel *P34* found the survivors of *Queen* and signaled that there were German destroyers in the area. This was received correctly by *Lawford*, which at last began to move south from the Downs. There were other British forces converging on the barrage at the time the German Ninth Flotilla approached it, but their actions demonstrated continuing confusion. The destroyer *Nubian* sighted and challenged the Seventeenth Half-Flotilla, but initially believing they were from the Harwich Force, only realized the units in sight were hostile after two torpedoes had been fired at her. Primitive fire control arrangements and lack of preparedness for night fighting meant that only *Nubian*'s forward gun fired, word never getting to the torpedo tubes or the after gun mount. Another German torpedo blew away most of the front half of the ship, although the remainder remained afloat.

Her sister ship, *Amazon*, made the same assumption that the ships sighted were British *L*-class destroyers. So sure was *Amazon* her response to being fired upon was to issue the challenge. She was lucky to survive with heavy damage. A division of three other *Tribal*-class destroyers fared little better. They also issued the challenge and were met by gunfire that damaged *Mohawk*. Her rudder jammed, *Mohawk*'s movements confused the situation so much that her consorts could not turn around in time to give chase to the fast-disappearing Germans. By 0100 the latter were clear of the British defenses, with no chance of being overhauled. All the British could do was pick up survivors and attempt to salvage the stricken *Nubian*. Despite the best efforts of *Lark*, the destroyer's remains drove ashore on the South Foreland. *Nubian*'s construction must have been robust, because the wreck endured the pounding effects of two gales before being salvaged and brought back to Dover. By the time this was done, *Nubian*'s sister ship, *Zulu*, had her stern blown off by a mine on 8 November. *Zulu* was found by the French destroyer *Capitaine Mehl* and towed into Calais.[12] The remains of both ships were taken to Chatham dockyard and the bows of *Zulu* successfully mated to the stern of *Nubian*. Aptly and cheerfully renamed *Zubian*, the resulting conglomeration was back in service in June 1917 and did good work.

The Germans had mixed feelings about their success. While they conducted the operation without loss, the results were limited, particularly against Allied transport vessels. Despite the care taken to separate the four formations, on at least two occasions German units sighted each other and very nearly fired on their own side. Night combat remained risky for all concerned. In the meantime, it was clear to the British that the Channel was vulnerable. The barrage was no obstacle to surface vessels and the Dover Patrol's strength insufficient to be certain of an effective response to a night raid. The French could not help. Even with reinforcement units from the Atlantic and the Mediterranean, they could provide only five 800-ton destroyers and a handful of torpedo craft, useful against submarines, but not of a capability to face the German flotillas with any surety of success.[13]

The affair also contributed to growing concerns about the Admiralty itself. German raiders striking so close to British shores and escaping unscathed struck further at public confidence in the Royal Navy. British credibility was not helped by the Admiralty claiming two German torpedo craft had been sunk. The First Lord, Arthur Balfour, hedged on the assertion a few days later, stating there was "ground for thinking" two ships had been destroyed by mines—but none for their destruction by gunfire.[14] The Germans quickly denied they had suffered any losses. A complete lack of supporting evidence eventually forced the Admiralty to drop the claim, adding fuel to the campaign against the Balfour-Jackson regime that was under way in press and parliament.[15]

Bacon's losses were made up by transfers from other local flotillas in the south, while the Harwich Force was ordered to detach yet another division of destroyers to the Channel. Tyrwhitt was less than pleased by this further reduction in strength. Not only was his offensive capability substantially depleted, but the "Beef trip" convoys depended upon the availability of destroyers. With so many units operating in the Dover area, he could safely conduct only one round-trip a week. Tyrwhitt's concern that there were other problems than Dover was confirmed when the German Ninth Flotilla mounted an attack on shipping off the Dutch coast on 1 November. The British had been alerted by Room 40 to the German sortie but did not know what Michelsen's ships intended. Tyrwhitt was forced to dispatch his remaining destroyers to reinforce Dover, while he took his cruisers to patrol off the Scheldt in case the High Sea Fleet flotillas were on their way home. The Germans had originally intended to repeat the attack on the Channel, but the combination of an aircraft report of a substantial British fleet off the Gravelines and radio intercepts by the Flanders Command intelligence center made them believe the British were warned and ready. There was justifiable (and correct) scepticism in von Schröder's headquarters regarding the aircraft's assessment that it had sighted eleven battleships, but the report had to be given some weight. Believing that all the flotilla would find would be alerted enemy cruisers and destroyers, the sortie was canceled and a sweep for shipping on the shipping lanes to the Netherlands substituted.

The Ninth Flotilla succeeded in capturing three ships, all of which were dispatched to Zeebrugge with prize crews embarked. Early on the morning of 2 November, their work was interrupted by Tyrwhitt's force, which intercepted the third prize, the Dutch merchant ship *Oldambt*, and shortly afterward sighted five German torpedo boats, themselves in pursuit of another Dutch vessel. The old problem of identification raised its head and Tyrwhitt himself had to be persuaded the ships in sight were neither Dutch nor French.[16] A sharp little action followed, but the range was never less than eight thousand yards and rapid deployment of a smoke screen by the retiring Germans meant neither side suffered any damage before contact was lost. The belief the British had strongly reinforced their units in the south to match the German strength on the Flanders coast confirmed the decision to send the Third Flotilla home. It sailed on the night of 2 November and was in German waters the next day. The British were not alerted to the movement, but eventually realized there had been a transfer of forces back to the North Sea. This reduced the pressure on the Dover Patrol and the Harwich Force, but the continuing presence of the Ninth Flotilla in the Flanders ports suggested the Germans had further operations in mind.

Operations in the North Sea

To the north another saga was unfolding. On the evening of 2 November *U30*, operating off the Norwegian coast, reported that her diesels had broken down and she required assistance. This message was taken in by *U20*, which joined her early the next morning, ready to take the stricken submarine in tow. The signal had also been intercepted by Room 40. The British immediately sent destroyers with cruisers as cover to intercept *U30*, but, unaware of the assistance the U-boat had received, the first group into the area looked too far north and the rendezvous for the other formations was set astern of the submarines' track. The British called off their effort when they decrypted *U30*'s report on the afternoon of 3 November that she had fixed her engines and was proceeding homeward at twelve knots. Reality in the U-boat's engine-spaces was nothing like so good. *U30* broke down repeatedly and her rate of progress overnight was closer to four knots.

After another temporary fix, speed was increased on the morning of 4 November, but at this stage a thick fog enveloped the Skagerrak. Uncertain of their position, the submarines were set much farther northeast than they realized. That evening both ran aground on the Danish coast near Bovbjerg. *U30* lightened herself enough to get clear, at the price of losing her ability to submerge, but *U20* was caught fast. The would-be rescuer now found that her own diesel engines were out of action. With battery exhausted, *U20* could not be refloated without help. When the news reached Admiral Scheer just after 2100, he ordered the outpost forces to sea under von Hipper in *Seydlitz*, reinforced by *Moltke* and no fewer than eleven battleships, including the Third Squadron, just returned from the Baltic. A half-flotilla of torpedo boats was sent ahead to attempt the salvage of *U20* and this was on scene early on the morning of 5 November. Repeated attempts to pull the submarine off failed and Scheer approved the boat's destruction. Conditions were calm enough to allow confidential books and equipment and even her remaining torpedoes to be removed before *U20* was blown up.

Dispatching substantial forces to cover the salvage attempt was a reasonable risk, since Neumünster advised that there was no indication that major British units were at sea. But there was a greater hazard in the relatively small number of torpedo craft available to screen the major units. Although von Hipper's two battle cruisers and his light cruisers each had a torpedo boat in company, the battleships had only a handful between them. Matters were not improved by the heavy ships running a north-south line as they waited on developments, doing so at twelve knots to make life easier for the escorting torpedo boats. This was a gift for a submarine. *J1*, under the command of Baltic veteran Commander Noel Laurence, had arrived in her patrol area on the morning of 5 November and dived for the day. Laurence, who put a torpedo into *Moltke* in the Baltic in 1915, was one of the Royal Navy's most skillful submarine commanders. He sighted four battleships on the submarine's starboard quarter in the haze at 1150. Laurence was forced to go deep and reverse course to get into an attack position. When he came to periscope depth again, conditions were so bad that *J1* broke surface, but Laurence forced her down without being spotted. When he had his boat under control and could take another look, it was clear the battleships had reversed course and were heading south and opening from *J1*. Laurence immediately fired all four bow tubes at a range of approximately three thousand yards. That he could launch a salvo this size demonstrated the capability of the newest submarines, such as the big and fast *J* class. That any weapons would hit when fired from such a range showed the increasing skills of the best submarine captains. One torpedo struck *Grosser Kurfürst* aft and a second *Kronprinz* forward.

Both ships suffered substantial damage, but managed to return to harbor without assistance, further confirmation of German capital ships' robust underwater protection and the British need for a heavier torpedo. However, the incident showed that the High Sea Fleet had failed to adjust to the new threat environment. Scheer's dispatch of capital ships with minimal escort was one questionable decision, but the risks involved were greatly increased by the on-scene commanders. The handling of the force by Behncke, the Third Squadron's commander, would have been understandable in August 1914, but not at this point of the war. Failure to zigzag combined with slow speed made the battleships a much more inviting target than they should have been, even if the Third Squadron was unfortunate in coming within Laurence's reach. These errors were indicative of the minimal seagoing experience the High Seas Fleet's operational employment allowed its leadership, but they also showed the same failure of imagination for which British admirals like Lewis Bayly were justly criticized in the wake of British losses in 1914 and 1915. Jellicoe may have consulted his fears too much in handling the Grand Fleet, but his opponents had clearly not thought through the submarine threat they themselves faced. The nineteen knots with which the Third Squadron hastily departed the attack scene should have been maintained for the entire operation.

The kaiser was highly critical of Scheer's decision to hazard the battleships to support the recovery of a single U-boat. Part of the C-in-C's motivation may have been to avoid handing the Allies the propaganda victory inherent in the destruction of the submarine that sank *Lusitania*, but he defended himself stoutly, arguing that the submarines were the German navy's primary fighting element and their crews needed to believe they would be supported by the fleet in every way possible. Scheer had a point, one the kaiser accepted after a personal interview. The C-in-C also noted that "English torpedoes have never yet proved fatal to our big ships," a statement not unreasonable in the circumstances, but which failed to address the tactical failures involved.[17]

Developments in the Main Fleets

The damage to the two battleships and the demands of the refit program were further restraints on major fleet operations over the winter months and Scheer accepted an operational pause. This allowed the First Scouting Group the opportunity for tactical training in the Baltic and the C-in-C to reorganize the remainder of the battle fleet. The encounter with *J1*, confirming the requirement for constant high speed, may have been the final nail in the coffin of the Second Squadron. With manpower required for the U-boats and the completion of the 38-cm gunned *Bayern* and *Baden*, the High Sea Fleet could be reconstituted, and in December the eight oldest dreadnoughts were placed in the First Squadron and the most modern divided into the Third and the new Fourth Squadron. One important German tactical doctrine changed with the departure of the pre-dreadnoughts, curiously at odds with the direction the Grand Fleet was taking. The Second Squadron's commander had authority to maneuver independently of the line of battle, "risking his force regardless of the consequences" if the likely results justified it. This discretion was specifically withdrawn with the formation of the Fourth Squadron.[18] The old *Deutschland* class may have been expendable, but the super-dreadnoughts were not.

Friedrich der Grosse remained fleet flagship until *Baden* became operational in March 1917. The Second Scouting Group and the Fourth Scouting Group were also reorganized and now contained only the most modern light cruisers, including the first products of the replacement program for the losses of 1914. The Fourth Scouting Group included the new cruiser-minelayers *Bremse* and *Brummer*, which would be among the most active offensive units during the remainder of the war. As for the Second Squadron, one ship was retained as the Baltic guard ship, while the others were disarmed for training or accommodation duties. That their guns were modified to serve as railway weapons on the western front was another indication of shifting priorities. Yet this stand-down of the fleet over the winter showed that neither the Admiralstab nor the High Sea Fleet were thinking through their multifront problem. The months in which the northeastern Baltic was under ice provided an opportunity to focus totally on the North Sea and the Channel, which the Germans never properly exploited. The winter of 1916–17 was particularly harsh but the social and morale problems that inadequate food and fuel were creating in the nation and in its navy might have not been so severe had there been more evidence of offensive activity against the enemy.

The British undertook their own reorganization. Resumption of the U-boat campaign against shipping in home waters combined with the continuing German and Austrian submarine operations in the Mediterranean to increase shipping losses substantially in October and again in November. The Admiralty seemed to have little answer to the U-boat, and its professional component was exhibiting neither the energy nor the judgment necessary to find one. Jellicoe himself pressed the need for action upon the First Lord, Arthur Balfour, as well as other politicians. (One of his informal channels was breakfasting with the daily dispatch carriers who were often younger members of parliament.)[19] The First Sea Lord, Jackson, recognized his own limitations and was willing to step aside. In the circumstances, the First Lord's only choice as his replacement could be Jellicoe and in late November the latter was offered and accepted the post. Jellicoe did so with reluctance, partly because he could never lead the fleet to the decisive action it sought. One of his staff officers believed Jellicoe left the Grand Fleet on "the bitterest day of his life."[20] Experienced in Whitehall, he had no illusions as to the workload or the infighting to come. The reality was even worse than he expected, for only a few days later, David Lloyd George became prime minister at the head of a coalition government, whose other changes included Balfour's transfer to the Foreign Office. Jellicoe respected Lloyd George's energy, but he neither trusted nor liked a man who was too political an animal for the tired admiral. That Balfour's replacement as First Lord, Sir Edward Carson, proved a congenial colleague would not, in the end, be enough. Despite Jellicoe's misgivings, Beatty was his only logical successor as C-in-C. Jellicoe's first choice, Madden (who, though older, was junior to Beatty as a flag officer), was made second in command and commander of the First Battle Squadron. Both were appointed acting full admirals with "war seniority" to ensure they remained senior to any routine promotions. This was necessary because, although two of the squadron commanders—Burney and Jerram—were replaced, Sturdee remained in the Fourth Battle Squadron.[21]

A key change was in the battle cruisers, which reverted under their new flag officer, Rear Admiral Sir William Pakenham, from being the "Battle Cruiser Fleet" to the "Battle Cruiser Force," a designation from the first days of the war. That Beatty should have endorsed this reduction in the status of the Grand Fleet's advanced formation is significant. Although the new commander had worked closely with him as flag officer in the Second Battle Cruiser Squadron, Beatty clearly believed that he required closer control than Jellicoe had imposed on the battle cruisers. In Beatty's correspondence in 1917 and 1918, there is evidence he intervened, albeit generally through private conversation or personal letter, in affairs within the Battle Cruiser

Force much more frequently than his predecessor as C-in-C. As a first step in such closer supervision, Beatty obtained the Admiralty's agreement to the battle cruisers' temporary transfer to Scapa Flow. This was to give them the concentrated gunnery training difficult to conduct at Rosyth and the opportunity for a tactical exercise with the battle fleet. It would also allow Beatty to ensure that Pakenham understood his C-in-C's intentions.

There were many other changes in the Grand Fleet. Jellicoe took several of his closest subordinates to the Admiralty, while Beatty brought most of his staff to *Iron Duke*. This was inevitable and, although there was renewed energy to pursue some key issues, the change was more of manner than matter. Beatty knew he had much to learn. The challenges of operating the Grand Fleet were outside his experience—as they were for anyone except Jellicoe himself—and Beatty was shrewd enough to hold fire on matters such as the *Grand Fleet Battle Orders* until he had settled in. This settling process also included gaining both the confidence of his immediate subordinates and the Grand Fleet as a whole. Jellicoe had his own charisma and Beatty was very much on trial as far as the battle squadrons were concerned. Awareness of this attitude on board *Iron Duke* may have contributed to his desire to transfer his flag to the larger, faster, and more heavily armed *Queen Elizabeth*. On board her, Beatty's grander manner would not be contrasted unfavorably with that of his quiet predecessor.

The Grand Fleet's exercises were marred by the loss of two destroyers in the early hours of 21 December after a collision that demonstrated the hazards of the new antisubmarine weapons. Sailing in close formation,

Photo 7.1   **HMS *Tiger* and HMS *Renown* at sea**   *Royal Navy Historical Branch*

Hoste's rudder jammed. Her unexpected turn brought *Hoste* across the bows of *Negro*, which ran into her stern. Serious damage became critical when *Hoste*'s two depth charges were dislodged and went overboard. Both exploded, breaking *Hoste*'s back and flooding *Negro*'s engine room. With the weather worsening, attempts were made to take the crippled *Negro* in tow, but with her bulkheads collapsing, the destroyer suddenly sank by the stern just after 0400. Despite desperate efforts, only thirty-four of her crew were saved. *Hoste*'s ship's company fared better. Heavy seas eventually tore the destroyer's stern off, but her consort, *Marvel*, repeatedly got alongside in a considerable feat of seamanship and took off *Hoste*'s crew. Oil pumped on the water by another ship helped reduce sea and spray, although a heavy swell remained for what was no easy task. Three died, caught between the hulls, and one was injured. Remarkably, when a lone survivor suddenly appeared on *Hoste*'s upper deck after *Marvel*'s captain had thought his grueling task was done, the evolution was repeated and the tardy sailor saved.

The absence of the battle cruisers in the north between 10 and 21 December worried the Admiralty. The High Sea Fleet's reorganization had not yet been detected and Scheer's program of exercises was not immediately recognized for what it was. There were false alarms about the High Sea Fleet's movements when it was simply assembling to practice the new commanders and their formations. Scheer had plans for minor forays, but the stormy weather marking the start of a hard winter meant these were repeatedly delayed and then canceled outright. Given that the light cruisers of two scouting groups, the Second and the Fourth, and the torpedo boats were now the C-in-C's key offensive force, this dependence on good weather was inevitable. The German battle cruisers, like their opposite numbers at Rosyth, were now on much shorter apron strings than had been the case before Jutland. The only substantial operation was on 27 December, when four light cruisers and the bulk of the High Sea Fleet flotillas were dispatched to the Great Fisher Bank to intercept merchant traffic. The weather was so bad *Regensburg* was forced to send the light craft home. Finding no targets, the cruisers turned back soon afterward. *Regensburg*'s liberal use of radio gave the British a reasonable idea of what was going on through a combination of direction finding and decryptions, but their assessment was greatly helped by Scheer himself continuing to use radio in harbor for changing the readiness of the fleet as whole.

To be fair, the continuing anxiety within the Admiralty was justified by the assessment that the Germans would use the short periods of daylight and poor weather to slip surface raiders through the blockade. This was correct, but by the beginning of December the first two raiders had already sailed, *Möwe* via the Kattegat on 23 November and *Wolf* on 30 November. *Möwe* beat the British at their own signals intelligence game and gleaned sufficient information from the Tenth Cruiser Squadron's radio traffic to dodge around its patrols. *Wolf*, on her third attempt, was helped by poor weather and went through undetected.[22] Initially shepherded by U-boats, she risked the ice of the Denmark Strait to minimize the chance of contact. It was months before her activities made it clear to Allied authorities there was a raider in the Indian Ocean. Matters had been confused for the British by a report an outward-bound German raider was expected to pass Christiana on 12 December. This was a local misinterpretation of the merchant ship *Prinz Friedrich Wilhelm* attempting to get to Germany through Norwegian waters. Although forces were deployed to the Norwegian Sea to intercept the expected movement, there was no raider and *Prinz Friedrich Wilhelm* escaped, helped by the fact the British cruisers and destroyers were looking the wrong way.

The British feared there were more raiders to come and they were right. The Germans adopted the novel solution of converting a sailing vessel with auxiliary propulsion for the attack on commerce. *Seeadler*'s departure was delayed by the fracas over *Prinz Friedrich Wilhelm*, but things quietened sufficiently for her to clear the Heligoland Bight late on 21 December. Disguising *Seeadler* as a Norwegian timber carrier bound for Melbourne proved effective. She was stopped and examined by the armed boarding vessel *Patia* and allowed to proceed. In the new year *Seeadler* started her work in the South Atlantic. The combined global efforts of the three raiders were a continuing distraction for the Admiralty during 1917 as they took a substantial toll of Allied shipping and diverted large numbers of cruisers and patrol vessels to fruitless searches of the world's oceans. Not one was intercepted. *Möwe* returned home in March 1917, the more cautious but wide-ranging *Wolf* in January 1918, while *Seeadler* was wrecked in the Society Islands in the Pacific in August 1917.

Problems in the Channel

The closing weeks of 1916 suggested that the Belgian Coast and the English Channel would be the most active areas of war for surface forces. Both sides faced problems in balancing their local efforts, although the British, increasingly preoccupied with the submarine threat, had more to be worried about.

Matters were not helped by divided command arrangements. The return of a detachment of the Ninth Flotilla to Harwich from Dover renewed Tyrwhitt's concerns about their employment by the Dover Command—and Bacon's fitness for his job. Bacon insisted on ships at anchor remaining "almost entirely at instant or 10 minutes' notice for sea," for "seventeen days in succession" without allowing opportunity for rest or maintenance.[23] Tyrwhitt remonstrated with the admiral but got nowhere. Finally, despite Bacon's vast seniority, Commodore (T) wrote directly to the Admiralty, stating firmly, "Even disregarding human endurance, it is obvious to anyone with the slightest knowledge of destroyers, that the mechanical element must inevitably deteriorate rapidly."[24] Bacon later defended himself by asserting that the war was a once in a lifetime event and "therefore everyone had to be prepared to expend the energy of a lifetime."[25] A destroyer's commanding officer disposed of the argument, "This is all very well, but there is a limit to human endurance."[26]

Notably, there is no record of Tyrwhitt being admonished by the Admiralty, despite his direct criticism of a senior officer. This may have been because Bacon's fixation on immediate readiness for action had embroiled him in a dispute about other elements of destroyer operations. Bacon's dispositions were generally endorsed by the Admiralty, but his piecemeal approach to dispatching his forces into the dark was rightly criticized. Part of the confusion of the night of 26 October resulted from the *Tribal*-class destroyers leaving their anchorage individually, rather than operating in divisions. Bacon supported this procedure, but a court of enquiry and the Admiralty pointed out this was a recipe for exactly the sort of problems the British had experienced. Professional opinion was turning against the admiral. Tyrwhitt's flag captain, Domvile, was scathing and told Vice Admiral de Robeck, new commander of the Second Battle Squadron, "the Rasher had made a priceless balls of everything the other night—I wish they would send him back to his sty."[27] As Tyrwhitt was similarly abusive on the subject of "the Streaky one," whom he described as his "bugbear" in private correspondence, it is clear feelings ran high in the Harwich Force.[28]

There were two wider issues at play. One, which also applied to the Harwich Force and other commands but manifested most clearly in the Dover Patrol, was the failure to allow ships enough time to work up and conduct weapon practices. So anxious was Bacon to have the maximum fighting strength available that little time was given his small ships to train, most notably to cope with the complexities of night warfare. The admiral was not alone in this attitude, and many local commands pressed new arrivals into service with little thought as to a ship's readiness for operations. What became even more apparent in the coming months was that lack of service-wide doctrine and procedures meant detachments from the major elements of the forces in home waters were unfamiliar with the practices of the new command they joined. There were many differences, big and small, explicit and implicit between the way the Dover Patrol, the Harwich Force, and the Grand Fleet did their business. Bacon made the local problem worse by his apparent inability to take criticism or counsel. He was less than encouraging of the initiatives of his immediate subordinates and no better when responding to external inquiries.[29] Yet Tyrwhitt, too, was not sufficiently sensitive to the need to indoctrinate new arrivals. One of the necessary changes to the British approach in the time ahead would be the achievement of a more coordinated approach to every aspect of operations in home waters.

On the night of 29–30 December, the minelayer *Abdiel* deployed an eighty-mine field across one of the swept channels in the Heligoland Bight. It caused the immediate loss of a German auxiliary and twelve days later, a narrow escape for *U57.* This was too early for such an operation to be considered the first swallow of spring, but it was a start.

Crisis at Sea

8

T
HE DEBATE OVER UNRESTRICTED submarine warfare became the
German navy's main concern as 1916 ended. The stalemate on land
brought the German army's leaders to believe an unrestricted campaign might be the only way to achieve decisive victory. While the motivations for this dangerous escalation contained as much emotion as reason,
there was an effort absent at the beginning of 1915 (which remained absent
when considering the zeppelins' bombing campaign) to base the argument
upon facts. The Admiralstab used civilian experts to produce a case that,
given the state of the global wheat crop, sufficient tonnage could be sunk
within six months to bring the United Kingdom to the brink of starvation.
The British would be forced to sue for peace, even if they survived the internal
dissent that would follow mass shortages of food. To figures of tonnage, the
Admiralstab added the old idea that the campaign would frighten neutrals
to the point they would withdraw their vessels from Allied shipping routes.

The argument accepted some risks and ignored others. It was based
on reasonable estimates of ship availability, including British and Allied
performance in repair and construction. The Germans understood the extent
to which the French, the Italians, and the Russians were dependent on British
supply by sea. The navy was prepared to accept the possibility of neutrals
entering the war, notably Denmark, about whose potential occupation
the Admiralstab was more sanguine than the army, as well as the United
States. Both Admiralstab and the army were dismissive of the capacity of the
Americans to contribute to the Allied effort. The politicians were much less
confident, but it was difficult to argue the point when unrestricted warfare's
key promise was that the desired results could be achieved in only six months.

There were other weaknesses in the German navy's case. Although
operational U-boats had increased to more than 100 by the end of 1916,
sustaining operations at the required level would strain the force to the

utmost. Mass production, however, was not part of the concept. Orders for only 45 UB-type boats and six larger units were signed around the time the unrestricted campaign started. Completions of existing orders, and high survival rates through the poor results of the Allied defense, allowed operational availability to pass 120 by the middle of 1917, but it hovered there for the remainder of the year. The U-boat force would need to manage with what it had. The Germans may also have been guilty of projection, assuming their own problems of industrial mobilization extended to the British. They had justification, given the obvious fall in British merchant ship production. The same assumption extended to the British ability to manage their national food supplies on an equitable basis, something Germany had so far failed to do, starkly demonstrated during the coming "turnip winter." That the British might be able to combine political will and administrative capacity to solve both problems seems to have been outside the imagination of the Great General Staff and the Admiralstab and of their civilian experts. The Germans also underestimated not only the ruthlessness with which the British would deal with anxious neutrals, but how much America's entry to the war would strengthen the Allied position. In effect, full control of global resources and transport passed into Allied hands. The United States would have no interest in making profits from the Central powers, and neutrals would be under much greater pressure to comply with the Allies. The half-million tons of interned German merchant shipping lying in U.S. and South American ports were another potential resource that the German shipping magnate Albert Ballin feared would be put to good use.[1] The Admiralstab believed these ships would be rendered useless by sabotage before the Americans could take control, but this proved another false judgment. Perhaps most dangerous for the navy's and for Germany's leadership was that they were staking their remaining credibility with the German people on the promise of success in six months. It should not have escaped the German admirals that they were taking the same risk within the navy itself.

The Allied Response

The Allies were aware of the German dilemma, as were the Americans. While the diplomatic and military attachés of the United States in Berlin were increasingly isolated from both official and personal contacts, their reports to Washington demonstrated a good understanding of the progress that proponents of unrestricted warfare were making. The bell was already tolling for the British, confirmed by Jellicoe's reluctant translation to Whitehall. The war on trade had become the greatest problem for the Allies at sea. The rate of sinkings had increased rapidly between October and December 1916, to an average of some 300,000 tons every month. The steep rise by comparison with the previous prize warfare campaign was largely because so many more U-boats were operational than in 1915. The Allies were being overwhelmed. The Admiralty's access to signals intelligence was imperfect, but enough to be sure that claims of U-boat sinkings by forces at sea were still often wrong, even when the evidence on scene seemed overwhelming.

The new organization at the Admiralty had many problems to fix, and the Anti-Submarine Division got no breathing space before difficult decisions had to be made. The first requirement was to improve coordination of patrol forces and the multitude of local commands around the coast. An early step was reorganization of the Auxiliary Patrol, to standardize procedures and share experience. The compartmentalization between local commands reflected a wider problem of excessive restrictions on disseminating information, particularly intelligence, and the Admiralty tried to open channels of communication. The problem was exacerbated by continuing reliance on independently sailed merchant ships, each of which needed to be kept informed of danger areas and safe passages. As the Admiralty staff history commented, "the great defect of routeing [sic] lay in its powerlessness to control traffic in the light of an immediate situation."[2] Further, not all local authorities received the information they needed for planning or the short-term diversions that might have been possible. The processes for passing on signals intelligence and other information about U-boat activity had also to be placed on a systematic basis.

The Admiralty and Jellicoe have been heavily criticized for their failures in the campaign against the U-boats. Some of this was justified. The Admiralty was tragically slow to adopt convoy and did not think through the fundamental advantages of the system (an intellectual exercise arguably not formally undertaken until after World War II). Nevertheless, the work to coordinate action within the navy and encourage the efforts of the nation was fundamental to eventual confinement of the problem. As early as January 1916 Jellicoe had urged the Admiralty to "persuade the Government to build merchant ships."[3] It may be that the new First Sea Lord's inability to achieve real improvements in this area during his first months in Whitehall was as significant a personal failure as his reluctance to convoy. The revival of merchant shipbuilding and drastic improvements in repair times would be vital factors in holding the line against the U-boats. This work of coordination was so important because, although some innovations proved extremely useful in combating the U-boats, no real solution to the combined problems of detection, classification, and destruction was available before the end of the war. There was no silver bullet in 1914–18.

Defensive arming of merchant ships was accelerated, the Director of Naval Ordnance noting in November 1916 that he was "busy trying to take up every available gun."[4] This was reasonable, given the proportion of U-boat attacks conducted on the surface and it got high priority, extending to the selective removal of 4-inch guns from the Grand Fleet's older capital ships, more useful in merchant ships than as a last-ditch defense against torpedo craft. Much hope was attached to disguised "Special Service Ships" (or "Q Ships"), which also relied upon their attacker approaching on the surface. By the end of 1916 at least five U-boats had fallen victim and, although the Germans were increasingly alert to the threat, their desire to economize on torpedoes and the "stop and search" nature of prize warfare still gave the Q Ships some opportunities. Another tactic that had potential was a submerged submarine under tow by a decoy vessel. On the latter being attacked, the tow would be slipped, allowing the submarine to maneuver and attack the U-boat.

There were technological developments that promised to give the anti-submarine forces some ability to fight back, but it was difficult to be sure just what worked—and none, even in combination, were a panacea. On 6 December, the destroyer *Ariel* attacked a surfaced U-boat southwest of Land's End. A depth charge dropped on the diving position failed to explode, but the destroyer deployed armed paravanes, one of which fired. The Admiralty later assessed this as a "possible." The boat concerned may have been *UC19*, although this is not certain. Postwar analysis suggested it might have been *UB29*, but that boat was caught off the Goodwin Sands by the destroyer *Landrail* on 13 December. In a night encounter that also started with the submarine on the surface, *Landrail* forced *UB29* under. On this occasion, aided by shallow water that prevented the U-boat's ability to go deep, depth charges were employed with what seemed to be success. This appeared to be the first loss of a German submarine to a depth charge but could only be assessed as a "possible" as no wreckage was initially found. The wreck was finally located in 2017, sixty miles closer to Zeebrugge. Rather than being sunk by a depth charge, the already badly damaged *UB29* seems finally to have fallen victim to a mine.[5]

The initial allocation of two or four depth charges to each ship was inadequate. At 40, 80, and even 120 feet, the early hydrostatic settings also proved largely ineffective except in shallow water. Given the very limited lethality radius of the charges, all a submarine had to do was to dive quickly and deep enough to avoid damage. By early 1917 work was in hand to allow activation down to two hundred feet. Equally important, production was increased tenfold, although it was well into 1918 before the allocation of depth charges to dedicated antisubmarine craft was increased to the thirty to fifty necessary.[6]

Hydrophones were beginning to be manufactured in numbers. Their first use was as coastal detection systems, with arrays of hydrophones monitored from ashore. Their logical weapon was the controlled mine, triggered when the submarine was directly over the hydrophone. Such systems' effective detection range was inevitably limited by background noise, including that of local shipping. As for hydrophones at sea, during World War I they were more useful to submarines. The latter were relatively quiet when operating on batteries underwater and could minimize self-noise to improve detection ranges (and reduce the range at which they themselves could be heard). For the Germans, with their much smaller antisubmarine challenge, listening devices for U-boats were the priority. By 1917, German submariners were becoming increasingly expert in their use. The problem for surface vessels, although the solution of streamlined bodies containing hydrophones towed clear of the ship was eventually identified, was that moving at any speed reduced the hydrophones' detection ranges to practically nothing. In effect, a ship had to stop each time its hydrophone operators needed to listen. This meant hydrophone barrages, both permanent and temporary ones made up by ships in line, became a favored method of searching for a U-boat or

Photo 8.1   **HMS** *Truant*   *Royal Navy Historical Branch*

attempting to block its passage. In the open sea, given that the submarines could well detect the surface ships first, such lines of observation were easy to avoid. At this stage of technology, while a submarine's bearing and movement could be estimated and triangulation across a base line of multiple hydrophones was possible, a moving target could not be located precisely enough to give any of the available underwater weaponry a significant chance of achieving a killing blow.

This limitation in hydrophones had another important effect. The only submarine detection method for a warship moving at a speed necessary to escort even the slowest merchant ship was what is now colloquially termed "the Mark One Eyeball." This was an abiding element in any discussion over the merits of the direct protection of merchant ships—convoy. What should never be discounted, but has not always been highlighted in subsequent analysis, was the concern that the merchant ships in convoy would be targets that their escorts would be unable to protect. The fear the escort could do little more than stand by as its charges were attacked was at the root of some of the objections to grouping merchant vessels together. This also underlay at least part of the Admiralty's concern about attempting to convoy neutrals, since these ships could be surrendering what little remaining privileged status they had for a false promise. It may also have underlain the collective objections of many merchant captains to being convoyed, a view firmly expressed to Jellicoe at a meeting on 22 February 1917.[7] Himself the son of a master mariner, perhaps the First Sea Lord gave their views too much weight. It was not yet understood that the great strength of the convoy system, even in the absence of effective escorts, was that convoys, by concentrating ships in such small areas, reduced the likelihood of detection by comparison with widely distributed single ships, and confined the U-boats' opportunities for attack. The seas emptied with the introduction of convoy and each submarine realistically only had one clear chance of firing before it would be forced deep and left astern. Small convoys, even if heavily escorted, were as a system much less effective in this respect than large ones.

Efforts to solve the submarine problem, despite ingenuity, devoted service, and huge mobilization of men and material, were hindered by two other continuing misapprehensions, which also contributed to the tardy acceptance of convoys. These were the insistence on "hunting" submarines because such offensive operations were considered the most effective way to deal with the U-boat menace. The second was the idea of patrolled areas with individual ships moving within them. The latter concept was refined to become "patrolled lanes," but even this idea of fixed routes with concentrated surveillance and response was doomed to at least partial failure. It reduced the submarines' success rate, but only to a limited extent. Patrol lines with units distributed at five-mile intervals looked good in theory and on a small-scale chart, but the intervals needed to be much smaller even against U-boats operating under the prize rules. Submarines could destroy their targets and escape before the antisubmarine forces could get to the scene—two ten-knot armed trawlers would take fifteen minutes to converge on an incident midway between their patrol stations. This would be even more true when unrestricted warfare began, with its increasing proportion of submerged attacks. Although fog could hinder the U-boats as much as their enemies, the normal moderate visibility around British waters limited the range of detection of submarines on the surface by patrol forces much more than it did U-boats looking for large, sometimes smoky, merchantmen. U-boats also were more likely to spot the smallest warship before being seen themselves. Even if a patrol vessel was early on scene, the submarine could still dive too quickly for the latter to have any serious chance of destroying it.

The difficulties that surface forces had in attacking U-boats intensified the Admiralty's concern that it did not have enough escorts for a convoy system to work. In part, this was based on a false understanding of the numbers of major merchant vessels involved, but even with the correct figures that eventually came to light, it was a legitimate issue. Furthermore, although the total tonnage losses were always the metric of concern, together with the associated number of large oceangoing ships, the U-boats took a heavy toll of a much larger number of small coasters, sailing vessels, and fishing vessels. *UC17* was one of the most successful of the Flanders-based boats, but of the 96 ships that the submarine sank over two years from November 1916 to October 1918, 42 were under 500 tons and 34 were under 200 tons.[8] These vessels also deserved protection and it seemed, given the numbers and the complexities of management, that keeping them within well-defined, heavily patrolled coastal areas was the most workable approach.

The fishing industry was becoming a major concern. By the beginning of 1917, the combined effects of taking into naval service some 1,400 of the 1,900 British trawlers, along with the toll taken by enemy action to reduce the national catch to dangerous levels, threatened supply of one of the staple foods of the working class. Losses were not being made up because shipowners were unwilling to order new construction likely to be requisitioned by the Admiralty. Means had to be found to increase the take and provide better protection for the fishing fleets. This was the subject of much discussion in the first months in 1917. In part, these problems were already perceived and much was hoped not only from the *Flower*-class sloops that were appearing in increasing numbers, but the smaller, and at twenty knots, faster *P*- and *PC*-class patrol boats. Additional units were ordered in January 1917, with the *PC* class built to resemble small merchant vessels as another form of Q ship. Because the supply of civil craft was effectively exhausted, 250 trawlers were ordered in November 1916 to three standard designs and 150 more would be ordered in 1917. When completed, these ships were shared between the Auxiliary Patrol and the minesweeping service.[9]

Crisis point in the submarine war had already been reached for the French. The loss of many of their own coalfields to the Germans made them dependent upon supply from British fields at the rate of more than 1.5 million tons a month. Much of this was carried in Norwegian colliers, which hitherto had not been integrated into the warning and route control system organized for Allied ships. Their losses were heavy and the reduction in the amount of coal arriving in France was made worse by the standard response to a high U-boat threat, suspension of sailings. The French naval staff did its own analysis and rapidly formed the view that the suspensions equated to a blockade of up to 40 percent effectiveness. By the end of December, the French were pressing for the introduction of convoy, a plea also made by the British Committee for the Supply of Coal to France and Italy. The French argument put by Commandant Vandier had a sting: "You yourself will be forced to form convoys and to escort them in order to continue to trade. We forced you to do it twice in the past, with our pirates. You will be forced to do it once more. This organisation of the French coal trade that I am requesting will be a trial run for you."[10]

Although the Admiralty tried to mask the status of the Norwegian colliers and other neutral ships by designating the procedures that were rapidly agreed as "controlled sailing," there was no ambiguity about the actual arrangements. Convoys would be dispatched daily from Swansea, Portland, and Dover under escort. The scheme was approved on 22 January 1917 and the first convoy sailed on 10 February. The coal convoys' low loss rate was a factor in the Admiralty's change of thinking on convoy in coming months. Another, which has received less attention, was the careful work of the French naval staff in defining the problem and proposing a practicable solution. This provided an example for the Admiralty that may well have been critical.

The subject of convoy was also being aired for the Scandinavian trade. Norwegian shipowners had become increasingly concerned at their losses and were putting pressure on the Foreign Office and the Board of Trade. Britain could underwrite their insurance, but this was obviously not enough if the German attacks continued. The Admiralty worried about the legal problems of providing armed protection for neutral vessels. On this matter the Foreign Office, bearing the brunt of Norwegian complaints, was more robust than the navy. Since the Norwegian government itself would provide no assistance, the British had to find a method that met both operational and legal requirements. Eventually, a system of controlled sailings was set up that combined the maximum use of the dark hours for crossing the Norwegian Sea with the provision of escorts when close to British waters. These arrangements would help a little, but the Scandinavian problem had not been solved. It certainly concerned the new C-in-C. Beatty was frustrated by the failures to intercept either the raiders that left German waters at the end of 1916 or the homeward-bound *Prinz Friedrich Wilhelm* and other merchant ships. He began to argue for the imposition of British control over Norwegian territorial waters to the extent necessary to prevent their use by the Germans. The War Cabinet's rejection of the proposal was a setback for the increasingly frustrated Beatty, but he did not abandon his campaign.

Grand Fleet Operations

The Grand Fleet was settling into a new pattern of operations that continued for most of the war. In part, the reduction in the capital ships' activity was driven by shortages of fuel. While oil supply was being hit particularly hard by the U-boats, the demand for coal by a battle fleet based so far north represented a significant burden, particularly as the new C-in-C maintained the view of his predecessor that enough colliers had to be in the fleet anchorages to allow the immediate resupply of every major unit—effectively a collier for every battleship. The distance to Scapa Flow and the strain on both shipping and the railway system were strong arguments for the move to Rosyth.

Beatty sought to make operation of the Grand Fleet as a whole more flexible with the issue of his first *Grand Fleet Battle Instructions* in March 1917 and progressive modification of the voluminous *Grand Fleet Battle Orders*. Although the first release of *Instructions* was only a few pages in length, it eventually became clear that, even as principles for guidance, the size and complexity of the fleet required them to be highly detailed. By late 1917, work was in hand to incorporate Beatty's plans for fighting his fleet into an expanded set of *Instructions*, while the systems for maneuvering the force and conducting routine operations were incorporated into the new *Grand Fleet Manoeuvring Orders*. The new system finally came into force in February 1918.[11]

In some ways, this focus on the main fleet was increasingly irrelevant. There was another aspect to the fleet's new operating modes, a shift to formations of the lighter, high-speed vessels supported by individual squadrons of capital ships. These new arrangements were still immature, but the transition was under way and the deployment patterns of the Grand Fleet's squadrons would reflect this in the months ahead. One indication of the change was that responsibility for maintaining a presence in the North Sea fell increasingly on the light cruisers. Partly triggered by continuing reports of German raider movements, it was also because light cruisers provided the best mix of fighting capability with limited commitment. Powerful enough to deal with most threats, they were also fast enough to escape heavier metal and agile enough, despite the experiences of August, to be very difficult targets for submarines. The availability of the new antisubmarine paravanes provided another justification for ventures into the North Sea to hunt errant U-boats. There were, however, not enough light cruisers to protect this sort of destroyer work and be available to support the Grand Fleet should the battle squadrons deploy. Such operations were also not without their cost in the terrible winter of 1916–17. Recent changes in the command of squadrons and ships may have contributed to casualties in both *Southampton* and the newly arrived *Sydney* and *Melbourne*. The latter two ships suffered multiple dead and injured during the heavy weather of 21 December,[12] while *Southampton* lost her first lieutenant and three ratings on 18 January. Through inexperience, the ships were probably driven too hard in appalling conditions. *Southampton*'s gunnery officer's testimony suggests a chapter of errors, his new captain being unaware there were personnel working in darkness on the forecastle to secure gear that had gone adrift.[13] The squadron itself was certainly steaming at too high a speed for the prevailing weather. Goodenough had only recently been replaced in command of the Second Light Cruiser Squadron by Commodore Cecil Lambert, who had not been to sea since before the war.[14]

February saw the new routine of the Grand Fleet continue. The battle squadrons were not wholly idle. The protected waters of Scapa Flow were employed for tactical exercises and subcaliber firings, while full-caliber shoots were conducted in Pentland Firth. The British routine was sustained in other ways. Light cruisers conducted seven sweeps into the North Sea and the Norwegian Sea in February. They had no more success than their predecessors in either intercepting German iron ore traffic from Norwegian ports or detecting any German surface traffic. The weather was still intensely cold, punctuated by storms that more than once forced operations to be curtailed or cancelled outright. The only sortie by the fleet as a whole was north of the Shetlands to test the fleet's response to encountering the enemy battle squadrons in unfavorable conditions. The mismatch between the speed and effective gun range of the most modern battleships and those of the original 12-inch gun dreadnoughts proved an increasing problem. Attempting to mass the entire firepower of the Grand Fleet almost inevitably involved delay and thus the loss of tactical opportunities. More encouraging was the first trial in such an environment of the newly joined K-class submarines. The flotilla was not yet at full strength, but Beatty thought that the new type had real potential in a fleet action. The possibility that the submarines could be positioned on the disengaged flank of the enemy was attractive—any turn away by the High Sea Fleet would leave it open to a mass torpedo attack.[15]

The other focus of Grand Fleet operations was the mining effort in the Heligoland Bight. The shortage of suitable mines continued to bedevil the British but work to create a barrier across the Bight began in earnest with seven fields laid in January. These amounted to only 912 mines, a drop in the bucket compared with the estimates of between 60,000 and 80,000 that the Grand Fleet and Admiralty staffs calculated would be required. The pace increased in February, with nine fields with 1,464 mines being laid, but not only were many of these fields deliberately given short lives with sinking devices, but defects and natural attrition meant the British were only just beginning to create a credible level of mine threat in German waters. The developing British effort did not go unnoticed, however. The Germans were anxious that the U-boat passages into the North Sea should remain clear and aware what an effective British effort could do to close them off. They were also alert to the submarine minelayers. The latter could individually lay few mines but, as U-boats were demonstrating on the other side of the North Sea, skillfully handled, they could seed weapons in areas hitherto thought safe and whose closure, however temporary, created significant disruption. From the beginning of 1917, the mine clearance forces of the Bight were strengthened, an effort that continued until the end of the war, but which had a price. The minesweeper M56 went down in February, while M15, M16, and M26 were sunk in March.

The War in the South

The Channel again became the center of the surface war in late January. The High Sea Fleet dispatched the Sixth Flotilla to reinforce the Flanders command on 22 January. Radio traffic was intercepted by the British, who suspected Zeebrugge was the flotilla's intended destination. The Harwich Force of six light cruisers, a flotilla leader, and ten destroyers immediately sailed, with another leader and six destroyers dispatched from Dover in support. Tyrwhitt's dispositions were relatively straightforward. He divided his cruisers into two divisions, well to seaward of the Dutch coast across the most likely German line of passage south. The destroyers were distributed much closer inshore, with seven ships to the north and the remainder in two divisions led by *Nimrod* and *Simoom* to the south. These arrangements created the chance the British could have two strikes at the Germans if the latter continued to make for Zeebrugge, but they depended on each British force retaining a good idea of where it was—and where the other friendly forces were. It was very dark, but relatively clear on what veterans would remember as the coldest night at sea of the entire war.[16]

The first encounter took place at 0240 when Tyrwhitt's own cruiser division, consisting of *Centaur*, *Aurora*, and *Conquest*, was sighted by *V69*, leader of the Sixth Flotilla about two thousand yards ahead. Although the German ships were on the starboard quarter of the British, the latter were sufficiently alert that their sighting of the torpedo boats was almost simultaneous. A sharp and inevitably confused action followed. The British light cruisers avoided the German torpedoes, but the torpedo boats' immediate use of smoke made them very difficult targets, particularly as the British did not take the risk of shining their searchlights. What did help was the old coal burner problem of flaming funnels as the German torpedo boats' furnaces were stoked for higher speed, giving "quite a reasonably good point of aim."[17] Only *V69* was hit—seriously enough to jam her rudder—taking the torpedo boat across the bows of her consort *G41*. Subsequent damage from the collision was relatively superficial for *V69*, but *G41* was harder hit, her speed reduced to eight knots. In the melee, *V69*, *G41*, and *S50* separated from the rest of the flotilla. The eight remaining boats kept in touch with each other and, out of sight of the British, resumed their passage to Zeebrugge. The undamaged *S50* also turned south when she was sure the British were not in the way, while the two damaged boats limped for the coast. Contact having been lost with the Germans, all Tyrwhitt had to go on was the apparent withdrawal of the disabled *V69* to the northeast, which he reported by radio before beginning his own search in that direction. *S50* may have been seen fleetingly by *Aurora*, but the cruisers found nothing, not even the disabled torpedo boat they expected to encounter when they returned to the scene of action a few minutes later.

The second cruiser division—consisting of *Penelope*, *Undaunted*, and *Cleopatra*—had seen the flash of guns on the horizon and its commander, Captain Hubert Lynes, sensibly moved to block the most likely German course of withdrawal. The decision soon paid a dividend when the cruisers encountered *V69*. The unfortunate torpedo boat suffered at least four hits in rapid succession, killing the flotilla commander, Max Schultz, and many of the bridge personnel and blowing away the after funnel. Temporarily dead in the water, *V69* appeared so badly damaged the British thought she was sinking and left her to seek other targets. Heavily hit as she was, *V69*'s survivors managed to control the damage and get under way again. As she was in no condition to return to Germany or risk facing the British forces that lay between her and Zeebrugge, the only alternative was a Netherlands port and *V69* made for Ymuiden, into which she struggled the next day. The Dutch did not intern her, as the torpedo boat was legally allowed to make the repairs essential to become seaworthy again. *V69* eventually limped home to Germany, monitored by Dutch warships while she remained in Netherlands waters. The Dutch had no intention of permitting a British coup de main.

The night was not yet over. Tyrwhitt directed all his forces to remain in their patrol areas, since this still gave the best chance of another encounter. The damaged *G41* passed through the northern destroyer patrol lines a few hours before dawn but remained unseen. The Sixth Flotilla's main body also avoided being detected by either of the destroyer groups in the southern patrols, probably because the latter had not yet regained their stations as directed by the commodore. So far honors rested with the British, despite the success of the German evasions. At 0413, however, the destroyer *Simoom* encountered an enemy torpedo boat cutting across her bows at close range. This was *S50* following her consorts to Zeebrugge. *Simoom* turned to ram, but passed close astern of *S50*, thereby opening herself up to the inevitable torpedo, which struck home. *Simoom*'s forward magazine exploded, rendering her immediately hors de combat. What followed demonstrated once more the problem of dispersed friendly forces at night. The two British destroyer formations in the south were much closer to each other than either group realized. Consequently, when *Simoom*'s consort, *Starfish*, took up the pursuit, the first ship seen was immediately assumed to be enemy. Shaping course to ram, only the sudden showing of her British fighting lights by *Moorsom* gave *Starfish* enough time to recognize her error and steer clear, "missing our [*Moorsom*'s] stern by inches."[18] *Nimrod*'s division had seen the initial encounter and themselves made fleeting contact with *S50*, but any chance of pursuing the German after *S50* passed down the British line at only four hundred yards distance was spoiled by two things. First, the night was so cold that many guns were "seized up with solid ice."[19] Second, was the sudden manifestation of *Starfish*. By the time the situation was sorted out, *S50* had disappeared. Damaged and with casualties from *Simoom*'s gunfire, she turned for Germany and home. *S50* was safe in the Ems early the same afternoon. The even more badly damaged *G41* had been brought into Zeebrugge that morning by her consorts and sent to Bruges for repairs.

Simoom's battered stern section remained afloat. After the survivors were removed, there were attempts to take the wreck in tow, but neither *Nimrod* nor *Matchless* could get *Simoom* under control. Commodore Tyrwhitt arrived on scene just after dawn. With a German seaplane observing proceedings and the force vulnerable to submarine attack, Tyrwhitt directed that *Simoom* be sunk with "despatch." Gunfire from *Matchless* quickly made an end to what remained. There were few new lessons for the British, although the need had been confirmed for effective star shell to illuminate the enemy without creating the aiming point that searchlights did. Tyrwhitt again emphasized that night fighting differed from day action in one key respect. Friendly forces could not converge uncontrolled on an action without creating confusion.

The Germans' Sixth Flotilla did not spend much time licking its wounds and undertook two sorties in the following week. The first was a bombardment of Southwold. The Germans fired ninety-two rounds into the town, badly damaging some buildings but causing no casualties. So brief was the fusillade at three minutes, the British were uncertain whether the attack had been by a U-boat or surface craft. The Germans knew the destructive effect of the torpedo boats' main armament was minimal and were focused on undermining local morale. Their communications security while operating from Zeebrugge was so much better than that of the High Sea Fleet the British had no idea that the flotilla, supported by units of the First Half-Flotilla, had been at sea at all. As it was, when school resumed at Southwold, the main excitement for the children was picking up pieces of shrapnel in the playground.[20] The Germans took advantage of a lull in the weather to conduct another night sortie on 29–30 January. This did not proceed far into the North Sea. Looking for enemy shipping and isolated patrols, it found nothing. Like the first venture, radio silence meant the operation passed unnoticed by the British.

In the meantime, the German die was cast. On 31 January 1917, the German government informed the United States that unrestricted submarine warfare would be resumed the next day in a zone encompassing British and French waters, the Western Approaches, much of the North Sea, and the Mediterranean. The Americans broke off diplomatic relations on 3 February. On 2 April, the president sought a declaration of war against Germany from Congress; this followed on 6 April. Perhaps the best indication of what lay ahead for Germany was the immediate and well-executed seizure of its merchant ships that had been sheltering in American ports since 1914.

Spring in the North Sea

9

THE HIGH SEA FLEET SPENT A QUIET WINTER. Sea training was constrained by intense cold, which saw ice invade the Kiel training areas. The fleet had to wait until March, when *Baden* took over as fleet flagship, to train with all three battle squadrons in the Baltic. The newly repaired *Kronprinz* and *Grosser Kurfürst* had not improved their welcome back to the fleet by colliding in the Heligoland Bight due to a misunderstood turning signal.[1] Both missed the Baltic exercise as they were again under repair, *Grosser Kurfürst's* "crooked and bent nozzle [bow]" amusing at least one observer.[2] The Baltic presented more problems than ice. Exercises were repeatedly delayed by thick fog, with the inevitable near-misses with other traffic. Visibility improved only briefly before the fog returned and planned weapon firings were not completed before the ships returned to the North Sea.

The battleships' limited activities made torpedo boats available for the Flanders Command. This allowed reinforcement of the Flanders flotillas in February with six large and four small torpedo boats and Scheer's eventual consent that the Third Flotilla be permanently reassigned there. The Sixth Flotilla had not yet been recalled to Germany, which made the local forces particularly strong in late February. Continuing poor weather, however, meant they were not very active. Although the British were aware of the accession of German strength and took precautions, another German sortie passed unnoticed, again through a combination of communications security and the absence of encounters at sea. With good reason to expect another strike against the Dover Barrage, the British reorganized to meet a night attack. The vulnerable drifters were replaced after dark by a division of destroyers, individually distributed along the barrage. A light cruiser and another destroyer division were anchored off Deal, with a larger force of destroyers kept at Dover. Monitors protected the merchant ship anchorages in the Downs. The Germans dispatched six boats of the Sixth Flotilla and four of the First Flanders Half-Flotilla on the evening of 25 February, with instructions to attack the units protecting the barrage, bombard British ports if the opportunity arose, and, in the case of the First Half-Flotilla, attack shipping in the Channel. Three boats of the Second Half-Flotilla were ordered to the vicinity of the Maas light ship as a diversion, to attack merchant shipping. Despite the poor weather, aerial reconnaissance had given the Germans a good idea of British dispositions around the barrage, so Lieutenant Commander Tilleson in *S49* and Lieutenant Commander Albrecht in *G95* knew what to expect.

At 2230, the destroyer *Laverock* sighted a torpedo boat on her port bow, two thousand yards away and closing. *S49*'s sighting of *Laverock* was practically simultaneous. She immediately opened fire and launched a torpedo. With an alert officer of the watch, *Laverock* avoided the weapon but was subjected to a fusillade of gun and torpedo fire. She replied in kind. Only one of the six torpedoes launched by the Sixth Flotilla struck home. In the heat of action, its impact was not noticed. The weapon failed to explode and only the next day was a dent in the destroyer's hull identified. In the darkness, with both sides blinded by flash and exploding shells, contact was quickly lost without serious damage to any unit. Thinking he had been engaged by a full division of destroyers and having intercepted *Laverock*'s enemy contact report, Tilleson believed he had lost the advantage of surprise. He swept back through the barrage, hoping to encounter other British units but finding nothing, turned for home.

The Second Half-Flotilla drew a blank off the Maas, while the First Half-Flotilla did not do much better. A drifter off the northern entrance to the Downs sighted the torpedo boats at 2300 and sent up a flare, just as Albrecht began to bombard North Foreland and Margate. Forty rounds were fired. Since neither North Foreland lighthouse nor wireless station was hit, there was no military effect. The damage was to a cottage further inland, with a mother and two children killed and other children injured. Curiously, the cottage was close to Elmwood, country house of the newspaper proprietor Lord Northcliffe, that also suffered shrapnel hits. Northcliffe was convinced the attack was aimed at him, understandable in the circumstances, but a ploy more sophisticated than Flanders Command was capable of devising.[3] Nevertheless, Northcliffe's scare may well have contributed to the animus his newspapers displayed against Jellicoe and the Admiralty in later months. Standby units from Deal arrived on scene within forty minutes, but they saw nothing of the First Half-Flotilla before the latter withdrew.

Admiral von Schröder was reasonably sanguine about the operation. Little was achieved in material terms, but it was "desirable to remind the English as frequently as possible of the presence of German naval forces directly before their coast."[4] Now that unrestricted submarine warfare had resumed in earnest, any efforts that diverted Allied forces away from anti-submarine operations were worthwhile, particularly if aimed at interrupting the enemy's supply lines. The window for night operations would open again in two weeks. Meanwhile, Scheer had his own ideas for an attack on the Netherlands-England traffic, utilizing the scouting groups, covered by the battle squadrons. He planned to employ transiting U-boats to create a barrier against British forces in the north, although the speed-time-distance equation was such that his forces could strike and be back in the Heligoland Bight before the Grand Fleet could intervene—provided he achieved surprise. Scheer's problem was that intelligence relating to convoy movements was very short term, which meant he could not deploy the zeppelins ahead of time to confirm the absence of British heavy forces. Scheer was prepared to take his chances, even if the weather was so bad the zeppelins could not go out, and he sent a warning order to the fleet on 10 March. The C-in-C told the Admiralstab of his intentions, which inevitably involved informing the kaiser. The response from the "All Highest" was unambiguous. The sortie

Photo 9.1   German torpedo boats in formation   *German Naval Association Archive*

was not to take place unless accompanied by zeppelin surveillance. Unsurprisingly, the weather of mid-spring in the North Sea did not allow this. Scheer's sortie was never carried out.

The Admiralty decided to take advantage of additional new destroyers to transfer existing units from the Harwich Force to Dover, replacing them in Tyrwhitt's command with new construction. A full flotilla of sixteen *M*-class destroyers would eventually be based at Dover, with some of Bacon's older destroyers transferred to local flotillas in the major home ports. This accession of strength meant, in theory, that Dover Command had sufficient ships to defend against a thrust by the Flanders flotillas at full strength and still allow for boiler cleaning and repairs. Dover Command also needed enough resources to focus on what remained the greatest threat—the U-boat. It remained to be seen how well the new arrangements worked.

Operations in the Norwegian Sea

The watch on the Norwegian Sea gained new priority with reports that a raider was homeward bound. While patrolling ships found nothing in early March, the British were still alert to the prospect of transits and with good reason. *Yarrowdale*, captured as a prize by *Möwe*, had arrived in Germany at the end of December. Fast and modern, she was ideal for conversion into a raider, which was undertaken at Kiel early in 1917. Equipped with two torpedo tubes and 150-mm guns transferred from decommissioned ships, *Leopard* was ready in early March. Unfortunately for the raider, the British patrol lines had recently been strengthened, and *Leopard* was sighted just before noon on 16 March by the armored cruiser *Achilles* and the armed boarding vessel *Dundee*. This tactical group combined the cruiser's heavy metal with the auxiliary's relative expendability. In this situation, it proved very effective. After a lengthy chase, the unknown vessel, posing as the Norwegian steamer *Rena*, was brought to by an increasingly suspicious *Dundee*. *Achilles* remained clear while *Dundee*, carefully holding herself on *Rena*'s quarter, dispatched a boarding party. The Germans did their best to convince the latter of their bona fides because it was nearly an hour before *Leopard* revealed herself by opening fire with guns and torpedoes, just as the boarding party's empty boat came into *Dundee*'s sight. The much more lightly armed *Dundee* was well prepared and immediately sent a hail of 4-inch and 3-pound gunfire into *Leopard*, while maneuvering to keep the German at a disadvantage. *Dundee*'s 3-pounder was directed at *Leopard*'s bridge and its twenty hits may well have wiped out the German command team at the outset.[5] *Leopard*'s crew may also not have been fully trained. Despite the range, their fire was ineffective. Although *Leopard* fought on, the combined efforts of *Dundee* and *Achilles* soon reduced her to a flaming wreck, with *Dundee* expending all her ammunition and having "the time of her life."[6] The raider rolled over and sank at 1632, taking with her the entire crew and *Dundee*'s unfortunate boarding party. Fear of submarines prevented a search for survivors, although the boarding party's boat was found by a merchant ship several months later. The British were pleased by their success, but the estimate that the sunken ship was the successful Atlantic raider of December 1916 was wishful thinking; *Möwe* had not been intercepted.[7] The little action was one of the few successes enjoyed by an armored cruiser during the war. The type's increasing obsolescence was reflected in the ironic greeting given *Achilles* on her return to Scapa Flow—a battleship's band struck up "Any Old Iron." *Achilles*' musical response was just as pointed: "And the Green Grass grew all round my Boys."[8]

British Submarine Losses

Small ship losses mounted steadily. The destroyer *Pheasant* blew up on a mine and sank with all hands off Stromness on 1 March. The British ascribed the sinking to an old floating mine, but it was one of four laid by *U80* six weeks before. The submarine *E5* failed to return from patrol off the Ems in early March. She had experienced a series of encounters with German surface forces during her sortie. These included the entire First Scouting Group, conducting exercises in the Bight on 5 March. *Seydlitz* and the torpedo boats in her immediate vicinity sighted a submarine, which the light forces attacked with depth charges. This was a fleeting contact at best. *E29* later reported sighting *E5* north of Juist Island on 6 March. The submarine's wreck was finally located in 2016, farther west, off the Dutch island of Schiermonnikoog. With no discernible hull damage and open hatches, the cause of *E5*'s sinking is unlikely to have been the mine to which both the British and Germans later ascribed her loss.[9]

The British submarine force was under strain. A succession of losses since late in 1916 hit the forward deployed forces hard, although Tyrwhitt denied this when taxed with the matter by Beatty.[10] Before the loss of *E5*, her sisters *E30*, *E37*, and *E36* had all been sunk by unknown causes since late November, while the modification of several boats for minelaying promised even greater hazards. Other submarines were being employed on antisubmarine patrols around the British coast and across the expected passage routes of the U-boats. These had their successes, such as *G13*'s destruction of *UC43*. In theory, this was less dangerous work than operating in the Heligoland Bight, but *E49*'s loss off the Shetlands on 3 March confirmed that there were few safe areas. Just after leaving her temporary base in Balta Sound, the submarine's bows were blown off by a mine laid by *UC76* a few days earlier. She went down with all on board. The question of safe areas also arose with increasing frequency in relation to friendly surface forces. Both *G12* and *J1* were attacked by mistake and forced to dive to avoid destruction. *G12* was lucky to survive, as her conning tower was damaged by gunfire. The submariners were increasingly concerned about the tendency of the surface ships to shoot first and ask questions afterward. German submarines represented an additional threat for any boat on passage, not only with mines but torpedoes. In some ways, the transit to and from a home port was becoming more dangerous than periods spent in an operating area. There was another pressure: seventeen big, new *K*-class submarines commissioned before the end of the year, requiring expert commanders and large crews. This stripped many of the older boats of experienced personnel. The steam machinery of the *K* class was a formidable proposition, requiring retraining of existing submarine personnel and the transfer of artificers and stokers from the surface fleet. The demand for submarines for coastal patrol and antisubmarine work meant even the elderly *C* class had to remain in operation, although the submarine service rid itself of the handful of even older and smaller *B* class when they were converted to surface patrol vessels in the Mediterranean.

Operations in the South

The dark nights of mid-March provided a new opportunity for the Flanders flotillas. Seven torpedo boats of the Sixth Flotilla under Werner Tillessen and eight more from the two Zeebrugge half-flotillas were dispatched on the evening of 17 March. The Sixth Flotilla was to attack the western side of the barrage and the First Half-Flotilla the eastern side, while the Second Half-Flotilla attacked the northern entrance to the Downs. The British arrangements were much as they had been in February, with a division of destroyers patrolling the barrage; a light cruiser, a flotilla leader, and four destroyers off Deal; and a reserve of a flotilla leader and five destroyers at Dover. Two monitors were stationed off Ramsgate, covering the Downs. The first encounter came at 2247, when Tillessen sighted a destroyer broad on his port bow. *Paragon* was less alert and did not see anything until the

Germans were well on her beam. Disastrously, instead of engaging straight away, *Paragon* challenged the newcomers. Tillessen responded by opening fire and *Paragon* was almost immediately hit amidships by a torpedo. She managed to launch one in return before a second torpedo struck her engine room. Possibly hit by a third weapon, *Paragon* was torn in two and sank within minutes. The tragedy was complete when a depth charge detonated as the ship went down, blowing off their raft the handful of survivors who had taken refuge there. Only ten men survived. In a counterstroke of luck after the experience of *Laverock*, *Paragon*'s single torpedo may have struck home on a German ship but failed to detonate. It was found without its warhead, which could have broken off without detonating if the weapon struck a glancing blow.[11]

The Germans had their own confusions. The rearmost units lost touch with Tillessen as he maneuvered to engage *Paragon*, evidence a six-ship formation was too big for night fighting. Their commander sensibly withdrew on realizing his situation. Tillessen himself swept back toward the wreck of *Paragon* a few minutes after the action and began to withdraw. The affair was not finished, however, for the destroyers *Laforey* and *Llewellyn* saw the explosions and converged on the scene. Neither ship appreciated that *Paragon* had been engaged by surface forces. Their immediate response was to search for survivors and this involved the fatal step of using their searchlights.

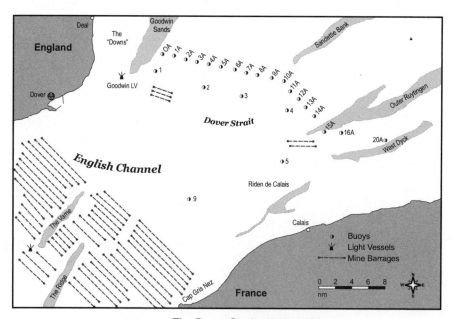

Map 9.1   The Dover Strait, 1917–1918

These Tillessen saw astern of his formation and he immediately turned his ships around. The British, occupied with rescue and night vision impaired by their searchlights, had no idea they were being approached by German torpedo boats. The latter were intelligent enough not to use their guns. *S49* and *G87* fired torpedoes, one of which passed close astern of *Laforey* and hit *Llewellyn*, blowing off her bows forward of the gun mount. Tillessen then circled around and withdrew, undetected. The British destroyers still did not realize they had been subject to a surface attack. *Laforey* reported that the torpedo was fired by a submarine and confined her efforts to searching for it. Meanwhile, despite the German intent to maintain separation between their forces, the First Half-Flotilla had been set further west than planned. Having seen the searchlights, which had to be British rather than German, the First's commander was approaching the scene when, to their mutual surprise, the Sixth Flotilla and the First Half-Flotilla sighted each other. Fortunately for the Germans, each made the correct identification. Tillessen combined the groups and withdrew.

The British took some time to sort out what had happened and were fortunate that the Germans did not guess at the confusion, which could have allowed an equally effective second attack. Early reports seemed to indicate at least one enemy submarine was active near the barrage, and the assault's true nature became clear only when *Paragon*'s survivors had been interviewed. That it had been a multipronged attack became apparent when reports came in of an enemy formation off Margate. The Second Half-Flotilla was spotted by the destroyer *Paramount*, which fired flares and alerted other units in the vicinity. The Germans sank the already disabled merchant ship *Greypoint* and damaged a drifter, but their bombardment of Ramsgate and Broadstairs was superficial, with only three houses hit and no casualties. The Second Half-Flotilla then withdrew, well before the cruiser *Canterbury* and the destroyers sent from Deal could catch them. One small consolation was that *Llewellyn* got safely back to Dover for repairs, albeit stern first.

The British again revised their night arrangements. The first change was to concentrate the destroyers into two formations, one on the eastern side and one in the west, rather than distributing them along the barrage. The second and more important step was that issuing a challenge was no longer the default action on sighting an unidentified unit at night. "Destroyers were not to hesitate to use torpedoes at once."[12] Admiral Bacon closed his report with the comment, "I am very hopeful that we may yet give . . . [the enemy] . . . a lesson, and one serious blow will, without doubt, make him less eager to carry out these raids."[13] The Admiralty had reason to take the Flag Officer Dover's predictions with a grain of salt, but this time he would be proved correct. The Germans were also making changes. The Sixth Flotilla returned to Germany on 29 March, but not before the Third Flotilla had arrived in Flanders, together with additional units to make up the First Half-Flotilla to full flotilla strength. The big new torpedo boats were not the only reinforcement. Von Schröder had been pressing hard to get a fair share of the smaller craft being produced, both for minesweeping and for short-range offensive operations. A lightning raid on Dunkirk on 24 March that cost the Allies two merchant ships showed what the small torpedo boats were capable of, even if only as an irritant.

The torpedo boats' presence gave new priority to sustained air attacks by the British on Bruges and other German installations. British aircraft's growing capabilities ensured these became more than an irritant. They caused substantial damage, forced the Germans to begin building covered pens for the U-boats and, as Dover Command became aware, to start the practice of moving the torpedo boats to berths or anchorages seaward of Zeebrugge. This created a potential opportunity for the squadron of Coastal Motor Boats, under Lieutenant W. N. T. Beckett, that had been operating from Dunkirk for a few months. In the meantime, Bacon had other plans for both defense and offense. The unreliable monitor *Marshal Ney* lost her 15-inch turret to the new *Terror*, but the admiral seized upon the ship as a permanent guard for the Downs. Rearmed with six 6-inch guns and additional antiaircraft weapons when she returned in early April, *Ney*'s weapons and bulges made her a formidable proposition.

Bacon was also interested in cutting off the water access to Zeebrugge and Ostend from Bruges by destroying the Bruges Canal's lock gates. The Flanders ports had been the subject of intense debate in recent months. Tyrwhitt was inclined toward a direct assault on the two ports, but this was rejected by both the Admiralty and Bacon.[14] They were working on an even more ambitious scheme to eject the Germans from Flanders in cooperation with the British Expeditionary Force. This was a plan that Jellicoe strongly supported, as he had become convinced the U-boat threat was directly related to German possession of the bases on the Flanders coast. A British army offensive would be mounted later in the year. At the right time, Dover Command would mount a divisional size amphibious assault with three massive pontoons, pushed by monitors, each disgorging a brigade at intervals between Westende and Middelkerke.[15] Additional troops would be inserted over the following days, with the intent that the landing forces link up with the main advance on land, forcing a full German retreat. The first pontoon was successfully tested at the end of March while the second and third units were under construction.

In the meantime, Bacon proposed a bombardment to maintain pressure. Because of the continuing air attacks on the ports, Bruges' ability to take both submarines and torpedo boats for repair with relative immunity was critical to the continuing operations of the Flanders squadrons. The lock gates were a small target, invisible from the sea. Given the capabilities of the German coastal batteries, even the 15-inch gun monitors, with their extended-range mountings, would be working at their limit, but Bacon believed it was worth a try, at much less risk than a direct assault. The operation required the ideal combination of visibility, tide, and sea state to allow units to be in position by dawn and for the essential air spotters to be able to do their job. Bacon would also need reinforcement by the Harwich Force to guard against the German flotillas. At best, the window was only open for a day or two every fortnight. While 1917's spring brought better weather, poor visibility stymied Bacon's first attempt of 25 March, while conditions were too rough on 8 April. Ten days later, a third try failed through a succession of problems, culminating in *Marshal Soult* (whose engines, marginally more reliable than those of *Marshal Ney*, could not be trusted for an operation this precise) breaking her tow line. Not until May would the bombardment be carried out in full. Bacon, disliked by so many other officers, was criticized for his "spasmodic" efforts,[16] but his opportunities were indeed few and far between. Furthermore, much of the admiral's time was taken up by the detailed planning for the amphibious assault intended later in the year. Although the Flag Officer Dover delegated too little, Bacon was becoming a victim of the practical impossibility of balancing the day-to-day demands of command with preparing complex future operations. Many judgments made about the inadequacies of the naval staff organization at the Admiralty are more rightly aimed at this level of British naval planning and command in general, and Dover in particular. Bacon's successor, Keyes, experienced the same problems, although he does not seem ever to have understood this.

The CMBs got their chance on the night of 7 April, when the squadron attacked German torpedo boats anchored outside Zeebrugge. In shallow water and with a bright moon, the Germans believed themselves secure from both submarine and destroyer attack and focused on supplementing Zeebrugge's antiaircraft defenses. The CMBs were working at the absolute limits of their capability in deteriorating weather, but tiny and hard to see, they achieved surprise under cover of three seaplanes, which bombed Zeebrugge in succession at twenty-minute intervals. The Germans heard the CMB engines, but assumed the sound presaged another air raid. Despite two CMBs suffering from engine trouble, Beckett in No. 4 hit *V81* with a torpedo which did not explode. No. 9 succeeded in sinking *G88* with a single weapon. The torpedo boats thought they had been attacked by a submarine, despite the very shallow water. Only later was the attackers' true nature understood. The affair was a fillip for the CMBs, but the German assessment that the fast boats' success owed much to their being completely unexpected was fair.[17]

The Germans waged their own air war against the British at sea, even if engagements against other aircraft were consuming ever increasing resources. Like the Baltic, Flanders Command received a flight of the new torpedo carrying seaplanes and four of these were dispatched on 19 April to attack the Downs. Poor visibility dogged the aircraft, which lost contact with each other and conducted abortive attacks on *Marshal Ney* and merchant ships. The depth of water was not enough to prevent the torpedoes hitting the bottom on being dropped. Furthermore, as in the Baltic, the fragile and underpowered seaplanes were not up to the mission. When this and a more successful sortie that torpedoed a merchant ship were reported to the Admiralty, however, their significance was recognized. On 2 May a letter was sent to the Grand Fleet to warn of the development and of its possible extension in range "by use of a seaplane carrier."[18] The report fell on fertile ground in a fleet increasingly aware of the importance of the air.

The next German attack on the Dover barrage came on 20 April. Two groups of torpedo boats were dispatched, with the primary mission of sinking any units protecting the barrage and a secondary task of bombarding Dover and Calais. With this sortie, Flanders Command introduced a new system of command and control. It was believed the onshore signals intelligence organization could provide a sufficiently timely assessment of British activities that the flotillas would be most effectively coordinated from ashore. This was a good idea—in theory. Both the Fifth Half-Flotilla to the west and the First Half-Flotilla to the east passed through the barrage without sighting any British units and proceeded immediately to their bombardments. The First's firing on Calais at 2315 was the first indication to Dover Command of the enemy, swiftly followed by the bombardment of Dover itself by the Fifth Half-Flotilla. Neither attack was particularly effective, a stable being the main victim of the Fifth's efforts, further confirmation of something the

British already understood: small-caliber naval guns were useless for shore bombardment. Gautier of the Fifth soon turned back toward the barrage in the hope of encountering British surface forces.

The British standby destroyers sailed from Dover, but, with four destroyers and the flotilla leaders *Swift* and *Broke* already on patrol, they and Admiral Bacon were concerned to prevent confusion. The units in the strait reporting that they saw nothing, Bacon recalled the standby ships. They played no further part. The Fifth Half-Flotilla cast about for enemy units from shortly after midnight. Finding nothing, they turned for home at approximately 0036, no longer expecting an encounter. *Swift* and *Broke* had been roving back and forth southwest of the barrage in the hope of finding something. By 0030 they were heading westerly at twelve knots. At 0045 *Swift* sighted torpedo boats on her port bow, steering in a nearly opposite direction. *Swift's* commander, Peck, did not hesitate, increasing to full speed and turning to ram. Unfortunately, flash from *Swift's* 6-inch gun temporarily blinded her captain and the destroyer leader passed close astern of the Germans. Torpedoes fired by both sides missed. From behind her consort, *Broke* sighted the Germans and increased to full speed, but the trio of torpedo boats were rapidly drawing left and out of sight. *Broke* followed *Swift* to the southwest, both ships moving at nearly thirty knots. Within minutes their advance carried them into the second line of Germans. Alerted, the leader, *S53*, hit *Broke* with a 105-mm round and knocked out a gun mount. *Swift* turned hard and got a torpedo away into *G85*, bringing the German to an immediate stop. *Broke* rammed *G42* abreast her after funnel. The two ships were locked together and a confused hand-to-hand action followed before *Broke* pulled clear. Circling around to the south, Gautier's boats were sighted by *Swift*, which turned in pursuit. Although *Swift* had suffered significant damage, she clearly carried much heavier metal than the remnant of the Fifth Half-Flotilla and Gautier turned away to the east. *S53* also managed to escape into the night, not before scoring further hits on *Broke*. Despite her own severe damage, however, the latter finished off the crippled *G85* with a torpedo.

Swift did not continue her pursuit past the barrage, and the early hours of 21 April were spent rescuing survivors from the two German boats and ensuring *Broke* was kept afloat and clear of the burning wrecks. Eighty-nine were saved from *G42* and *G85* and 71 killed, while the British had 22 dead and 29 wounded. The action was a considerable propaganda success, helped by the fact that Commander E. R. G. R. "Teddy" Evans, a celebrated Antarctic explorer and thus already good "newspaper copy," was made more so by his new label "Evans of the *Broke*." The Germans thought they had sunk at least one British destroyer, while the British hoped that they had sunk not two, but three of their enemy. Although both British ships required extensive repairs, the destruction of two German boats provided a morale boost and the Admiralty made the most of the rare success.

The Flanders flotillas had wounds to lick; it was clear the new British arrangements were capable of a concentrated response to a sally against the barrage. An associated problem for the Germans was that the Dutch convoys had escorts of sufficient strength to be a match for the depleted torpedo boat flotillas, while, if the British were given any warning, the Harwich Force could be concentrated in the area. The choice was thus between finding the seas clear of shipping if no convoys were at sea or running the risk of encountering superior forces. The German solution was to use the small and fast torpedo craft in hit-and-run raids against the more vulnerable ports on the French side of the Channel and around the Thames while the larger vessels worked to cut the shipping lanes between the Netherlands and England. In the early hours of 25 April, four torpedo boats of the Second Half-Flotilla bombarded Dunkirk. The monitor *Lord Clive* and the destroyer *Greyhound*, stationed off La Panne, attempted to cut off their retreat, but could not get close enough. The Germans encountered the small French destroyer *Etendard*, which blew up and sank with all hands after being torpedoed by *A39*. The trawler *Notre Dame de Lourdes* was also hit hard but managed to make port. The German torpedo boats were convinced they had been attacked by CMBs during their approach to Dunkirk, but there is no report in the British records to substantiate this theory.[19]

Convoys and Admiralty Reform

One of the most significant developments of the naval war came in April with the establishment of a Scandinavian convoy system. The existing arrangements still failed to provide sufficient protection, and Norwegian pressure for the British to do more was growing. A conference between Grand Fleet and area commanders in east Scottish waters had already resulted in a recommendation to start a convoy regime. The depredations of *U30*, *UC76*, and *UC45* in the Norwegian Sea in mid-April added new urgency to the problem. Thinking in the Admiralty continued to evolve and that month, key personnel including Oliver, Chief of the War Staff, and Duff, Director of the Anti-Submarine Division changed their views. Most importantly, they were now prepared to accept large convoys with relatively few escorts. Formal approval for Scandinavian convoys was issued on 24 April, while northeast coast convoys began to operate from 29 April. Work to adopt a more comprehensive convoy system throughout the North Atlantic was already well under way. The new scheme was submitted to the First Sea Lord on 26 April and approved the next day.[20] In both material and political terms, this step was taken just in time. When the prime minister visited the Admiralty on 30 April, he was "gratified to learn" of the new policy, even if the naval staff continued to have reservations.[21] The prime minister's visit reflected growing concern in the War Cabinet that the U-boat problem was not being well handled. The Admiralty's credit would depend greatly upon the speed with which the new arrangements were implemented—and their results.

There were pressures from other directions and changes already in the wind. A new dynamic was developing between the Grand Fleet and the Admiralty. Beatty was also increasingly dissatisfied with the naval staff's performance and vented his feelings on the prime minister and the First Lord at a meeting on 14 April. The combination of the "driblets" of mines placed in the Heligoland Bight, rather than the vast numbers planned, and time it had taken the Admiralty to accept convoy, as well as the delays that seemed to dog implementation of any new measures were justification for Beatty to argue for a reorganization of the Admiralty and for the Grand Fleet's staff to be brought much more closely into the planning system.[22] Beatty had a case, and some of his ideas were reflected in the changes at the Admiralty that followed in the next few weeks, with Jellicoe formally taking on the role of Chief of Naval Staff and Oliver becoming his deputy. The prime minister did force the installation of a civilian, albeit with temporary rank as a vice admiral, as controller. Sir Eric Geddes, a railway expert who had reorganized the transport networks supporting the western front, was brought in with a mandate to reform shipbuilding to meet not only the needs of the navy, but the more pressing demands of the merchant marine. Geddes brought new energy to the task but was soon discontented by the lack of leadership from the First Lord, Carson, while increasingly uncertain of Jellicoe's performance. Carson's days were numbered, since Geddes had the prime minister's ear and support from other elements in government and the army. In July, Lloyd George shifted Carson to a position without portfolio in the War Cabinet and installed Geddes as First Lord.

Beatty, however, was becoming increasingly "imperial" in his outlook. While the Admiralty was prepared to humor him, the Grand Fleet could not deal with the complex, whole of government issues that practically any major initiative involved. Whatever the pretensions of Beatty and some of his officers, they could not act as an alternative naval staff. Nevertheless, the Grand Fleet's frustrations were justified in two areas. Mine warfare was on the brink of resolution at last with the introduction of an effective near-copy of a German mine, designated the H2. From a poor start in 1914, the Admiralty and its associated establishments had not given development of reliable mines the priority required. The second area would be a source of future ill feeling. Naval aviation was Beatty's focus almost as soon as he arrived in the Grand Fleet and he had sponsored extensive work to identify the right lines of development for air defense, for reconnaissance, and for strike. In early 1917 aviation was in a state of flux and the problems of coordination between departments, conflicts over resources, and the difficulties of dealing with breakneck technological development that could give one side or the other overwhelming, if temporary, advantages were coming to a head. With the German example (albeit on a small scale), the Grand Fleet was beginning to understand that only a mass torpedo attack on the High Sea Fleet in its anchorages would work. This required both capable aircraft and suitable ships to launch them. The apparent inability of the Admiralty to give these ideas the priority the Grand Fleet thought they deserved did not help relations in the months ahead.

Some of the most important work done in the naval staff came through the efforts of the Convoy Committee, established on 17 May. This board consisted of a small group of officers from the Trade Division, supplemented by a junior officer from the Anti-Submarine Division, and (critically) Norman Leslie, an expert from the Ministry of Shipping. Leslie had already made a key contribution to the recalculation of the shipping statistics that allowed the Admiralty to understand the true scale—and manageability—of the convoy problem. The committee's report was completed on 6 June. It set out a plan for the creation of an Atlantic convoy system, its management, and the scale of protection required. Convoy itself created two problems. One was the strain it put on the limited numbers of destroyers. The need to detach them for escort work represented an additional constraint on the operations of the Grand Fleet, a problem that would eat away at Beatty's own morale. In part, convoy had been accepted because of the Admiralty's expectation that the Americans would send destroyers and other craft to reinforce the effort to counter the U-boat threat. The second was that convoys across the Norwegian Sea and on Britain's east coast were very attractive targets for German raids. An escort capable of warding off a submarine could well be defeated in detail by a more powerful surface force, leaving the convoy to be annihilated. The possibility that Atlantic convoys might become the target of surface raids could also not be discounted.

The creation of an independent Convoy Section under the direction of the Assistant Chief of Naval Staff, and within it a chart room that could track and direct the passage of each convoy was a vital step. What made this prototype "U-boat Tracking Room" particularly powerful was that parallel reforms to the signals intelligence organization brought Room 40 at last under the control of the Director of Naval Intelligence. This allowed a much more open approach to the use of both cryptographic work and direction finding. As the staff history noted, "The door was now opened wide enough to permit of intercepts and directionals being plotted on the Convoy Chart."[23] The Convoy Section could arrange convoy diversions to avoid areas of high threat, something practically impossible with individual merchant ships, some of which did not have wireless, while many others could not maintain a twenty-four-hour radio watch. Fleet Paymaster Eldon Manisty was appointed organizing manager of convoys, an inspired selection, and a welcome move by the Royal Navy away from the idea that only seaman officers could fulfill such roles.

Enter the Americans

10

N EITHER THE U.S. NAVY'S FORCE STRUCTURE nor much of its planning had prepared it for the maritime conflict it was entering. The USN was not ready for war at sea. Spending had been devoted to a numerous and extremely powerful battleship force, but although destroyers were rapidly increasing in numbers and capability, their strength was in no way adequate, even for the "decisive battle" construct on which the USN was centered. The submarine force was in a similar state, while naval aviation was only starting to get the resources it needed. Yet the USN's potential was formidable, as was its ability to innovate and expand. This reflected not only the high quality of its personnel and their training, particularly in technical disciplines, but America's industrial base, its educational systems, and the mechanical aptitude of its population. A basis of expansion had already been laid with the Naval Act of 1916. This organized the Naval Reserve into components that aligned with many of the demands that would soon be made. Another measure was to pay dividends. U-boat operations in the western Atlantic had drawn attention to the likely requirement for coastal patrol craft if the United States entered the war. The navy had conducted a census of civilian small craft and arranged for small-boat enthusiasts to join the reserve while it undertook initial design studies for small antisubmarine vessels and prepared to place its own orders for vessel types already being built under Allied contracts.

The reality of the naval plight of its allies came as a shock to the USN, even though it had already identified the U-boat as its likely priority.[1] As America moved toward a declaration of war, the Anglo-French naval mission dispatched to Washington sought destroyers and other light craft to reinforce the antisubmarine campaign in European waters. This plea was quickly supplemented by the reports of Rear Admiral William S. Sims, sent to liaise with the Admiralty. Jellicoe had not hesitated to take Sims into his confidence as to the severity of the U-boat problem. Sims quickly recognized that protection of shipping was the overriding priority—and thus for their new partner. It was apparent the main operational theaters would remain the British Isles and the Mediterranean. The Germans could divert resources to American waters as an irritant, but the long transits involved would reduce the effectiveness of individual U-boats.

The American naval staff were willing to commit a flotilla of destroyers, but to do more required accepting that there was no need to maintain a fleet to protect the American homeland. Detachments to Northern Europe would quickly denude the battle squadrons of their necessary flotilla craft. The USN's instinctive aversion to this step was allied to an underlying concern that Japan could not be trusted in the Pacific. A second obstacle was probably just as important: both the USN and America's political leadership hankered for an offensive approach to the war at sea. President Wilson favored close investment of the German coast and attacks on the German bases. The American naval staff had similar views and were discontented with what they believed was an excessively defensive mindset in the Allied naval commanders. It required all Admiral Sims' powers of persuasion, together with the united pressure of British and French political and naval authorities to change this attitude in Washington. Perhaps Sims' greatest success was encouraging the USN into a partly subordinate posture rather than the early ideas of a fully independent role.[2]

To be fair to Washington, a first division of six destroyers was followed at rapid intervals by three more. By 1 June 1917 there were twenty-four American destroyers at Queenstown, and by 1 July twenty-eight units were in European waters—out of only fifty-two available in the entire USN.[3] The selection of the first division's senior officer was shrewd, reflecting the same good judgment that sent Admiral Sims on his way. Cdr Joseph K. Taussig was not just an experienced destroyer captain, with the combination of tact and drive essential to ensure his force integrated successfully. He was also, as a veteran of the 1900 Boxer Rebellion, a member of the curious freemasonry of officers who served in that multinational campaign. Wounded in China on the same day as Jellicoe, he was well known to that officer, and a warm personal letter from the First Sea Lord was waiting for him at Queenstown.[4] Taussig was acutely aware that he and his ships were on trial, thus his legendary response to Vice Admiral Sir Lewis Bayly when asked on arrival when his ships would be ready to sail. Taussig allegedly replied that his destroyers could sail as soon as they had fueled, and this was taken up by the British and American press. Taussig himself could not remember being so direct, claiming a few weeks later, "It is possible that in conversation with [Bayly] I said we were ready for immediate service, but there was not any-thing spectacular about it."[5] That the destroyers had made their way across the Atlantic without refueling was already tribute to their capabilities, but the truth was all needed maintenance and time to study local conditions. In a clever move (at Sims' suggestion), Jellicoe sent "Evans of the *Broke*," whose ship was under repair after the Channel action, as liaison and mentor for the new arrivals. Evans' combination of combat success, Antarctic experience, charm, and personal magnetism meant that he was listened to closely and without resentment. That another side of this first RN-USN operational partnership worked so well came as a surprise to many. The apparently irascible and difficult-to-please Bayly quickly gained the confidence of the captains and officers of Taussig's destroyers.[6] From the first, Bayly "in no way" interfered with the internal administration of the American forces.[7] The admiral designated the captain of the destroyer tender *Dixie* (Capt. Poinsett Pringle) as his American chief of staff and left him to it. A second factor was that Bayly and Sims quickly established a firm friendship. Bayly kept Sims informed of the performance of individual USN units and their captains, but any move to counsel or even replace poor performers was left wholly to the American admiral. Later, Bayly asked Sims to take command at Queenstown during the British officer's absence on leave.

The first American destroyer patrols started on 8 May. Fitted with depth charges and with masts cut down, paint schemes modified to suit local con-ditions, and a general effort to reduce top weight, the American units were soon ready for work. The Admiralty very sensibly agreed that the British dockyards were to take on American repairs in the same way as they did for British units, maintaining a record of costs that could be reconciled and paid, as they were, after the war. Although the USN units required such dockyard support, it rapidly became apparent the American ships had a greater capac-ity for self-repair than their British equivalents. The destroyer tenders that soon arrived and took on much of the maintenance work were also notably well equipped. They were early products of the USN's dawning realization of the likely demands of a Pacific conflict and the vast distances involved.

The American crews had much to learn, but they possessed an élan and a freshness of outlook increasingly rare among the hard-pressed British units, now entering their fourth year of war. By this time, many British patrol units were feeling the strain of practically constant seagoing, in which officers and men "hardly ever get ashore & seldom get a night in."[8] Indeed, the American presence may have contributed to improved morale and performance in the Royal Navy. Bayly certainly believed that a competitive element had entered, the Americans determined to prove themselves and the British anxious not to be shown up. In one small way adjusting from peacetime to operational conditions proved unexpectedly easy for the Americans. The oil fuel shortage resulting from the efforts of the U-boats had forced the British to impose much tighter restrictions on high-speed steaming than had applied since 1914, a source of much frustration. The Americans were still accustomed to such constraints. The USN was also adjusting its building programs to meet the emerging need and by late May 1917 there were sixty-one destroyers contracted for. Further orders followed but industry took time to mobilize and only thirty-nine of the new destroyers entered service during the conflict.[9] The burden of the next eighteen months fell on the existing force. Sims continued to urge that the USN dispatch every available destroyer and patrol vessel. He remained a strong proponent of convoy, but if the passage of American troops to France was to be protected against U-boats, the USN destroyers already in European waters would be barely enough to provide the necessary escorts in the submarine danger zone. They could not, as became obvious in June, meet this requirement and support other patrol and escort activities around the British and French coasts at the same time.

Operations of the Grand Fleet

Admiral Beatty was determined the Grand Fleet should make a greater contribution to the antisubmarine campaign than simply detaching destroyers to reinforce local forces. He yearned to go on the offensive, and if his intended approach did not derive from his passion for foxhunting, it certainly owed something to shooting game birds. The Admiralty had similar enthusiasm for an offensive approach. Operation BB proposed to employ destroyers as "beaters" to force U-boats passaging around the north of Scotland to dive. The hope was that having evaded the surface forces, they would surface to be attacked by submarines positioned farther south. Reasonable in theory, the operation from 15 to 24 June nevertheless took up fifty-three out of eighty-six available destroyers and their leaders, together with seventeen submarines. The British believed that they made twenty-six sightings and conducted eight destroyer and three submarine attacks. Some were against phantoms, although *K1* may have succeeded in hitting *U95* with a dud torpedo. In other encounters, the British submariners learned how difficult a target a submarine made; the need for surprise meant most attacks were conducted at very long ranges. *J1* (no longer commanded by Laurence) fired four torpedoes at a surfaced U-boat at ranges between forty-five hundred and five thousand yards. They missed. The British believed the operation seriously interfered with the U-boats' antishipping operations on the east coast and in the Norwegian Sea, but there is no evidence that it made any real difference. Furthermore, the operation's scale meant it could not soon be repeated, although Beatty was eager to do so. The Grand Fleet had to content itself with less ambitious projects. Operation CC, conducted over five days beginning on 5 July attempted to integrate kite balloons with a small force of destroyers, five of which had balloons in tow. Deployed north of the Shetlands across one of the U-boats' transit routes to the Atlantic, conditions were favorable, with the light winds and high visibility all too rare in that area. Arguably, they could not have been better for the hunting force. One submarine was sighted, but the U-boat concerned dived well before the destroyers could get into her vicinity. The price of the extended horizon of the kite balloon was its visibility at long range to an enemy observer on the surface. A second operation a few days later produced the sighting of a U-boat and an attack by the destroyer *Patriot*, which the British thought successful on the evidence of oil and an explosion underwater. The actual fate of the boat in question (*U69*) remains uncertain.

This period saw another important change. America's entry to the war altered the nature of the blockade and made it much more a regime of port control than examination at sea. The units of the Tenth Cruiser Squadron were not required in the same numbers as before. They were also increasingly vulnerable to U-boats using the northern route and represented potentially useful merchant tonnage, as well as possible ocean convoy escorts. The squadron's numbers were reduced in June 1917, initially to provide for Atlantic convoy work. There were further detachments in September, while submarines picked off a unit at intervals. By November plans were in train to reduce the patrol to a handful of ships, operating with the Second Cruiser Squadron. By the start of 1918, the focus of the "Northern Patrol" would be almost wholly on antisubmarine work.

The naval war in the air continued. Beatty's efforts to improve the aviation capabilities of the fleet were slowly bearing fruit. As an antizeppelin measure, three light cruisers, *Cassandra*, *Dublin*, and *Yarmouth*, were fitted with platforms to launch a Sopwith Pup. This provided a response aircraft to three of the light cruiser squadrons. An encounter between the light cruisers *Sydney* and *Dublin* and eight destroyers with *L43* on 3 May confirmed that a zeppelin at twenty thousand feet was very difficult to hit with antiaircraft guns, while its bombs fell uncomfortably close. *Sydney*'s captain, J. S. Dumaresq, played an important role in coming months in developing efficient methods of launching aircraft from cruisers and capital ships.

In the meantime, entry into service of four "Large America" flying boats with greater endurance and weapon load than any previous naval aircraft meant the British could take the offensive against the airships. They capitalized on the extensive use the zeppelins made of radio. Cued by Room 40 and direction finding, the Admiralty could order a sortie and provide the aircraft's crew with a fair idea of their quarry's location. Operating from Yarmouth and Felixstowe, the new machines quickly made their presence felt. On 14 May, No. 8666 shot down *L22*, with the loss of all on board. The Germans had no idea what caused the airship's destruction, ascribing it to antiaircraft fire from surface forces. They might have understood the threat when attacks on *L40* on 24 May and 5 June failed, but on both occasions the German airship commander assumed his assailants were seaplanes operating from parent ships.

L43 was destroyed off Terschelling by No. 8677 on 14 June, but it was only *L46*'s escape from No. 8666 the same day that finally alerted the zeppelins to the danger. The immediate response to such an attack was to climb, something the newest airships could do rapidly, but which heavier-than-air machines found challenging. But being able to gain height rapidly was

Photo 10.1   *Orion*-class battleships with   *Maritime Quest and Michael Pocock*
                  the Sixth Battle Squadron

not enough. If a zeppelin was caught operating at low level, the practice for mine-spotting and antisubmarine work, a flying boat could attack before the airship climbed too high. The resulting order to operate above a height of thirteen thousand feet negated much of the airships' value in supporting the minesweepers. Fighter escorts could be provided, but they were an expensive resource and, with limited endurance, could not be available all the time.[10] The seaborne antizeppelin capability proved its worth on 17 August, when *Yarmouth* launched a Pup against *L23*, shadowing the First Light Cruiser Squadron off the coast of Jutland. The force steamed north to draw the zeppelin on before the Pup was launched. The little aircraft succeeded in getting over *L23* and sent the zeppelin crashing into the sea in flames. There were no survivors and, although *L23* had reported she was being pursued, no indication to the German command what caused her loss.

The zeppelins remained valuable, if carefully handled, as scouts against surface forces, but their utility was diminishing rapidly. They were soon the subject of debate within Germany. In late July the General Staff proposed that zeppelin production be discontinued in favor of aircraft. This Scheer would not accept and the problem was eventually placed before the kaiser, who decided largely in favor of the army on 17 August. The navy's production of airships did not stop, but its reduction by 75 percent to one every two months created serious constraints. The Naval Airship Division was limited to eighteen operational units and losses could not soon be replaced. Strasser was still devoted to the bombing campaign against England, but the compromise implied that the zeppelins' priority would be scouting for the fleet. In the coming months, the airships' employment reflected both the increasing threat and the need to husband the force.[11]

Operations in the South

Farther south, Vice Admiral Bacon faced new problems with the Dover Strait net barrage. The mines laid on its southern side during the previous winter had proved no more suitable in the strong currents and tides than previous fields. By spring, despite being fitted with additional sinkers to hold them in position, many had dragged into the nets. They soon claimed ships and lives. By May, Bacon and the Admiralty agreed the mines had to go and over the next three months more than a thousand were swept. This could not account for every weapon, however, and Bacon decided to cut his losses and redeploy the net barrage farther south, well clear of the main danger area. New minefields were needed, provided they were located farther away from the barrage and had better mooring systems, but sufficient units would not be available until near the end of 1917.

In the meantime, Flanders Command had been trying to get a clear idea of the cycle of the "Beef trip" convoys. By early May, it was confident enough to dispatch practically its entire force of torpedo boats on a search and destroy mission. Under Commander Adolf Kahle, the Third Flotilla sailed on the evening of 9 May, with eight units, together with four more from the First Flanders Half-Flotilla. Twelve torpedo boats from the other Flanders flotillas would search to the west and southwest, to give warning of any movement by forces from Dover. The main target was what the Germans believed was a large westbound convoy. The Germans were not relying on intelligence alone; scouting aircraft were deployed as soon as there was enough daylight, but the aviators failed to make any reports to Kahle's formation.

The Harwich Force was out in strength, with the advantage that the convoy movements it was protecting had been completed. Once again, German communications security was tight, so the British had no idea that they were at sea. Leading three light cruisers and four destroyers, Tyrwhitt sighted Kahle's force to the south just before 0400 on 10 May. With sunrise only twenty minutes away, visibility was excellent and the enemy units in clear view at 16,000 yards. Tyrwhitt altered course to close, while the Germans turned south to run for Zeebrugge. The early detection proved a disadvantage for the pursuit. Kahle's ships quickly began making funnel smoke and deploying smoke floats while they engaged in a gunnery duel that did more credit to the Germans than the British. The latter thought they were making hits, but did no significant damage, made obvious when it became apparent the German force was increasing its distance from the British cruisers. German 105-mm fire straddled the British several times, although a lone torpedo fired by *G91* went nowhere. Tyrwhitt attempted to send his destroyers ahead, but the order was slow to be transmitted; some of his signalmen had been knocked out by blast. The position of *Centaur*'s No. 2 mount abaft the bridge meant firing it on a forward bearing created hazards for personnel.[12] Even after they understood what the commodore wanted, however, the destroyers were slow to increase speed, a serious matter as the Germans were rapidly approaching the security of the Flanders coast batteries. While Tyrwhitt's cruisers turned away on reaching the Thornton Ridge, *Stork*, leading the destroyers, at last began to gain on the Germans, but still too slowly. This was a source of comfort to Kahle, concerned for the safety of the slower, coal-fired units in his force. The situation briefly improved for the British when the leader *Lightfoot* and four destroyers, returning from seeing their convoy into the Netherlands, approached from the northeast. Kahle had moved to attack *Stork*, but the arrival of *Lightfoot*'s unit forced his retreat. He turned easterly to parallel the coast, just clear of the Wenduyne Bank, as soon as he was inside the protective cover of the coastal defenses.[13]

The lesson for the Germans was that the timing of attacks on Anglo-Dutch shipping had to be precise. On 17 May, with more accurate information to hand, Kahle took out sixteen torpedo boats. It was not a good night for operations, with no moon and a thick fog. Since there were three British cruisers at sea, with three more due to sail in the early hours of 18 May, as well as destroyers distributed between the cruiser forces and the eastbound and westbound convoys, the Germans may have been lucky the weather was so thick. Visibility was less than a thousand yards in the late evening and reduced even further as the night wore on. Kahle divided his ships into four groups, accepting the risk of misidentification in the murk in the hope of increasing the chance of finding his quarry, but also separating the formations as much as possible. One group succeeded in sinking the small British merchant ship *Cito*. Two boats shortly afterward encountered the British destroyer division protecting the eastbound convoy's rear. The division's leader *Sylph* practically ran into the lead German, *V71*, and the latter was almost as surprised. The Germans opened fire, albeit not very accurately, but did not stay for *Sylph*'s answering shots, delayed by the breakdown in onboard procedures all too frequent in British ships at night. After the Germans disappeared, *Sylph* pursued them but lost touch with the remainder of her own division. This proved disastrous when *Sylph*'s captain realized too late that a new contact looming in sight was not the enemy. *Sylph* went full astern and turned to starboard in a desperate attempt to prevent a collision but struck the destroyer *Setter* a heavy blow on her starboard side, immediately flooding the engine room. *Sylph* attempted to take *Setter* in tow, but the latter's after boiler room bulkhead collapsed and she sank at 0030 on 18 May. Ironically, when she crossed *Sylph*'s bows, *Setter* had been extricating herself from a near-collision with *Recruit*, another member of the same division. The Germans did not go entirely unscathed. *S55*, belonging to one of the other formations, was rammed and badly damaged by a merchant ship, whose identity remained unknown. *S55* made her own way home, but the night provided another sharp reminder how difficult operations in poor visibility were to coordinate. This did not stop the Flanders flotillas from trying again with another sortie on 23 May. This initiative, however, was also stymied by thick fog.

The smaller torpedo boats' turn had come on 19 May when Lieutenant Günther Lütjens led five torpedo boats toward Dunkirk.[14] There they encountered four French destroyers. The two sides were evenly matched in gun and torpedo fire. Although the Germans maintained the initiative throughout, their torpedo attack failed, even at the practically ideal range of less than five hundred yards. Matters were confused by the coincidence that both sides' night recognition lights were identical. This particularly affected the French, beset by the constant preoccupation of the Allied forces in the Channel that friend should not be mistaken for foe. *Bouclier* was badly damaged and her captain killed, while *Capitaine Mehl* was also hit. The Germans were more helped than hindered by French searchlights working from the shore and had scant difficulty making out their targets. They got home with little damage. The French believed the action had been observed by British destroyers, unable to intervene because of the proximity of a Dover Command minefield.[15] There is, however, no mention of this in the relevant British records.[16]

On 11 May, Dover Command made another attempt to bombard the canal lock gates. *Terror* and *Soult* had the southern gate as their target, while *Erebus* took the north. Only one of the planned trio of spotting aircraft managed to get on task, but it did good work for the forty-five minutes it remained overhead. The three monitors fired 175 15-inch shells, 21 of which landed within 50 yards of the key targets, the gates and the associated dock pump houses, but no direct hits were scored, confirming how difficult such targets were for naval guns.[17] Nevertheless, the operation demonstrated that such attacks remained possible, provided there was sufficient protection for the monitors in the form of supporting surface forces, minesweepers, and—as was becoming increasingly important—air cover. The Germans responded by improving their smoke-making devices and by holding spotting aircraft for their shore batteries at short notice to fly when a bombardment seemed likely.

Bacon's attempts to repeat the effort were frustrated by unfavorable weather and defects. A full bombardment was abandoned on 26 May, but the Germans were on the alert and sent out four units of the Second Flanders Half-Flotilla. They found the 12-inch gun *General Wolfe* and two smaller monitors conducting experimental firings off the Ratel Bank. Their only close escort was the aging "30 knotter" destroyer *Leven*. The heavier guns of *Wolfe*, *M24*, and *M27* may have made the Germans unduly circumspect. They conducted a torpedo attack at very long range and almost immediately withdrew. Although one weapon missed *M24* by only a hundred yards, the results should have been no surprise. *Leven* shadowed until the Germans' superior speed took them out of sight.[18] After further disappointments with the weather, Bacon finally managed to bombard Ostend Dockyard on 5 June. This area target proved much more suitable than the lock gates, and the combined efforts of *Erebus* and *Terror* caused significant damage. This included sinking *UC70*, which (although eventually salvaged) did not return to service for nearly a year, while the torpedo boat *G41* was also badly hit. Bacon wanted more, notably the yard's two floating docks, and he hoped for a chance to resume the bombardment.

Tyrwhitt had reason to be pleased with at least this Dover Command operation. As the British force approached the coast, Tyrwhitt's ships ran into the torpedo boats *S15* and *S20*, which had been conducting one of their semiregular night sweeps toward the Thornton Bank. A brisk action followed as the Germans fled to the coast. *S20* suffered a hit on her bridge, killing her captain, and was crippled by two further hits in her boiler rooms.[19] The British continued to chase *S15* but, despite severe damage, the torpedo boat got close enough to the coastal defenses that Tyrwhitt called off the British destroyers. Lieutenant Hamilton in the newly completed *Taurus* claimed, "If we had only had another 10 minutes at him we should have had him for keeps."[20] *S15* was fortunate that a division of *A-II* torpedo boats was also at sea and she was eventually towed to port. *S20* was finished off by the destroyer *Satyr*. The German press asserted that *Satyr* deliberately left survivors in the water when she withdrew and that her boats' crews had refused to embark them while there were still opportunities to do so. Tyrwhitt pointed out that *Satyr* was only 16,000 yards away from the shore batteries and under constant fire, "her boats and upper works being hit by splinters" from the shells falling around. Tyrwhitt himself had recalled her.[21] The few remaining personnel from *S20* who survived were eventually rescued by German seaplanes. The controversy continued for some weeks, with Tyrwhitt demanding and eventually receiving formal guidance from the Admiralty that "no action should be taken which hazards one of H.M. Ships or the lives of the crew for the sake of picking up survivors. This applies particularly to circumstances in which it would be dangerous for ships' boats to pick up more survivors than they could properly carry."[22]

The bombardment convinced Admiral von Schröder that Ostend was too vulnerable, and he began to prepare Ghent, farther inland, as an alternative base.[23] It was also clear that the torpedo boat force was being steadily worn down. The pleas of Flanders Command for additional units were emphasized by the loss of G96 to a mine on 25 June. On the western side of the Channel, Flag Officer Dover also had many things on his mind. Forces for the planned assault on the Flanders coast began to assemble in the Thames in the middle of July. Six of the original big-gun monitors, with a seventh in reserve, were allocated to the pontoons and practiced in their operation, while the First Division of the Fourth Army was brigaded at Dunkirk, the intended embarkation point. The 12-inch-gun monitors could easily be spared, since they lacked the range to contest the German Flanders coastal batteries, but it was too early for the associated armada of support, escort, and bombardment units to assemble. The assault itself had to wait not only upon the offensive on land, which began on 31 July, but the combination of a sufficient advance inland (ten miles) and the alignment of weather and tide to place the pontoons close enough to the shore.[24] In the meantime, Dover Command sought to constrain the Germans with new minefields and an additional net barrage. The war off the Belgian coast intensified, with the British attempting to maintain and extend their minefields and nets, while the Germans worked to clear sufficient water to keep their freedom of maneuver. It was also more than ever a three-dimensional conflict, with aircraft being employed for reconnaissance and (increasingly) bombing attacks. The submarine threat seemed pervasive, particularly for the British, and both sides faced the ubiquitous danger of the mine.

While waiting for the amphibious assault, Bacon organized the 15-inch-gun monitors on a rotating patrol designated "BO" to back up the light forces protecting the barrage, but also to conduct bombardments of the German shore facilities when conditions allowed. The monitors' work was supplemented by increasingly effective air raids. Aircraft had yet to prove capable against moving targets in a seaway, but they were a growing threat to ships in harbor. S53 was damaged in July, while A13 was sunk by a bomb at Ostend on 16 August.[25] A44 was hit at Zeebrugge a few days later and a night raid on 3–4 September damaged two large and two small torpedo boats, as well as UB54, which was out of action for two months. The coastal bases were becoming untenable; this was confirmed when Soult put twenty-eight rounds into Ostend dockyard on 4 September. Terror followed with two further bombardments before the end of the month, which did more damage—the one on 22 September was particularly effective. The newly salvaged *A13* and the *A45* were trapped when their floating dock was damaged and sank at one end.[26] Although both were eventually freed, *A13* (hit again in November) never returned to sea.[27]

An action that accompanied the deployment of the new net barrier off the Thornton Ridge on 25 July illustrated the problems that both sides faced. The Allied force included not only every fighting unit that Admiral Bacon could muster, but also a division of French destroyers, together with the leader *Nimrod* and eight destroyers from the Harwich Force. Sixty-two drifters were required to lay the first fifteen miles of nets and their distribution over a wide area demanded a high level of protection (particularly in that morning's poor visibility). The British were wise to take these precautions because *G91* and *S55* were at sea. The two torpedo boats approached to investigate and a running action followed once the Germans recognized the weight of metal against them. As *G91* and *S55* made for the shelter of the coastal batteries, they exchanged intermittent fire with *Broke* and other Dover and Harwich destroyers. Conditions were very difficult and although each side thought it scored hits, this was not the case. Once under the cover of the batteries, only heavy weapons could reach the torpedo boats. *Terror* straddled the German boats at least once but failed to hit them. In return, the Flanders batteries dropped some forty heavy rounds onto the Allied force, straddling *Terror* in their turn, but also failing to score a hit. The action resumed later in the morning, with *G91* and *S55* reinforced by *S54* and *V70*. There was sporadic firing at long range between the Germans and a group of six British destroyers led by *Faulknor*. Attempts by the British to close found the Germans retreating under the cover of their own batteries. In worsening visibility the exchange was repeated in the afternoon, but neither side got near enough to make any hits. It was a standoff, something that would remain the case in the weeks ahead.

Ashore in Flanders, the Third Battle of Ypres descended into the mire of Passchendaele. Despite renewed efforts in August and September, the British offensive failed, stymied by appalling weather and the sheer difficulty of achieving gains in the conditions prevailing. The amphibious forces waited with diminishing hope as one tidal window after another opened and closed. The attack could not go ahead without the consent of the British army C-in-C, Sir Douglas Haig, and that depended on the land offensive advancing the necessary distance. To be fair, Haig allowed the land elements of the amphibious venture to remain in reserve for many weeks, when there were increasing calls for reinforcements for the main offensive. At one point, Bacon proposed a less ambitious raid to destroy the most dangerous coastal batteries, but Haig was unwilling for his troops to be used for a purpose that did not contribute directly to his primary aim—clearing the Germans out of Flanders. At the beginning of October, the monitors and pontoons were dispersed and the supporting forces taken off their notice to move. The most substantial amphibious project in the North Sea or Channel of the First World War was stillborn.

Whether the assault would have succeeded remains uncertain. Dieppe in 1942 showed the dangers of attempting a direct amphibious attack on an extensively fortified area and the operation carried some very high risks. It certainly depended upon ideal tide, wind, and visibility. Nevertheless, with such a combination and the achievement of surprise, it is possible a successful assault could have been staged. By this time the ability to generate smoke screens to mask advancing units from enemy guns was reasonably sophisticated, while it is unlikely the German shore defenses would have had sufficient light weaponry in the right positions to prevent mass disembarkation of the British troops from the pontoons. As has been suggested, the real problems would have arisen a few hours afterward, when the landing forces faced German formations dispatched to repel them.[28] Like the Battle of Arnhem in the next war, the amphibious pontoons might have represented "a bridge too far" for a division that could not be readily reinforced. There were only three miles between the western landing and the Allied front at Nieuport, but, in the conditions of 1917, that may have been three too many.[29] The indefatigable Bacon did not give up and began plans for a direct attack on Zeebrugge to destroy the lock gates. He spent much of the autumn refining this scheme. He also developed proposals to use the 18-inch guns available from the conversion of *Furious* to carry aircraft. Bacon was particularly interested in the 18-inch guns because, with sufficient elevation, their shells could reach Bruges when fired from outside the effective range of the most capable German coast battery.

The Germans in Flanders had their own problems in the second half of 1917. The British nets and minefields were having a similar effect to the mining campaign in the Heligoland Bight. The Germans were feeling the strain. The minesweepers were constantly at work but risked being attacked by British patrols if they were not supported by the torpedo boats. This commitment was not only a drain on the flotillas but carried its own hazards: there was a steady toll in damaged or sunken ships. The British did not fully appreciate, nor did the Germans admit, that this pressure greatly constrained Admiral von Schröder in ordering further raids on the Dover Strait, but that was the case. The ability of the High Sea Fleet to provide reinforcement for Flanders was further restricted by the Baltic commitment in the autumn of 1917 to Operation Albion, which itself involved additional losses in the torpedo boat flotillas.[30]

Mine Warfare and the Grand Fleet

The Grand Fleet was not idle during this period. The minelaying effort in the Heligoland Bight continued, if too slowly. To continuing restrictions on the availability of effective mines had to be added the constraint of long summer days and the increased risk of detection they brought. Only five fields were laid in June and five in July, the majority by submarines. The total was no more than 849 mines and only one field claimed any victims—a patrol vessel and a minesweeper. Nevertheless, the British were determined to press ahead. Smaller and older light cruisers were already being employed on the task, but it could be performed just as efficiently by destroyers. The leader *Abdiel* was already operational and had done good work. The Admiralty ordered that two of the new, large *V*- and *W*-class destroyers be modified during build; fifteen more were similarly altered in later months.[31] At the beginning of 1917 the new *Telemachus* and *Tarpon* were converted to carry forty mines, as were the older *Meteor* and *Legion*, as well as a handful of still older (and slower) destroyers. The after gun mounts and torpedo tubes could be exchanged for mines within a few hours, thus retaining the ability to employ the ships concerned as destroyers. Their retention in conventional flotillas reflected this duality, probably caused by the continuing shortage of destroyers. It was not ideal; Dorling of *Telemachus* in the Battle Cruiser Force's Thirteenth Flotilla commented, "We never quite knew whether we were a destroyer or a minelayer."[32] The same observation was not made by *Royalist*'s captain, but judging by the amount of time spent in 1917 shipping and unshipping mine rails, the cruisers modified for minelaying were equally schizophrenic.[33] Until early 1918, only the destroyer leader *Abdiel* could confine herself to the single task. Techniques also changed. Instead of long, single-line fields, from early 1917 the minelayers deployed shorter, compact fields with an alteration of direction during the lay to confuse minesweepers, a tactic also adopted by the Germans.[34]

On 14 July, the destroyers sailed from Dunkirk with a strong escort to lay mines overnight off the Middelkerke Bank in preparation for the net barrage that Dover Command would deploy eleven days later. The lay itself passed off without a hitch, although *Telemachus* received a scare when surface craft appeared, heading on an opposite course at high speed. They were clearly enemy and are likely to have been *G91* and *V70*. Neither was sufficiently alert to notice the startled British minelayer, while the latter could not provoke action until the lay was complete. By the time all forty of *Telemachus'* "eggs" were away, the enemy were out of sight. *Tarpon*, the next unit west of *Telemachus* had just completed her work when she exploded a mine under her stern, blowing off the starboard propeller. *Tarpon* survived, towed into Dunkirk by *Thruster*, but the cause of her damage remained a vexed subject.

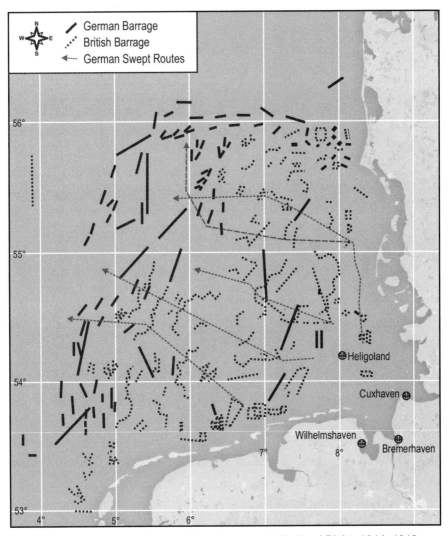

Map 10.1 **British and German Mine Barrages Heligoland Bight, 1914–1918**

Dorling thought that she might have been torpedoed, but the German torpedo boats did not fire any weapons that night. It is most likely *Tarpon* hit an old British mine, either adrift or dragged from a field laid farther west in 1916. What made any conclusion difficult was the uncertainty of navigation (i.e., the discrepancies between *Tarpon*'s estimated position, that calculated by her consorts, and a third reconstructed during the enquiry were nearly three miles) when there were little more than four miles between the old minefield and the Middelkerke Bank.[35] *Tarpon* was not operational again until early 1918, but *Telemachus* joined the light cruisers *Blanche*, *Bellona*, and *Royalist* for the only surface minelaying sortie into the Heligoland Bight of July. On the 25th of that month the quartet laid 280 mines north of the Horns Reef, just clear of Danish territorial waters. This was quickly discovered by the Germans, and it indicated what was to come.

The Grand Fleet was shocked by the loss of the battleship *Vanguard*, which blew up and sank at anchor in Scapa Flow on the evening of 9 July. Only three men were found alive, one of whom died two days afterward. The loss of practically the entire ship's company was mitigated by the fact that personnel were on advance leave in preparation for the ship's forthcoming refit and fifteen officers were attending a concert on board *Royal Oak*, but there were also visitors on board *Vanguard*. An embarked observer from the Japanese navy was one of the dead. A midshipman whose life was saved by a last-minute invitation to the concert recalled his narrow escape: "Everyone spoke in hushed tones and treated us almost with reverence."[36] The cause of the explosions that tore *Vanguard* apart was never confirmed. It was almost certainly aging cordite, but there was evidence magazine temperatures varied considerably and not all magazine regulations had been enforced.[37] The result was an effort to rid the fleet of overage propellant and tighten up magazine procedures. The tendency to ascribe such events to sabotage received a boost with the discovery that the charge hand of the ordnance fitters embarked to prepare the ship for a coming refit had been on board the armored cruiser *Natal* on the day of her explosion in 1915. The unfortunate foreman was cross-examined closely. There was "nothing suspicious" in his testimony, although the report to the Admiralty said something about the state of the naval dockyards' workforces when it stated "he had displayed remarkable ignorance of the general details of magazines."[38]

Beatty was moving in new directions. He had increasing reservations about Pakenham as commander of the Battle Cruiser Force, commenting in May that "he does not seem to possess the right flair. . . . But for the life of

Photo 10.2   HMAS *Melbourne* and HMS *Southampton*   *Sea Power Centre, Australia*

me I don't know a soul who would do it better."[39] Although he successfully urged Pakenham's promotion to acting vice admiral in June, the following month Beatty assigned command of all the Grand Fleet's light cruisers to Rear Admiral Trevylyan Napier, who also received promotion to acting vice admiral. Beatty's justification was that the Light Cruiser Force's creation affected Pakenham "only in matters of administration, which had become too big for him to deal with and required decentralising."[40] Beatty's flag captain, Ernle Chatfield, urged the step to help improve the cruisers' gunnery; the changes were tactically significant, as Chatfield knew and in spite of Beatty's disclaimer.[41] In part, they recognized the potential of the new "large light cruisers" *Courageous* and *Glorious* under Napier's command in the First Cruiser Squadron to support the scouting forces with their high speed and 15-inch guns. But they also reflected the increasing practice for the units of the Battle Cruiser Force, as well as the advanced units directly attached to the Grand Fleet, to deploy in smaller formations, such as single battle cruiser or light cruiser squadrons, strongly supported by destroyers. Pakenham was thus more just one tactical commander among others than had been the case for Beatty, even if he retained his oversight of all the battle cruisers.

There were other matters in train. The evidence suggests that Beatty had his own signals intelligence unit within the Grand Fleet. Jellicoe always had a strong signals and wireless staff, but their numbers increased under Beatty as did the number of clerks in what was a more decentralized staff system than in 1914–16.[42] What is most likely is that the organization started in 1916 and was expanded in the new regime, focusing on at-sea exploitation of tactical signals. Beatty himself displayed a sophisticated understanding of the importance of signals intelligence, derived partly from his close relationship with Reginald Hall, director of the Intelligence Division.[43] Both had cause for anxiety. Although interception and direction-finding capabilities continued to expand and the capacity of Room 40 developed apace, the Germans were improving their communications security. They introduced a new major units' code in May 1917 and replaced their entire call sign system. These measures were largely driven by recognition of the British direction-finding capability, accompanied by understanding that individual units could be "fingerprinted," first by their call sign and then the characteristics of individual radio transmitters and their associated operators. The British feared that the Germans might realize that their cyphers had been compromised, although two things suggested this was not the case. The first was that the Germans used the same code book in the Baltic as the North Sea and free use of the new *Flottenfunkspruchbuch* (FFB) in that theater gave Room 40 the entry it required. The second was that continuing liberal use of radio and the *Allgemeinesfunkspruchbuch* (AFB) code for small ships and U-boats indicated the Germans had no idea of their full vulnerability.[44]

The Baltic in 1917

11

THE LEADERSHIP OF THE BALTIC FLEET and the Royal Navy's submarine flotilla regarded the prospect of spring and the renewal of sea
warfare with some optimism. Although *Letun* had been mined in
November, there were now twelve of the fast *Novik*-type destroyers in the
fleet, with more under construction. There were also eleven new *Bars*-class
submarines, with several additional boats expected to commission in 1917.
Recent completions and the arrival of the five American-built *AG* units in
late 1916 allowed the Baltic Fleet to decommission some of its older, less
satisfactory submarines. There were also hopes that the first of the new light
cruisers, *Svetlana*, could be completed before the end of the 1917 fighting
season. Major vessels such as *Slava* were being modified over the winter to
give their main armament greater elevation and thus extended range. Above
all, it was possible that Admiral Nepenin might at last receive approval for
more active employment of the four dreadnoughts.[1]

Unfortunately, the political situation was deteriorating steadily in
Petrograd and Kronstadt. The base commander there privately admitted
as early as September 1916 that he was not in effective control of the
80,000 men under his command, while the navy minister, Vice Admiral
Grigorovich, had been rebuffed by the tsar in November when he expressed
concern over the unrest in naval shore establishments and dockyards,
where recurrent strikes were interfering with new construction and refits.[2]
The entire country was slowly becoming ungovernable as the overloaded
transport system inched closer to failure and many centers ran short of
food and fuel. Revolution was regarded by some officers as a probability
and many more were unsure how they should respond to insurrection.
This uncertainty was reflected in the relatively light sentences meted
out to sailors who were rounded up in October and accused of political
subversion.

179

The revolt began in Petrograd and spread successively to Kronstadt, Helsingfors, Reval, and the other bases of the Baltic Fleet. From the uprising's start around 8 March, events moved quickly.[3] Admiral Wiren, commander at Kronstadt, was one of the first victims, murdered by revolutionary sailors. Petrograd and Kronstadt nevertheless soon returned to a semblance of calm as a provisional government took charge and the tsar's abdication was announced. Helsingfors, however, descended into temporary chaos. Admiral Nepenin declared his support for the provisional government, but this was not enough for the newly emboldened sailors, and Nepenin was shot dead after being forced to accompany an armed mob. The opportunist flag officer torpedo craft, Vice Admiral A. M. Maksimov, had already offered himself as an alternative commander, a proposal reluctantly endorsed by the provisional government after Nepenin's murder. In reality he held his command at the pleasure of the newly formed and still chaotic sailors' councils. Many officers tried to make the best of the new situation, but death and wounds removed much of the senior leadership, while some no longer wished to serve in the navy at all. Others still were in a stupor, so shocked that they were incapable of taking a further lead. The ships' companies were themselves divided. There was already no love lost between the crew of the *Slava* and her inactive division mates. Matters were not improved when sailors from *Imperator Pavel I* threatened *Slava* with the ship's 8-inch secondary armament if her crew did not adopt a more active role in the insurrection.[4]

Although the number who died is practically impossible to establish with certainty, at least forty-five officers were killed at Helsingfors.[5] The reasons for their deaths range from opportunistic displays of resentment at the ruling class, to individual and group efforts to settle scores with officers considered particularly brutal or unsympathetic. While the older battleships were at the center of the organized rebellion and had their share of atrocities, much smaller ships were also involved in bloody reprisals. Destroyers and other light craft usually had much higher morale and cohesion across the ranks than the capital ships, but poor leadership and personality conflicts sometimes had other results in the close quarters involved. The Baltic Fleet had lost at least 10 percent of its officer corps—and this was only the beginning. Many extended-enlistment sailors went home, while many warrant officers felt as alienated from the new regime as their seniors, some falling victim to the insurgents. Vice Admiral Maksimov bowed to pressure from the sailors' committees and presided for the next few months over a revolving door of command changes. The lack of continuity and the belief the officers were operating only by favor of the committees meant there was almost no chance of refocusing the navy on its proper tasks.

That the ice remained so thick contributed to the steady deterioration of the fleet over the next few months. There was no prospect of an early resumption of operations, which made the fleet "a sitting target for the revolutionaries."[6] It is difficult to determine how strong the revolutionary groups were in the Baltic Fleet at the beginning of 1917 (or the actual distribution of Social Revolutionaries, Bolsheviks, and others). What is apparent is the political consciousness of the sailors grew by leaps and bounds and that the Bolsheviks made the navy a focus of their attention. Operationally, the requirement was to salvage as much as possible from the mess. The Stavka issued a directive to Maksimov in early April to achieve "the quickest possible restoration of the battle-readiness of the fleet," but this was easier said than done.[7] For most of the year to come, control of the fleet was disputed between its commander, the fleet's central *Tsentrobalt* committee, ideologically divergent ship soviets—in which the Bolsheviks played an increasing part—and the disorganized and often irresolute provisional government. The soviets had also gained control of large amounts of cash, which strengthened their position with many sailors, who looked to them for largesse.[8]

The Naval Situation after the Revolution

If Russia, as the provisional government intended, were to continue the war, the key naval questions were when the Germans would decide that holding their hand was no longer worthwhile and at what point they would come to believe that Russian capability had deteriorated to the point that a renewed attack on the Gulf of Riga and of Finland was feasible. The British, under Commander Cromie, did what they could to ease the situation in Reval and were largely successful in maintaining good order among the Russian personnel directly assigned to the British flotilla. They also worked closely with the Russian submariners. Many of the big ships were probably a lost cause, but Cromie hoped the minesweepers and minelayers could be made active and with them, both the Russian and British submarine forces. He had an important ally in the form of Rear Admiral Dmitrii Verderevsky, Nepenin's choice as submarine force commander, who was installed as deputy to Admiral Maksimov in early April and soon afterward took over as fleet commander. This initiative seems to have resulted from Petrograd's eventual realization that Maksimov was ineffective. Kolchak from the Black

Sea Fleet was an earlier choice by the provisional government but refused the appointment.

Verderevsky did not enjoy a long period in command, but his initiatives were sensible. He supported preparation of the submarines for operations as soon as the ice had thawed, and he organized a new mining campaign to reinforce and extend both the Advanced Position and the Central Position. One consolation for the new fleet commander was that there were plenty of mines in store and the organization for their arming and loading on board the minelayers still operated. This was important because many of the second-line elements of the Russian navy were disintegrating even faster than the fighting ships. The repair organization was increasingly unreliable, while the availability of stores steadily declined. The British submariners could do a lot of self-help, but they were acutely aware their operational readiness and that of the Russian units still willing to fight depended upon at least minimal support from ashore. The bulk of the fleet remained at least semioperational in mid-1917, but it was steadily expending its limited capital of serviceability.

The Germans were watching closely but were unsure what was going on in Russia. They had their own problems, for the privations of the "turnip winter" resulted in increasing industrial unrest and many were beginning to fear that revolution in Russia showed what lay ahead for Germany. The Baltic forces had their own example of changing times. The *Augsburg*, one of the cruisers permanently assigned to the Baltic, had suffered underwater damage from a rogue practice torpedo, but her repairs were delayed by a dockyard strike in Kiel, in which the workers called for more bread.[9] While this was settled relatively quickly, local commanders suspected that political influence rather than welfare concerns had been the trigger for the strike.

The Germans decided not to embark on offensive operations on any substantial scale, in the hope this would help persuade the Russians to sue for peace. In any case, both sides had to wait on the sea to open. The severe winter affected the Germans' activities much more than in previous years. With so much ice in the Baltic, many units scheduled for Libau had to wait in Swinemunde. Even in late March, the temperature in Libau fell as low as −20° Celsius, while at Kiel it was −6° Celsius. Admiral Hopman owned that he was "embarrassed" by his own inability to deploy forward to Libau.[10] Since the German strategy was one of "wait and see," Hopman decided the best approach would be renewal of the offensive minefields in the northern

Baltic. A large minefield laid in May 1916 between the Swedish coast and Dago Island was reinforced from 18 to 26 April with more than two thousand mines, sowed by *Deutschland* and *Nautilus* and the torpedo boat *V77*. Hopman was concerned enough by the possibility of a Russian attack that he escorted the minelayers with *Augsburg* and *Strassburg*. This field would protect the iron ore convoys running along the Swedish coast, an important factor because Hopman's limited forces were insufficient to provide full cover for the merchant ships in addition to conducting other operations.

Russian shipping routes to Sweden remained a legitimate target, particularly as continuing shortages in Petrograd and other cities might contribute to anti-war sentiment. Hopman deployed U-boats as soon as the ice cleared. The brand-new *UC78* laid eighteen mines south of the Aland Islands. The next to deploy, the even more recently completed *UC58*, laid a few mines and went on to sink or capture nine small Swedish-flagged vessels. She was followed by *UC57*, which laid another minefield and sank four tiny Russian vessels and an equally small Swedish sailing vessel, as well as taking two larger British merchant vessels as prizes. These were pinpricks, but the German boats were nevertheless more successful than the Russians. The latter sailed four submarines on 19 May, but none achieved any successes against the well-organized German convoy system. One, *Bars*, did not return from patrol. The circumstances of her loss remain uncertain. It is not known whether she fell victim to German depth charges off the coast of Sweden or was rammed and sunk in error by a Russian destroyer outside the Gulf of Finland. Her wreck has not been located. Sorties in June fared no better as the German antisubmarine forces proved more than a match for the Russian boats. *Pantera* was attacked by an airship and received sufficient damage to force her return to base, while the fate of *Lvitsa* remains unknown. The submarine was most probably destroyed south of the Swedish skerries on 11 June by gunfire and depth charges dropped by antisubmarine forces, including the minesweeper *M31*. One source suggested debris from *Lvitsa* was found by *E19* south of Gotland and that *Lvitsa* may have been destroyed by a mine, but there is no supporting evidence for this, including in the British records.[11]

These were heavy blows to an increasingly dispirited Russian force and they were not helped by the loss with all hands in early July of *AG14*, under the command of Lieutenant A. N. von Essen, the late C-in-C's son who had worked with the British and was one of the most dynamic and competent Russian junior commanders. *AG14* was almost certainly sunk by a mine.

Photo 11.1   Russian submarine *Lvitsa*   *Sergei Vinogradov*

Her wreck is believed to lie off the Swedish island of Gotska Sandoen, north of Gotland, suggesting *AG14* was on her way home from her patrol area off Libau.[12] A few days later, an accident in harbor saw the sinking of *AG15*, with eighteen deaths. Although the submarine was eventually salvaged, this was clear indication that professional standards were dropping. The one ray of light was *Vepr's* sinking the small merchant ship *Friedrich Carow* in the Gulf of Bothnia on 8 August. Attacks on convoys by both *Tigr* and *Gepard* in the following weeks were dismal failures, with malfunctioning torpedoes and increasingly disaffected crews.

The mining campaign was more straightforward. The winter's severity meant the operation to renew the fields began over a month later than usual. The focus was entirely defensive, with attention devoted to blocking the Gulf of Finland against further U-boat intrusions. In addition to more than four thousand mines, antisubmarine nets were deployed to seaward of the Central Position as additional obstructions. The minelayers *Pripyat*, *Nina*, and *Elena*, supported by light craft, renewed the Advanced Position with nearly 3,000 mines, while fields were laid to provide additional barriers to U-boats and protect the coastal defenses in the Gulf of Finland and the Gulf of Riga. The work continued largely uninterrupted well into September. Given the many disruptions, it is remarkable that the Russian mining campaign in the Baltic in 1917, a total of 13,318 mines, represented more than a third of their entire effort of the war.[13]

The minesweepers started their work a few days before the minelayers. The elderly craft allotted to the sweeping force had more than their share of maintenance problems, but they attempted to clear as much operating water for Russian forces in both gulfs as they could, as well as respond to the German mining campaign in the Gulf of Bothnia, given the threat this posed for the link with Sweden. The minesweepers' task was made harder by the fact that U-boats did not find either the additional minefields or the antisubmarine nets a serious problem in forcing entry into the Gulf of Finland. As with the Dover and Otranto Straits, such barriers were much less dangerous than their creators hoped. Given the size and minimal armament of the elderly minesweepers, they themselves were vulnerable to gun attack by an enterprising U-boat.

The Germans continued to watch and wait. The main offensive effort remained minelaying sorties by the small U-boats and a small but significant minelaying campaign by aircraft in and around the Gulf of Riga. This paid dividends when the small destroyer *Okhotnik* was sunk by an aerial mine on 26 September in the Irben Strait, the first-ever victim of such a weapon. After the appalling winter, the summer (at least in the Baltic) proved surprisingly gentle, allowing the German airship fleet of two older naval units and four army ships to conduct patrols over much of the sea. Unchallenged by the now moribund Russian air arm, they patrolled at heights ideal for detecting submarines at or near periscope depth as well as minefields, while they could provide early warning of any surface venture.[14] German aircraft embarked on a campaign to harass the Russian forces on Ösel and Dago islands. They could not drop a great weight of explosives, but their increasing numbers—and skill—helped wear down Russian morale. They achieved an important material success on 30 September when an ammunition store near the 30.5-cm battery at Zerel in the south of Ösel blew up. The Baltic was becoming something of a German lake.

The decline of the Russian fleet continued. The failure of Russia's July offensive on land meant the disintegration of much of the army. The Kornilov affair in later weeks further disrupted what remained of effective government. This had serious effects in the fleet, with the arrest and murder of officers who refused to swear a new oath to the provisional government, yet more new command appointments, and continuing muddle. Another change of fleet commanders brought in Rear Admiral A. V. Razvozov, whose situation was no more certain than his predecessor. The new fleet commander nevertheless succeeded in dispatching reinforcements, including *Slava*, to the Gulf of Riga at the end of August. *Slava*'s crew,

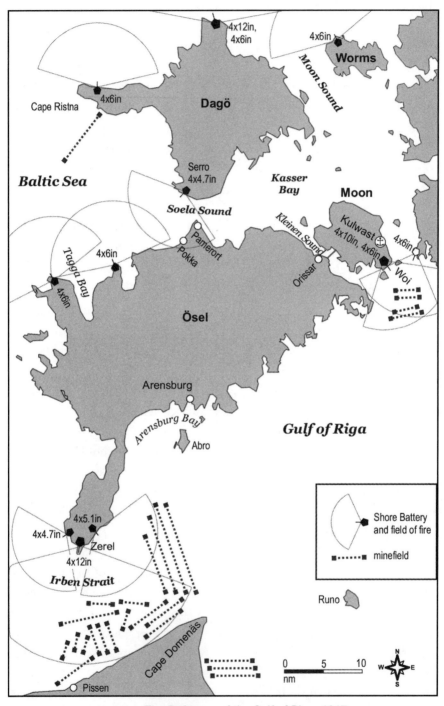

4x12in,
4x6in

4x6in

Worms

4x6in

Moon Sound

Cape Ristna

4x6in

Dagö

Baltic Sea

Serro
4x4.7in

Kasser
Bay

Moon

Kleinen Sound

Kulwast
4x10in, 4x6in

4x6in

Soela Sound

Pamerort

Woi

Tagga Bay

4x6in

Pokka

Orissar

4x6in

Ösel

Arensburg

Gulf of Riga

Arensburg Bay

Abro

4x5.1in

4x4.7in

Zerel

4x12in

Shore Battery
and field of fire

minefield

Irben Strait

Runo

Cape Domenäs

0   5   10

nm

N

W   E

S

Pissen

Map 11.1   The Defenses of the Gulf of Riga, 1917

disaffected by close association with the events of the revolution, took some persuasion before they agreed to sail, but the ship was on station by 26 August.[15] The Russian forces in the Gulf were under the command of Vice Admiral M. K. Bakhirev in the cruiser *Bajan*. Bakhirev was formally senior to Razvozov, but he was less acceptable to the provisional government and was thus made the latter's subordinate. The new arrangement depended very much upon Razvozov's tact. Bakhirev had under his control both *Slava* and her near-sister, *Grazhdanin*, formerly *Tsesarevich*, although the latter lacked *Slava*'s modified long-range main armament, as well as some cruisers and a strong force of destroyers, supplemented by the British C-class submarines.

Invasion of the Baltic Islands

It was increasingly clear the Gulf of Riga was the most likely target for a German attack. The German army had embarked on a limited offensive to secure Riga, resulting in its capitulation on 3 September, although there was no intent to push farther toward Petrograd. The Germans were content to wait for the final collapse of the Russian state and a direct thrust at the city might revive the Russians' fighting spirit. The General Staff were, however, interested in the capture of the islands at the entrance to the gulf, with Ösel Island as their first priority. With this in German hands, Riga and other ports in the southern gulf would be opened and supply lines to the front made more secure, vital if the land offensive had to be renewed in 1918. The threat of an attack on the Germans' coastal flank in the gulf would also be removed. By late September, from both signals intelligence and British reports, the Russians were aware that elements of the High Sea Fleet were entering the Baltic and they built up an accurate picture of German intentions.[16] Their ability to respond was crippled by the parlous state of the Russian submarines, while both *E9* and *E19* had run aground and withdrawn to Reval for docking. Where more could have been done, a point repeatedly made by the commanders of the British C-class submarines maintaining a watch on German activities in the Gulf of Riga, was to interfere with the increasing small-ship traffic passing in and out of the southern gulf.[17]

German joint-service planning began tentatively in mid-1917 but only gained real momentum in August. The navy had mixed feelings about a commitment that would require a substantial part of the High Sea Fleet as well as a massive effort by already hard-pressed minesweeping forces. On the other hand, the recent mutinies had created a new consciousness of the flagging morale of the major units and of the importance of finding constructive activities for them. The state of discipline in the big ships remained a concern up to the start of operations.[18] The light forces could also do with a major success as their spirit was beginning to lag. For both elements of the navy, achieving a victory before the lull of winter would be psychologically very important. Furthermore, although some in the navy regarded the operation as a sideshow, its success would further confine the Russian navy—including its submarines—and ease the pressure on the Baltic forces.[19] It would certainly reduce the mine threat and thus allow diversion of sweepers to support the North Sea units.

The question of command in the Baltic again raised its head.[20] Despite his claims to overall direction, Prince Heinrich was sidelined and the naval commander designated as vice admiral, Erhardt Schmidt in the battle cruiser *Moltke*, with Rear Admiral Behncke as his deputy. *Moltke* was accompanied by some of the most modern battleships of the Third and Fourth Squadrons; they were supported by a substantial force of light craft. However, the overriding need to keep the Heligoland Bight open meant only a handful of minesweepers could be transferred from the North Sea. Although every available mine warfare unit from the Baltic command was mustered, the mine would prove to be the Achilles heel of the German effort.

Overall command of the joint operation was vested in the Eighth Army at Riga, but the soldiers had enough sense to work closely with the navy to organize the seaborne elements.[21] These were necessarily improvised, with merchant ships of all sizes requisitioned as transports. Some had been lying idle for years and rendering them operational proved no easy task for the hastily assembled crews. Loading had to be carefully managed because many of the bigger transports drew too much water to operate in the assault area when fully laden. The number of ships available was not enough to allow the entire force to be lifted at once, so two waves were organized. This put a premium on the rapid disembarkation of the first assault group and an equally rapid turnaround of the transports. The naval forces were to cover the landing of a reinforced division, supplemented by a brigade—a total force in the order of 25,000 men. This was considered sufficient, given the state of the Russian coastal defense formations, which were grossly understrength, with poor training and in an equally poor state of morale. Despite the disruptions that the Russian fleet continued to experience, its ships and crews were in a much better fighting state than the troops ashore. Critically, however, although Bakhirev's own command was capable of something, the situation continued to deteriorate at Helsingfors and Reval. By mid-October, although there was wishful thinking that the season was getting too late for the Germans to attempt a landing, the state of the fleet was such that only a handful of submarines—largely through British efforts—remained fully operational.[22]

The primary target of what was designated Operation Albion was Ösel Island, but this was only the starting point for capturing Moon Island, while the later occupation of Dago Island was always a possibility. Certainly, once Moon Island was secured, the Russian fleet's access to the Gulf of Riga could be cut completely. This would make German command of the gulf simply a matter of eliminating whatever Russian units remained. The minefields in the Irben Strait and the heavy gun batteries in the south of Ösel Island meant the initial landing had to be in Ösel's west, at Tagga Bay. The landing itself, although in an area less dominated by coastal artillery, required active protection against Russian light craft from Kassar Bay. To achieve this, German light forces would enter the bay through the Soela Strait as soon as the batteries that covered its western entrance could be disabled. To provide access, a secondary landing at Pamerort on the strait's southern side would take place at the same time as at Tagga Bay. The Germans also intended that a channel be swept through the Irben Strait to allow entry of their heavy forces into the gulf as soon as Ösel's southern battery could be neutralized. A passage for deep draft ships had already been cleared outside the range of the Russian guns and only a few days' uninterrupted work would be required to do the rest of the job.

The German advance toward the islands was hindered by a combination of weather, which broke toward the end of September, and the limitations of the minesweepers. Much time could not be allowed for preliminary mine-sweeping because it would—and did—immediately alert the Russians to the imminent invasion. Despite the apparently chaotic situation in Russia, the Germans could not be sure that the Russians would not immediately reinforce the islands and deploy whatever naval forces they could muster. On the other hand, the scratch fleet of transports needed sufficient clear water for its approach and no ambiguity about where to go, necessitating temporary light ships and buoys that could only be laid close to the Russian coast at the last possible moment.[23] The one benefit of the delays for the Germans was that they allowed more time for preparing the transports and for a simple amphibious rehearsal near Libau.[24]

The main force sailed on 11 October and was in position off Tagga Bay early the next morning. The operation was soon behind schedule, but the first real hitch came shortly after the designated bombardment units moved to take up their stations. The limitations of German precursor minesweeping became rapidly clear when, at 0507, *Bayern* (designated to support the Pamerort landing) was mined, followed two minutes later by *Grosser Kurfürst*.[25] Both could continue with their immediate tasking. *Grosser Kurfürst*'s damage was relatively limited and the flooding soon contained, but *Bayern* rapidly took on over a thousand tons of water forward. Well down by the bows and with substantial internal damage, she started home for Kiel in the afternoon. The weather soon worsened, however, and with the battleship's bulkheads threatening collapse, *Bayern* was forced to withdraw to Tagga Bay for repairs.[26] Had the battleship been caught in the open sea, it is likely she would have sunk. *Bayern* took no further part in the operation and her voyage to Kiel after temporary repairs became something of an epic. *Grosser Kurfürst* also successfully completed her bombardment and was detached to return to Germany for repairs.

This substantial reduction in the capital ships assigned to Operation Albion must have worried Schmidt and his subordinates. Apart from the continuing mine threat, the remaining forces were arguably only just superior to the main Russian fleet, and the Germans could not be sure whether the latter remained capable of action. Fortunately, only one of the transports, *Corsica*, had been mined and her crew beached her after the troops had been taken off. In one innovation, the bombardment units and the approaches to the transports' anchorage were ringed by light craft equipped with hydrophones to listen for approaching submarines. Given the noise generated by activities on the surface, it is unlikely these units could have detected a submarine, but they provided reassurance to both major warships and the transports. The monitoring units were soon supplemented by an antisubmarine net laid at the entrance of Tagga Bay.

The initial landings were a success, while the bombardments silenced the Russian coastal guns looking west, although more than one battery seems to have been incapable of firing at all. The naval elements of the landing force at Pamerort immediately set about surveying and buoying the channel into Kassar Bay to allow the German flotillas' transit to contest control of the sea areas to the east. Delighted to find that Soela Sound (which was an access to the Baltic for Russian light forces) had not been mined or obstructed, the Germans started to push ships through as quickly as they could, led by four of the fast, shallow-draught *A-II* type torpedo boats.

Admiral Bakhirev understood the significance of the German threat to Kassar Bay as soon as the form of the German assault became clear.

He immediately decided on mining Soela Sound and, in the meantime, dispatched two small destroyers to patrol the approaches. The pair reported that German light craft had passed through the sound and, in a brisk action, succeeded in forcing the torpedo boats back to seek reinforcements. The German units were protected close to the sound itself by the guns of *Bayern* and the light cruiser *Emden*. Bakhirev progressively dispatched the gunboat *Grozyaschcy* and additional large destroyers, led by Rear Admiral Stark in *Desna*. Their arrival was timely as the Germans soon reinforced their *A-II*'s with more powerful destroyers. The result, with minor damage to both sides, was something of a standoff. The Russians had no idea that *Bayern* had been forced to withdraw and would not venture within the assessed range of the German heavy guns, although the Germans soon replaced her with *Kaiser*. The Germans for their part knew that the Russians could muster overwhelming strength if they attempted to push east.

The events of 13 October confirmed the situation. Stark, now in *Novik*, had assembled a strong force of destroyers, too powerful for any German force that could pass through shallow waters of the sound. The latter were forced to reorganize, with *Kaiser* being carefully positioned so her guns could range farther into Kassar Bay than the Russians would expect. For his part, on the evening of 13 October Bakhirev sent a block ship and the minelayer *Pripyat* to close the sound. The block ship *Latvia* ran aground, while *Pripyat*'s crew refused to proceed with the operation. The ship's council objected to being asked to take on such risks. This was a clear indicator of increasing indiscipline in the fleet, although *Pripyat*'s crew were the subject of general scorn when their behavior became known. Bakhirev had little difficulty assembling a replacement crew (which may have included some original *Pripyats* seeking to expiate their fault), but the opportunity of shutting the sound completely was lost that night. By the next day, the Germans were ready to move.

Kaiser's salvoes in the late morning came as a shock to the Russians and the destroyer *Grom* received a direct hit in the engine room, which disabled her. The gunboat *Khrabryj* attempted to tow her clear, but a confused action followed between the Germans and the Russian destroyer force. The Germans had the advantage of numbers, despite having lost the services of *G101* in a grounding. Units on both sides suffered damage, but the key problem for the Russians was that *Grom* and *Khrabryj* were steadily lagging behind, a situation worsened when the tow parted. With the Germans concentrating on *Grom*, all *Khrabryj* could do was to go alongside and take off the destroyer's crew, whose discipline was rapidly breaking down. *Grom* was on fire and listing heavily, but still afloat. The Russians failed to destroy their confidential books, and as *Khrabryj* and the remaining Russian destroyers retreated, the Germans boarded *Grom* and removed a large amount of material. Critically, this included an up-to-date chart of the local minefields and coast defenses, which proved a godsend in determining where the German forces would have freedom to maneuver in the coming days. *Grom* was taken in tow by *B98*, but soon after she heeled over to port and sank, leaving much of the wreck above water. This was an important success for the Germans and the beginning of the end for the Russians. Nevertheless, German light forces were feeling the heat. *G103* had been sufficiently damaged during the day's action to require her withdrawal, while *G101* was also too badly hurt by her grounding to remain operational. The Russian minelaying effort in Kassar Bay may have been too late to be decisive, but it claimed a victim on 15 October when *B98* had her bows blown off. Attempting to keep clear of the mine danger area, some of the other destroyers ran into shallow water. *B110* got off with slight damage, but *B112* suffered punctured fuel tanks and sufficient hurt to her propellers that she, too, had to withdraw.

The next two days were something of an impasse. The Germans could not operate very far east before they came within gun range of the heavy ships in Moon Sound such as *Admiral Makarov*, but the Russians were only willing to venture westward into Kassar Bay under the cover of night. The exchanges of gunfire that occurred during daylight hours were at extended range and achieved little. Both sides found the shoal waters a menace, with two Russian destroyers suffering propeller damage on 16 October. Bakhirev considered a night attack with his remaining flotilla craft but was overruled by a combination of his commanding officers and the sailors' councils, who had what he later bitterly described as "a self-preservation complex."[27]

Meanwhile, the focus of operations shifted south. The gun batteries at Zerel that dominated the Irben Strait continued to make life difficult for the minesweepers, despite repeated bombardments by German battleships. However, the Germans had advanced far enough on land to make capture of the battery only a matter of time. Morale was rapidly breaking down among the artillery crews and their supporting infantry as they contemplated their situation. On 15 October, a small Russian force led by *Grazhdanin* appeared off the southern coast of Ösel Island, but—too weak to provide serious opposition to the German dreadnoughts—it could not prevent the battery from being abandoned after an attempt to destroy the installation.

While her consorts embarked a handful of survivors from the garrison, *Grazhdanin* bombarded the ruins of the battery to ensure nothing useful remained for German use.

The way now open for the German minesweepers, they succeeded in clearing a passage northeast toward the southern entrance to Moon Sound. The channel was only a few hundred yards wide, but the minesweepers swept a passage more than fifty nautical miles in length by sunset on 16 October. By that evening, the battleships *König* and *Kronprinz* were at anchor to the west of Ösel Island, with supporting craft anchored along the channel. Their transit had not been without danger. The British submarine *C27* had entered the gulf from Moon Sound and was on patrol when she detected the German force. *C27* avoided both the mine breakers and the destroyers screening ahead of the capital ships and attacked *König*. Lieutenant Douglas Sealy underestimated the battleship's speed, however, and fired his torpedoes too close. Seen by the battleship at the last minute, they passed clear underneath. *C27* then lost depth control and broke surface astern of *König*. The Germans later claimed that the submarine was not attacked because they feared it was one of their own coastal units, which superficially resembled the British C class.[28] By the time *König* informed her escorts that she had seen the tracks of two torpedoes, it was too late. *C27* had got under again and was reloading her tubes. A second attack, on the depot ship *Indianola*, was more successful. Sealy crippled her with a single torpedo.[29] Considering the average depth of water where these attacks were conducted is barely ninety feet, it was a remarkable feat. Sealy displayed even more skill over the next two days. With only one torpedo left, he decided to escape from the gulf. On 18 October he succeeded in using *Indianola* as both his guide and cover as the depot ship was towed to be beached near Arenburg. This got him near enough to the Irben Strait to make his break. Once clear, *C27* made her way through thick fog—and at least one minefield—before arriving in Hango on 19 October.

C32, which emerged from Rogekul to take station further southeast in the gulf, was less successful. She sighted the Germans in the afternoon of 16 October, but her attempt to close for an attack on Hopman's cruiser force the next day was stymied by a seaplane, which spotted the submerged submarine in the clear water. Its bombs missed, but *C32* was forced to wait for darkness before taking up a new position south of Moon Sound. This seemed to her captain, Christopher Satow, to have the most potential. Over the following two days, *C32* unsuccessfully attacked a transport and the net-layer *Eskimo*.

Detected by *Eskimo*'s escorts, *C32* was depth charged and damaged. Critically, her compass was knocked out and the impossibility of finding a way through the maze of minefields in such condition forced Satow to consider scuttling the boat. He put her ashore outside Pernau, on the gulf's northeastern shore, only to discover that the port was still in Russian hands and *C26* was already sheltering there. By this point it was too late to salvage *C32* and the hull was demolished with explosives.

The German plan for the next day was for the cruisers *Kolberg* and *Strassburg* to push into Kleinen Sound between Ösel and Moon Island. There they could support the forces fighting on Ösel, as well as cut off any retreat by sea for the Russian forces trapped in the southeast of the island, while the battleships pressed on toward Moon Sound itself to destroy the batteries and the Russian surface forces waiting for them. Bakhirev only became aware of the German moves in the south after daylight on 17 October, but his response was immediate. While Stark's destroyers and gunboats were instructed to keep Kassar Bay secure, he gathered *Bajan*, *Slava*, and *Grazhdanin* and moved to Moon Sound's southern entrance. Bakhirev did not know that the Germans had a complete picture of his defensive minefields, but even with this advantage the advancing German forces were operating within very tight constraints. The captured Russian charts were a help, but Behncke could not trust them completely. Available sea room rapidly diminished in the approaches to Moon Sound, while the battleships and cruisers had to remain within the water cleared by the minesweepers. Bakhirev's concept was thus to use his heavy ships and the coastal batteries to keep the German sweeping effort under fire. Bakhirev's firepower, even with the batteries ashore, was much inferior to that of Behncke's two dreadnoughts, but he had an ace in hand in *Slava*'s extended-range armament. The longer a German advance could be delayed, the more options remained open to the Russians to reinforce their defensive efforts on land and weaken the German naval forces. The latter remained vulnerable to both submarines and mines, while the Russian surface forces retained considerable strength.

The morning did not start well for the Germans. *Grazhdanin* and the Moon Island and mainland batteries engaged the minesweepers. The latter continued their work, concealed as much as possible by smoke screens laid down by accompanying torpedo boats. Behncke's plan to suppress the Russian fire with the guns of his battleships received a check. When *Slava*'s shells fell close to his ships, it rapidly became apparent the elderly pre-dreadnought outranged both *König* and *Kronprinz*. Until the minesweepers

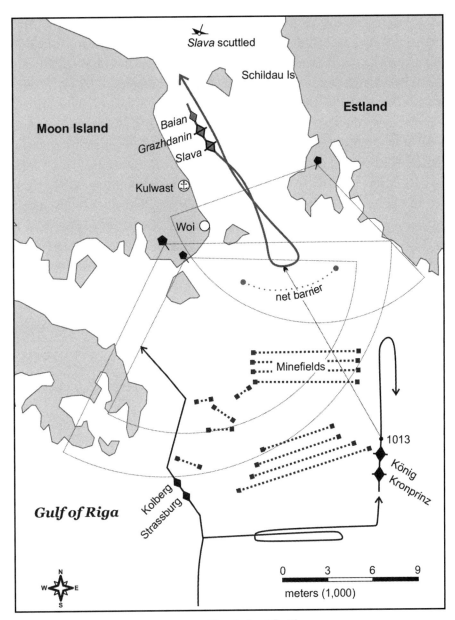

Map 11.2 *Slava*'s Last Battle

had cleared more water to the north, Behncke's battleships thus ran the
risk of being exposed to crippling fire with little room to maneuver and no
ability to reply. Behncke therefore withdrew out of range to buy time. This
was a wise decision. Although the German minesweepers were under the
combined fire of the Russian battleships, the cruiser *Bajan*, and the shore
batteries, they made steady progress. At this point, the Russian suffered a

heavy loss when *Slava*'s forward turret became unserviceable. Nevertheless, although *Slava*'s capabilities were central to the Russian effort, their tactics had already doomed them to defeat. Possibly because he could not rely on them, Bakhirev failed to make full use of the light forces in Moon Sound. If the eight available destroyers had been deployed against the German minesweepers the resultant melee would have made the German situation much more dangerous. It might even have forced the dreadnoughts to retreat. Bakhirev may have been hoping that the British submarines could make a difference. The last of the three *C* boats in the theater, *C26* under Lieutenant Basil Downie had entered the gulf through Moon Sound and was on patrol in the sound's southern approaches.

As it was, when the minesweepers had cleared a large enough area, Behncke advanced to unleash the full firepower of the two dreadnoughts. *König* engaged *Slava* while *Kronprinz* took on *Grazhdanin*. *König*'s third, tightly grouped salvo scored three hits on *Slava* and sealed her fate. Her hull penetrated, much of the fore part of the ship flooded rapidly, causing the battleship to take on a 9-degree list to port. Counter-flooding succeeded in reducing the list, but the damage accumulated rapidly as *Slava* suffered four more hits over the next half hour. She was reduced to firing occasional shots from her after turret in local control. *Grazhdanin* suffered two hits, which did some damage, but did not disable her. If the engagement continued, there could be only one end and Bakhirev ordered a withdrawal. The battleships were the first to get out of range of the Germans and the latter consequently

Gefecht im Moonsund, schwerer Einschlag am Bug vor „Kronprinz."

Photo 11.2   SMS *Kronprinz* under   *German Naval Association Archive*
                    fire in the Gulf of Riga

shifted their fire to *Bajan*, Bakhirev's flagship. The cruiser suffered one 30.5-cm hit forward, which started a large fire and forced the flooding of the forward magazine. *Bajan*'s 8-inch guns did not have the range to respond to the German battleships, although they had earlier done good work in discomfiting the minesweepers. The situation was not helped for the Russians by an attack by six German seaplanes, although these concentrated on the light forces rather than the big ships. Despite her damage, *Bajan* won clear.

Bakhirev decided on a general withdrawal. His immediate problem was *Slava*. With her extensive damage, the old battleship was in a bad way and any hope of getting her out of the Moon Sound was soon extinguished. She was drawing too much water to pass through the dredged channel. Bakhirev ordered that she be scuttled to block the passage as soon as *Grazhdanin* and *Bajan* had cleared the area and anchored in the north of Moon Sound. What followed had the same combination of bravery with muddle and dereliction of duty that had marked so many Russian operations in the previous few days. Discipline broke down among large elements of the crew during the evacuation, with the machinery spaces being prematurely abandoned. *Slava* did not block the dredged channel but grounded on one side. Charges were set in her after magazine, which blew the roof of the 30.5-cm turret off and effectively made the ship unsalvageable. Destroyers tried to finish the job with six torpedoes. Although four apparently hit, only one exploded, confirming Admiral Bakhirev's concerns about the overall readiness of his ships.[30]

Photo 11.3   *Slava* scuttled   *Sergei Vinogradov*

The German dreadnoughts made relatively short work of the coastal defenses after Bazhirev's ships cleared to the north. Within an hour, the batteries' resistance had ceased. This was just as well, because Behncke faced a new submarine threat. Although a false alarm was the cause of his getting his battleships under way again and into the midst of an antisubmarine screen, he faced *C26*, which was maneuvering to attack. The British submarine was even less fortunate than her sisters and went hard aground while trying to get into position. Forced to blow ballast to get off the shoal, *C26* broke surface and was immediately set upon by the German escort forces. She was lucky to survive the extended hunt, at one point becoming entangled in an antisubmarine net. *C26* was eventually able to get clear, but surfacing after dark, Downie realized his boat was too badly damaged to resume operations. *C26*'s only remaining refuge was Pernau, to which Downie headed the submarine in the hope of making temporary repairs. This marked the effective end of the submarine campaign against Operation Albion. The Germans had run considerable risks in bringing capital ships into the Gulf of Riga while a submarine threat still existed, but they paid off. Further, neither the British *E* class nor the Russian submarines that sortied into the Baltic had any significant successes. The repaired *E9* conducted an unsuccessful attack on two transports, while *Tigr* and *Tur*, which sailed a few days later, achieved nothing.

The withdrawal of the big ships made the position of the Russian light forces blocking Kassar Bay untenable. Admiral Stark organized the deployment of two minefields, one at the eastern end of the bay by *Bureya*, closing the access to Moon Sound and the other in the sound itself by *Pripyat*. It was too late to do anything in Kleinen Sound. By this time, the Russians had decided, with Ösel effectively lost, on complete abandonment of Moon Island. Evacuation was ordered for the next day. The Germans were eager to follow up their success. Despite the spectacular explosion of *Slava*'s after magazine, they could not be sure of the ship's condition or whether there were still major Russian units in the southern Moon Sound but they believed the Russians must be vulnerable. Three boats of the Thirteenth Half-Flotilla were therefore dispatched on a raid from Seolo Sound by Commodore Heinrich. It did not go well. *S64* struck one of *Bureya*'s mines and was immediately disabled. *S61* made a valiant attempt to tow her away, but *S64* soon went aground. It was clear that the torpedo boat was effectively a total loss. Although she damaged her own hull in getting alongside, *S61* embarked *S64*'s survivors and finished off the wreck with explosive charges. As *V74* had also suffered damage from running aground, both boats needed repair when they returned to the western end of Kassar Bay. In any case, from the evidence of *S64*'s mine strike, the way to Moon Sound was closed until the new field could be cleared. The Russians did their best to block the southern end of the dredged channel in Moon Sound by sinking four merchant ships over the next two days. In the meantime, the direction to evacuate Moon Island and destroy any remaining facilities including the base at Rogekul on the mainland had been confirmed. Bakhirev's force was increasingly vulnerable to a German attack from the north, which was precisely what Vice Admiral Schmidt was contemplating. A warning of Schmidt's intentions was issued by SNIS, and this presented an immediate problem for the Russians.

Although German operations on land were progressing well, with the invasion of Dago beginning on 19 October and meeting little resistance, the situation was more complicated for the navy. The light forces were shocked when the destroyer *B111* ran on to one of the remaining mines from the field *Pripyat* had laid a few days earlier. The weapon had been missed by the German sweeping effort. Although *B111* survived, her bows were almost ripped off, snagging the bottom and holding the ship fast until the wreckage finally broke away the next morning.[31] *B111* eventually got back to Germany for repair, but the flotillas were suffering. Repeated groundings required renewed efforts to buoy navigable channels. German and Russian light forces continued to clash. The Russian gunboats and large destroyers had an edge over their opponents, and it was apparent the German torpedo craft would need heavy support if they were to seize control of the western end of the bay and the southern waters of Moon Sound. Poor weather was making the continuing effort to sweep the sound's southern approaches very difficult. It certainly contributed to the confused positioning that resulted in the unnecessary mining of *T66*. The Germans also faced the net barrier, which lay across the part of the channel navigable by heavy ships. However, Behncke had a stroke of luck when *A62* found the big ship gate in the barrier and succeeded in opening it. By the evening of 18 October, *König* was at anchor at the entrance to Moon Sound.

The Fall of the Baltic Islands

With the Germans considering a thrust north of the islands and the Russians debating whether they should dispatch reinforcements or withdraw completely, the high commands on both sides were not finding it easy to determine a way ahead. The German operation to cut off Bakhirev's ships from their escape, employing the battleships of the Fourth Squadron, was contingent on a minesweeping effort to create sea room. The deteriorating weather delayed the start of this work by twenty-four hours, but it is doubtful, given the limitations in German numbers and capabilities, whether it was ever a practicable proposition. In any event, after an "ill tempered" signal complaining about the poor quality of Schmidt's reports, the Admiralstab intervened on 19 October to forbid the sortie outright.[32] With two battle-ships already damaged and the main operation, with its attendant risks, still under way, this was understandable. As for the Russians, Admiral Razvozov decided that he had to face the Germans if they appeared off the Gulf of Finland and dispatched preliminary orders to bring the dreadnoughts out of Helsingfors to an anchorage in the skerries. The other main formations of the fleet were also to move west to be ready to reinforce the First Battleship Brigade. Curiously, opposition to Razvozov's plan came from the Supreme Command. The latter had the old fixation on defending the Central Posi-tion and feared a major defeat at sea would open the way to Petrograd for the Germans. Razvozov's orders were canceled. The Baltic Fleet would not intervene. Ironically, the real threat to the Central Position and to the secu-rity of the capital lay not in a possible defeat at sea, but in a renewed German offensive on land. If the latter were to capture the last island of the group, Worms, and then move to the mainland, the Russians faced the loss of Reval, a lynchpin of the defense of the Gulf of Finland. Without the base and the coastal fortifications to its west, the Central Position would be untenable in the face of a sustained attack.[33]

Any prospect of a fleet action in the Baltic died with the two decisions against fleet deployment. As a "might have been" it is very difficult to judge the likely outcome. The Germans would have been running very serious risks from the Russian minefields. Even if they remained unscathed from the underwater threat, whether the Fourth Squadron's five battleships would have had a decisive tactical advantage over the four Russian dreadnoughts and any units mustered to support them is an open question. While it is highly probable the increasingly poor material state of the Russian ships would have combined with the near-chaos of their internal organization, there may have been sufficient remaining capability to make a contest of it. Russian gunnery had been as good as that of the Germans in the past (and would still be quite good in the operations of 1919 against the British),[34] and they had the advantage of a large and strong destroyer force. The Russians would have been fighting in their home waters and in direct defense of the motherland. The Admiralstab's caution may have been even better advised than it seemed at the time. With the existence of at least one minefield unknown to the Germans and the Russians' performance to that point, the British signals intelligence history has a point when it asserts, "it is not possible to dismiss the Russian fleet with a sneer."[35]

The Russians were now bent on full withdrawal from Moon Sound. Admiral Bakhirev argued that light craft should be left in the area, operating from the mainland, to contest the northern sound and prevent the Germans using the islands as a jumping-off point. He was overruled and final evacuation began on the afternoon of 19 October. It went undisturbed. With no German surface units in the vicinity, the only possible threat came from mines—continuing U-boat operations meant that the Gulf of Finland was no longer safe—and the U-boats themselves. Schmidt had deployed the three UC boats but, probably because of concerns about the Russian minefields, they were positioned too far west and north. UC58 observed and reported the movements of the Russian formations but could not get into an attack position.[36] Bakhirev sent back some small craft to help take off any remaining troops from the islands, but they could do little to reduce the chaos that saw the capture of large numbers of Russian soldiers and much equipment. Ösel, Moon, and Dago were all soon in German hands.

With Arenburg being rapidly developed as an advanced base, the German army content with its gains, and little prospect of further naval encounters, Vice Admiral Schmidt was happy to wind up his command. Although Ostfriesland and Thuringen from the First Squadron would soon arrive to replace the units sent home for repair, Schmidt proposed the battleships be withdrawn as quickly as possible. The majority of Third and Fourth Squadron units left for Kiel over the following few days, escorted by the destroyers. Apart from Schmidt's own flagship, Moltke, only Markgraf remained to support operations in the Gulf of Riga. Admiral Hopman, the senior officer with the best local knowledge, thought even this limited commitment was "pointless" when comparing the value of such ships against the pervasive mine threat.[37] Markgraf left for home on 29 October but struck two mines in the swept channel in the Irben Strait. The damage was relatively minor, however, and the flooding soon contained. Markgraf continued her voyage and repairs were relatively quickly made after the ship's return to Wilhelmshaven.[38] Nevertheless, the incident was a reminder that the theater continued to hold many dangers for the capital ships, whose utility in the new situation was in any case doubtful. Schmidt remained on station in *Moltke* for only three days more before taking his departure in company with *Ostfriesland* and *Thuringen*. On 3 November, in Danzig Bay, Schmidt shifted his flag to *Ostfriesland* and detached *Moltke* to return to the North Sea. The "Special Unit" was no more and the Baltic could be left to the cruisers and light forces that had held it for most of the conflict.

The German operation had been much more a matter of improvisation than the product of systematic doctrinal or operational developments. Nevertheless, just enough had proved good enough and the hazard of deploying a land force not of the theoretical strength required to overcome the defenses justified. The navy had accepted serious risks and three battleships had been mined, while at least two battleships and a cruiser touched ground. One torpedo boat had been sunk and two destroyers severely damaged. Eight destroyers or torpedo boats ran aground, some suffering severe damage, while no less than nine minesweepers were sunk, as were several other light craft. Many more suffered damage from shellfire, mines, or grounding. It was a list Hopman viewed with dismay.[39] Things could have been much worse, however, and the German repair bill was arguably a moderate one. Hopman's doubts about the operation were reasonable, but its value soon became clear. That Operation Albion helped undermine the last foundations of the provisional government is almost certain. The Bolshevik revolution followed the occupation of Dago Island by only a few days. An important factor in the insurgents being able to summon the armed support they needed to overthrow Kerensky and his cabinet was the promise of ending the war.

A footnote was provided by the submarine *C26*. The British feared Pernau would fall to the Germans before they could get the boat seaworthy again. Repairs were made over the next few weeks, but *C26* had to return to Pernau twice before making a success of a third departure. Even then, among other makeshifts, the submarine's main petrol pump was run by a wooden pulley. Nevertheless, *C26* got through the Irben Strait, arriving safely in Hango on 13 December, with a greatly relieved and very tired crew.[40] Her departure from Pernau was only possible because the British agreed the submarine would take no offensive action during her passage. The new revolutionary government had begun peace negotiations and wanted no possible disruption to their progress, particularly as the Germans had made it clear that ending British submarine operations in the Baltic was one of their highest priorities.

C26's quiet departure from the Gulf of Riga marked the effective end of the war at sea in the northern Baltic. The German fleet would return to these waters in 1918 as its government sought to capitalize on the dissolution of the Russian empire, the independence of Finland, and the uncertain future of the Baltic provinces. The German navy would provide cover for the occupation of the Aland Islands and find itself in an uncomfortable standoff with the Swedish fleet, but the naval conflict with Russia was essentially at an end. In the spring, after the signing of the Treaty of Brest-Litovsk, German intervention in Finland provided the final trigger for the scuttling of the British submarines outside Helsingfors. The remnants of the Russian fleet fled their old forward bases for the relative safety of Kronstadt in an operation nicknamed the "Ice March," the final echelon sailing from Helsingfors only a few days before the Germans arrived. The only other option the Germans had allowed them was their disarming and inactivation. The navy of the new Soviet state was down, yet it was not out, and 1919 would see the renewal of naval warfare in the Gulf of Finland and the northern Baltic. But this time it was the British, not the Germans, who were the enemy.

Twists and Turns

12

AS 1917 CAME TO A CLOSE, both British and Germans faced crises of strategy and command. The root cause of both problems was growing unease over lack of return on the resources being expended on the war at sea. The Allies were still suffering heavy shipping losses. Even if there were glimmers of light with the introduction of convoy and more effective antisubmarine weapons, there appeared to be a lack of initiative and resolution within the Admiralty. As for the Germans: however impressive the tonnage the U-boats claimed, they had yet to force the British to the negotiating table; there was increasing evidence that Allied antisubmarine efforts were holding the line. The campaign had become yet another facet of the war of attrition with no end in sight. The six months' deadline had long since been discredited and the implications of the convoy system began to sink in as early as July.[1] U-boats losses became an anxiety.[2] September was a particularly bad month, with ten boats sunk by comparison with five in August and five in July.[3] October provided only temporary comfort before losses rose again in November. New construction could keep the numbers up, but only just. The navy admitted reality as early as June when orders for ninety-five U-boats were placed. The majority were the small and relatively quickly built *UB* and *UC* types, although ten large "cruiser" boats were included to increase pressure on the Americans in their home waters. Labor and materials were in short supply, however, and the Reichs-Marine-Amt had to reorder its priorities and seek support from the army high command. Even this program would not be enough if U-boat losses continued at the increased rate, since it would only provide replacements without achieving an increase in numbers and the attendant ability to sink Allied shipping at a higher rate.

There were other consequences. According the U-boats priority meant something had to give. The High Sea Fleet added only the battle cruiser

Hindenburg in 1917. It would get no more big ships. Construction of the last two *Bayern*-class battleships stalled, as did that of the new battle cruisers. The light cruiser and torpedo boat programs also slowed significantly. Only one cruiser joined the fleet in 1917 and two in 1918. Even if Russia left the war, removing any threat in the Baltic, the disparity of strength between the British and the German battle fleets would only grow. The British, however, consistently overestimated Germany's production capacity, believing reports that the yard concerned was "forcing work on the battleship *Saschen* night and day."[4]

There was also a psychological element at play. The promise of a six-month campaign had been accepted by the fleet and by the German population as well. All now faced the prospect of a conflict with no apparent end in worsening conditions. The strain showed itself in mutiny on board the battleship *Prinzregent Luitpold*. At the end of July fifty stokers broke out of the ship in protest against additional drills. Although they soon returned, a number were confined and this triggered a mass walkout by junior sailors. Unrest spread to other ships in the Fourth Squadron, including the former fleet flagship, *Friedrich der Grosse*. This was what the High Sea Fleet's command feared. There had been rumblings of discontent during the "turnip winter," with inadequate food and dispiriting routines at the center of both individual complaints and occasional collective disobedience, and they became louder after the events in Russia. Although Admiral Scheer permitted establishment of a "Food Complaints Committee" in each big ship, the first Russian revolution and the part played in it by sailors loomed much larger in the minds of many. While the High Sea Fleet's command remained insensitive to the indiscipline's root causes, it was acutely aware of the need to maintain its authority and equally alert to the significance of events in Russia. Scheer's response to the unrest was immediate, with heavy sentences meted out to the mutineers, culminating in the execution of two ringleaders. They were shot on 5 September in what many regarded as judicial murder, and much of whatever confidence the lower deck of the High Sea Fleet's major units still had in their leadership died with them.[5]

There was no shadowy fleet organization behind the events of July and August 1917, just deepening discontent and longing for the war to end.[6] Measures were taken to improve the sailors' food and moderate officers' privileges, but the fundamental causes of discontent particular to the High Sea Fleet remained and were combining with the war-weariness of the civilian population. The fleet's frequent presence in Wilhelmshaven and

Kiel meant its junior personnel had opportunities to interact with elements ashore and the lower deck's political awareness increased steadily. The fleet's leadership was dimly aware of this development but ascribed it to external subversion, probably funded by the British. There were more disturbances in the autumn, although on a much smaller scale. They were also dealt with harshly; sentences to punishment battalions in Flanders were common.[7] Only the deployment of a good part of the fleet to the Baltic for Operation Albion and its success, albeit at a price, achieved a temporary improvement in morale.

The British were not immune to trouble on the lower deck, but their problems related more directly to the way the war at sea was being fought—and how this appeared to government and people. The immediate U-boat crisis had passed, although the toll in shipping and the continuing absence of fully effective weapons and sensors remained sources of anxiety. The first difficulty for the Admiralty was that much of the navy's work was unspectacular. Even its offensive measures were largely indirect in effect, as evidenced by mine warfare. The war of attrition now included the struggle over the Heligoland Bight, as the British sought to close it and the Germans tried to keep open passages for their submarines. The British minelaying effort was not random. The Germans understood the intent of the British declaration on 25 June that the "Notified Mined Area" in the Bight had been extended by one degree to 57° N and westward to 4° E. Hopes that the neutrals would force the British to revoke the declaration were soon dashed. A compromise reached in late July reduced the notified area only marginally and brought the establishment of a buoyed and lit channel along its western edge maintained by the Dutch. This channel resulted in further controlling the movement of merchant shipping—as well as providing useful navigational aids to the British. The effect of the British move, Scheer noted, was to extend the channels Germany required to be kept clear by twenty to twenty-five miles. This was a serious matter. He commented, "We barely had sufficient ships to ascertain where mines were laid."[8] By the end of 1917, minesweepers were operating up to 150 miles away from the main anchorages.

Room 40 worked to understand the location of the German passages and their patterns of use through analysis of the U-boats' signals reporting their movements and the U-boat command's messages arranging for them to be escorted through the swept channels. However, the British mining effort could accelerate only slightly after the fallow months of summer. Production of the new H2 mine increased steadily but slowly, while minelayers had to be modified to carry it. Even then, problems were encountered as the new weapon was heavier than its predecessors.[9] Nevertheless, the 4,169 mines laid between August and December were enough to burden the German minesweeping forces. Their own losses were still moderate but they were accumulating, while British mines took a toll of the escorts essential when the sweepers were operating so far out. *G37* was sunk by a mine in November. The strain was beginning to tell.

The British soon appreciated that minesweepers were targets. A fleeting engagement on 16 August followed a Harwich Force sweep to find German sweepers along the western side of the mined areas in the southern Heligoland Bight. The destroyer *Surprise* unexpectedly encountered *A36* and the British unsuccessfully chased the torpedo boat to the edge of the mined area. Tyrwhitt was beginning to withdraw when one of his ships sighted what the Harwich Force "took to be three German battle cruisers" (although he only admitted to "cruisers" in his report).[10] The British immediately laid down a smoke screen and prepared to flee westward, but realized their opponents were merely German minesweepers and turned to pursue them. The chase was confused by the British smoke and repeated phantom periscope sightings. Although *M4*, *M37*, and *M65* were hit, Tyrwhitt was forced to withdraw when his ships again approached the mined area. The German ships had a narrow escape, one that they only tentatively ascribed to the British fear of their own minefields.[11] Von Hipper was displeased with the commander of the covering force, Commander Regensburg in the light cruiser *Frankfurt* failed to intervene with his two light cruisers and torpedo boats. Regensburg was removed from command.

The entrances to the northern German channels were discovered by the submarine *E31* in mid-August and this information provided an important boost to the mining campaign, with a major operation on 20–21 August. Hitherto, the British had concentrated on the southern routes, largely because these provided the shortest passage to the U-boats' favored operating areas. Nevertheless, as shown by the earlier sweeping operation, the ability to operate in this area was an abiding concern for Beatty and he intervened to cancel at least one major lay later in the year to maintain that freedom of maneuver.[12] This was the other element to the British effort, typified by the Battle Cruiser Force's sortie on 5–6 September to cover a sweeping operation to the Horns Reef by new Flower-class minesweeping sloops. This was intended to create sea room for the British to cut German surface forces off from the Bight if they were detected operating closer to the

Photo 12.1   German minesweeper at sea   *German Naval Association Archive*

British coast. The tension between maintaining operational space to allow offensive surface action and prosecuting the mine campaign was never fully resolved. By late 1917, Commodore Tyrwhitt believed "he could not be off the German coasts with his light cruisers because he could not now get there."[13] Time-limited mines with soluble plugs that would cause the mines to sink after a specified number of days (usually thirty-eight) were an attempt to fix this problem, but inherent navigational errors and the limits of technology meant it could not readily be solved.

Crisis at Sea—Crisis in Whitehall

Given the continuing challenge of the U-boats and that the mining campaign was largely unknown, the Royal Navy's bank of credit with politicians and public had eroded substantially. A series of failures that raised doubts as to the Admiralty's grip on the operational situation further undermined the position of the First Sea Lord and his key associates. The first was one of omission. Despite continuing turmoil in Russia, naval intelligence links remained strong. Kerensky, leader of the embattled Russian government, knew the British were well informed regarding the probability of a German attack on the Baltic islands before winter set in. As the German force was assembling in October 1917, Kerensky appealed for a diversionary operation against the Germans in the Baltic on a scale that would force them to abandon their amphibious venture. Jellicoe ordered a review by the Plans Division. Their report rejected an attack on the Baltic passages by major units. The judgments about the effort required for either an amphibious assault or a purely naval raid were fair, but the study went on to dismiss very much more limited efforts. The Grand Fleet might conduct demonstrations in the North Sea and the Kattegat, but nothing more. After the Baltic islands fell, the First Lord's declaration in parliament on 1 November that a British attack on the Baltic would have been "madness" did not leave a good taste in the public's mouth.[14]

Another failure was embodied in the successful German surface attack on a westbound Scandinavian convoy early on the morning of 17 October. Intelligence had been accumulating about the convoys between Scotland and Norway, and the High Sea Fleet believed a raid would disrupt an important transport route and take the initiative away from the British when German forces in the North Sea had been reduced to provide for the Baltic. The fast minelaying cruisers *Brummer* and *Bremse* were selected, as much for their heavy 150-mm armament and superficial resemblance to British light cruisers as their speed. The British had enough intelligence about a possible German move to deploy every available light cruiser squadron, accompanied by destroyers, as well as the carrier *Furious* into the North Sea. With German intentions uncertain, the Harwich Force was also sent out in strength. The British assumed a minelaying operation was intended. Unfortunately, although later intercepts began to build a picture of a much more ambitious operation, the Admiralty failed to pass on its developing appreciation to the C-in-C in good time—and may have failed to make the necessary connections itself.[15] Although some later commentary suggested the problem was Room 40 did not have access to the operational plot showing the British formations and convoys, "This entirely begs the fact that Operations did keep such a plot and did have the benefit of all Room 40's information."[16]

Brummer and *Bremse* fell on the convoy before dawn on 17 October. The twelve merchant ships and their escort of two destroyers had little hope, although the pair of accompanying trawlers were more fortunate. The response of *Strongbow* and her consort *Mary Rose* suggested not only that the Germans achieved complete surprise but the destroyers were ill prepared for surface attack. *Strongbow*, astern of the widely scattered convoy, sighted unknown ships to the south. Her captain and his officers could not identify the new German ships, at first thinking they might be British or even Norwegian.[17] *Strongbow* repeatedly attempted to challenge but went to action stations only as the Germans made a makeshift response to the third challenge by light. This was too late. *Brummer* and *Bremse* opened fire and rapidly disabled

Strongbow, which was unable to make an effective reply. The German ships then looked for the convoy and soon disposed of nine of its twelve ships. *Mary Rose*, well ahead of the rest of the formation, heard the gunfire but had little idea what was happening. Her captain may have believed a U-boat attack was in progress when he turned back. The undermanned destroyer was first sighted by *Brummer*, which opened fire at a little over eight thousand yards. *Mary Rose* replied in kind and the Germans reported she "shot remarkably fast and well," hitting *Brummer* once, although causing only superficial damage.[18] There could only be one end; struck at least fifteen times and so enveloped in smoke and flames her opponents thought *Mary Rose* had deployed smoke makers, the British destroyer rolled over and sank. The German cruisers then sought to finish off the stationary *Strongbow*. Their commander, Leonhardi, decided to withdraw after the British ship had been rendered completely hors de combat, although still afloat. *Strongbow* was eventually scuttled by her crew rather than risk the ship being made a prize. Survivors from both destroyers were picked up by the antisubmarine trawlers that went unseen by the Germans. Reports of the action only got through to British authorities after the trawler *Elise* found the escort of the eastbound convoy. The information was too late to give much chance of intercepting the homeward-bound Germans. All but one of the British cruiser-destroyer groups were west or north of the intended track of *Brummer* and *Bremse*, making any interception a stern chase that could not succeed. Only the ships of the Sixth Light Cruiser Squadron, originally just sixty miles off the coast of Denmark, might have straddled the German track in time, but they headed west when they should have turned east. Given that the British effort included all three "large light cruisers," as well as no less than twenty-seven light cruisers and fifty-four destroyers, it was a dispiriting result.

Beatty summed up only part of the problem when he declared, the destroyers "were not very bright, never expecting a thing, they never having seen one [an enemy surface ship] during the past 3 years, and became an easy prey."[19] *Strongbow*'s response was certainly tardy, but the case against *Mary Rose* is less clear. In their post-action assessment, the British were critical of the failure of both ships to buy the necessary time to report the presence of the enemy force; but, probably still concerned with the U-boat threat, *Mary Rose* did not understand what she faced until she sighted *Brummer*.[20] She made a report, but the first transmission, while heard by a shore station, was incomprehensible. *Brummer* jammed the repeated message, an action that was standard German procedure and for which they were well prepared.

The real concern was that the British had failed to take adequate precautions against a contingency increasingly likely when the Scandinavian convoy system proved effective. Criticism in the press was justified, whatever the difficulties of preventing such hit-and-run raids. With the opportunities the long darkness of winter gave German raiders lying ahead, the British had to provide effective cover. This was not simple, given the strain on the forces available. The immediate response was to assign the First Cruiser Squadron to protect the first convoy cycle after the raid. Armored cruisers were a longer-term solution, but while this provided a role for units of otherwise limited utility in the North Sea, more would be needed if the Germans attacked again. There was also the requirement to ensure that escorts knew what to do. Beatty closed the stable door a fraction with explicit instructions that the primary task in the event of a surface attack was not a defense against odds but to report the presence of the enemy. He also impressed upon ships the need for greater alertness to the possibility that any unidentified surface contact might be hostile. This was fair enough, but the British had yet to solve the admittedly complex problem of ensuring full awareness of the presence of other friendly forces among the units at sea. There were still too many unexpected encounters.

The convoy debacle was quickly followed by another incident that showed information sharing lacked the systematic approach essential under the new conditions. Partly in response to the German raid and partly to do something to support the Russian defense of the Baltic Islands, Beatty determined upon a sweep into the Kattegat to attack the antisubmarine patrols and torpedo boats believed to be escorting merchant ships and transiting U-boats. Five light cruisers and thirteen destroyers would conduct the operation, covered by the First Battle Cruiser Squadron. Delayed by a week, Operation AG got under way on 1 November.[21] The small armed merchant cruiser *Kronprinz* and ten trawlers (most of which were fishing boats, not patrol vessels) were sunk by destroyers of the Fifteenth Flotilla, but this was not the result wanted, either materially or morally.[22]

The Second Battle of Heligoland Bight

Thus, when the Admiralty believed it had strong intelligence of minesweeping operations well to seaward in the Heligoland Bight, the opportunity to attack not only the sweepers but the light cruisers protecting them could not be missed. There were repeated attempts to stage such an operation in early November, but these were stymied by the precautionary movements required by reports that the Germans intended to raid the east coast.[23] The British units finally sailed on 16 November and approached the Bight in the early hours of 17 November. Covered from the west by the First Battle Cruiser Squadron, reinforced by *New Zealand*, the First and Sixth Light Cruiser Squadrons and their destroyer flotillas were also supported by *Courageous* and *Glorious*. Vice Admiral Napier in *Courageous* was effectively in tactical command, given that Pakenham was so far astern. Napier's flag commander claimed many years later, "We did not know we were acting on practically certain information that the cruisers and sweepers would be there. It was the usual routine sweep,"[24] but the contemporary evidence suggests otherwise. Aware that the sortie was "based on fairly definite information of the enemy's movements," ships such as *Glorious* were expecting action.[25]

Two critical factors would be the minefields and the U-boat threat. The Royal Navy's promulgation of mine danger areas turned out to be extraordinarily hit-and-miss for this stage of the war. All concerned had very different ideas of the parameters of their safe operating areas. Only the C-in-C and the battle cruisers' commander had a full picture. Napier's knowledge was incomplete. Although he had enough information to allow him to go east past "Line A," which was the usual prohibition, and believed he also had sufficient knowledge to move if necessary past "Line B," which made provision for recent British minefields, he was governed by a direction not to proceed farther east than "Line C," which encompassed an area starting a few miles east of longitude 6° 30′ east. The charts of the two light cruiser squadron commanders were different again and did not include Line C. Furthermore, there was little information as to the nature of the mined areas. That covered by Line C related to British mines laid as long before as 1915, but Napier had no details of this.[26] By this time, the deficiencies of the older British mines was so well known that even the most cautious commander could discount their lethality after more than two years in the water.

The Germans had deployed fourteen minesweepers and two mine breakers, escorted by eight torpedo boats of the Seventh Flotilla and four light cruisers of the Second Scouting Group, commanded by Rear Admiral Ludwig von Reuter in *Königsberg*. The battleships *Kaiserin* and *Kaiser* (known as "the married couple") were providing heavy cover, although at sixty miles away, they were stationed much farther south east than was ideal. Contact was made just before dawn. Conditions were relatively good, with slight seas and little wind. Although the morning was hazy, the British had the initial advantage that the rising sun was behind the Germans and

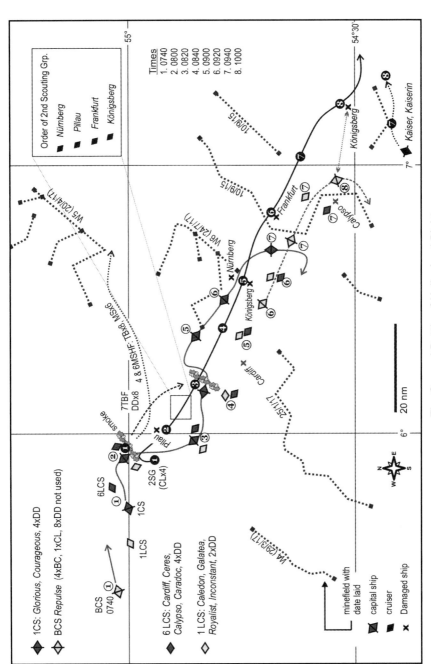

Map 12.1 The Second Battle of Heligoland Bight

silhouetted them, but they would have preferred an initial contact at closer range. Further, the British had hoped to find the Germans to their north, offering the possibility of cutting them off from their bases, but they saw them in the east. Like the Dogger Bank in 1915, this would be a stern chase, although the British took some time to realize it. Opening fire at ranges between 10,000 and 12,000 yards, *Courageous* and *Glorious* took on the enemy light cruisers with the First Light Cruiser Squadron's support, while the Sixth Light Cruiser Squadron initially went for the sweepers and light craft. Napier maneuvered to clear his big ships from each other and from the light cruisers, desperate to see what the Germans were doing. He did not take advantage of the large light cruisers' speed of over thirty knots, never ordering them to more than twenty-five. Given Napier's need to keep clear of the smoke screens, this meant he could not close the range quickly enough. Although at one point the admiral took the brave step of pushing directly into the smoke, failure to exploit the large light cruisers' speed was significant since the British light cruisers, particularly the newer *C*-class units, had little or no speed advantage over their German opposite numbers. Walter Cowan, commanding the First Light Cruiser Squadron, complained, "I tried & tried but each time you altered in they drew ahead & guns wdn't [*sic*] bear. . . . My telegraphs were put full speed when we sighted them & never touched until after we'd fled West again."[27]

Surprised as the Germans were to find 15-inch shells falling among them, von Reuter's light cruisers moved to protect the minesweepers. All the German units rapidly made smoke or deployed smoke canisters, creating exactly the problems for British gunnery and maneuvering they were meant to. Matters were not helped for the British by repeated false sightings of diving U-boats, which would be a threat should a British unit close their position. What followed over the next two hours was a long-range action in which the British forces never succeeded in getting to grips with the enemy, while the Germans made their retreat at the cost of only one trawler in the early stages of the battle. Von Reuter took risks, delaying his own withdrawal to ensure that none of the light craft were left behind and deliberately taking his ships through waters believed dangerous because of British mines. Nevertheless, within fifteen minutes of the first encounter, "all enemy vessels were well hidden"[28] and this largely remained the case. The British were frequently baffled by the thick smoke, which they did not again risk breaking through. They were torn between the assumption that the Germans were retreating along their own swept channel, which could be considered safe water, and the fear the smoke screens would conceal either waiting torpedo craft or U-boats. Still unsure what von Reuter was doing, when Napier arrived at Line B just before 0840, he turned and headed northeast for twelve minutes before deciding to resume the chase until Line C. The German light cruisers had continued their retreat, however, and the gain of four miles they made from Napier's turn was crucial.

Meanwhile, the fast and heavily armed battle cruiser *Repulse* had been detached by Pakenham and allowed to move ahead. Her four-knot speed advantage could be very important and she used all of it. Napier's turn at 0840 meant *Repulse*, now to the south of the First Cruiser Squadron, took the lead from *Courageous* and *Glorious*, drawing farther ahead as her extra knots told. The First and Sixth Light Cruiser Squadrons, largely unaware of the mine restrictions that preoccupied Napier, also continued onward. Rear Admiral Phillimore, in *Repulse*, received a warning from Pakenham about mine danger at Line B, but ignored it, asking for a repetition of the signal to buy time.[29]

Pakenham in *Lion* was increasingly worried by the growing risks of continuing southeast. At 0908 he issued a general recall. Napier, believing the Germans had received reinforcements and that his move inside Line B committed him to seize what chances offered from the risk he had accepted, decided to continue, reported to Pakenham that there were additional enemy units, and remained in contact. Napier would have known that the chase could not continue much longer. The closer the German coast, the greater the danger. A disabled ship would soon fall prey to forces emerging from the inner Bight. The ever-greater proximity of the land was confirmed by the appearance of aircraft that bombed the British ships. They were only an irritation (some British captains thought they were causing damage) but further complicated an increasingly complex situation.[30] The British had reason to worry. The battle cruisers *Hindenburg* and *Moltke* had sailed at 0840 and they were followed out at 1000 by the battleships *Friedrich der Grosse*, with Vice Admiral Souchon embarked, and *König Albert*.

Although von Reuter's tactics to this point had been wholly defensive, he clearly hoped to cripple his opponents, so they could be finished off by these reinforcements. He had some justification. *Cardiff* of the Sixth Light Cruiser Squadron had already been hit several times. In the First, *Caledon* had been struck, while *Royalist*'s flying-off platform was clipped by a 150-mm shell. The British believed they were scoring hits themselves, despite the ineffectiveness of the 4-inch carried by the older light cruisers.[31] While expenditure of 6-inch ammunition was substantial, more than 2,500 rounds being fired, the results were limited. *Pillau* took a 15-inch shell on one of her 150-mm mounts; it did not explode but knocked the gun out of action and caused nine casualties. *Frankfurt* suffered two 6-inch hits, with twenty-three casualties. Although the British destroyers tried to position for torpedo attacks, the geometry did not allow it and only one weapon was fired. The Germans, on the other hand, fired several torpedoes, but the range and a piecemeal approach did not help. *Galatea* may have been struck under the bridge by a torpedo that failed to explode, but the Germans made no other hits. When wakes were seen, the British frequently assumed the torpedoes had been fired by U-boats, while both *Glorious* and *Repulse* thought they had seen submarines (*Glorious* later admitted these were small craft). No unit on either side had yet been disabled—but if this occurred it would immediately change the entire situation.

The action approached its culmination at approximately 0930, when *Kaiserin* and *Kaiser* finally came in sight of von Reuter from the southeast. Captain Kurt Grasshof in *Kaiserin* saw his task as covering the advanced forces' retreat, not taking offensive advantage of the situation. He may have been overly conscious of the weight of metal he faced. The Germans were well aware of the superiority of the 15-inch gun over the 30.5-cm, but this discounted the battleships' heavy protection. Furthermore, this was the nearest thing yet to the defensive action in the Heligoland Bight the High Sea Fleet had always wanted. Von Reuter attempted to order Grasshof to advance northwest, but the admiral's signals were not received and the battleships almost immediately turned east, toward the Second Scouting Group. Under the circumstances, a frustrated von Reuter had to continue his retreat. Only the British light cruisers continuing their advance allowed the battleships to engage the Sixth Light Cruiser Squadron at approximately 0948. Just before this, the Germans scored their most important hit, one that confirmed the risks the British were running. Although *Caledon* was shortly afterward struck on the waterline by a 30.5-cm shell that failed to explode, it was a 150-mm round that hit *Calypso*'s forward superstructure, killing her captain and most of her bridge personnel. The ship was kept under control by the gunnery officer in the foretop, who used the transmitting station to pass orders to the wheel in the lower conning tower.[32]

In the meantime, at 0932 Napier had reached Line C and turned south. This was not well received in *Glorious*, where "Our Captain 'Dusty' Miller fumed up and down our bridge. Apparently we had direct orders not to follow up and everybody was waiting to rush in."[33] Napier's quandary was reflected in his inquiry to the light cruiser commanders whether they could achieve a successful conclusion to their pursuit, while at the same time he ordered *Repulse* to advance no further; the battle cruiser may have been as unaware as the light cruisers of the existence of Line C. In any event, Rear Admiral Phillimore continued the pursuit and eventually brought the Second Scouting Group under fire, providing important support to the British light cruisers. It is possible that had *Repulse* not been present, Grasshof in *Kaiserin* might have been more enterprising—particularly as the German force was now joined by four destroyers of the Second Flotilla just returned from a sweep to the Dogger Bank. Von Reuter would certainly have acted differently. *Repulse*'s only material achievement was a single hit on the *Königsberg*, but this had important consequences. Penetrating a bunker and damaging a boiler room and all three funnels, the shell started a serious fire, which soon enveloped the cruiser in smoke. With *Königsberg*'s speed reduced to seventeen knots, the situation on board was confused and von Reuter's ideas of turning to face the pursuit at least temporarily frustrated. *Königsberg*'s problems contributed to the difficulty of convincing Grasshof to be more aggressive, but von Reuter's direction to his ships to continue south-southeast itself meant the action was effectively over. Rear Admiral Alexander-Sinclair in *Cardiff* had responded to the battleships' salvoes by turning away and Commodore Cowan in *Caledon* followed suit. The opposed forces opened rapidly from each other, while the sudden descent of thick fog ended any chance of the action's immediate resumption. *Hindenburg* and *Moltke* had made their best speed to join—the aging *Moltke*, ominously, could not keep up with her new squadronmate—but they did not venture farther after they found von Reuter. The Germans finally turned back to the northwest only after Admiral Souchon arrived with his two battleships in the afternoon. This was possibly in the hope of finding British stragglers, but there was nothing to be seen and the force returned to harbor that evening.

The Germans had their own recriminations. Von Reuter was concerned by the state of training in his light cruisers, believing the loss of experienced sailors to U-boats contributed to signaling problems. Apart from *Kaiserin* and *Kaiser* being too far south to provide effective cover for von Reuter's forces, they had also lost an opportunity to inflict punishment on the advanced British cruisers that might have achieved an important success for the Germans. Although both Admiralstab and the fleet command were critical of Grasshof's performance, he was let down lightly, soon being sent ashore as senior German naval officer at Pola. The British may have drawn satisfaction from reports that Captain Grasshof had been relieved of command and court-martialed, but they had their own problems to deal with.[34] Napier was subjected to bitter criticism. Much was justified, but opinion was not unanimous. Pakenham was particularly critical of the risks taken by Phillimore in *Repulse*, although Beatty endorsed his actions.[35] The British were once more forced to recognize that neither their doctrine nor their exercises had prepared ships for such difficult conditions. Where Napier had clearly erred—in the view of Admiralty, C-in-C, and the service's opinion—was in failing to use the speed of *Courageous* and *Glorious*. His somewhat lame explanation lends credibility to a later comment, "as a light-cruiser admiral he was accustomed to think of 25 knots as the battle speed and forgot how much faster he could go if he wanted to—which seems rather feeble."[36] Despite his own disappointment, Beatty mixed his official strictures with private reassurance to Napier that, "I have perfect confidence in your ability and determination to deal with any situation that may arise in the future."[37] The deficiencies in planning and tactics that had been revealed could not be concealed, even if public criticism was directed at the Admiralty, rather than the Grand Fleet, where blame really lay. While censorship limited commentary, it could not constrain the wider press campaign against the Admiralty—or close the fissure developing between Eric Geddes (the new First Lord) and Jellicoe. The latter had to fight off Geddes' attempts to make Napier an immediate scapegoat. The First Lord even suggested Lord Fisher lead an inquiry, a step that Jellicoe pointed out would create "great ill feeling in the fleet." Geddes acquiesced, but then dispatched a telegram to Beatty that seemed to criticize the C-in-C and cast doubt on his ability to convene a disinterested court. It was not well received.[38]

The Germans Respond

Scheer set new constraints for the minesweeping operations, which included the requirement for air surveillance to be available. Because of the problems with zeppelins, this provided new impetus to modifying additional seaplane carriers. The High Sea Fleet's light forces in the North Sea had got back to full strength by the beginning of December, with the return of the flotillas from the Baltic and the completion of repairs to the units that had grounded or suffered action damage there. Scheer now approved a raid by the Second Flotilla, whose big destroyers were proving very effective offensive weapons.

This would be two-pronged, with one half-flotilla attacking shipping in the war channel on the northeast coast of England, while the second had another crack at a Scandinavian convoy. The cruiser *Emden* led out the eight destroyers that were detached when the formation reached the North Dogger Bank lightship. *B97, B109, B110,* and *B112* made for the coast north of the Tyne. As they approached, Heinecke, their commander in *B97,* was provided by Neumünster with reports of the forces operating in the area which, critically, declared that a southbound convoy was due to leave the Firth of Forth. There were convoys heading south in the war channel, but these were farther away from the Firth than Heinecke's information led him to expect. In poor weather and without coastal lights—itself indication there was no convoy in the immediate vicinity—the German formation groped its way along the coast, at last encountering the Danish steamer *Peter Willemoes,* a straggler from a convoy thirty miles ahead. They sank the ship with torpedoes, although *B97* suffered the mortification of firing two weapons that failed to explode before *B112* made certain of the job with two more. The Germans later sank another straggler, the Swedish *Nike,* and destroyed a small coastal steamer with gunfire, but did not find the main body from which the stragglers had come. With dawn approaching, the half-flotilla could do no more, and at 0440 Heinecke turned for home. It took the British many hours to piece together the story and realize that a surface force had operated so close to the coast.

Meanwhile, the Third Half-Flotilla under Lieutenant Commander Hans Kolbe, consisting of *G101, G103, G104,* and *V100,* had been heading north to close the Norwegian coast and cross the convoy route. They encountered an eastbound convoy of six small merchant ships escorted by the destroyers *Partridge* and *Pellew* and four armed trawlers. The searchlight on board *Partridge* required to make a long-range challenge in daytime was defective and ten minutes were consumed before *Partridge* could be certain that the unknown ships were hostile. In the lee position with a strong northwesterly in their teeth, the gunnery of the British destroyers was much less effective than that of the Germans, recently subjected to intense training by their commodore.[39] While *G104,* limited in speed by a leaking condenser, worked around to attack the convoy, the other three made short work of *Partridge.* Her main steam pipe severed, she was soon stopped and helpless. *Partridge's* survivors succeeded in firing a torpedo, which they believed struck a German unit but failed to explode, while others made sure of the ship sinking as the enemy approached. The Third Half-Flotilla had no intention of making a capture, however, and finished *Partridge* off with torpedoes. *Pellew*, meanwhile, had been partly disabled by hits that opened up her port engine room. Flooding rapidly, *Pellew* was enveloped by a merciful squall. With little hope of achieving anything against a force so superior, she made her way toward the Norwegian coast. Kolbe did not attempt to relocate *Pellew*, but focused on his principal target, the six ships of the convoy. They and their escorting trawlers were rapidly finished off. Kolbe did not hang around; he turned south to clear the area.

Partridge did her job in one important respect. She sent an enemy contact report that, even if vague in detail and mutilated in transmission, made it clear there was an enemy force close to the convoys' eastern rendezvous. The Germans did not completely succeed in jamming its transmission. The message was taken in, not by its intended recipient, the C-in-C, but by the cruiser *Shannon*. This was senior ship of the covering force consisting of two armored cruisers and four destroyers meant to defend the convoy against such attack but, being sixty miles to the west, it was too far away. The Germans completed their destruction only seventy-three minutes after first sighting the smoke of their quarry.[40] Furthermore, neither *Pellew*, the senior officer, nor *Partridge* had been aware of the covering force. This continuing failure to make units aware of the full "friendly picture" was one reason for units to be fatally slow to identify an unknown contact as the enemy. Although Captain Molteno in *Shannon* headed east as fast as he could with his armored cruisers and sent the destroyers ahead, there was no hope of intercepting the Germans. That task rested with the Third Light Cruiser Squadron patrolling farther south off the Norwegian coast. *Partridge*'s report was taken in by *Rival*, listening out on the destroyer wavelength and passed to *Birkenhead*, senior ship of a force of three cruisers and four destroyers. Captain L. C. S. Woollcombe turned his force north-northwest and spread his ships out as an observation line. Despite well-judged dispositions, Woollcombe missed Kolbe by a few miles. The latter, concerned by heavy weather approaching from the northwest and worried that *G104*'s machinery might give up altogether, decided to make for home through the Kattegat. This put his course close to the Norwegian coast and meant he passed unseen to the east of the British force about an hour after sunset. Only an hour later, Woollcombe realized he must have missed the Germans and put his ships into night formation. The sole survivor of the convoy, *Pellew*, was forced to shelter overnight in Norwegian waters, where her severely depleted engine room staff made repairs; she was assisted by the destroyer *Sabrina*, sent to help by *Shannon*. There were some complications about the status of *Pellew* in a neutral port, but she was allowed to complete her repairs and leave. The two destroyers found *Shannon* later that day, after which all the covering force could do was protect the still crippled *Pellew* as she made her way back to Scapa Flow.

Beatty had sent out other units as soon as *Partridge*'s report (relayed by *Shannon*) came in, a move backed by the Admiralty when it became aware of the east coast action. Since *Partridge*'s signal gave no indication of the enemy force's composition, both C-in-C and Admiralty had to assume a movement by the High Sea Fleet was in progress. Thus, not only were substantial elements of the Battle Cruiser Force dispatched as quickly as possible, but the remainder of the Grand Fleet and the Harwich Force were brought to short notice for sea. This was not rescinded until what had happened was understood. The British had much to chew on. The press seized upon the new reverse to cast further doubt on the Admiralty's competence, while the operational commanders had to consider very carefully how to prevent further failures of this kind. Beatty himself was shocked; he had not thought the Germans would send destroyers out so far by themselves. He also felt that neither intelligence support nor the Admiralty's coordination efforts had been efficient, points put forcibly to Rear Admiral Hall, the DNI, a few days later.[41] For the Germans, the two sorties had been well worth the risk, even if the results from the east coast raid were limited. The recurrence of *G104*'s condenser problems was a worry, as it was largely due to the deteriorating quality of the metal in pipes and valves, indication of the problems of machinery reliability the High Sea Fleet now faced.

The Harwich Force and Dover Command under Strain

A week after the convoy disaster, the Harwich Force suffered its worst night of the war. Two divisions of destroyers were protecting the "Beef trip" on the evening of 22 December, with the leader *Valkyrie* and four destroyers escorting an eastbound convoy, while *Nimrod* and four more destroyers provided cover to the north. Unknown to the British, the previous evening thirteen units of the Flanders flotillas had emerged, taking advantage of the longest night of the year to deploy 144 mines across the assessed route of the convoys, close to the Dutch coast but outside territorial waters. The mission was conducted successfully, without the British picking up any hint that the Germans had been at sea. *Valkyrie* was the first to trigger two mines, at 2215. The ship was lucky to stay afloat, her back almost broken aft of the bridge. *Sylph* stood by the *Valkyrie*, providing medical assistance and eventually taking the stricken destroyer leader in tow to Harwich. Worse followed. *Nimrod* and her consorts were circling the rendezvous north of the Maas Light Buoy in the early hours of 23 December as they awaited the ships in the westbound convoy. Shortly after 0200, as the force headed south to find their new charges, the destroyer *Torrent* exploded a mine. *Surprise* and *Tornado* immediately turned to give assistance. *Torrent* had already developed a heavy list and was sinking when she struck a second mine, which finished her off. The British did not appreciate the true threat, believing *Torrent* had been torpedoed by a U-boat. This at least meant that *Radiant* stayed clear of *Torrent*'s vicinity while she searched for the enemy. While *Surprise* continued to pick up survivors, *Tornado* moved to join *Radiant*. She was no sooner out of sight of *Surprise* when she detonated two mines and sank. *Surprise* then also struck a mine and quickly sank, her captain only surviving because he was blown overboard and picked up by the ship's whaler, already in the water.

Radiant's captain did not hesitate to return for the survivors. While this may have been because of the belief the work had been done by a submarine, *Radiant*'s action meant the handful who escaped the sinkings survived. As it was, there were 252 dead from the three lost destroyers, while *Valykrie* had suffered 19 more fatalities. The captain's brother, an army officer, was on board *Radiant* as a passenger. In the aftermath, the latter declared "he would rather go through the biggest 'push' in France than take part in an affair like that again!"[42] The British continued to think a U-boat was the cause of the losses, rather than mines. This was a problem, because it created the idea in the public (and the government) that the disaster had been "a sort of repetition of [the *Aboukir*,] *Hogue* and *Cressy* show,"[43] with the implication the navy had failed to learn the war's most basic lessons. By late December 1917, the Royal Navy's credibility was low and confidence in its leadership approaching crisis point.

Dover Command provided the catalyst. The units in the Channel were working hard but seemed to be achieving little. The Germans had enjoyed a series of small successes in the autumn, which forced the withdrawal of two of Admiral Bacon's most valuable units for repairs. On the night of 18–19 October, seven *A*-type torpedo boats under Lieutenant Commander Assmann left Zeebrugge to bombard Dunkirk. The operation started off badly with a collision between *A48* and *A58*, which forced both back to harbor. The situation was exacerbated by *A59*'s loss of contact with the remainder of the force. Assmann nevertheless continued the sortie. He evaded Allied patrols and attacked Dunkirk, damaging ships in the harbor, as well as facilities ashore. The sortie achieved complete surprise, something apparent after Assmann detected a large contact in the darkness. When illuminated it proved to be the monitor *Terror*, at anchor. The ship was effectively helpless and Assmann did not hesitate to take advantage of the situation. The bombardment was immediately halted and *A60*, *A61*, and *A49* each put a torpedo into *Terror*'s port side. There might have been a fourth, but *A50* started a private war with an imaginary submarine, delaying her attack. *A50* believed she eventually scored a hit on *Terror*, but this was not the case.

The Germans withdrew to Zeebrugge unscathed, despite the efforts of alerted Allied patrols to find them. *Terror*, severely hurt by the torpedoes that struck forward, was in a bad way. Her bulge meant that the third hit, much further aft, did little damage but with the forward fifty feet of the hull below the main deck blown away, the British had to beach the ship near Dunkirk. Despite attacks by German aircraft, *Terror* was given temporary repairs and floated off. Nearly lost in bad weather while on passage to Portsmouth for a full repair, *Terror* was not back in action until January 1918.[44]

Flanders Command had also been trying to use the cable-controlled explosive motor boats that had arrived earlier in the year. They were of immediate concern to the Allies. The French recovered the wreckage of a boat in March off Nieuport and made the material and their assessments available to the British straight away.[45] The destroyer *North Star* and her consorts destroyed another on 3 October, but a substantial achievement came on 28 October. *FL12* struck the monitor *Erebus* and exploded against her starboard side, ripping open fifty feet of her protective bulge. Although her inner hull was largely unhurt, the shock seriously damaged the electrics.[46] *Erebus* was out of service for nearly a month.[47]

These actions removed Admiral Bacon's two most effective offensive units when he was under increasing pressure to produce better results. The reconstituted Plans Division in the Admiralty under Rear Admiral Roger Keyes had looked closely at the apparent inability of the barrages to stop U-boats moving into the western Channel. Although signals intelligence already made the problem clear, the extent to which U-boats were making free of the Dover Strait was confirmed through the salvage of *UC44*, sunk off Ireland by one of her own mines on 4 August. The boat was brought ashore in late September and by early October extensive material on U-boat operations was in Admiralty hands.[48] There were other indications all was not well. Stationing a British submarine at the approaches to the barrage resulted in *E52* sinking *UC63* on 1 November, but the difficult conditions of the Channel meant the British boats could not keep clear of the defensive system. *E31*'s captain noted he was "swept through the barrage three times by mistake, twice on the surface, and once submerged, without coming to any harm. Not a very effective trap for the Germans."[49] Keyes was firmly backed by Geddes through the formation in November of a Channel Barrage Committee, which Keyes chaired. The fundamental point of difference that emerged between the committee and Bacon was not over deployment of the new deep barrage of mines, which finally began in November, but the committee's insistence that the strait be fully illuminated to force the U-boats to abandon surfaced night transit in favor of submerged passage through the minefields. Bacon accepted the idea of illumination but proposed alternative methods that would take much longer to put in place.

There were other less important differences, but the dispute assumed symbolic importance. Jellicoe strongly supported Bacon, but the latter was resentful when dealing with Keyes and the Plans Division, even though willing to make some of the changes required. Given his unpopularity with all but Jellicoe (Keyes and many others were eager to see Bacon go) the admiral's position was extremely vulnerable.[50] This was confirmed on 19 December when the new illuminations were finally in place. Bacon had protested, but he finally organized the illumination program at Jellicoe's explicit direction, the result of which was that *UB56* was forced to dive and was destroyed by a mine. Geddes felt that Bacon could not continue in his post. Jellicoe had successfully protected other officers in the past, but Geddes was now convinced the First Sea Lord also had to go if the navy's performance was to improve. On 25 December, the First Lord wrote to Jellicoe to relieve him of his appointment. The new First Sea Lord would be Admiral Sir Wester Wemyss, hitherto Jellicoe's underutilized and frustrated deputy. Bacon's sacking followed immediately.

The Grand Fleet and the Sixth Battle Squadron

In the meantime, arrangements for the Scandinavian convoys were subject to intense review. Command and control were tightened up to improve coordination, while the western terminus was shifted from Lerwick to Methil at the entrance of the Firth of Forth, shortening the route but putting it closer to the Germans. This required a much stronger covering force, although reducing the frequency of sailings reduced the problem somewhat. Beatty accepted the need for the cover to be at battle squadron strength even though he had considerable concerns about the possibility of a detached formation being overwhelmed in an unexpected sortie by the High Sea Fleet. There may have been other factors in allowing the battle squadrons to be employed in this way. The transfer of the fleet to Rosyth, finally due for April 1918, reduced the pressure on the transport system and allowed more liberal coal expenditure, even if oil remained in short supply. The battleships also needed to do more. None took part in operations in August 1917, while activities in September were confined to a few days of fleet exercises. They were idle again in October. November was busier, but even this meant only four days at sea for the First and Second Battle Squadrons and two for the remainder.[51] Further, the Rosyth areas did not allow the same opportunities for "day running" exercises as the safe internal waters of Scapa Flow.

The C-in-C's readiness to accept the risk may have been partly due to the Grand Fleet's new accession of strength. American capital ships had finally arrived. Over the later months of 1917, a protracted debate was conducted over a British request for American battleships. The Admiralty's initial motivation was simple enough. The status of the Third Battle Squadron, long based near the Thames Estuary, was increasingly being questioned. The squadron consisted only of *Dreadnought* herself, together with a handful of *King Edward VII*–class pre-dreadnoughts. A contingency force in the event of an unexpected move south by German heavy forces, its utility was doubtful, particularly as the squadron was not strong enough to stand up to a major detachment of the High Sea Fleet. The urgent need to expand the antisubmarine forces made release of manpower from these older battleships an attractive proposition. As early as July, Admiral Sims relayed a British request that four coal-burning battleships join the Grand Fleet. This would allow transfer of four British dreadnoughts south and decommissioning of the *King Edward VII*–class ships. Despite Sims' advocacy, the USN was initially unenthusiastic. That the American battle fleet remain concentrated continued to be Washington's policy. It was only after the seagoing C-in-C, Admiral Mayo, visited the United Kingdom for discussions with both the Admiralty and the Grand Fleet that this approach began to change. Mayo's support was a factor, but there was another element at play.

Mayo had crossed the Atlantic with a mandate to bring about the more offensive approach sought by President Wilson. The Admiralty produced at least one plan for an attack on the German anchorages and canvassed the sort of help required to mount such an operation. This may have been a diversion because in their briefings the British emphasized the complexities and dangers of the operational environment in German littoral waters. The extent to which mines and submarines dominated the situation, as well as the strength of Germany's coastal defenses, may have been a revelation to the American admiral. At any event, while Mayo remained dissatisfied with what he viewed as an overly passive British campaign plan, he forwarded the Admiralty's request for a division of battleships. Opinion was beginning to change within the USN about such a deployment, not least because the closer look at British systems allowed the Americans in recent months made it clear the Grand Fleet was well ahead of USN practices in several areas.[52] There was another factor, particularly as the overall American war effort began to ramp up. If the battle fleet was not seen as an active contributor, the navy risked its political position in a future postwar environment when budgets would be subject to much more debate.

The Chief of Naval Operations Admiral Benson visited Britain in November, and his endorsement of the proposal finally persuaded the American government to act. The USN then moved quickly. Four units of Battleship Division Nine under Rear Adm. Hugh Rodman sailed from the United States on 25 November. The force had no easy passage, suffering damage and being scattered in a storm in which "it blew as hard as I have ever seen it, and the seas were the worst I could recollect."[53] The USN was encountering the differences between discretionary peacetime navigation and the demands of war the Royal Navy had experienced since 1914. It took twenty-four hours to collect the force at the rendezvous with their British guide, the cruiser *Constance*. The Americans arrived at Scapa Flow on 7 December to a warm—if carefully staged—welcome. They were conscious they had to integrate tactically in full with the Grand Fleet and this was Rodman's priority from the start. Their status was reflected in the division's immediate designation as the Sixth Battle Squadron. Already equipped with British signal flags and selected British texts, the process was rapidly completed with the full issue of Grand Fleet instructions and signal books, while Royal Navy signals and radio liaison staff were allocated to each ship. Even so, observers remarked on "the at times somewhat startling manoeuvres of the American 6th Battle Squadron" in its early days.[54]

There seemed a lot to do before the Sixth Battle Squadron was fully fit for operations. Each ship required modification, particularly the fit of

Photo 12.2   Sixth Battle Squadron arrives   *Sea Power Centre, Australia*

minesweeping paravanes, while early gunnery practice suggested problems with excessive spread in some of the salvo firings.[55] This was likely due as much to the American practice of firing both guns of a turret at once (as opposed to the British system of each gun firing alternately) as to actual problems with material. More critical, as USN officers were quick to admit within their own service, was getting out of the mindset of preplanned firings that did not reflect the reality of war. There were also basic things to learn, particularly in coaling. The British emphasis on the work being done immediately on return to harbor may have been a shock to the USN. Junior British officers were scornful about the alleged response of the American battleships to the direction to coal immediately after arrival, while the battleships took longer to refuel (admittedly their bunkers were practically empty after the transatlantic passage—*Arkansas* arrived in July 1918 with only twenty-four tons left) and clean up than they would on later occasions.[56] The need for much improved watertight integrity also quickly became apparent to the USN. There were, in short, "all sorts of little odds and ends, all sorts of things that needed attention."[57] It had been just the same for the British in 1914. Beatty allowed what he believed to be adequate time for the American units to get fully up to scratch and sought every opportunity to exercise the new squadron with the fleet. It is possible to read too much into his comments about the USN; Beatty's assessments of his RN subordinates have much the same, often patronizing, tone. Wisely, despite a considerable element of the Royal Navy's inherent assumption of superiority, Beatty concealed his concerns from Rodman, with whom he quickly developed a warm relationship. The latter, a rather straightforward man, was another wise choice for command in a complex situation. Rodman's positive attitude ensured the transition would be relatively smooth. And it was.

The C-in-C's caution, as well as the new commitment to the Scandinavian convoys, contributed to his unwillingness to reduce the British battleship strength of the Grand Fleet, despite the earlier ideas of transferring a division south to replace the old, now decommissioned battleships. Nevertheless, overall integration of the American units was achieved very quickly in both tactical and harbor environments. Their cleanliness (and ease of keeping clean), better crew facilities, and ability to do much of their own deep maintenance were soon noticed by the British. While interaction between the lower decks was largely through sporting activities—the USN doing better in soccer, and baseball arousing much more British interest than anyone expected—the officers' social scene was very active. American

Photo 12.3   **Admiral Rodman and staff**   *Sea Power Centre, Australia*

ships had recently been made "dry," so USN officers appreciated a drink on board a British ship, although some were struck by the amounts consumed and viewed their own austere situation with more favor than before. On the other hand, more than one British officer may have enjoyed a libation on board a USN unit in the privacy of a friend's cabin. Perhaps not surprisingly, close relationships developed between the Americans and the Australian units with the Grand Fleet.[58] Although the latter were much more closely integrated with the Royal Navy and had many British personnel on board, they were also strangers in a strange land.

A Scandinavian convoy generated the Sixth Battle Squadron's first semioperational task. It sailed in company with the Fifth Battle Squadron, effectively on leading reins, on 16 December for three days. Beatty in *Queen Elizabeth* accompanied the sortie, which concluded in Rosyth. This allowed the C-in-C to conduct key meetings, while the American crews saw something of Edinburgh and the authorities at Rosyth dockyard began to assess the modifications that the new arrivals required. They would remain a month before returning to Scapa Flow.

1918 Opens in the North Sea

13

THE NEW ADMIRALTY REGIME SET TO WORK. Admiral Sir Wester Wemyss seemed a new broom, but "there is no easy division between the work done by the Staff under Jellicoe and that done under Wemyss."[1] The basis of much of 1918's operational effort was laid in 1917, even if the directing personalities were very different. One shift in relationships would prove important. Wemyss got on well with Beatty and was older (and once senior in rank), but he was junior as a flag officer and did not enjoy the same prestige. This made for a very different relationship than Beatty had with his predecessor. Further, Geddes had expended political capital, even with the prime minister's support, in removing Jellicoe. He could not afford to repeat the move with Beatty, however difficult the latter became. The C-in-C was thus in a strong position. Beatty set his face against reductions in the Grand Fleet, particularly its destroyer force, which the naval staff sought to provide more capacity for antisubmarine work. Beatty had Wemyss' sympathy in maintaining the Grand Fleet's strength and readiness for action, but the First Sea Lord was always loath to overrule the C-in-C if he could avoid it.[2] Beatty's desire to preserve his fleet meant final rejection of Wemyss' attempt to resuscitate the battleship force in the Swin. The *King Edward VII* class had been paid off and *Dreadnought* was sent to the Grand Fleet to replace the broken-down *Superb*.

Despite his insistence on maintaining the strength of his fleet, Beatty admitted the need for caution, particularly as Russia's collapse ended the Germans' three-front problem. The C-in-C would not seek battle at any cost but preserve the fleet as the covering force for the Allied campaigns at sea. British offensive measures would focus on the mining campaign. Beatty had legitimate concerns about meeting the High Sea Fleet in unfavorable circumstances, particularly if the Germans chose a moment when they could deploy their maximum strength. The Grand Fleet's light cruisers and destroyers were in high demand, often for operations that meant they were not immediately available to support the battle squadrons. This was Beatty's main worry, but he had others. British heavy shells remained unreliable and it would be months before the new armor-piercing units became available.[3] Yet some of Beatty's fears were created by overestimation of German shipbuilding. Beatty's claims of his battle cruiser force's relative weakness assumed that *Mackensen* was operational and other ships would soon be completed. The reality was otherwise. *Mackensen* was launched in April 1917, but work proceeded so slowly due to labor and material shortages she would still be more than a year from completion in November 1918. *Graf Spee*, launched in September 1917, was no further advanced.[4] The battleship program was even worse off. The C-in-C's estimates were consistently less optimistic than the Admiralty's, whose reports were, if inconsistent, generally closer to the truth.[5]

The Admiralty started the year by adjuring units at sea to increase the destruction rate of U-boats. This was because Admiral von Capelle had admitted to the Reichstag that the monthly production rate was expected to be between eight and twelve boats. The Admiralty estimated that U-boat losses since September had averaged nine a month[6] and urged the navy to exceed an average of 2.25 sinkings a week, emphasizing, "the more that this is increased the sooner will the end come."[7] The Grand Fleet itself got off to a bad start on 12 January with the wreck of the destroyers *Opal* and *Narborough*. Both were driven ashore on South Ronaldsay during a heavy storm. There was only one survivor. This followed the loss with all on board the destroyer *Raccoon* on the coast of Ireland only three days before.[8] Beatty's flag lieutenant noted, "Destroyers and light craft have had an awful winter, poor devils."[9] Nevertheless, despite continuing poor weather, the minelaying campaign accelerated in the new year. Operation A25, launched on 25 January, included a new twist, with *Princess Margaret* laying dummy mines in addition to a live field deployed by *Abdiel* and cruisers near Terschelling.[10] The idea was that such mines would be detected, probably by aircraft, and divert German effort away from the real fields, while the British also hoped their use would disguise the extent of British knowledge of the German-swept channels.[11] Given that minefields, if discovered, were generally left in place if possible, the dummy fields could also provide safe channels for the British while the Germans thought they were functioning as additional barriers. The Germans, who did much of their sweeping at night and did not collect many mines for examination, only discovered the stratagem after the war.[12] Beatty's concern over the diversion of light cruisers from their primary tasks and completion of the destroyers' modifications brought the creation of a minelaying destroyer flotilla and an end to the routine use of light cruisers for minelaying. The C-in-C was not pleased to lose more destroyers from his escort force, but this was better than nothing. Operating from Immingham, the new Twentieth Flotilla included eight ships. The group was led by *Abdiel*, whose captain, Berwick Curtis, was the most experienced in this work in the Royal Navy.[13]

On 31 January, units from Rosyth sailed into thickening fog for exercises with the Grand Fleet. Accompanying the heavy ships were the newly formed Thirteenth Submarine Flotilla, led by the flotilla leader *Ithuriel* and including five *K*-class submarines, and the Twelfth Flotilla, comprising the light cruiser *Fearless* and four more *K*-class. As the force approached the Isle of May at the entrance to the Firth of Forth, the movement was straightforward until the Thirteenth Flotilla became entangled with a group of minesweepers. In attempting to avoid them, *K14*'s rudder jammed; within minutes her turn brought *K14* across the bows of *K22*. Both boats were badly damaged. *K14*, despite being holed forward, got clear of the remainder of the force; but the *K22* did not and found herself in the path of *Inflexible*, rear unit of the Second Battle Cruiser Squadron. *Inflexible* struck *K22* a heavy blow that ripped off the submarine's external ballast tanks but did not sink her. In an increasingly confused situation, the signal reporting the first collision did not get through to the flotilla's commander until an hour later. By this stage, the battle cruisers knew there had been an accident and detached a destroyer to assist the crippled units. Unaware of this, Commander E. W. Leir in *Ithuriel* decided to turn his flotilla back to assist. This was a disastrous step in the prevailing fog. The turn put the flotilla in front of the battle cruisers and the formations behind them. *Australia* just avoided running down *K12*, but the Twelfth Flotilla was not so lucky. *Fearless* struck *K17* amidships; the submarine sank eight minutes later. Although her crew got clear of their boat, they became victims of the melee that followed as the remaining submarines tried to avoid each other. *K6* and *K4* did not succeed and *K4* went down with all hands. *K7* scraped the sinking *K4* and in maneuvering forced many of *K17*'s survivors under, drowning them. Only eight survived the night.[14]

The "Battle of May Island" struck a blow at the fleet's morale, but also contributed to unease over the *K* class. The undoubted tactical promise for fleet operations of these difficult-to-handle boats was increasingly masked by accidents the class experienced. *K13* was lost on trials (although salvaged and recommissioned as *K22*), while *K1* was sunk after a collision with *K4* during a sweep off the Danish coast on 18 November 1917. This accident was caused by confusion between different formations and machinery problems on board *K1* due to salt water entering the fuel system. Had the incident occurred on the other side of the North Sea, the submarine could have been saved, but the risk of attack was too great and *Blonde* sank *K1* with gunfire. Some of the *K* boats' defects, such as their poor sea keeping, could be fixed, but developing the experience to operate such large boats with their complex machinery as integral components of a surface fleet would take more time than the war allowed. As the captain of *K12* noted, the class was "built and designed for battle only and the type . . . had to share the fate of the Grand Fleet battleships which never got a fair chance at the enemy."[15]

February found the Grand Fleet sailing into heavy weather in the hope of intercepting a reported sortie by the First Scouting Group. Conditions were so bad that twelve men were swept overboard, including one from *New York*. The inability to recover the man was another demonstration to the USN of the hazards of war.[16] *Delaware* suffered a total power failure and substantial upper deck damage; several British ships were similarly battered. Fog also remained a hazard and the Sixth Battle Squadron soon had experience of its challenges. Approaching a rendezvous of his battleships with light cruisers before meeting a westbound Scandinavian convoy on 11 March, Admiral Rodman was faced by a bank of fog. He tried to alter course, but before the order could be executed, visibility dropped to almost nothing. With uncertainty about the force's base course, "there were some very narrow escapes in collision." No harm was done, but in the confusion, *Texas*, *Wyoming*, and *Florida*, as well as four destroyers, became separated. The squadron and its escorts did not reassemble until the next morning. Much had been learned, something apparent in Rodman's frank admissions to the C-in-C.[17]

Operations in the Channel

Appointed acting vice admiral, Roger Keyes took up duty as Flag Officer Dover on 1 January. Left in no doubt about his position by the new First Sea Lord, it was Admiral Oliver who made the point most succinctly, telling Keyes, "It is up to you to deliver the goods."[18] The Flanders Command would not remain passive, particularly as Allied antisubmarine measures were proving increasingly effective. January was a bad month for the U-boats, with ten sunk or missing. Nevertheless, the command had to accept that the British mining campaign in the Heligoland Bight meant Flanders no longer had a high priority in the eyes of the High Sea Fleet. Admiral von Schröder was not given promised reinforcements, while units sent to Germany to refit were not returned, Scheer viewing his own needs as greater. The situation was not helped by the Allied bombing campaign, which became increasingly effective as the year went on, severely affecting the ability to undertake repairs—and get rest.[19]

Despite the success of the mining sortie on 22 December, the Flanders Command could not launch another surface operation until 14 January, when fourteen torpedo boats were dispatched to attack shipping, with the contingency of a bombardment of Lowestoft and Southwold if they found no quarry. Von Schröder wanted to maintain the pressure the Royal Navy was clearly feeling after the losses of the previous months. The British were alerted to the raid and Keyes naturally assumed the Dover barrage was the target. Matters were complicated by a British plan to lay a minefield north of Zeebrugge the same night. Keyes decided this should continue, as it could be placed across the line of German withdrawal, while he put to sea in the light cruiser *Attentive*. Accompanied by ten leaders and destroyers, he deployed his ships in two divisions, one at the eastern end of the barrage and the other to the west. The drifters that usually patrolled the barrage were sent inshore, while the remaining units were placed on alert but continued their antisubmarine work. Tyrwhitt, newly appointed an acting rear admiral, was also ready in Harwich.

German signals intelligence had detected that the British were

Photo 13.1
Admiral Keyes
Sea Power Centre, Australia

expecting a surface attack and had reinforced the Dover Strait and emptied the Channel of traffic. The Germans still ascribed British foreknowledge to other causes than decryption but decided to make the best of the situation. Although there was likely to be no merchant traffic to attack, they would be operating well north of where the British expected. This maintained the chance of achieving surprise, not only with the bombardments—now the operation's principal aim—but also in intercepting any local patrols. Weather once more decided events. By midnight a gale was blowing from the SSW, with limited visibility and the short, steep seas that made North Sea operations so difficult for small craft. None of the three German formations achieved anything of significance. Group 1, assigned to attack Lowestoft, found itself instead off Great Yarmouth and made the best of things by bombarding the town for five minutes, firing approximately fifty shells and causing four deaths. The submarine *H9* was in harbor and got under way within fifteen minutes but found nothing when she put to sea. Group 2, allocated to attack shipping farther north, found none. Group 3 did not locate Southwold at all. Some of this formation sighted two enemy patrol vessels but lost them in the darkness before they could attack. In the foul weather, the British units saw nothing.

The Harwich Force sailed on receiving news of Yarmouth's bombardment, while Keyes, realizing the attack was directed elsewhere than the Channel barrage, changed his dispositions to intercept the homeward-bound enemy. In these conditions, it was a forlorn hope and neither side made contact. So uncertain was the operational picture that Keyes believed the German flotillas "had come from the Heligoland Bight, and returned there."[20] They had not, but their passage to Zeebrugge proved fraught. Several units were badly damaged in the heavy seas, losing masts and gear. At the time, Tyrwhitt's ships were making no more than ten knots and were hard put to avoid damage themselves.[21] The British minelaying operation was undertaken in equally difficult conditions, with at least two of the minelayers unable to deploy their weapons, but bore almost immediate fruit when *V67* detonated a mine. This blew off her bows and killed twelve of the crew. Despite the damage, the torpedo boat struggled back to Zeebrugge escorted by *G95*. Never again fully operational, *V67* was scuttled when the Germans withdrew from Belgium later in the year. Keyes was inclined to blame a failure of intelligence, but his accompanying complaints about the poor weather were more apt.[22]

An inconclusive engagement took place on 23 January when four torpedo boats encountered the net vessel *Clover Bank* and her escort, the small monitor *M26*. The Germans mistook *M26* for the much more powerful *Erebus*, which was also at sea, and kept their distance in hazy conditions, worsened by both sides laying smoke.[23] Both thought they scored hits on their opponents, but no one suffered damage. Given the likely appearance of British reinforcements, the German torpedo boats did not linger. When the destroyers *Melpomene* and *Marksman* arrived on the scene, they found nothing. Keyes felt that the captain of *M26* should have been more aggressive, but it is difficult to see what more a slow monitor armed with a single 7.5-inch gun could do against a half-flotilla of torpedo boats.[24]

The Dover barrage's increasing success was reflected in the High Sea Fleet's decision to allow the North Sea U-boats to take the longer passage around the north of Scotland. The Flanders boats were also finding the Channel transit increasingly dangerous and losses were mounting. If they needed to take the northern route as well, the advantage of forward bases in Belgium no longer existed. Something had to be done and a sortie by the Second Flotilla was organized by the High Sea Fleet. *Emden* led the destroyers out on 13 February, but heavy fog forced Commander Heinecke, leading the flotilla, to rejoin *Emden* and anchor. When the ships got under way again on 14 February, visibility was at the other extreme and Heinecke became concerned his passage was being reported by one of the many fishing vessels in sight. His outlook was not improved by the need to detach the lame duck *G104*, which had yet again developed condenser trouble. Heinecke nevertheless decided to continue. In the early hours of 15 February the eight destroyers, divided into two divisions, made their descent. The Fourth Half-Flotilla would attack the northern side of the barrage and the Third Half-Flotilla, the south.

The barrage was protected by destroyer patrols, while seventy-two trawlers, drifters, and other light craft patrolled the deep minefields and provided the illuminations to force U-boats to dive. A monitor was stationed near the Varne Shoal as heavy cover, although on the night of 14–15 February the guard ship was *M26*, not one of the big-gun units. The assembly was an inviting target. Bacon had specifically warned Keyes of its vulnerability to surface attack and Keyes later stated he was fully aware of the risks. Despite Keyes' claims of a new approach, the night dispositions had not significantly changed from those ordered by Bacon. Although he asserted he had been successful in immediately instilling a new spirit of enterprise, Keyes failed to ensure the patrol forces were mentally ready for a German sortie, even though he expected the barrage's success would "provoke reprisals before long."[25] His hope that Room 40 could provide warning of a sortie may have become an assumption that it would. Significantly, Keyes believed that such advanced notice would allow him to put to sea to take control of operations himself. This suggests he had little understanding of the need to be positioned to coordinate the responses of what were widely dispersed—and disparate—forces.

The Germans arrived at the barrage without triggering any alarms. Part of the British unreadiness for surface action lay in their focus on U-boats. Keyes had been warned of the passage of a crack submarine he was eager to destroy, and a possible U-boat was sighted just before midnight. The idea that this had triggered an engagement colored British appreciation of the situation. The Germans began their attack at 0030 when they detected the minesweeper *Newbury*. The ship was quickly disabled and left in what the Fourth Half-Flotilla thought was a sinking condition. Failing to work up minor war vessels after refit raised its head once more—*Newbury* had not sorted out her stores and the green flares to give warning of surface attack were not at hand. Confusion reigned among the British. Units did not interpret the gunfire they heard as a surface attack, thinking that it was coming from ashore or related to an air raid—or even the detonation of mines. The barrage's lighting was another factor. The brilliant flares and illuminations meant that few personnel had any night vision.[26] Most critically, the green flares that would have indicated the nature of the attack were not fired in the first encounters. The Germans were thus able to destroy a trawler and seven drifters and damage as many more. Both half-flotillas thought they had done twice as well, being misled by explosions of the magnesium flares on board their victims, which "gave the impression that the whole ship had blown up."[27] The Third Half-Flotilla was not as active as the Fourth, largely because *G103* had also developed condenser problems, limiting the force's speed. The Third Half-Flotilla's onslaught eventually triggered the firing of green flares, but the British response remained disjointed. *M26* moved to investigate, but her search was inconclusive and her captain did not report. Some of the small craft might have made the situation clear, but they also failed to make any coherent reports. The French did not do much better. The German southern force was seen by the small torpedo boats *344* and *350*, but these were not close enough to attack, while it is doubtful they recognized the contacts as hostile. Neither they nor the shore station at Cape Gris-Nez, which also saw the Germans, made sighting reports.[28] Although Keyes was alarmed by the repeated sound of gunfire and started to get the standby forces in the Downs under way, he gained the impression all was well and reversed his orders.

Worse followed. The Third Half-Flotilla was seen by the destroyer *Amazon*, rearmost unit of *Termagant*'s four-ship division. She repeatedly challenged but got no response and the strange ships rapidly passed out of sight. Constrained by the struggling *G103*, Kolbe would not risk a night action against destroyers and had turned away. Despite the lack of response, *Amazon*'s bridge team were convinced the ships were British and therefore did no more than pass a message up the line that they had seen three friendly destroyers. By the time *Termagant* questioned *Amazon*'s identification—a process slowed by a signals mix-up—it was too late. The Germans were clear away, although *G102* detonated a mine approaching Zeebrugge. Patched up, she followed her consorts home a few days after they returned to Germany. The Second Flotilla had not remained in harbor at Zeebrugge for a single night, perhaps due to fear of air attack. The Germans had other concerns, particularly their machinery's increasing unreliability. While they drew considerable satisfaction from the apparent success of the sortie, it would not be repeated by High Sea Fleet units. Believing the British were vulnerable to an immediate follow-up, von Schröder dispatched the Flanders torpedo boats on another raid the following night. They found nothing, despite Keyes' declaration that the barrage was manned and fully illuminated. It has been suggested the Flanders' units did not proceed as far southwest as Heinecke's forces, while the barrage lighting seems to have been considerably reduced following the raid.[29] Low visibility may have limited the horizon of both sides. The Channel at night in winter remained a difficult environment.

Admiral Keyes vented his wrath on those he considered negligent. He was backed by the Admiralty, and the captains of *Termagant*, *Amazon*, and *M26* were superseded—despite A. A. Mellin of *M26* having received the DSO and Bar and special promotion to commander for his work in Q ships. Perhaps these rigorous measures were needed to set an example. Keyes later railed at the role played in the defeat by unfortunate legacies of the Bacon regime.[30] There was some justice in his claims, but systemic problems of readiness and training extended more widely than the Dover Patrol. Destroyers did not have enough practice in night warfare, with all its challenges and uncertainties. The RNR captains of small craft were splendid seamen but had little indoctrination in many aspects of operations that bore upon their naval tasks in ways they did not understand. *Newbury*'s unreadiness confirmed that small ships were not receiving the unit training essential on commissioning or after a long period in refit. Nevertheless, after six weeks in command—coming with the benefit of time in the Plans Division—Keyes must bear much of the blame. An attack should have been expected within days, and it was Keyes' responsibility to ensure that the Dover Patrol understood this. Too much of his attention may have been on preparations for the attack on Zeebrugge and Ostend that was another element of his new regime. He had not thought through the implications for the Germans of the barrage's success, as well as the extent to which the changes exposed his ships to a surprise attack on the surface. He certainly displayed no understanding of the problems of situational awareness in the illuminations' glare.

The Attacks on Zeebrugge and Ostend

Keyes' morale recovered quickly from the reverse, sustained by evidence of further U-boat sinkings and a successful minelaying sortie by four CMBs on the night of 7–8 February. Although two got lost and the other two were very nearly caught, the latter pair managed to lay mines off Ostend, one of which claimed the small torpedo boat *A10*. The admiral also had other fish to fry. An attack on Zeebrugge and Ostend had been debated over many months. Ideas of a direct descent were put in abeyance in favor of the divisional assault on the Flanders coast planned in 1917, but the land offensive's failure brought them back into consideration. Different schemes developed by Tyrwhitt and Bacon had been considered and rejected. There was no consensus about the practicability of gaining surprise and achieving the main purpose of any attack, destroying the ability of the German light forces and U-boats to employ the canal and lock system between Bruges and the open sea. By September 1917, with Beatty expressing support, Jellicoe had authorized new Admiralty studies. Keyes' arrival as Director of Plans injected, arguably, a much more positive outlook. On 3 December Keyes submitted a plan, which Jellicoe soon endorsed.

Preparations were overtaken by Keyes' appointment to Dover. He quickly moved to revise key aspects. Keyes differed from Bacon in having less faith in 12-inch gun monitors and more in block ships placed to close the canal channels. There were two elements to this difference of opinion. Bacon and Keyes agreed that an assault on the mole that sheltered Zeebrugge harbor was essential to allow the ships attacking the canals to do their work. The canal at Ostend, being much more open to the sea, did not present the same problems. Bacon had intended a specially equipped monitor strike the Zeebrugge mole head-on, disgorging troops over a brow fitted for the purpose. Keyes' objection was that the underpowered monitor was limited by its extra gear to four knots, inadequate in the current around the mole. His preference was to put a more maneuverable and faster ship alongside and disembark the force on as many gangways as possible. Keyes' scheme also recognized that an assault force could be rapidly overwhelmed if German forces on the mole were reinforced. To prevent this, the viaduct that connected the mole to the land would be breached by CMBs filled with explosives.

Differences in the methods of closing the canals were more fundamental. Bacon believed destruction of the lock gates by close-range heavy gun-fire would be more effective than block ships alone and determined that a monitor should bombard the locks from inside the harbor. Keyes was convinced that properly positioned hulls sunk in the channels could close them if enough block ships were assigned—three for Zeebrugge and two for Ostend. Filled with cement, the sunken ships would be hard to remove. The objections to this assessment were that the combination of the width and slope of the channels, the large tidal range (fourteen feet in spring tides), and the relatively shallow draft of their torpedo boats and submarines meant the Germans would soon be able to work around whatever obstacles were placed in their way. Keyes argued that the natural silting to which the canals were prone would rapidly build around the block ships, creating a problem impossible for the Germans to solve for many weeks.

The Admiralty considered the revised plan for Operation ZO at the beginning of March. Achieving surprise and disrupting any German response required not only the right combinations of moon and tide, but weather good enough to allow every unit, however small, to do its work. It was also key to have wind blowing in the right direction to deploy the smoke screens essential to mask the last stages of the assault force's approach. Moon and tide created windows of only a few days each lunar month; sea state and wind would limit the opportunities even further. Much was hoped from the operation. The final comments by the Admiralty attached great importance to the moral effect of the venture inside and outside the navy. Bacon's ideas of using army troops were rejected in favor of using RN and RM personnel, including large numbers from the Grand Fleet itself. This was a deliberate effort to find an outlet for the most enthusiastic (and frustrated) officers and ratings, who flocked to volunteer; the division between ships was made as even as possible, with HMAS *Australia*'s contribution of eleven being typical.[31] Keyes had hoped to mount the attack in mid-March, but neither all the conversions nor the smoke devices were ready. The Admiralty became particularly anxious the element of surprise would be lost, since it was difficult to conceal the preparations from German aerial reconnaissance.

Flanders Command did not detect the buildup of British forces, perhaps due to its own preparations to support the great offensive the German army was about to initiate, which included diversion of its aircraft to scouting and combat farther inland. A preliminary reconnaissance of the French coast was conducted by torpedo boats on 19 March, two nights before the offensive's planned start. Early on the 21st, the Germans sailed in three groups and began to bombard the French coast as firing began on the western front. Five boats under Lieutenant Commander Assmann attacked Dunkirk at 0348, but rapidly became aware that there were strong Allied forces in the vicinity. The monitors *Terror* and *M25* opened fire in response and the explosion of *Terror*'s star shell above his ships convinced Assmann that immediate withdrawal was necessary. Collecting two smaller torpedo boats positioned as navigational markers, Assmann made for home. Steering to cut him off were the destroyer leader *Botha* and four British and French destroyers that had slipped their cables in the Dunkirk anchorage on hearing the firing. The two formations made contact in mist at approximately 0440, *Botha* confirming with star shell the Germans' presence on her port bow. At close range, the two sides exchanged fire with main armament and light weapons. *Botha* suffered a pierced steam pipe. With his speed falling off, Commander Rede turned toward the German line and rammed *A19*, cutting her in two. An attempt to follow up by ramming *A7* failed, although *Botha*'s gunfire quickly reduced the little torpedo boat to a wreck. Torpedoes fired by Assmann's units did not find their mark, but their smoke screen proved more effective. Not only did Assmann's five bigger boats make a clean break, in the confusion the French destroyer *Capitaine Mehl* mistook *Botha* for the enemy and put a torpedo into her as she emerged from the smoke. Holed in her boiler room, *Botha* came to a halt. Since the Germans had disappeared, all the Anglo-French force could do was finish off *A7* and escort the crippled flotilla leader back to Dunkirk. *CMB20* spotted the German force and succeeded in getting a torpedo away, despite being under heavy fire. The CMB's crew thought they hit the fourth in line, but this was not so. The other German bombardments did not achieve anything significant, although Commander Albrecht's units covered the last stages of Assmann's withdrawal.

Botha's crippling was an embarrassing end to an otherwise encouraging engagement and a reminder of the conclusion drawn by a French officer, "Numbers are often a disadvantage at night."[32] As *Morris* had also fired a torpedo at what she thought was an enemy, it took the discovery of "a piece marked Creusot" inside *Botha*'s boiler room to confirm who had done what. Keyes worked hard to patch up the Anglo-French relationship.[33] This was already under strain, since a week earlier the French airship *AT-0* had mistaken *D3* for a U-boat off Dieppe. When the airship failed to recognize the submarine's recognition signals and closed to attack, *D3* dived, but not quickly enough. In one of the very few successes of the air against submersibles, six 114-pound bombs sank *D3*. The submarine broached before finally sinking, leaving four survivors in the water, but all drowned before they could be rescued.[34] In the meantime, the admiral was determined the enemy venture would not pass without a response, particularly as the Allied armies were retreating from the devastating German offensive. On the afternoon of 21 March *Terror* bombarded Ostend, putting thirty-nine rounds into the waterfront, withdrawing only when the German shore batteries became too accurate. Although no ships were hit, the accuracy of the shooting from both monitor and batteries confirmed how far fire control techniques had developed with the help of air spotting, sound ranging, and increased navigational accuracy. Over the next few weeks, despite their desire to support the land offensive, the Flanders surface forces were constrained by the need to keep the approaches to Ostend and Zeebrugge clear for the U-boats, as well as serviceability problems and continuing air attacks. Later sorties to bombard the French coast in April achieved nothing more than the first effort, although the Germans avoided contact with Allied forces at sea. For its part, the Dover Patrol was not only maintaining the barrage and preparing for the attack on the enemy ports but also protecting the flow of reinforcements as the British combed the United Kingdom for troops to shore up the front. The Admiralty, fearing the prospect of the loss of the Channel harbors—and perhaps the entire coast of northern France—to the German offensive began to prepare for the destruction and blocking of the ports concerned.[35]

The old cruiser *Vindictive* was selected for the attack on Zeebrugge mole and refitted to carry gangways and additional light weapons to suppress the defenses. The Mersey ferries *Iris II* and *Daffodil* were also requisitioned to carry the remainder of the force assigned to the mole. The old *Apollo*-class cruisers *Intrepid*, *Iphigenia*, and *Sirius* were allocated to block Zeebrugge, while *Brilliant* and *Thetis* were designated for Ostend. Instead of CMBs, two *C*-class submarines were assigned to blow up the viaduct, each being packed with five tons of explosives. The survivors of *A7* and *A19* also played a part. Their interrogations provided useful details of the arrangements at Zeebrugge.[36] The combined Royal Marines–Royal Navy unit formed to attack the mole received intensive training, but they lacked battle-experienced officers and their preparation was unsophisticated, emphasizing hand-to-hand combat (bayonet drills) that seemed out of place in 1918.[37] The landing force joined the assault ships in the Swin anchorage on 6 April to wait for the first attack window. This opened on 11 April and the force got under way at 1600. The ships successfully moved along the succession of buoys laid to ensure there were no mistakes of navigation; but at the position from which the attack force would separate from the covering forces, Keyes detected the onset of a southerly wind that would make the smoke barrage ineffective. As the covering smoke was fundamental to a successful attack, Keyes had to order a return to the anchorage. *CMB33* may not have received this order, as it approached Ostend too closely and went aground. *CMB18* also did not survive, being run down and sunk as the force turned for home. Keyes was initially undismayed, but poor weather forced him to turn back once again on the 13th, the last day of his window for April. Faced by the probability the Germans would realize what was in train, a probability that could only increase, Keyes rethought his preconditions. As he argued to the First Sea Lord when Wemyss visited him on the 14th, if the smoke were as effective as expected, even a full moon would not make much difference to the Germans' ability to see what was going on. The attack could therefore take place on the next spring tide—only nine days away. Wemyss had intended canceling the operation outright, but accepted Keyes' proposal and with it ultimate responsibility for the raid.[38]

The Germans quickly salvaged *CMB33* and found material that made it clear Ostend had been the intended target of some form of attack. That a descent on Ostend could be combined with a simultaneous venture against the more difficult target of Zeebrugge did not occur to Flanders Command, possibly because of the scale involved. Furthermore, von Schröder's resources did not permit him to put constant night patrols to sea. Uncertain what the British intended, the admiral's response was to alert the coast defenses and rely on his artillery as the first response.[39] Concerned to keep the Germans off-balance and inure them to offensive British activity, Keyes ordered a diversion for the night of 17–18 April when all three 15-inch gun monitors and the 12-inch gun *Prince Eugene* bombarded batteries to the west of Ostend.

On 22 April, Keyes tried again, aware that the new window almost certainly represented his last chance. More than 160 ships, big and small, were under way by late afternoon. It is possible Keyes would have gone ahead whatever the weather and conditions at first favored him, the large force disguised by mist and squalls, the wind in the right direction, and the sea low enough to allow the passage of small craft and ships under tow. The one problem was the weather did not allow the planned air raid against the enemy ports. Movement along the line of illuminated buoys went without a hitch. *C1*, one of the two submarines designated for the viaduct, had to drop out, but the remainder of the force went on. Deployment of the smoke screen started at 2130 and continued over the next few hours. Just before 2330, *Erebus* and *Terror* began their bombardment. This was key to the deception plan, even more important because of the absence of bombing aircraft. In addition to the damage that the 15-inch shells could do, the barrage forced the German gun crews and garrison troops into shelters, reducing their readiness for an assault, while the more routine nature of bombardment by monitors lulled them into thinking this was the main event for the night.

The British achieved almost complete surprise at Zeebrugge—the key word being "almost." Although the smoke screens successfully concealed the force until the final stages of the approach, a wind shift just before midnight revealed *Vindictive* three hundred yards off the mole. The Germans, suspicious enough they had already closed up at their fighting stations, were ready to respond. Despite the efforts of CMBs to suppress the defenses of the mole and disable the torpedo boat *V69*, berthed on the mole's inshore side, *Vindictive* came under heavy fire. Critically, positioning the old cruiser correctly in the strong current proved as difficult as some of the senior officers who reviewed the scheme had feared. Her captain, Alfred Carpenter, was a specialist navigator, but he could not avoid placing *Vindictive* three hundred yards farther along the mole than planned. An intense engagement ensued in which the British were hamstrung by problems disembarking from the cruiser, the increased distance the assault parties had to cover to reach their objectives, and the difficulty of suppressing the enemy's fire. The battle included an extraordinary duel over the mole between *Vindictive* and *V69*, which culminated in the German disabling *Vindictive*'s fighting top on her foremast, the only weapon position in the ship with the height to enjoy a clear field of fire. In the heavy current, *Vindictive* was kept alongside by

Daffodil pushing her bodily against the mole while *Daffodil's* assault parties used the cruiser as their bridge ashore. *Iris II* was berthed farther along the mole but suffered so many casualties and had so much trouble getting her people onto the mole that she finally repositioned alongside *Vindictive*. The one clear success for the British was *C3's* successful breach of the viaduct. Contrary to instructions, Lieutenant Richard Sandford and his crew stayed with their boat until she had rammed the viaduct under full power. They set fuses and got away in a small skiff under heavy fire. Although they were still within a few hundred yards when the charges detonated, the explosion's effect on the German defenders gave the crew enough breathing space to be rescued by a motor launch (commanded by Sandford's brother Francis).

Meanwhile, the first block ship, *Thetis*, was approaching. She entered the inner harbor but became entangled in the protective nets. While she succeeded in clearing a path for her consorts, the nets fouled *Thetis'* propellers. Losing way, the cruiser could not enter the canal. Commander Ralph Sneyd ordered *Intrepid* and *Iphigenia* to pass ahead, waiting until they were clear before he swung the ship across the channel for scuttling. *Thetis'* task had been to ram the lock gate, probably the only practicable way of achieving the blockage the British sought, but no contingency orders were in place. *Intrepid* therefore continued her mission of blocking the entrance channel. Lieutenant Stuart Bonham-Carter positioned his ship well, grounding her by the stern. *Iphigenia*, which followed, tried to fill the remaining gap between the *Intrepid's* bow and the side of the canal. The effect was to push *Intrepid* into a position less directly across the line of the channel, while the *Iphigenia* drifted back to seaward before scuttling charges took effect. The result was that the ships lay at angles across the middle of the channel, impeding passage but not preventing it completely.

Action around the mole continued. The destroyer *North Star* entered the inner harbor to attack any targets she could find. Subjected to devastating fire as she withdrew, *North Star* was left stopped and burning only a few hundred yards off the mole. The destroyer *Phoebe*, covered by the smoke screens that were again proving effective, labored for nearly an hour to tow *North Star* away. She failed at this task but succeeded in taking off all but a few of the crew. This incident may have provided a helpful diversion for the withdrawal that began just after 0100. Despite the hazards of being alongside the mole, moving away from its shelter put *Vindictive* and the two ferries under even more intense fire from the surviving German positions. *Iris II* in particular suffered heavy casualties. *ML558* did extraordinary work in covering her with yet another smoke screen. This was typical of the vital part played by small craft in the operation, not least in their protracted efforts to rescue survivors from the various elements of the force.

Despite the casualties, the Zeebrugge operation appeared to have achieved its goal. The assault against Ostend was less fortunate. The change of wind that disrupted the protective smoke screens occurred at an earlier stage in the operation, leaving the block ships exposed. The final stage of the approach and the turn toward the canal entrance depended on the Stroom Bank buoy outside Ostend as a marker. Although the British had designated a motor launch to stand by the buoy as an additional mark, they were unaware the Germans had shifted it as a routine precaution only the night before. Commander Alfred Godsal could not see the low-lying shore in the mix of smoke and mist and turned more than a mile short of his target. *Sirius* and *Brilliant* ran hard aground a few minutes later. Although they were lying under the German fortifications, the evacuation of both ships was achieved by a group of motor launches with relatively few casualties. Here the presence of *Marshal Soult* and three 12-inch gun monitors may have been critical. Anchored offshore, they exchanged fire with the German coastal batteries over several hours. Although their initial targets were the heavy batteries, they shifted to take on the lighter guns that were the principal threat to the withdrawal. The monitors did not do much damage, nor did they suffer from the German return fire, but they certainly provided some of the diversion required.

Photo 13.2   **Sunken block ships at Zeebrugge**   *German Naval Association Archive*

The attack on Ostend was obviously a failure, but Keyes never wavered from his claim that Zeebrugge had been successfully blocked. Room 40 rapidly developed a contrary view, while aerial photography and local intelligence also confirmed the Germans could get their coastal U-boats and smaller torpedo boats around the sunken hulls. The bigger units made a transit on 14 May, although they had to do so at high tide. Perhaps more inconvenienced was the seaplane force, which could no longer move its aircraft by rail to enter the water by crane from the mole and had to use the weather-bound beach.[40] But Keyes was correct in his appreciation of the enormous effect on morale within the Royal Navy and in the country and allied nations. The operation was in the finest traditions of the Royal Navy and it came at a time when the war news had been bad for many weeks. The affair restored the navy's lagging confidence, as well as much of the confidence of Britain.

The Travails of Flanders Command

The psychological effect on the Germans was also significant. It took time to determine the extent of the damage and von Schröder was criticized for the absence of night patrols. He pointed out how few resources he had to meet his tasks and his resultant inability to divert units to guard against such contingencies. Minesweeping had to take priority if the U-boats were to continue operating from Flanders.[41] The admiral's litany was justified. In addition to losses in the mine fields, air raids in March and April had damaged three torpedo boats, as well as UB30. The Flanders Command was slowly buckling under the combination of Allied pressure and its diminishing resources. When the Admiralstab did permit the return of the refitted quartet of the Sixth Half-Flotilla, the operation did not go well. The torpedo boats sailed on 19 April preceded by minesweepers. Their passage proved difficult, dogged by the discovery of minefields. It became clear that the force could not get far enough along the coast to make the final approach to Zeebrugge at night. Lieutenant Commander Gautier decided to turn back, but his sweeping force found itself unexpectedly entangled in yet another minefield. After M95, M39, and M64 struck mines and sank in rapid succession, Gautier's only course was to anchor and ask for additional minesweepers. These arrived the next morning and began to clear a passage.

The Harwich Force had intelligence of German sweeping activity that was confirmed by flying boat reconnaissance. What was now designated the "Striking Force" was dispatched. The day was one of "marvellous visibility" and Gautier sighted the British early enough to get his half-flotilla underway and send the sweepers east under cover of a smoke screen. His torpedo boats proceeded to lay smoke as five British destroyers led by *Thruster* approached. A long-range engagement with heavy expenditure of ammunition ensued. The British labeled Gautier as "unenterprising" because he maintained the range at over eight thousand yards and withdrew as soon as the minesweepers were safe.[42] The British seemed just as cautious, but the destroyers had already crossed the limiting east longitude that Tyrwhitt had ordered because of the British A36 minefield.[43] The light cruisers covering the destroyers to the west could not intervene, while the destroyers did not follow the Germans farther because they believed they had "sighted their backing-up force." This was the Fourth Scouting Group, but its advance west was halted by urgent advice from the minesweepers.[44] The British were fortunate this was the case, since the destroyer *Sturgeon* was disabled by a 105-mm hit in her engine room and had to be taken in tow. Within the Harwich Force Tyrwhitt was highly critical of the destroyers' "foolhardy action" in crossing A36 but covered for *Thruster*'s captain in his report: "He did all that could be done, the extraordinary visibility defeating any chance of surprise."[45] The naval staff's post-action analysis did not miss what had happened, however, and the Admiralty called Commander George Gibbs to account. To his great credit Tyrwhitt closed the matter, pointing out he had already dealt with Gibbs and "cautioned" his commanding officers.[46] The minefields that littered the southern North Sea had once more proven to be an overriding constraint. The incident confirmed another development. An increasingly active naval staff in the Admiralty was conducting more sophisticated analysis of operations than had been the case earlier in the war. This was both necessary and correct, particularly as it would help identify deficiencies in information flows and coordinating remote operations that had dogged the British since 1914. Nevertheless, it must have been galling to officers like Tyrwhitt, accustomed as they were to operational autonomy. A note of black humor was sounded after the war. During the encounter, the Germans were puzzled by the British advance across one of their own minefields. When they discovered the existence of dummy mines, the explanation seemed to be that A36 was not a live field, but it was.[47]

The Second Assault on Ostend

Keyes was determined to renew the assault on Ostend. He still had a few days of the right tidal conditions and the battered *Vindictive* was available for conversion to a block ship. A galvanized Dover Command and support units patched up the old cruiser and filled her with cement in time for an attempt on 27 April. Keyes understood the heightened risks of this second venture and insisted on the smallest crew possible on board *Vindictive*.[48] Worsening weather forced another delay. This allowed the depot ship *Sappho*, another elderly cruiser, to be converted as an additional block vessel, but also meant the raiders had to accept a shorter period of darkness to cover the attack and withdrawal. The operation went ahead on the night of 9–10 May. *Sappho* had to drop out with a boiler defect soon after the force sailed from Dunkirk, leaving *Vindictive* to continue alone. The preliminary bombardment began just after 0140, this time supported by a bombing raid. The final approach went well until a thick fog suddenly descended, forcing *Vindictive* to grope her way along the coast while the German gun batteries, alerted by reports from torpedo boats picketed to seaward, searched for their target. As a last resort, the British illuminated the canal entrance to show *Vindictive* the way, but this also made the cruiser visible to the shore defenses. Under intense fire, *Vindictive* (whose captain, Alfred Godsal, was dead) approached the entrance just before 0200 and grounded by the bows on the eastern side of the channel. The plan had been to ground by the bow on the other side, allowing the tide to swing the stern across the passage, but *Vindictive* finished up practically parallel to the side of the canal. The blocking attempt had failed again.

Two motor launches extracted *Vindictive*'s survivors under a hail of fire. *ML254* was so badly damaged that she only just made it to Keyes' flagship, the destroyer *Warwick*, lying offshore. Keyes had brought the ship close into the coast to look for any "derelicts." This was a risk justified by the results, but just after *Warwick* began her passage home, the destroyer detonated a mine. The ship's back was broken and her stern only held on by the mine rails fitted over the quarterdeck. The struggle to save the crippled ship was an anxious one. The disabled *Warwick* was first towed alongside by *Velox* and then by *Whirlwind*. Even after Keyes' ships had got out of range of the German batteries, there remained the possibility of a surface attack. The British believed a flotilla of High Sea Fleet destroyers had been dispatched to Flanders, although their intelligence may have confused the aborted return of the command's own units, which resulted in the action of 20 April. Delayed by weather, these did not arrive at Zeebrugge until 12 May.

Keyes would not give up and developed yet another proposal to block Ostend, this time using *Sappho* and the stripped and lightened pre-dreadnought *Swiftsure*, whose armor and size would make her a much more formidable proposition for the defenses, as well as a substantial obstacle to place in the canal. The operation, however, was canceled by the Admiralty just before it was due to take place in June. The personnel concerned were "bitterly disappointed"[49] but the British no longer believed the Bruges-Ostend canal justified the casualties inevitable in a third attack, while they knew the Germans had laid additional mines around the approaches to the port.[50]

The focus of British offensive effort was shifting in any case. Although Keyes became intensely frustrated by his reduced control over the air elements that followed the establishment of the Royal Air Force on 1 April 1918 and the incorporation into the new service of the RNAS, the bombing campaign against the Flanders bases was increasingly effective.[51] One of the Zeebrugge lock gates was put out of action for a week at the end of May, while several torpedo boats were severely damaged in the same month. Further, continuing improvements in range-finding techniques meant the monitors were more effective than ever. On 9 June, *Marshal Soult* and *Terror* bombarded Zeebrugge. Their primary targets were the dredgers attempting to widen the channel, but they achieved the hit that Bacon had sought for so long when the newly repaired lock gate was again put out of action. This time the caisson was so badly damaged the canal was unusable for a month.[52] Driven off by the increasingly accurate coastal batteries, the British do not seem to have realized their achievement.

The Dover barrage's consolidation and perfection of the night illumination organization completed the effective closure of the strait to U-boats, adding to von Schröder's woes. The Allied air offensive could be met in part by reinforcement aircraft and the reallocation of squadrons already in Flanders; but the Germans were finding it increasingly difficult to maintain mine-free passage for the U-boats, and increasingly active British and French surface forces required the submarines to have escorts. The problems with the canals and the cumulative effects of the bombing campaign meant the Flanders Command was hard put to field enough operational minesweepers and torpedo craft, while some of the small *A* boats had to take on minesweeping to compensate for the losses of more suitable units.

Sortie by the High Sea Fleet

The High Sea Fleet was also feeling the pressure. The light cruiser *Stralsund* had been severely damaged by a mine in the Heligoland Bight on 12 February, while *A57* and *A56* were sunk by mines early in March, with *M91*, *M36*, and *M40* falling victim later in the month. On 30 March, *G87*, *G93*, and *G94* were caught in a minefield laid only the previous day and sank within less than an hour of each other, highlighting the risks of supporting the minesweeping operations. Scheer determined that a new northerly mine-free route should be established. This could be done, but it would only be a matter of time before the British deduced the existence of another passage and turned their attention to it. The one active step was to embark on a new program of defensive minelaying. During April and May, five thousand mines were deployed around the swept channels, placed across the expected approach axes of the British minelayers. It would be some time before this effort paid dividends.

The navy was also under pressure to do what it could to support the Army's offensive on the western front. The *Handelskrieg* was not going well. While the loss rate of U-boats dropped sharply in February and remained relatively low at six boats in both March and April, the average tonnage sunk by each unit also declined. The requirement to pass around the north of Scotland was one factor, so was the difficulty in maintaining operational availability. Finally, although there were still targets to be found, convoy was proving a significant challenge. The army's high command had lost faith in the ability of the U-boats to end the war but appealed for a special effort against the shipping carrying reinforcements to France. This was easier said than done, but Scheer believed the High Sea Fleet could strike a heavy blow.

Photo 13.3   **U-boat and battleship in ice**   *German Naval Association Archive*

The possibility of attacking in the south was canvassed, but Scheer found the kaiser would not allow the risk. The admiral was particularly critical of the Admiralstab's influence in this decision, contributing to his own belief that the German navy should be put under one commander alone. Despite the closer proximity of the Grand Fleet, however, a sortie north was acceptable to the kaiser and the Admiralstab. The British had increased the interval between the Scandinavian convoys until by April they ran every five days. This made their protection less onerous, but also enlarged the convoys and thus their attractiveness as targets. Scheer's staff had gathered intelligence about the operating cycle from U-boats, although not apparently from local agents in Norway.

The plan was for von Hipper to attack the convoy with his battle cruisers. The Germans were aware that a division or squadron of the Grand Fleet's capital ships would be at sea as cover. If Hipper were unable to brush this force aside, he could call on the support of the complete High Sea Fleet, which would follow him into the North Sea. Poor weather forced the cancellation of a sortie planned for 10 April, but the raiding forces finally sailed early on 23 April. Although briefly delayed in the Heligoland Bight by fog, the High Sea Fleet was on its way by daybreak. German communications security on this occasion was excellent. Scheer and his admirals had at last stopped using radio to pass preparatory messages, adopting the British practice of passing such directions by hand. Security was helped by the recent issue of new call signs and a change in the cipher key on 21 April, which Room 40 did not break for three days.[53] There were scraps of signals intelligence, notably orders to zeppelins to scout the North Sea, but not enough to convince the British a major sortie was under way. Five British submarines were on patrol in the Bight, disposed to detect and report such a sortie. One of the submarines—*J6*—operating off Horns Reef, sighted the German force on the afternoon of 23 April. Unfortunately, her captain decided—admittedly in poor visibility—that the ships he saw were forces covering a British minelaying operation of which he had been warned and neither reported his sighting nor made an attack. Perhaps it was an improvement in British procedures that *J6*'s captain had been informed of friendly forces, but it is clear that the information was either insufficiently precise or not well understood.

What the Germans did not understand was that their own intelligence was poor. They had timed their attack for a gap in the schedule. The irony was the greater because the covering force that returned to Rosyth on 24 April was the most vulnerable of any element of the Grand Fleet: the Second

Battle Cruiser Squadron, comprising the four oldest and weakest of the type. The scouting groups also had to do their own reconnaissance. The zeppelins *L41*, *L42*, and *L63* launched late on the 23rd, but were recalled in the early hours of the following morning because of rising winds.[54] This forced Hipper to proceed near 60° N to search for the convoy, farther than any capital ships of the High Sea Fleet had been during the entire war.

The scouting groups' progress was not without difficulty. *Seydlitz* shut down her starboard engine for two hours due to a condenser defect. The poor quality of the battle cruisers' coal also caused problems, forcing frequent furnace cleaning and limiting speed—*Von der Tann* could barely manage

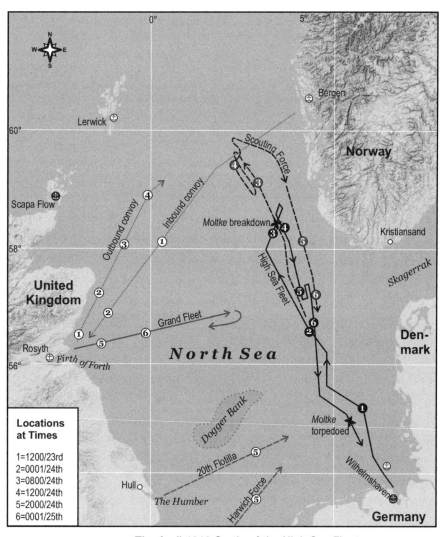

Map 13.1 **The April 1918 Sortie of the High Sea Fleet**

twenty-one knots.[55] Worse followed. At 0410 *Moltke*'s inner starboard shaft snapped due to the failure of a thrust block. The outboard end of the shaft and the propeller broke off and despite efforts to use the overspeed shutdown, the starboard high-pressure turbine ran away, shattering the turbine, and scattering debris that penetrated pipes and machinery. The midships engine room and the dynamo room rapidly flooded as the *Moltke* took in sixteen hundred tons of water. Since the auxiliary condenser pipes had been breached, the feed system rapidly salted. The ship could still manage thirteen knots, but it was only a matter of time before she lost motive power.[56] Hipper was unaware of the full extent of *Moltke*'s problems when he detached her to join Scheer and was alarmed to receive the crippled ship's 0543 signal that she was restricted to four knots. Sent at high power, this was a major breach of radio silence, but justifiable in circumstances that saw the ship at risk of being stopped and helpless in the open sea. The signal took time to get through to Scheer and *Moltke*'s initial text confused the situation with an incorrect position. While this was being sorted out, Scheer detached *Strassburg* to assist *Moltke*. Hipper initially turned back to support his lame duck but resumed the search for the convoy when he became aware the main body was dealing with the cripple.

Moltke's 0543 signal was picked up by the British, their first clear indication something was amiss. At this stage, the text was not decrypted, but Room 40 was sure of the call sign. Unfortunately, the directionals placed *Moltke* inland in Norway, an ironic assessment given the positional error in the original signal.[57] Although the Admiralty immediately informed Beatty of the intercept, uncertainty as to its credibility delayed an order to sail by nearly two hours. However, by this point Room 40 was in little doubt that something was up. This was confirmed by decryption of a Neumünster signal reporting its own analysis that the British were not aware of German forces at sea. The inference was clear. This information was sent to Beatty at 0955 and he first directed the battle cruisers and then the remainder of the fleet to prepare to sail. The Admiralty ordered the Grand Fleet out at 1047. Despite the Firth of Forth being enveloped in thick fog, a frequent condition and one of the long-standing objections to Rosyth as a fleet base, the entire fleet departed without incident in less than three hours.

Even without the problem of *Moltke*, the High Sea Fleet was not going to linger in the north. The force still included torpedo boats with very limited operational endurance and these could not remain out another day without eating into their operational reserves, vital to retain in case the enemy was encountered. The clear weather eventually left no room for doubt the intelligence was mistaken, even if Neumünster still claimed a convoy was due to depart Bergen on 24 April. After sighting the Norwegian coast, the First Scouting Group turned for home just after 1500. *Strassburg* and then the battleship *Oldenburg* had taken *Moltke* under tow, while her engineers worked to flush the boiler tubes with newly distilled fresh water. When von Hipper caught up, his ships took station around *Moltke*. By 1600, the battle cruiser's portside shafts were turning and there were prospects of bringing the outer starboard shaft into operation using the low-pressure turbine. The tow was maintained, but von Hipper and Scheer could be reasonably confident they had a clear run to the Bight.

The geometry of the situation was probably obvious to Beatty as he sailed. The Grand Fleet could not get across the North Sea in time to intercept the Germans once the latter turned south. That they had done so was made clear by a signal from the Admiralty at 1625, which gave the position of the German flagship steering a course SSE. Perhaps to Room 40's amusement, it decrypted a signal from *U19* that reported "11 old enemy cruisers" in a position that matched that of the High Sea Fleet. *J6* was not the only muddled submarine on patrol, although the U-boats had the benefit of warning by "catchword" signals that their fleet would be at sea—a clue Room 40 realized it had missed.[58] The Grand Fleet continued its sortie into 25 April, but the High Sea Fleet was well ahead of it, helped by practically perfect weather conditions that allowed *Moltke* to maintain speed through the combination of tow and engines. Only at 1640, by which time *Moltke* could manage thirteen knots, was the tow cast off. This was timely as the fleet was well into the Heligoland Bight, trammelled by mine fields and the submarines the Germans knew to be on patrol. The minesweeper *M67* had already hit a mine and sunk, while there had been at least one submarine sighting.

J6 did no better a job on the High Sea Fleet's return. Between 0400 and 0715 Lieutenant Commander Geoffrey Warburton observed substantial components of the German fleet on their homeward course. He did not attack but surfaced and reported the sightings. However, orders that gave priority to reporting were intended for outward-bound contacts; *J6* should have attacked the homeward-bound German fleet. The British had a last chance with *E42*, dispatched to lie across the swept channel that the Admiralty thought most likely the High Sea Fleet would employ. Forced to submerge and bombed by a seaplane, Lieutenant C. H. Allen was fortunate to spot smoke in the northeast in the late afternoon of 25 April. A dash southeast brought him in contact with *Moltke*'s formation. Allen fired his two bow and two beam tubes in succession at a range of over two thousand yards and was rewarded by a single explosion.[59] *Moltke* spotted a torpedo on her port bow and turned to avoid, but it struck abreast her port engine room at 1838. More than seventeen hundred tons of water flooded in, forcing immediate counter-flooding and threatening *Moltke*'s ability to move. The battle cruiser responded with gunfire in the torpedo's direction and called for help. Over the next few hours, torpedo boats and destroyers supplemented the battle cruiser's escort as she struggled to get home. *E42* was hunted, and an estimated twenty-five or more depth charges were deployed against her, but she escaped unscathed. In addition to strenuous patrols, smoke screens were deployed around the battle cruiser. These were so effective they embarrassed the late-arriving Second Flotilla, which was lucky to avoid any collisions. Good damage control and further hard work by her engineers meant that *Moltke* never lost steaming power, although she was once again under tow that evening. *Moltke* was safe in Wilhelmshaven anchorage by the morning of 26 April, but her damage meant she would not be fully operational again until mid-September.[60]

The Grand Fleet returned to harbor after the Admiralty assessed that the High Sea Fleet was on its way home and could not be caught. Beatty had already decided to allow the convoy cycle to resume without delay, although he strengthened the covering force. The incident confirmed the C-in-C's misgivings over the requirement to protect the convoys with a detachment of heavy ships. What is clear is that his strictures about the potential weakness of the Grand Fleet were not justified. There were thirty-one capital ships in the force that left Rosyth, despite the absence of the Second Battle Cruiser Squadron and at least three other dreadnoughts. Room 40 carried out its own postmortem. The signals intelligence system could certainly have done better but had not done that badly. Confirmation Room 40 could not be relied upon to provide warning on every occasion heightened the concern of senior officers, but perhaps the greatest failure lay in *J6*'s captain's poor assessments.

One theory sometimes raised by historians is that a previous convoy cycle had been protected by the Sixth Battle Squadron.[61] It is true that the destruction of the American force, when thus isolated from the Grand Fleet, would have been both a material and a psychological disaster for the Anglo-American relationship. Von Hipper's battle cruisers, however, would have found Rodman's quartet of powerful dreadnoughts a hard nut to crack, even if the German problems with coal and machinery did not eliminate their speed advantage, while Rodman would have had to make a succession of unlikely errors to become entangled with the main body of the High Sea Fleet. He and all the Grand Fleet's admirals were acutely aware of the risk of defeat in detail and Rodman drew Sims's ire when he expressed his concerns a little too openly later in April.[62] Scheer had already taken his fleet farther north than it had been since July 1914. He would have no appetite for a chase toward the Scottish coast, a chase that in any case the light forces of his fleet could not have long continued.

End Game in the North Sea

14

THE HIGH SEA FLEET DID NOT REPEAT the attempt against the Scandinavian convoy. Scheer later wrote "it was unfortunately the last which the Fleet was unable to undertake," but he failed to explain further.[1] Why the North Sea forces were so passive over the next six months had several causes. The opportunities opening in the Baltic with the Russian peace were one. The diversion of dreadnoughts and their escorts to occupying the Aland Islands and operations in the Baltic provinces was not huge, but still significant. Another factor was the two influenza pandemics that struck later in the year. The navy's material state was an even greater concern. The fleet was accumulating defects that the repair system could not fix.[2] A dearth of nonferrous metals combined with shortages of skilled manpower in the dockyards meant ships were either going without repair at all or the work was, at best, makeshift. *Moltke*'s shaft failure was the result of hull damage incurred entering Wilhelmshaven in December 1916, which caused cracking in the shaft tunnel.[3] A two-week repair period followed, but the work was a temporary solution that had to answer "all requirements until it gave way in April 1918."[4] *Moltke* was not alone in her troubles on the April sortie. Apart from the poor coal quality, which affected other battle cruisers, *Seydlitz* suffered condenser problems that forced her to shut down both port and starboard engines at different times.[5] Even if shortages of fuel were overcome, Scheer had to face the possibility his fleet was not fully seaworthy, let alone battle ready.

Another problem was the mine threat. Maintaining access to the North Sea for the U-boats was vital. The ability of the British to fuse intelligence of the German swept channels with deployment of their own mine fields was creating the prospect of a Heligoland Bight that was completely shut off from the open sea. By March, homeward-bound U-boats were returning through the Baltic and in June the battle cruisers conducted navigation exercises to familiarize them with using the Little Belt.[6] Keeping even one channel open in the Heligoland Bight consumed much of the capacity of the minesweeping force and the scouting groups and battle squadrons that covered them. Contrary to the historical image, the High Sea Fleet in this period went to sea, just not very far. The battle cruisers did the most work, but even the battleships provided close or distant cover two or three times a month. Over the summer, there were variations on clearing a passage, including the creation of a new channel at the end of July. This involved nine half-flotillas of minesweepers, supported by the First Scouting Group and the Third Squadron, with substantial numbers of escorts. Only *U96* was immediately present to proceed through the newly opened channel, but the passage remained useful until September. All this was better than nothing, but the essentially defensive strategy did not encourage high morale and left all offensive effort to the failing powers of the U-boats.

The British and the Americans, by comparison, were increasingly active. In addition to the antisubmarine campaign, there were four elements: convoy protection in the Atlantic, mining operations in the Heligoland Bight and Kattegat, creation of a northern mine barrage, and more ambitious efforts to employ aircraft and CMBs offensively. Each activity experienced setbacks, but there was an increasing sense as 1918 wore on that the initiative had shifted in the British and American favor. Only in one area did operational activity diminish. By the middle of the year, a battle squadron was no longer

Photo 14.1   HMS *Barham* with aircraft   *Sea Power Centre, Australia*

covering the Scandinavian convoy. This was delegated to light cruisers and then to armored cruisers, which—if close enough to the convoy—were certainly enough to deter a repeat effort by German light cruisers or destroyers. Whether armored cruisers would have followed the guidance to withdraw and report the appearance of superior forces is a moot point.

The American presence in the eastern Atlantic grew steadily throughout 1918. The High Sea Fleet's April sortie raised the specter of other ventures, notably the possibility that German battle cruisers might be sent into the Atlantic. British cruisers and armed merchant cruisers and American units were already assigned to convoy protection west of the submarine danger zone in the eastern Atlantic and these were certainly enough to deal with disguised merchant raiders. A battle cruiser was something else again. There were lengthy discussions within the Admiralty, in Washington, and in the Allies' consultative processes regarding how the transatlantic traffic should be protected—particularly the troops moving to Europe in increasing numbers. Much of the USN's additional destroyer effort was devoted to escorting this shipping within the submarine zone, with the French port of Brest becoming an important base of operations. But it was reasonable to think that the less effective the U-boats were against the flow of American men and materials, the more likely the Germans would be to try an alternative. The solution finally adopted was the dispatch of Battleship Division Six, consisting of *Nevada*, *Oklahoma*, and *Utah*, to Berehaven in Ireland in August 1918. There they were immediately available to cover convoys already in the eastern Atlantic if the German battle cruisers broke out. There would only be one alert before the Armistice (it occurred in October), but the battleships and their destroyer escort from Queenstown were in company with the convoy concerned little more than forty-eight hours after the initial warning. The system worked.[7]

The 1918 flu pandemic had a profound effect on the operational readiness of both sides and is a key reason why that year saw extended periods of inactivity by the main fleets. The sickness occurred earlier in the Royal Navy and its allies than the German navy. The first variety brought many down, but its effects were relatively mild. The second was more severe and often deadly. One British battleship had 270 cases in the first period in May without any deaths, and only 62 cases in October, but 8 deaths. Each outbreak lasted 11 days.[8] The Grand Fleet's first epidemic started in April and reached its peak on 15 May with 2,568 cases. More than 10,000 of the fleet's 90,000 personnel were struck down, although there were only 4 deaths in all. There were sporadic cases until September, when 5,381 were stricken, of whom 151 died.[9] The Sixth Battle Squadron was severely affected, particularly during the second round. *Arkansas* suffered most, perhaps because the ship was newly arrived from the United States and its crew had not yet acquired resistance through exposure to the first variety. She had 259 cases and suffered 11 deaths. The Grand Fleet was never completely out of action, but it was a near-run thing. Several ships, including the battle cruiser *Princess Royal*, had so many sick they could not have sailed had the fleet been ordered out. The pandemic affected the remainder of the navy at different times. By the start of July, three cruisers of the Harwich Force could not sail, *Concord* being typical with 170 sick.[10] The escort forces were hit hard as well. At least one destroyer had so many sick that replacement personnel had to embark at sea to bring her back into port. At one point *Termagant*, on standby at Dover, had only 26 out of 150 fit for duty.[11] The pandemic struck the Germans in June. *Seydlitz* had 104 sick at its peak on board early in the month, while the numbers unfit for duty in the minesweepers found them struggling to meet their commitments in July.[12] The German naval experience of the second wave that hit in September is less clear, but based on the experience of the army, it is likely that the pandemic contributed to the chaotic events of October and November 1918.[13]

The Mine War

British submarine minelayers continued their campaign along the German and Dutch coast, although losses mounted. *E34* struck a mine off Vlieland during her twenty-fourth mission on 20 July, and the British authorities feared she had hit a mine laid by *E51*. The thirty-eight-day plugs often failed to dissolve, menacing attempts to re-seed an area with a new field. Surface efforts in the late winter and spring included the Kattegat, as the British accumulated evidence that U-boats were using the Baltic passages as an alternative to risking the Heligoland Bight. The first operation in February was covert, with a field successfully deployed southeast of the Skaw. A repeat effort planned for March turned back when it encountered thick fog, but another attempt on 15–16 April was much more successful. The minelayers were covered by the First Battle Cruiser Squadron and the Fifth Battle Squadron, in addition to three light cruiser squadrons and twenty-four destroyers. The light forces conducted their own sweep well into the Kattegat, sinking ten German trawlers. This was a clear signal of British interest in the Baltic approaches, heightening the High Sea Fleet's concern about the Kattegat's security.

Operations again focused on the Heligoland Bight as the days lengthened. The mining task, already taken away from light cruisers, shifted from the big converted minelayers, such as *Princess Margaret,* to the newly formed Twentieth Destroyer Flotilla. This was well into its stride by mid-year. Seven operations were conducted in the Heligoland Bight in July. Although the total included sorties off the Belgian coast, the captain of *Telemachus* estimated his ship took part in thirty-six operations between February and 31 August 1918 and laid 1,440 mines.[14] The Flotilla's score for the Bight would be forty-two sorties and 12,939 mines.[15] Despite at least one near encounter in poor visibility, the destroyer minelayers initially went unscathed, oblivious that "much of the water . . . considered innocuous, and . . . gaily careered over at 25 knots, teemed with [mines]."[16] On 28 March, the Twentieth Destroyer Flotilla captured and sank three armed trawlers. The flotilla's luck ran out, however, on 2 August. An eight-ship formation was approaching its start position when at 2347, *Vehement* hit a mine. Her magazine went up, taking with it everything forward of the fore-funnel. Despite being blown four hundred yards clear by the explosion, the captain lived and managed to save one of his sailors from drowning. *Abdiel* took *Vehement*'s remains in tow and ordered the remainder of the flotilla out of the German minefield. *Ariel* did not get clear; at 0010 she also struck a mine forward, which blew her bows off, sinking her in less than an hour. There were hopes that *Vehement* could be saved, but the tow became unmanageable. Her survivors taken off, she was sunk by gunfire. There were ninety-seven dead from both ships.

This incident greatly slowed the minelaying campaign in the Heligoland Bight. The British had an idea the Germans had laid new fields from *E51*'s sighting a line of mines in April, but the fact that the Germans had laid such large fields had not been suspected—perhaps because little radio traffic was involved. Pure luck had allowed the Twentieth Destroyer Flotilla to avoid them on sorties in the previous few weeks. Although the flotilla was soon out again on operations off the Belgian coast, it only undertook four more sorties into the Heligoland Bight during the remainder of the war: one on 31 August, one in late September, and two in October (one on the night of 2–3 October and a final sortie on 27–28 October). All were just to the outer ends of the German channels. Until the British had a much better idea of the enemy fields, the Admiralty was unwilling to risk either destroyers or submarines far inside the Bight. Beatty accepted the step back only reluctantly; had the war continued, the effort would have been resumed. *E45* was actually dispatched for a lay in the inner Bight in November but was recalled after the armistice, to her captain and flotilla commander's great relief.[17] As it was, the residue of the British campaign was sufficient to give the Germans continuing trouble. A German mine explosion destroyed *M41* in September, *M62* was sunk by a British mine on 9 August, and *M22* would go down on 14 October. *M42* survived striking a mine the day before, while *M18* and *M78* were both damaged on 27 October.[18]

With the first use of a magnetic mine, the minelaying effort off the Flanders coast foreshadowed the next war. The early magnetic mines were not particularly reliable, frequently exploding when the magnetic trigger reacted to a false signal, but the British successfully deployed a small field off Zeebrugge on 7 August. This soon claimed victims, *V68* being sunk and *G94* badly damaged the next day. The minesweepers, many of which were wooden, had not actuated the mines, but the torpedo boats did. The experience of detonating mines in water already swept was unnerving for the escort forces. Repeated sweeping efforts produced nothing, but *G41* was badly damaged on 11 August. *A58* fell victim on 15 August, breaking in two and partially blocking the channel after the attempt to bring her in failed. By this point, von Schröder was suspicious that the British had developed a new triggering system for their mines. It was another blow to the steadily diminishing ability of the Flanders forces to keep their access to the open sea, let alone pose any significant threat to the Allies.[19]

The Northern Barrage was a wholly different venture to the Heligoland Bight operations. An American idea, its acceptance by the British was largely to allay concerns of the U.S. administration and the USN over the apparently defensive policies of the Admiralty. Acquiescing to the American proposal helped maintain the relationship and encourage their commitment to other, more vital activities. The scheme was a barrier of mines to close off the North Sea between Scotland and Norway. The initial American estimate was that 72,000 mines would be required to cover the 250 miles in sufficient depth, with the barrage divided into three areas. The longest, central position was designated "Area A," the flanking area off the coast of Scotland, "Area B," and that off the coast of Norway, "Area C." There were always problems, not least of which was the technology involved was still being developed while the barrage's details were being worked out. To catch submerged U-boats, the American barrage mines were fitted with floating antennae above and below the mine casing. From the first, there were concerns with their lethality range. Another difficulty was that the barrage limited the Grand Fleet's sea room. Beatty, who never liked the idea, objected most to the prospect of no passage on the eastern side of the Orkneys. His bid for a ten-mile channel was eventually reduced to three, but only after pleas by the First Sea Lord to accept the closure in the interest of Anglo-American amity.

The first field was laid by the newly formed British First Minelaying Squadron in March. This did not go well when the destruction of the sloop *Gaillardia* revealed that the mines—the effective new H2 model—were floating well above their intended depth of sixty-five feet and were thus a menace to surface ships. A total of 1,440 mines had to be swept and the operation begun again from scratch. The ten USN units assigned to the barrage arrived in Cromarty on 26 May. They were designated the Second

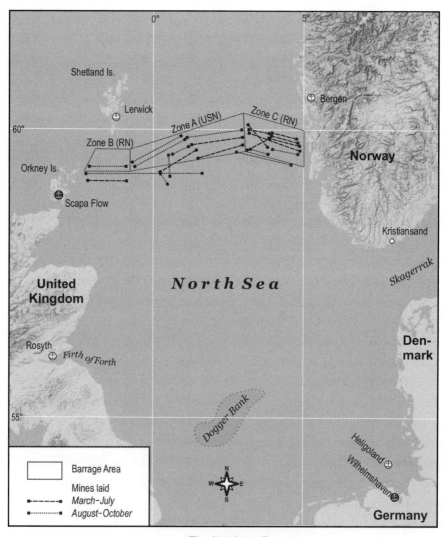

Map 14.1 **The Northern Barrage**

Mine Laying Squadron (Mine Squadron One in the USN). Both British and American squadrons conducted laying operations at roughly fortnightly intervals over the next few months.[20] The industrial-scale effort eventually resulted in more than 70,000 mines being laid, of which 56,570 were put down by USN units.[21] Its results were mixed. The American mines proved prone to detonate soon after being laid. This problem was never really fixed. The *Australia*, providing cover for Operation M14 on 27 September, estimated that a detonation occurred every two minutes over a six-hour period, with some individual detonations resulting in three or four other explosions. During Operation M15 a week later, the *Australia* recorded another 287 detonations.[22] On 26 October, the ships of Mine Squadron One themselves recorded an average of 140 explosions seen or heard that day, 28 believed to have caused countermining.[23] Apart from the problems with the mines, the patrols that were essential in forcing the U-boats to transit the mine danger area submerged were never put in place. It remains uncertain whether any submarines were sunk by these mines, although a much later Admiralty study suggests that up to five may have been caught.[24] Nevertheless, the barrage added to the U-boats' burdens and represented a formidable demonstration of America's resources and determination. It could certainly have become progressively more effective, particularly as the Norwegians, after much pressure, finally agreed in October 1918 to mine their own territorial sea to prevent its use by U-boats for covert transits.

British Offensive Operations

Tyrwhitt's forces had acquired a new capability in the form of lighters, each carrying a single flying boat; they could be towed at high speed by destroyers. The Harwich Force hoped this would provide a combination of mobility and capability against zeppelins and other fixed-wing aircraft that the British had not enjoyed before. The first deployment was on 19 March, when three were taken into the Heligoland Bight. The Harwich Force repeated the operation at two-week intervals over the next two months. The lighters proved more weatherly than expected, but the aircraft were still constrained by wind, sea, and swell and frequently could not get into the air, much to the Harwich Force's frustration (in August, Captain Domvile noted, "the seaplanes failed to fly, as usual").[25] Even so, a cat-and-mouse game was being played against the increasingly vulnerable zeppelins. A British flying boat operating from a shore base succeeded in damaging *L56* on 19 May, but it was storm or perhaps sabotage that downed *L62* the same day.[26]

The Harwich Force's sweeps in May and June had the additional intent of securing a copy of the new German signal book. This was at the behest of the DNI, who sent Commander Vivien Brandon (imprisoned between 1910 and 1913 by the Germans for espionage) from NID's German section on the first sortie. Operation F3, covered by the First Battle Cruiser Squadron and other formations, did not go well.[27] No signal book was captured and on 31 May the Harwich Force found itself in a minefield. Although at least five mines were cut by cruisers, paravanes did not protect the destroyer leader *Shakespeare*, which struck a mine and was severely damaged.[28] The operation was notable for one thing. The launch of a Sopwith Camel from the cruiser *Sydney* and its interception of a German seaplane, albeit without shooting its opponent down, was the first engagement by a ship-launched aircraft of another heavier-than-air machine.[29] Two weeks later, on another of what Tyrwhitt's flag captain described as "one of the fool expeditions," the cruiser *Centaur* was damaged by a mine, going home stern first.[30] As *Conquest* struck a mine near Harwich the same day, Tyrwhitt's ships were feeling the pressure.

CMBs were another element of the Harwich Force sorties. Carried in the cruisers, they were taken southeast of the Dogger Bank, launched, and sent toward the Ems for overnight sorties. Their targets were the minesweepers operating off the German coast but they held the faint hope of finding larger prey in the form of covering forces. The CMBs were almost as weather limited as the flying boats and more than one sortie was canceled before it began. While there were interactions with the German sweepers, darkness and the CMBs' limited horizon meant they often returned to their parent ships without having seen anything. Breakdowns were frequent and one crew was lucky to be picked up by a trawler after thirty-six hours adrift in open water.

The first real success of mid-1918 was not achieved by the Harwich Force, but by the aircraft carrier *Furious*. The importance of the Grand Fleet's air arm had been acknowledged by the appointment of Rear Admiral Phillimore as Admiral Commanding Aircraft in March at Beatty's behest. The newly modified *Furious* wore his flag. Great hopes were held for the new aft landing deck in *Furious*, despite the turbulent airflows created by her superstructure. Although there were some initial successes, it was soon confirmed that landing on *Furious* was too hazardous. Nevertheless, *Furious* could carry and launch reasonable numbers of aircraft and keep up with the battle cruisers and light forces. During the early summer, she accompanied elements of the Grand Fleet on several sorties, her aircraft shooting down a German seaplane on 19 June. The supporting destroyers had developed procedures, subject to sea state, to recover ditched aircraft. These were sometimes collected in better condition than the pilots, who frequently suffered broken noses from the Camel's tendency to pitch forward when ditching.

A more ambitious venture was in train. *Furious* was not the only advance in the fleet's aviation capability. In addition to flying-off platforms fitted on capital ship gun turrets that could be rotated to launch aircraft into the wind without necessarily requiring an alteration of course, light cruisers were now fitted with rotating platforms offering the same advantage. Practically every major unit now had a fighter embarked. The zeppelins' climbing ability, however, made them very difficult targets. Continuing sweeps into the southern North Sea in the hope of intercepting one seemed a waste of effort. The air staff of *Furious* proposed an alternative, a raid on the Tondern zeppelin base. The proposal was enthusiastically endorsed by Phillimore and Beatty. Seven Camels were equipped to carry 50-pound bombs and the pilots trained in low-level flying. The first attempt at the end of June was canceled when the weather worsened, but *Furious* and her escorts sailed on 17 July for a second try. Once again, poor weather forced postponement on the 18th, but the force remained at sea, hoping conditions would improve and sheltered from German air reconnaissance by the same bad weather. Notably, Admiral Phillimore delegated the decision to proceed to the air group commander. The weather cleared overnight and just before dawn, all seven aircraft were successfully launched, each carrying two bombs. The first three Camels to attack Tondern achieved surprise, successfully bombing "Toska" hangar and destroying the two zeppelins inside, *L54* and *L60*. The other aircraft damaged another hangar and set fire to a balloon, although some bombs failed to detonate. Two Camels returned to *Furious* and ditched successfully, a third was lost at sea, while the remainder were

Photo 14.2

HMS *Vega* with a recovered Sopwith Pup

Sea Power Centre, Australia

forced to divert to Denmark.[31] The Germans were fortunate in that the two zeppelins burned but did not explode, so damage to the hangar and base was relatively limited; still, it was a heavy blow that did not augur well for the future of the zeppelins. The Tondern raid marked another point in the airships' decline. Exposed to further attacks, the base was reduced to the status of an emergency landing ground.[32]

The raid was an important success and showed the way ahead for British carrier capability. Plans were set in motion to raid the much more challenging target of Ahlhorn, farther inland than Tondern. This required different, longer-range aircraft and the scheme did not come to fruition before the end of the war. The Grand Fleet nursed even greater hopes for the first "real" aircraft carrier, *Argus*, and her Sopwith Cuckoo torpedo bombers. While some technical problems had still to be resolved, the flat-decked *Argus* was capable of both launching and recovering wheeled aircraft. From before her commissioning in October 1918, plans were in hand to attack the High Sea Fleet in its anchorages. The strike force would not have been large enough to strike a decisive blow at the Germans, but it would have hit the High Sea Fleet hard and created a whole new set of problems for its defenses (as the Battle of Taranto so dramatically demonstrated in 1940).

The British had other innovations. The unsatisfactory performance of the flying boat/lighter combination inspired the idea of using the lighters to launch fighter aircraft. Trial and error confirmed a lighter could be modified to allow a wheeled fighter to launch with enough wind. On 10 August, after the system had been proved with a live flight, the Harwich Force sailed for another CMB raid, the destroyer *Redoubt* towing the modified lighter with a Camel embarked. Tyrwhitt was after a zeppelin and had good reason to be. A sortie on 1 August had seen the Harwich Force shadowed by two zeppelins. *L56* maintained her distance, but an inexperienced and aggressive captain in *L70* bombed the British ships. If such a close—and low—approach was to be repeated when a fighter aircraft was available, the airship would be very vulnerable. What Tyrwhitt could not know was the new capability would place the final nail in a coffin that was nearly sealed. On 5 August, Strasser led a four-ship raid on England. His command unit, *L70*, was intercepted by an Airco DH.4 off Norfolk and shot down in flames, killing all on board. The death of the dynamic Strasser and the loss of one of the most capable airships meant the end of the zeppelins' bombing campaign. The lead in this role had already passed to heavier-than-air aircraft, but the airships' days as naval scouting units were also coming to an end.

The Harwich Force sailed in perfect weather, which continued when six CMBs were launched by *Curacoa*, *Coventry*, and *Concord*. There was some anxiety that the operation was already being observed by German seaplanes as the CMBs headed toward the coast. The three flying boats that flew from Yarmouth to provide them air cover did not see the German aircraft and were unable to locate the CMBs, which were thus without the protection intended—and necessary—for a daylight operation. In the meantime, the cruisers and destroyers remained in the area until *L53* came in sight. Alerted by signals intelligence and the flying boats (which had at least spotted the zeppelin), Tyrwhitt was ready. He turned north and laid smoke to draw *L53* on. The ploy was successful and the Camel was launched shortly afterward. Despite *L53* operating at 19,000 feet, the Camel's pilot was eventually able to get within 300 feet of his prey. One of his guns jammed, but the other poured bullets into *L53*'s belly. The zeppelin went down in flames—there were no survivors. The Harwich Force was repeatedly bombed by seaplanes, but it was pleasantly surprised when Lieutenant Stuart Culley reappeared from his mission, ditched, and was rescued.

The CMBs did not fare well, being caught off the Dutch coast by seaplanes. A running fight followed, during which additional aircraft joined the fray. The CMBs were bombed and strafed, the Germans making effective use of the sun. While they replied with light machine guns, shooting down one airplane, the CMBs eventually exhausted their ammunition and, forced to

Photo 14.3   Coastal motor boat on a cruiser davit   *Sea Power Centre, Australia*

remain at maximum speed, ran low on fuel. They eventually turned toward the Dutch shore to find refuge, but although two damaged boats made it into Dutch territorial waters, four others were sunk or scuttled. An increasingly anxious Harwich Force called for aircraft from England to search for the CMBs, but nothing was found. The news that the crews were alive—albeit with one-third of them wounded—and in Dutch hands was a relief, but the affair confirmed that the fast motor boats could not operate in daylight without proper air cover. There would be no more CMB ventures into German waters without such support.

A New Approach to German Naval Command

The CMB affair occurred on the same day as a fundamental development in the command of the German navy. Scheer came ashore to replace von Holtzendorff at the head of the Admiralstab, but the change was much greater than that. Scheer insisted he be given full powers over naval policy and operations, receiving the designation of Chef der Seekriegsleitung (Chief of the Sea War Leadership). This stripped the kaiser of his authority and subjected the entire navy to Scheer, ending the compartmented arrangements that von Tirpitz had created to ensure his personal domination. Magnus von Levetzow was installed as Scheer's chief of staff, while von Hipper replaced Scheer in command of the fleet and von Reuter took over direction of the scouting groups. The German navy's new leadership had vast ambitions, incongruous in the context of the military collapse in progress on the western front and the navy's own problems with sustaining the *Handelskrieg* and finding ways to erode the enemy's growing supremacy at sea. The "Scheer Program" proposed a massive expansion in submarine construction, accelerating in 1919 and coming fully to fruition in 1920 with the monthly completion of thirty-three boats.[33] The program had an air of unreality, even if the Oberste Heeresleitung (Supreme Army Command) was prepared to release manpower and reallocate material to the shipyards. Scheer may have intended the project largely for propaganda purposes, to provide convincing evidence to domestic and international audiences of the navy's resolution, but it added immediately to the big ships' morale problems. Scheer having "to draw to an even greater degree than before upon the existing personnel of the fleet," could only be further confirmation of the High Sea Fleet's strategic irrelevance.[34] Scheer's insistence on placing his own supporters in key staff positions as he brought the navy under control had other effects. Nearly half the commanding and executive officers changed in the High

Sea Fleet's capital ships, creating disruptions in the seagoing leadership that contributed to the collapse of discipline later in the year.

The End of Days for the Imperial German Navy

After the "Black Day" of the German army at the Battle of Amiens on 8 August 1918, the tide had fully turned in the Allies' favor. Flanders Command made one last attempt at offensive operations. The German navy had followed the British in developing manned light craft and a flotilla arrived in Flanders earlier in 1918. Just after midnight on 23 August, six boats raided Dunkirk and attacked the destroyer *l'Obusier* and the torpedo boat *321*. The French ships avoided the German torpedoes and believed they damaged at least one of the attacking boats. *Terror* was at anchor but she used her guns in the later stages of the exchange, after which the German boats withdrew. The French official history concluded its narrative laconically, "*On ne les reverra plus*" (We will not see them again).[35] By late September, the German hold on Flanders was increasingly parlous and the British believed that their naval units' departure was likely. The German army formally advised a withdrawal on 28 September and von Schröder was given approval to prepare for an evacuation. He immediately began to send ships home. The smallest units, with as much war material as they could tow in barges, were dispatched through the canal system to Antwerp, but the bigger torpedo craft had to go by sea.[36] The British did what they could to stop this, but were aware of the German ability to remain under the protection of their coastal batteries before slipping into Dutch territorial waters. It is likely the experienced seagoing commanders did not expect to catch them. The Harwich Force sailed for a sweep along the Dutch coast on 30 September but found nothing and did not enjoy having to face gale-force weather. Sent out again the next day, after the Admiralty received additional intelligence of the evacuation, the Force "kept this up for a week, to all intents & purposes living at sea & waiting to catch the Hun leaving the Belgian coast."[37] The Twentieth Destroyer Flotilla placed minefields across possible escape routes, but as expected, both they and the Harwich Force failed to intercept their quarry. Eighteen German torpedo boats and two submarines sailed from Flanders on 1 October. Only a handful of serviceable units remained and these escaped over the next few days, with the last gone by 5 October. The unserviceable *G41* and *V74* together with four U-boats were sunk in the canals, while four more unseaworthy large torpedo boats were held in Ghent. Still unable to make the sea passage to Germany, *S61, V47, V67,* and *V69* were scuttled in early November when Belgium was completely evacuated. There was one moment of British hope—mixed with fear—when a sighting by an unaccompanied pair of destroyers suggested a much more numerous and powerful German force was in the offing. Escorting a "Beef trip" on 4 October, *Taurus* and *Mordaunt* thought they had detected a formation of German torpedo boats. Despite disquiet regarding their prospects against a superior enemy, they went in chase, only to find the Dutch navy out conducting maneuvers.[38]

The most important encounter in this period was further north in the Heligoland Bight. On the morning of 3 October, German minesweeping escorts waiting for some of the last submarines from Flanders ran into a British minefield laid the previous night. Just after 0200, *S33* struck two mines and went down, taking most of her crew with her. The torpedo boat's flotilla mates found the survivors after daylight, but the rescue was watched by the new British submarine *L10*. The latter successfully torpedoed *S34* after the German boat had picked up *S33*'s people. Unfortunately, perhaps because she was a new and untried design, *L10* reverted to the submariners' 1914 tendency of losing depth control after firing. She broached-to on the surface, at which *V26* and *V28* opened fire, damaging *L10*'s pressure hull and sinking her with all hands. This was some compensation for the Germans, particularly as attempts to tow *S34* home failed and she had to be sunk with a torpedo. *S122* was lost to a mine nearby on 5 October, confirming the western approaches to the Bight were still at hazard from the British effort.

Von Schröder's dispatch of his forces was just in time. Dover Command's bombardment ships spent most of August and September undergoing repairs and gun-barrel changes to ready themselves to support a new offensive by the allied northern armies. This began on 28 September. Over the following days the monitors conducted extensive bombardments for the forces ashore. The 18-inch gun carried by *General Wolfe* and the extended-range 9.2-inch guns of the newly completed *Gorgon* were indicative of growing material superiority. Although they had other targets in the following days, both could have made the German navy's position in Bruges untenable. The offensive ground to a temporary halt in early October and the monitors were not required again until the attack resumed on 14 October, joined by a second unit fitted with 18-inch guns, *Lord Clive*. There would not be many more firings. By the 19th the Belgian coast was empty of the enemy. The significance of that achievement was immediately recognized—the refit of *Prince Eugene* to take the third and last 18-inch gun was halted on 22 October.[39]

The collapse of the Oberste Heeresleitung's resolve to continue the war and the attempt to secure an armistice by appeal to President Wilson had almost immediate effects for the German navy. Suspension of the campaign against commerce was an essential precondition to ending hostilities. Scheer resisted the chancellor's insistence that the U-boats be called off, but he eventually gave way. The concession put to the president on 20 October was that submarine commanders would not attack passenger ships, but this amounted to the effective end of unrestricted warfare and Scheer knew it. The submarines were recalled the next day. This withdrawal of the U-boats and their order to return to Germany crystallized thinking within the navy's leadership about the need for a final effort to strike at the British. Justified in part as an attempt to strengthen Germany's position, it was much more a scheme to restore the navy's credibility and protect its political position in a postwar nation. Mixed with any rational motives was a curious muddle of emotion and wishful thinking that welcomed the prospect of a "death ride" but also harbored undefined hopes of achieving victory even in this final hour.

The chief of the Seekriegsleitung would not subject his plans to the approval of government or kaiser and Scheer's directions were conveyed by word of mouth to von Hipper, who immediately set about organizing the new venture. Plans had been in preparation within the High Sea Fleet staff since early October. Operation Plan No. 19 was partly a revival of the scheme to strike at the British in the south, which had been canvassed in March but rejected in favor of the abortive attack on the Scandinavian convoy. Scheer returned to his last initiative with the idea that large numbers of U-boats would be deployed to the North Sea. On 22 October, returning U-boats with sufficient remaining endurance were ordered to concentrate off the Firth of Forth. By the 28th, seven had arrived. Other submarines were sent out, although a number suffered defects and others had difficulties finding a safe route out of the Heligoland Bight. By the end of the month, there were twenty-two boats in the North Sea. Cruisers and torpedo craft would attack shipping in the Thames estuary while other units bombarded the Flanders coast. The First Scouting Group would serve in close support; the battle fleet would follow. The aim was to draw the Grand Fleet south to force a confrontation off Terschelling, a position the Germans judged to be their most favorable battleground. The Fourth Scouting Group, the raider *Möwe*, and some torpedo boats would lay minefields across the expected advance, the idea being that these, in combination with the fields already laid by U-boats off Britain's east coast and buttressed by attacks by the submarines themselves, would deplete the Grand Fleet's strength before it made contact with the German battle squadrons. It remains unclear how far north the High Sea Fleet would have been willing to go to meet the Grand Fleet, or how long it could have remained off Terschelling to offer battle. Von Hipper conceived that the junction would take place in the late afternoon of 31 October—a significant time, because there would be little daylight remaining, allowing the German fleet the cover of darkness to withdraw, while the flotillas made a mass attack on the British line.

Beatty would have sought action, notwithstanding the cautious policy he had maintained for so long. The U-boats might have achieved something against the fleet, but they did not have the numbers to gain more than isolated successes. The greatest problem would have been the mine threat. Despite this, it is likely the Grand Fleet would have arrived off Terschelling largely unscathed and in formidable strength. It is also likely that advances in gunnery, particularly the British ability to concentrate the fire of two or more ships on a single target and their practice under demanding conditions, as well as their improved heavy shell would have had a devastating effect on the High Sea Fleet. The Germans had learned much from Jutland but had experienced nothing like the same rate of technological or tactical progress.

Orders for Operation Plan No. 19 went out on 24 October and the High Sea Fleet began to assemble over the next few days. There were cover stories about fleet maneuvers, but the reality could not be concealed. The secrecy within which the plan shrouded itself contributed to fomenting mutiny. Since commanding officers were briefed at the last moment, they and their officers could only conjecture as to the reason for the obvious preparations for a fleet sortie and that uncertainty rapidly flowed to the lower deck. The dispirited sailors were willing to fight in direct defense of their homeland but would not embark on a venture simply to maintain the honor of their officers at a time when Germany's defeat was staring them in the face. The fleet was fully assembled on 29 October. By the next day it was apparent the crews of many capital ships would not take part in Operation Plan No. 19. Mass refusals of duty were occurring around the battle squadrons. Von Hipper was forced to delay the fleet's departure and finally, a few hours later, he canceled it. He issued an appeal to the High Sea Fleet, denying that it was being sent out "frivolously to satisfy the enemy's order for our destruction."[40] This did not wash. The men no longer believed their officers and the hitherto "hermetically sealed" executive officers had to accept they had lost the confidence of their crews.[41] While the small ships and submarines generally

Photo 14.4   The admirals of the Grand Fleet, 1918   *Sea Power Centre, Australia*

Back row (left to right): Commodore Tweedie, Rear Admiral Everett,
Rear Admiral Fergusson, Rear Admiral Halsey, Rear Admiral Goodenough,
Rear Admiral D. R. L. Nicholson, Rear Admiral Bruen, Rear Admiral Brand
Front row (left to right): Rear Admiral W. Nicholson, Rear Admiral Phillimore,
Rear Admiral Cowan, Vice Admiral Pakenham, Vice Admiral Leveson,
Admiral Madden, Admiral Beatty, Vice Admiral de Robeck, Vice Admiral Napier,
Rear Admiral Rodman (USN), Rear Admiral Oliver, Vice Admiral Brock, Rear Admiral Borrett

remained loyal, the capital ships and many of the light cruisers did not. The C-in-C and his admirals agreed to disperse the squadrons in the hope that calm could be restored and the men returned to their duties. On the advice of the Third Squadron's commander, von Hipper agreed these ships could go to Kiel. There they would be the trigger for revolution.

Events moved rapidly from this point, yet the breakdown of discipline in the German navy was never complete. Units led by the *Königsberg* deployed into the Heligoland Bight as late as 9 November in response to a false report that a British sortie was under way. But it was fundamental to the downfall of the German regime and the final acceptance of Germany's defeat. During negotiations for the armistice, the Royal Navy insisted on the internment of the U-boats and of the bulk of the High Sea Fleet. The First Sea Lord had to argue hard for such harsh conditions, particularly in relation to the surface forces, facing down generals who thought the battle fleets were an irrelevancy and politicians anxious not to make the terms so severe that Germany would refuse to accept them. Admiral Wemyss got his way, but the obvious collapse of the Imperial German Navy as a fighting force must have played a large part in the new German government's willingness to accede.

The U-boats began to arrive in British ports on 20 November, British observers commenting that some were clean, serviceable and with disciplined crews, while others were dirty and ill conducted.[42] The High Sea Fleet itself sailed for internment on 19 November, crews only being found for the ships by dint of a substantial bonus in pay. Early plans for sending the German ships to a neutral port proved impossible, because no country was willing to receive the fleet. They would go instead to the Firth of Forth, as a prelude to their final anchorage in Scapa Flow. One incident during the dismal passage of the German ships from Wilhelmshaven to Rosyth underlined the reality of how the war at sea had been fought: the torpedo boat *V30* struck a mine and sank on 20 November as the fleet left the Heligoland Bight. A British minefield had done its last war work.

The Grand Fleet, in an operation designated ZZ and carefully orchestrated by Beatty, met the Germans outside the Firth of Forth on 21 November 1918. It was an encounter staged not only for maximum psychological effect, but to create a photographic record as unassailable evidence of the Grand Fleet's final victory. A junior officer in the *Queen Elizabeth* recorded that his strongest impression of the day was of Beatty's "complete amazement" that the Germans had given up without a fight.[43] The admiral nevertheless produced some memorable quotations, saying to the crew of his flagship, "Didn't I tell you they would have to come out?"[44] The C-in-C's final order was equally to the point: "The German flag will be hauled down at sunset today, Thursday, and will not be hoisted again without permission." It would fly over the interned fleet only twice more, as a gesture of pride and defiance on the third anniversary of the Battle of Jutland and over the High Sea Fleet's mass scuttling on 21 June 1919.

Reflections

15

*A*FTER *J*UTLAND'S CENTRAL QUESTIONS ARE TWO: first, whether the navies achieved all they might have achieved between 1916 and 1918, given the capabilities and the limitations of the ships and weapons they had to hand; and second, if they did not succeed, why was this so?

The strategic failure which Britain's entry into the war on the side of the Entente meant for the very concept of the High Sea Fleet is beyond the scope of this book, but once the war had started, how effectively did Germany employ the navy it had created? The answer is *not well*. The German navy had missed its best opportunities in 1914–15 when the relative strengths of the forces in the North Sea were at their closest, but its fundamental error was initiation of the unrestricted submarine campaigns. Given the tactical advantages that submarines enjoyed in 1914–18, prize warfare alone could and did put a great deal of pressure on the Allies. The U-boats could certainly have been employed to attack Allied shipping, but it was never in Germany's interest to anger the United States or to create conditions that allowed Britain and France to justify tightening the blockade as reprisal for alleged German atrocities.

With or without an unrestricted submarine campaign, the surface forces should have been very much more active. The handful of disguised raiders showed what might have been achieved on the world's oceans to tie down Allied resources, all without much risk of alienating the Americans. More active use of the scouting groups and flotillas, properly supported by the battle fleet, would have made life very difficult for the British and French. This was particularly true during the crisis of the U-boat campaign in early 1917 when the Allies' situation at sea could have been made much more complicated and even more threatening than it seemed at the time.

But there must be doubt as to the German navy's ability to do much more than it did, at least over extended periods. This question must wait on research designed to clarify the exact nature of the navy's access to resources within Germany as the conflict progressed. The financial crisis of 1912 determined that the German army would have priority, while the navy entered the Great War with a budget already tightly restricted. The navy was a service under strain; its efforts to expand and its scale of operations—the U-boats excepted—appear extraordinarily restricted by comparison with the British rate of effort. We are left with the impression that the High Sea Fleet was always limited in fuel and material; it was certainly limited in personnel. The steady transfer of officers and men to the U-boat force and the minesweepers represented a drain of human capital from the main fleet that could not easily be replaced. By 1917, difficulties were mounting, and they manifested themselves most clearly in the engineering problems that dogged big and small ships alike. To what extent this was more the result of material shortages arising from an increasingly effective blockade or shortfalls in expert manpower in ships and dockyards remains unclear. Nevertheless, British and American observers were surprised by the poor condition of many of the major German units when they were interned; and the sad state of a substantial number of the U-boats at that time has already been noted. Warships deteriorate very rapidly when they are not looked after, but the implication is that things had not been well long before the mutinies of the previous month. The High Sea Fleet might have been hard pressed to be more active, even if its commanders had wanted to, and might have deteriorated even more rapidly had it tried to go to sea much more often.

The customary criticism of the British is that the Admiralty took an unconscionable amount of time to accept that convoy was the proper response to the U-boat campaign against merchant shipping. The truth is convoy was only one of the necessary responses, some of which the Admiralty did make, while dealing with many others turned out to require what we would now term as "whole of government" solutions. Further, had the Germans responded differently—and if the war had continued they would inevitably have done so—convoys would have been at the center of a series of battles that might have played out very differently to such encounters in the war of 1939–45. Some of the tools required to defeat mass submarine attacks did not yet exist. Late adoption of convoy was thus a critical, perhaps even egregious, failure, but convoy was not quite as simple a solution as it seems in hindsight.

The key missed opportunity for the Royal Navy may have been mine warfare. Deficiencies in British mine design, particularly when compared

Photo 15.1   SMS *Derfflinger* at the internment   *Sea Power Centre, Australia*

with those of the Russians and the Germans, were clear as early as the end of 1914. The defensive and offensive utility of mines in the emerging operational environment was also apparent from the very start of the conflict. This was acknowledged long before by Lord Fisher, although he shares a measure of blame for the situation in 1914. It should not have taken until well into 1917 for mass production of the relatively efficient H2 mine to start. Here, criticism of the Admiralty staff and their supervision of the navy's technical organization (in this case, the torpedo and mine warfare establishment, HMS *Vernon*) over the period 1915 to 1916 is justified. Too much time was taken to acknowledge the problems that British mines experienced and even more was consumed fiddling over alternative and unnecessary solutions.

As a form of attrition warfare, both geography and resources favored the British in mining. The Royal Navy could have started an extensive effort to mine the Heligoland Bight and the Kattegat at least twelve months earlier than it did, if an efficient model had been available at the right time. The evidence of 1917 and 1918 reveals that this would have achieved several things. First, it would have created growing stresses on the High Sea Fleet's minesweeping capabilities and on the main force itself through the need to protect the sweepers from attack; second, the transit of U-boats to their operational areas would have been made much more hazardous—as would the dispatch of any surface forces to attack the British coast. The combination of these demands may also have created more opportunities for British surface units to raid the Heligoland Bight and the Kattegat with a good chance of finding worthwhile targets. In short, if an effective mine had been produced earlier and the British had deployed it properly, the High Sea Fleet could have been worn down much more quickly than it was.

Another area the British might have pursued more aggressively is naval aviation, but the alternative scenario is less clear. The problems of operating aircraft from ships at sea were not only complicated, they kept changing as the aircraft evolved. The achievement of the Grand Fleet in moving as far and as fast as it did in 1917–18 to develop fixed-wing aviation may have been undervalued. The problem of recovery certainly persisted until means were found to recover wheeled planes on board *Argus* (*after* her completion, it should be noted), but the numbers and types of shipborne fighters and reconnaissance aircraft that the Grand Fleet carried in 1918 represented a formidable capability. If the Admiralty had given the Grand Fleet's proposals more priority in early 1917, a strike by torpedo aircraft on the High Sea Fleet in its anchorages would have been possible in 1918. But it is difficult to see how the required system-of-systems (torpedoes, aircraft, ships, launch and recovery techniques, marshaling in the air techniques, and at-sea operating experience) could have been brought into being and implemented on the necessary scale to be decisive in such a time frame. There is an analogy with the tank and its employment in the land war and the tension between the desire to employ it more or less piecemeal or wait until sufficient numbers were available to achieve a decisive victory. *Argus* could well have launched Cuckoo torpedo bombers to raid the High Sea Fleet anchorages in the summer of 1918, but it would have deployed no more than twenty aircraft. Admiral Beatty had much grander ambitions, it is true, but the aircraft that could do this job were no longer disposable in the manner of single-seat light fighters. They could not ditch after each sortie and be easily replaced.

Lack of strategic coordination between the British and the Russians has been another subject of criticism. To be fair, attempting to coordinate major operations in both the Baltic and the North Sea was probably always too much to ask. Here, the "Baltic Project" and the potential vulnerability of the Kattegat have tended to receive the most attention, but any British attempt to force their way into the Baltic would inevitably have involved

Photo 15.2   HMS *Orion* at the internment   *Sea Power Centre, Australia*

an amphibious operation on a grand scale, with the necessary involvement of large numbers of troops, confrontation with the German army on what was effectively home ground, and some very difficult decisions about the neutrality of Denmark, Sweden, and even Norway. After the Dardanelles, such a venture was unthinkable. But even if the Baltic passages are left out of consideration, much more could have been done to think how difficult life could be made for the Germans in the Kattegat if they were constantly being forced to deal with threats at sea in both the east and the west. Diversions and deceptions around the Kattegat could have played an important part in putting on pressure.

Here, the Russian failure paralleled the British. Even if its defensive fixation on the Gulf of Finland had some validity, the Baltic Fleet always had the resources—and as time went on, added to them—to wage a much more active campaign against German freedom of movement in the western and southern Baltic than it did. Mines, submarines (even with the environmental challenges), and surface forces could have done much to prevent the movement of shipping between Sweden and Germany, and German sea communications between Germany and Courland. Apart from restricting the flow of vital materials, particularly iron ore, this would have forced the Germans to make much greater naval efforts in the Baltic than proved to be the case. It is astonishing in retrospect just how weak the German naval forces in theater usually were; still, it was a gamble that repeatedly paid off in their favor, though it was not inevitable that this should have been so. One consideration for the British about the benefits of a more active Russian policy in the Baltic, allied to their own greater efforts in the Heligoland Bight and the Kattegat, is that the outpost of the Flanders Command would have quickly been targeted as a source of reinforcements for areas more critical to German survival.

Deficiencies in operations and tactics in all three navies are best examined from the British experience, though the conclusions are almost as certainly equally applicable to the other services. The causes of failure are related—largely the absence of support organizations to provide training, analyze battle experience, and develop doctrine and tactics to meet the new challenges. Far too much in the Royal Navy fell victim to a laissez-faire attitude. Inexperienced personnel were thrown into the sea war with their new ships and equipment untested and themselves untrained. Because there was no proper analytical organization, the problems of night fighting (among other things) festered and failures were repeated when they could have been avoided. Too much was expected of local operational commanders, given the span of their responsibilities and the tiny staffs they employed. At the end of the war, Tyrwhitt of the Harwich Force had only three operational staff officers, one engineer, and three administrative officers to manage his command. While he probably did not want it any other way, this was a seagoing battle staff, not an organization to do the detailed planning required for the multitude of complex initiatives that the Harwich Force attempted over the years. Bacon and Keyes at Dover were no better off, with staff sufficient to operate an around-the-clock operations room, but not to simultaneously plan ventures on the scale of the Zeebrugge and Ostend raids. The truth is that the Harwich Force, Dover Patrol, and other commands endured a hand-to-mouth existence in their planning and conduct of operations, and this was reflected in the results. That the Grand Fleet was eventually better organized was a combination of its greater scale and the relative inactivity of its major units. Even so, the main fleet labored throughout the entire conflict to create the full range of systems needed to support the training of all its components, conduct analysis, and identify the necessary lessons from exercises and operations. Many of the Royal Navy's problems that have long been ascribed to the Admiralty may have been as much the result of the inadequate organization of the operational commands as deficiencies in Whitehall.

The Royal Navy understood something of all these problems and it learned the lessons. The British sometimes made the mistake of over-staffing in later years, but the World War II period demonstrated that they had learned the difference between plans and operations. Establishment of the Tactical School in the 1920s was another answer. Notably—although it was only founded in 1942, more than two years after the start of the war—the Western Approaches Tactical Unit provided the type of doctrinal and tactical support to the antisubmarine forces of the Battle of the Atlantic that the night fighters of Dover and the Harwich Force so desperately needed. The need to train the mass of small ships and newly mobilized personnel was known in 1939. Early ideas for an Anglo-French training center were overtaken by the fall of France, but by the middle of 1940 there was an organization at Tobermory in Scotland that trained the crews of more than a thousand corvettes and frigates by the end of the war. That center was duplicated elsewhere in the United Kingdom and emulated around the world. The officers and sailors manning the destroyers, sloops, and patrol craft of the Great War would have envied their successors the experience of such training, however arduous, and the confidence it created in their equipment, their fellow crew members, and themselves.

While accepting the validity of these criticisms, we should also fully acknowledge the efforts in all navies to exploit emergent technology and the imagination and individual bravery that operating the new systems so often required. The anticlimactic end of the war at sea has largely disguised the progress made in so many areas of naval technology and operations since 1914. The U-boats and Allied submarines coming into service in 1918 were much closer in capability to the new construction units of 1939 than they were to their predecessors of 1914. This was certainly also the case for the surface fleets, and it was arguably true (in part) for aviation. It was not simply a matter of the technological progress of the war—although this had been at a breakneck pace—but also of operational advances in the employment of that technology. What is clear is that the operations of the Royal Navy in 1918 in particular were a remarkable advance on 1914, even if some of the concepts involved had been under consideration well before the outbreak of war. They foreshadowed the task forces of the next global conflict. The "Grand Fleet of Battles," which had been emerging before the Great War, had been replaced by fighting groups that had the same ideas of combined arms and mutual support but operated on a smaller scale that made the necessary coordination practicable. Largely oil-powered formations consisting of cruisers and destroyers, and supported by more workable single squadrons of fast capital ships rather than a ponderous battle line, all fitted out with as much aviation capability as they could carry or tow, ranged across the North Sea at high speeds. Things had moved very far from the Grand Fleet's seven-knot progress through the same theater in August 1914. A modern observer can mourn lost opportunities in the Great War at sea, but it is only fair to recognize just how much was achieved as well.

Notes

Introduction

1. As related to the author in 1979 by the late Captain F. H. Kennedy, son of the captain of the *Indomitable* (1912–16). The story seems to have been well known in the Royal Navy.

Chapter 1. June 1916—The War at Sea

1. The best recent English language history of the kaiser's navy is Nicholas Wolz, *From Imperial Splendour to Internment: The German Navy in the First World War*, trans. Geoffrey Brooks (Barnsley: Seaforth, 2015). The new German language study by Christian Jentzsch and Jann M. Witt, *Der Seekrieg 1914–1918: Die Kaiserliche Marine im Erstern Weltkrieg* (Darmstadt: WBG, 2016), is an excellent popular survey that deserves translation into English.

2. American Naval Observer Berlin, "Notes on Opinions Held by Admiral Scheer," 24 March 1921, p. 8, 8 Series 2, Box 116, Folder 3, USNWC Historical Collection.

3. Michael H. Clemmesen, "Otto Koefed-Hansen," Lecture to RN Museum Conference on the First World War. See also Michael H. Clemmesen, "Military and Strategy" (Denmark), http://encyclopedia.1914–1918-online.net/article/military_and_strategy_denmark?version=1.0; and Michael H. Clemmesen, "The Danish Navy, Expectations, realities and adjustments, 1909–1918," in *The Danish Straits and German Naval Power 1905–1918*, ed. Michael Epkenhans and Gunther P. Gross (Potsdam: MGFA, 2009), 107–28.

4. Commander Francis Cromie to Commodore Sydney Hall, Letter dated 10 October 1917. Nicholas Lambert, *The Submarine Service 1900–1918* (Aldershot: Ashgate/Navy Records Society, 2001), 335–37.

5. Russians generally delete "von," perhaps sensitive that one of the navy's most capable officers was of Germanic stock. A signed photograph presented to a British officer a few weeks earlier suggests he used "von" until his death on 20 May 1915.

6. Rear Admiral (later Admiral Sir Richard) Phillimore, diary, entry dated 11 November 1915, Phillimore Papers, IWM.

7. M. A. Petrov, "The Crisis of the Naval Command in 1916," *Morksoi Sbornik* 8 & 9 (August–September 1926): 13. I am indebted to Stephen McLaughlin for making this translation available.

8. Norman E. Saul, *Sailors in Revolt: The Russian Baltic Fleet in 1917* (Lawrence: Regents Press University of Kansas, 1978), 38. See "The Russian Navy: 1914–1918," *The Times History of the War*, vol. 16 (London: Times, 1918), 306.

9. "The Russian Navy," *Advertiser* (South Australia), 21 June 1916, http://trove.nla.gov.au/newspaper/article/6465821.

10. Gunnar Aselius, *The Rise and Fall of the Soviet Navy in the Baltic 1921–1941* (London: Routledge, 2004), 35–36.

Chapter 2. The Navies

1. Commander Eugene E. Wilson, Oral History, 121, 123. USNWC Historical Collection.

2. Commodore G. von Schoultz, *With the British Battle Fleet: War Recollections of a Russian Naval Officer*, trans. Arthur Chambers (London: Hutchinson, 1925), 299.

3. F. F. Raskolnikov, *Kronstadt and Petrograd in 1917*, trans. Brian Pearce (London: New Park, 1982), 127.

4. James R. Clifford, diary entry, dated 11 June 1918. Reproduced in *The Grey Funnel Line: Official Newsletter of the HMAS SYDNEY and VLSVA* 14, no. 3 (Mar–Jun 2008): 52.

5. Unsigned (Lieutenant Commander R. L. Edwards), "The Shibboleths of Peace," *Naval Review* 3, no. 4 (1915): 547.

6. Lewis R. Freeman, *Stories of the Ships* (London: John Murray, 1919), 167.

7. Captain (later Admiral Sir) Matthew Best, diary entry, dated 25–29 May 1918, Best Papers, Liddle Collection, Leeds University.

8. H. P. K. Oram, *Ready for Sea* (London: Seeley Service, 1974), 112.

9. Von Schoultz, *With the British Battle Fleet*, 230–31.

10. Jellicoe to Admiral Sir Frederick Hamilton (Second Sea Lord), letter, dated 16 April 1916. A. Temple Patterson, ed., *The Jellicoe Papers: Selections from the Private and Official Correspondence of Admiral of the Fleet Earl Jellicoe*, vol. 1, *1916–1935* (London: Navy Records Society, 1966), 238.

11. Grand Fleet Order 840, dated 23 May 1917, TNA ADM 137/2012.

12. Malcolm Brown and Patricia Meehan, eds., *Scapa Flow: The Reminiscences of Men and Women Who Served in Scapa Flow in the Two World Wars* (London: Allen Lane, 1968), 116.

13. Peter Jones, *Australia's Argonauts: The Remarkable Story of the First Class to Enter the Royal Australian Naval College* (West Geelong: Echo Books, 2016), 120–21.

14. Beatty to his wife, letter, dated 13 July 1917, B. McL. Ranft, *The Beatty Papers: Selections from the Private and Official Correspondence of Admiral of the Fleet Earl Beatty*, vol. 1, *1902–1918* (London: Scolar Press/Navy Records Society, 1989), 448.

15. Beatty to his wife, letter, dated 9 July 1917, BTY/17/43, NMM.

16. Oram, *Ready for Sea*, 179.

17. Anon. (Lieutenant Commander C. H. Rolleston), "Games," *Naval Review* 8, no. 2 (1920): 208.

18. Rear Admiral G. W. G. Simpson, *Periscope View: A Professional Autobiography* (London: Macmillan, 1972), 23.

19. Captain Lionel Lampart to Keyes, letter, dated 19 November 1918; Paul G. Halpern, *The Keyes Papers: Selections from the Private and Official Correspondence of Admiral of the Fleet Baron Keyes of Zeebrugge*, vol. 1, *1914–1918* (London: Navy Records Society), 515.

20. Admiral of the Fleet Viscount Cunningham of Hyndhope, *A Sailor's Odyssey* (London: Hutchinson, 1951), 88.

21. Grand Fleet Order 257, dated 15 November 1915, "Bread Ration," TNA ADM 137/2006.
22. "Reduction of Consumption of Food—Prevention of Waste," H. F. Memorandum 569/17, dated 10 March 1917, TNA ADM 137/2023.
23. Von Schoultz, *With the British Battle Fleet*, 343.
24. Grand Fleet Memorandum dated 18 June 1917, TNA ADM 137/2023.
25. Freeman, *Stories of the Ships*, 184.
26. Grand Fleet Order 369, undated, TNA ADM 137/2007.
27. Grand Fleet Order 542, dated 25 July 1916(?), TNA ADM 137/2009.
28. H. F. Memorandum 6/183, dated 28 February 1917, TNA ADM 137/2023.
29. Grand Fleet Fund, memorandum, dated 1 February 1916, TNA ADM 137/2022.
30. C-in-C Home Fleets, letter 1087/H. F. 1029, dated 5 June 1916, TNA ADM 137/2022.
31. Oram, *Ready for Sea*, 119.
32. Lieutenant J. K. Whittaker, diary entry, dated 22 May 1918, Whittaker Papers, NMM.
33. Simpson, *Periscope View*, 23–27.
34. "Supervision of Gunroom Officers," H. F. Memorandum 0012/37, dated October 1916, TNA ADM 137/2022.
35. Freeman, *Stories of the Ships*, 108.
36. Admiral Mark Kerr, *Prince Louis of Battenberg, Admiral of the Fleet* (London: Longmans, 1934), 147–48.
37. Christopher McKee, *Sober Men and True: Sailor Lives in the Royal Navy 1900–1945* (Cambridge, MA: Harvard University Press, 2002), 122.
38. Freeman, *Stories of the Ships*, 231.
39. Laura Rowe, "Counting Unrest: Physical Manifestations of Unrest and Their Relationship to Admiralty Perception," in *1917: Beyond the Western Front*, ed. Ian F. W. Beckett (Leiden & Boston: Brill, 2008), 71–96.
40. See for example, Best, diary entry, dated 9–20 January 1918, Best Papers, Liddle Collection.
41. Edward Hilton Young (later Lord Kennet), "Some Impressions of a Temporary Officer," *Naval Review* 8 no. 3 (August 1920): 325.
42. Commander (later Captain) the Honourable P. G. E. Acheson, diary entry, dated 19 February 1917, Acheson Papers, PGA/1, IWM.
43. Acheson, diary entry, dated 9 and 13 March 1917, Acheson Papers, PGA/1, IWM.
44. Sub Lieutenant (later Captain) A. W. Clarke, diary entry, dated 29 September to 24 October 1917, Clarke Papers, Liddle Collection.
45. Able Seaman William Lang, "Lower Deck and Wardroom," *Naval Review* 8, no. 4 (1920): 147.
46. Surgeon Commander R. W. B. Hall, "Eye-Strain in the Submarine Service," *Journal of the Royal Naval Medical Service* 5 (1919): 182.
47. Gilbert Hackforth-Jones, "Depot Ships," *Sixteen Bells: Stories of the Royal Navy in Peace and War* (London: Hodder & Stoughton, 1946), 230–34.
48. Vice Admiral Friedrich Ruge, *SM Torpedo Boat B. 110*, Warship Profile 27 (Windsor: Profile Publications, 1972), 50.
49. Wolz, *From Imperial Splendour to Internment*, 139.
50. Friedrich Ruge, *Scapa Flow 1919: The End of the German Fleet* (London: Ian Allan, 1973), 14.

51. Daniel Horn, ed., *The Private War of Seaman Stumpf: The Unique Diaries of a Young German in the Great War* (London: Leslie Frewin, 1969), 267.

52. Ruge, *Scapa Flow 1919*, 17.

53. W. F. Clarke and F. Birch, "A Contribution to the History of German Naval Warfare 1914–1918," vol. 1, pt. 2, 30–31 (annotated, 462–63), unpublished, compiled within NID 1919–1922, Ca9182/I, NHB.

54. Holger H. Herwig, *"Luxury" Fleet: The Imperial German Navy 1888–1918* (London: Allen & Unwin, 1980), 134.

55. Ruge, *SM Torpedo Boat B. 111*, 57.

56. Ruge, 62.

57. Evan Mawdsley, *The Russian Revolution and the Baltic Fleet* (London: Macmillan, 1978), 3.

58. D. Fedotoff White, *Survival through War and Revolution in Russia* (London: Oxford University Press, 1939), 130.

59. Mawdsley, *Russian Revolution and the Baltic Fleet*, 2.

60. Phillimore, diary entry, dated 8/21 November 1915, Phillimore Papers, IWM.

61. Phillimore, diary entry, dated 13 November 1915, Phillimore Papers, IWM.

62. Vice Admiral Leslie Ashmore, "Memoirs," 41, ASHM 1/1, Ashmore Papers, CCA.

63. White, *Survival through War*, 213.

64. Vice Admiral L. H. Ashmore, *Forgotten Flotilla: British Submarines in Russia 1914–1919* (Portsmouth: Manuscript Press, 2001), 118–19.

65. Raskolnikov, *Kronstadt and Petrograd in 1917*, 37–38.

Chapter 3. Operational Challenges

1. Nicholas Monsarrat, *The Cruel Sea* (London: Cassell, 1951).

2. Phillimore, diary entry, dated 16 November 1915. Phillimore Papers, IWM. Quote is from White, *Survival through War*, 75.

3. Commander L. Pitcairn-Jones, "Navigation in War of 1914–1918," 2, RN Staff College Lecture 1938, NHB.

4. "Taffrail" (Commander Taprell Dorling), *H.M.S. "Anonymous"* (London: Herbert Jenkins, 1920), 286.

5. Lieutenant (later Captain) Sir Philip Bowyer-Smyth, "Jutland," Bowyer-Smyth Papers, IWM.

6. Pitcairn-Jones, "Navigation in War of 1914–1918," 12.

7. Beatty to Wemyss, letter, dated 1 April 1918, in Ranft, *Beatty Papers*, 1:526.

8. Henry Oliver, Chief of the War Staff, claimed credit for organizing the system's development from those employed by cable-laying ships. See Henry Oliver, "Recollections for Rear Admiral R. D. Oliver," vol. 1, 128–29, OLV/12, Oliver Papers, NMM.

9. Captain Reginald Belknap, "Submarine Mines in War," 12, Belknap Papers, USNWC Historical Collection.

10. Admiral Sir Angus Cunninghame-Graham, *Random Naval Recollections* (Gartocharn: Privately published, 1979), 64–65.

11. "Taffrail," *H.M.S. "Anonymous,"* 61.

12. Admiralty Telegram no. 593 to Commodore in Charge Harwich, dated 6 January 1917, TNA ADM 137/2083.

13. "Navigational Notes," Commodore (T), letter 0050, dated 15 May 1916, TNA ADM 137/2083.

14. Rear Admiral Third Cruiser Squadron, letter no. 16, dated 22 May 1916, TNA ADM 137/2083.

15. See Vice Admiral Commanding Battle Cruiser Force, memorandum BCF 83C, dated 24 November 1917, TNA ADM 137/2138, asking for a much wider distribution of reporting codes for hostile airships.

16. Rear Admiral Third Light Cruiser Squadron, letter no. 712, dated 12 July 1917, Vice Admiral Sir Trevylyan Napier Papers, TN/1/1, IWM.

17. Vice Admiral Light Cruisers, letter no. 52, dated 6 July 1917, TNA ADM 137/1970.

18. HMS *Iron Duke*, letter 108/32, dated 6 April 1920, TNA ADM 116/2090.

19. Lieutenant Commander W. S. Chalmers, "Tactical Plotting," RN Staff College lecture, 14 August 1919, TNA ADM 116/2090.

20. Admiral Sir William Goodenough, *A Rough Record* (London: Hutchinson, 1943), 95.

21. H. F. Memorandum 1150/14, dated 20 July 1916, TNA ADM 137/2083.

22. Oram, *Ready for Sea*, 167–68.

23. Captain Lionel Dawson, *Flotillas: A Hard-Lying Story* (London: Rich & Cowan, 1929), 141–83.

24. Records of the Harwich Force, Pack 53, TNA ADM 137/2091, 137/2092.

25. Records of the Harwich Force.

26. Log of HMS *Attentive*, 5 March 1918, from "HMS *Attentive*: August 1917 to December 1918, Dover Patrol, Zeebrugge Raid, North Russia," *Royal Navy Log Books of the World War I Era*, http://www.naval-history.net/OWShips-WW1-06-HMS_Attentive.htm.

27. A. Thomazi, *La Guerre Navale dans La Zone des Armees du Nord* (Paris: Payot, 1924), 147.

28. Commodore (T) to Secretary of the Admiralty, letter, dated 22 March 1917, TNA ADM 137/2091.

29. Commanding Officer HMS *Dublin*, letter, dated 26 April 1916, TNA ADM 137/2138.

30. Naval Staff, Admiralty, *Narrative of the Battle of Jutland* (London: HMSO, 1924), 8.

31. Erich Gröner, *German Warships 1815–1945*, vol. 1, *Major Surface Vessels*, rev. ed. Dieter Jung and Martin Maass (London: Conway, 1990), 30.

32. Gary Staff, *German Battlecruisers of World War One: Their Design, Construction, and Operations* (Barnsley: Seaforth, 2014), 292–94.

33. Leading Seaman Edward Beaton, diary, entry dated 6 October 1916; David Stevens, *In All Respects Ready: Australia's Navy in World War One* (Melbourne: Oxford University Press, 2014), 226.

34. Lieutenant (later Admiral Sir) Louis Hamilton, diary, entry dated 19–22 February 1917, Hamilton Papers, NMM.

35. Commanding Officer HMS *Chester*, Report of Proceedings, dated 13 June 1916, Napier Papers, IWM.

36. "Taffrail," *H.M.S. "Anonymous,"* 194.

37. Cunningham, *A Sailor's Odyssey*, 92.

38. George Nekrasov, *Expendable Glory: A Russian Battleship in the Baltic, 1915–1917* (Boulder, CO: East European Monographs, 2004), 62.

39. Commodore (T) to Vice Admiral (Dover), memorandum no. 0070, dated 17 May 1916, TNA ADM 137/2085.

40. "Details of *S. 36*," dated 8 February 1917, TNA ADM 137/2085.

41. Ruge, *SM Torpedo Boat B. 111*, 55.

42. Norman Friedman, *British Destroyers: From the Earliest Days to the Second World War* (Barnsley: Seaforth, 2009), 146.

43. H. Graf, *The Russian Navy in War and Revolution 1914 up to 1918* (Honolulu: University Press of the Pacific, 2002), 79.

44. "Docking (Cruisers)," Admiralty Weekly Order (AWO) 330/1917, NHB.

45. Grand Fleet Order 373, dated 1917, TNA ADM 137/2011.

46. H. F. Memorandum 831/423, dated 17 November 1916, TNA ADM 137/2022.

47. Vice Admiral John L. McRae USN, Oral History, 90, USNWC Historical Collection.

48. Vice Admiral Lord Ashbourne, "Recollections," 2, Ashbourne Papers, IWM.

49. U.S. Office of Naval Intelligence, "Compilation of Data on British Navy," November 1916, 1, USNWC Historical Collection.

50. Staff, *German Battlecruisers*, 56–57.

51. "Taffrail," *H.M.S. "Anonymous,"* 101.

52. Norman Polmar and Jurrien Noot, *Submarines of the Russian and Soviet Navies, 1718–1990* (Annapolis, MD: Naval Institute Press, 1991), 239–41.

53. Ruge, *SM Torpedo Boat B. 111*, 67.

54. Lieutenant J. K. Whittaker, diary, entry dated 18 March 1918, Whittaker Papers, NMM.

55. Staff, *German Battlecruisers*, 189.

56. Staff, 53.

57. Engineer Commander Otto Looks, "The Engine Room Staff in the Battle of Skagerrak," trans. and ed. Engineer Lieutenant Commander D. Hastie Smith, RN, *Naval Review* 10 (1922), 312–13, 316–17.

58. Admiral Sir Ragnar Colvin, *Memoirs of Admiral Sir Ragnar Colvin 1882–1955* (Durley: Privately published, 1992), 38.

59. U.S. Office of Naval Intelligence, "Compilation of Data on British Navy," November 1916, 1, USNWC Historical Collection.

60. Captain A. W. Clarke (writing as "Onlooker"), "H.M. Navigation School, 1903–1968," *Naval Review* 56, no. 3 (July 1968): 258.

61. Naval Staff, Admiralty, *Naval Staff Monographs (Historical)*, vol. 19, *Home Waters*, pt. 9, *1st May 1917 to 31st July 1917*, 1.

62. "Watertightness of Compartments—Testing by Air Pressure," AWO 459/1916, NHB.

63. This model is in the Australian War Memorial. See "Ship's Structural Training Model of SMS *Emden* Showing Bulkhead, Decks and Fire Control," *Australian War Memorial*, https://www.awm.gov/au/collection/RELAWM00279.

64. "Earthenware Pans to Ship's Company Heads," AWO 2274/1917, and "W.C. Pans—Preservation against Gun Fire," AWO 3262/1917, NHB.

65. "Weights—Reduction (Destroyers)," AWO 1710/1917, NHB.

66. Clarke and Birch, "History of German Naval Warfare," vol. 1, pt. 2, 47.

67. Patrick Beesly, *Room 40: British Naval Intelligence 1914–1918* (New York: Harcourt Brace Jovanovich, 1982), 171.

68. Vice Admiral Battle Cruiser Force, memorandum, dated 4 July 1917, "Code for Reporting Positions of Hostile Airships," TNA ADM 137/2138.

69. C-in-C Home Fleets, Memorandum 0022/807, dated 23 August 1917, TNA ADM 137/2139.

70. Clarke and Birch, "History of German Naval Warfare," vol. 1, pt. 2, 95.

71. M. A. Partala and D. N. Simonov, "Radio Intelligence of the Russian Fleet in the Baltic Sea; the History of Its Creation," *Zaschita Informatsii Inside*, no. 1 (2005): 90–96, Stephen McLaughlin translation, 10.

72. Stephen McLaughlin "Russia"; Vincent P. O'Hara, W. David Dickson, and Richard Worth, eds., *To Crown the Waves: The Great Navies of the First World War* (Annapolis, MD: Naval Institute Press, 2013), 221.

73. Commodore (Flotillas), memorandum D007/5, dated 20 February 1917, "Methods Recommended for Carrying Out Searches for Hostile Submarines," TNA ADM 137/1975.

74. Commodore (Flotillas), memorandum 0059/21, dated 29 May 1917, TNA ADM 137/1975.

75. Commander G. P. Thomson, "Submarine Warfare," *Minutes of Proceedings of the Royal Artillery Institution* 48, no. 2 (1921): 51.

76. F. J. Dittmar and J. J. Colledge, *British Warships 1914–1919* (London: Ian Allan, 1972), 82–91; Robert M. Grant, *U-Boat Intelligence 1914–1918* (Hamden, CT: Archon, 1969), 182–83.

77. "Klaxon" (Lieutenant Commander J. G. Bower), *The Story of Our Submarines* (London: William Blackwood, 1919), 138.

78. Ashmore, *Forgotten Flotilla*, 92.

79. Gene C. Stevenson, "Russian 'Lake' Type Submarines and the Baltic War 1914–1916," in *Warship 1990*, ed. Robert Gardiner (London: Conway, 1990), 83.

80. Thomson, "Submarine Warfare," 46.

81. Lieutenant (later Captain) Oswald Hallifax, "Reminiscences," 1, Hallifax Papers, 85/41/1, IWM.

82. Technical History Section, Admiralty, "Submarine Administration, Training and Construction," *Admiralty Technical History* 2, pt. 21 (October 1921): 18–21.

83. Commanding Officer HMS *Birmingham*, memorandum 134/20, dated 15 July 1916, TNA ADM 137/2139.

84. T. M. Jones, *Watchdogs of the Deep: Life in a Submarine during the Great War* (Sydney: Angus & Robertson, 1935), 18.

85. Captain R. W. Blacklock, interview, dated August 1977, tape 448, 6, Liddle Collection.

86. Hallifax, "Reminiscences," 10, Hallifax Papers, 85/41/1, IWM.

87. Technical History Section, Admiralty, "Submarine Administration, Training and Construction," 9.

88. Thomson, "Submarine Warfare," 44–45; Norman Friedman, *Fighting the Great War at Sea: Strategy, Tactics and Technology* (Annapolis, MD: Naval Institute Press, 2014), 258.

89. Commander (later Vice Admiral Sir) Cecil Talbot, diary entry, dated 30 May and 10 July 1919, IWM.

90. Thomson, "Submarine Warfare," 53.

91. Thomson, 53.

92. Norman Friedman, *Naval Weapons of World War I* (Barnsley: Seaforth, 2011), 391.

93. Eric Grove, "Air Force, Fleet Air Arm—or Armoured Corps? The Royal Naval Air Service at War," in *British Naval Aviation: The First 100 Years*, ed. Tim Benbow (Farnham, UK: Ashgate, 2011), 41.

94. Major Georg Paul Neumann, *The German Air Force I Knew, 1914–1918: Memoirs of the Imperial German Air Force in the Great War*, trans. J. E. Gurdon, ed. Bob Carruthers (Barnsley: Pen & Sword Aviation, 2014), 96–98.
95. Neumann, 69.
96. For a discussion of national mines, see Friedman, *Naval Weapons of World War I*, 361–84.

Chapter 4. The Shadow of Jutland

1. Graham, *Random Naval Recollections*, 54–55.
2. Oram, *Ready for Sea*, 176.
3. Captain E. P. F. G. Grant to Rear Admiral C. F. Dampier, letter, undated [probably June 1916], Richmond Papers, NMM.
4. Captain J. M. Howson, "Memoirs," 81, Howson Papers, Liddell Hart Archive, KCL.
5. Stephen King-Hall (writing as "Etienne"), *A Naval Lieutenant 1914–1918* (London: Methuen, 1919), 159.
6. Phillimore, diary, entry undated, Phillimore Papers, IWM.
7. Commander George von Hase, *Kiel and Jutland* (London: Skeffington, 1921), 125.
8. Wolz, *From Imperial Splendour to Internment*, 116–17.
9. "The Battle of the Skagerrak, May 31 1916: Report of the Austro-Hungarian Naval Attache at Berlin, June 17 1916," free translation, U.S. ONI, February 1921, USNWC Historical Collection.
10. Friedman, *Fighting the Great War at Sea*, 170–71.
11. Ernst von Weizsacker, *Memoirs of Ernst von Weizsacker*, trans. John Andrews (London: Gollancz, 1951), 33.
12. Admiral Reinhard Scheer, *Germany's High Sea Fleet in the World War* (London: Cassell, 1920), 178.
13. Capitain de Fregate P. Chack, "The German Submarines during the Battle of Jutland," translation from *Revue Maritime*, *Naval Review* 13, no. 4 (1925): 706–7.
14. Staff, *German Battlecruisers*, 99 [*Moltke*], 56 [*Von der Tann*], and 187 [*Seydlitz*].
15. Walter Gladisch, *Der Krieg zur See 1914–1918: Der Krieg in der Nordsee*, vol. 6, *Von Juni 1916 bis Frühjahr 1917* (Berlin: Mittler, 1937), 50 [NHB translation].
16. Naval Staff, Admiralty, *Naval Staff Monographs (Historical)*, vol. 17, *Home Waters*, pt. 7, *From June 1916 to November 1916*, October 1927, 59.
17. Douglas H. Robinson, *The Zeppelin in Combat: A History of the German Naval Airship Division 1912–1918* (Atglen, PA: Schiffer, 1994), 387–88.
18. Robinson, 373.
19. Robinson, 187–88.
20. Von Schoultz, *With the British Battle Fleet*, 155.
21. Jellicoe to Jackson, letter, dated 5 June 1916, in Patterson, *Jellicoe Papers*, 1:271.
22. Innes McArtney, *Jutland 1916: The Archaeology of a Naval Battlefield* (London: Bloomsbury, 2016).
23. Nicholas A. Lambert, "'Our Bloody Ships' or 'Our Bloody System'? Jutland and the Loss of the Battle Cruisers, 1916," *Journal of Military History* 62, no. 1 (January 1998). See also Friedman, *Fighting the Great War at Sea*, 163–65. Naval Staff, Admiralty, *Naval Staff Monographs (Historical)*, vol. 17, *Home Waters*, pt. 7, 3–7, suggests that the author favored the Admiralty's

judgment. Significantly, an extract from the Director of Naval Construction's memorandum is at appendix A, 245.

24. See "Extract of Gunnery Practices in the Grand Fleet 1914–1918: Battleships and Battle Cruisers," TNA ADM 137/4822; and "Extract of Gunnery Practices in the Grand Fleet 1914–1918: Light Cruisers," TNA ADM 137/4823. Practically all the practices described were in 1917 and 1918. They include a shoot in June 1918 by American battleships.

25. C-in-C Home Fleets, letter 1483/H. F. 1187, dated 29 June 1916, TNA ADM 137/1645.

26. Admiralty, letter M 04524, dated 21 May 1916, TNA ADM 137/1645.

27. "Various Notes of Interest to the Bureau of Navigation," dated 1 January 1917, ONI Reports January 1917 (marked as p. 140, but ff. 52), USNWC Historical Collection.

28. C-in-C Home Fleets, letter 1483/H.F. 1187, dated 29 June 1916, see p. 2 (folio 160), TNA ADM 137/1645.

29. Jellicoe to Jackson, letter, dated 21 May 1916, in Patterson, *Jellicoe Papers*, 1:241–42. Jellicoe repeated the comment in a letter to Jackson dated 12 September 1916, in Temple A. Patterson, *The Jellicoe Papers: Selections from the Private and Official Correspondence of Admiral of the Fleet Earl Jellicoe of Scapa*, vol. 2, *1916–1935* (London: Navy Records Society, 1968), 2:80.

30. Rear Admiral Alexander Duff, diary, entry dated 21 September 1916, Duff Papers, NMM. For the report of the exercise, see "Grand Fleet Exercises— Operation 'Q'—21 September 1916," H. F. Memorandum 0037/73, dated 12 October 1916, TNA ADM 137/1994.

31. Robert M. Grant, *U-Boat Intelligence* (Hamden, CT: Archon, 1969), 15.

32. Grant, 183. The wreck of *UC 7* seems definitely located, *UB 13* provisionally. See *Wreck Site*, www.wrecksite.eu.

33. Commodore (T) to Vice Admiral (Dover), letter, dated 30 July 1916, TNA ADM 137/2085.

34. *The Murder of Captain Fryatt* was made by the Australian Famous Feature Company and released in February 1917.

35. "Taffrail," *H.M.S. "Anonymous,"* 141.

36. "Action off the Schouwen Bank Light Vessel (23rd July 1916)," Naval Staff, Admiralty, *Grand Fleet Gunnery and Torpedo Memoranda on Naval Actions*, Gunnery Division, April 1922, 54–55.

37. Naval Staff, Admiralty, *Naval Staff Monographs (Historical)*, vol. 17, *Home Waters*, pt. 7, 80.

Chapter 5. The Torpedoes of August

1. Tyrwhitt to Jellicoe, letter, dated 21 August 1916, in Patterson, *Jellicoe Papers*, 2: 46.

2. Captain C. B. Miller to Commodore William Goodenough, letter dated "Sunday" [but is 20 August 1916 from internal evidence], Goodenough Papers, IWM.

3. Lieutenant (later Admiral Sir) William Tennant, journal, entry dated 19 August 1916 [probably written up in 1919], Tennant Papers, NMM.

4. "Etienne" (Stephen King-Hall), *A Naval Lieutenant 1914–1918*, 172.

5. Naval Staff, Admiralty, *Naval Staff Monographs (Historical)*, vol. 17, *Home Waters*, pt. 7, 265.

6. Gladisch, *Der Krieg zur See: Nordsee*, 6:81, NHB translation.
7. Admiralty to C-in-C Signal, 19 August 1916, sent 1315, in Naval Staff, Admiralty, *Naval Staff Monographs (Historical)*, vol. 17, *Home Waters*, pt. 7, 267.
8. Anon. (Commander F. W. Talbot-Ponsonby), "Sweep of August 18th to 20th, 1916," *Naval Review* 9, no. 1 (1921): 75.
9. Scheer, *Germany's High Sea Fleet*, 181–84.
10. Gladisch, *Der Krieg zur See: Nordsee*, 6:90, NHB translation.
11. Talbot-Ponsonby, "Sweep of August 18th to 20th, 1916," 76.
12. Clarke and Birch, "History of German Naval Warfare," vol. 1, pt. 2, 173.
13. Acheson, diary, entry dated 19 August 1916, Acheson Papers, PGA/1, IWM.
14. ONI 7016, dated 15 September 1916, ONI Naval Attachés', Reports, November 1916, 18, USNWC Historical Collection.
15. ONI 7016, 17.
16. Commanding Officer HMS *Falmouth* report, "Loss of HMS *Falmouth*," dated 21 August 1916, Napier Papers, IWM.
17. Tyrwhitt to Jellicoe, letter, dated 21 August 1916, in Patterson, *Jellicoe Papers*, 2: 46.
18. "Fight for Submariners' Sea Grave," *BBC News*, http://news.bbc.co.uk/2/hi/uk_news/england/1628523.stm
19. Naval Staff, Admiralty, *Naval Staff Monographs (Historical)*, vol. 17, *Home Waters*, pt. 7, 124.
20. Lieutenant W. S. Chalmers to Captain H. W. Richmond, letter, dated 22 August 1916, Richmond Papers, NMM.
21. Jellicoe to Jackson, letter, dated 23 August 1916, in Patterson, *Jellicoe Papers*, 2:47.
22. "Submarine Exercises of 28 August 1916 and following days," H. F. Memorandum 40/15, dated 17 September 1916, TNA ADM 137/2022.
23. Captain (later Admiral Lord Mountevans) E. R. G. R. Evans, *Keeping the Seas* (London: Sampson Low Marston, 1919), 203.
24. "Conference, 'Iron Duke' September 13, 1916," in Naval Staff, Admiralty, *Naval Staff Monographs (Historical)*, vol. 17, *Home Waters*, pt. 7, app. L, 275.
25. Miller to Goodenough, letter, dated "Sunday" [but is actually 20 August 1916 from internal evidence], Goodenough Papers, IWM; and Tennant, journal, entry dated 19 August 1916, Tennant Papers, NMM.
26. Captain H. B. Freyberg, letter, dated 1966; Brown and Meehan, *Scapa Flow*, 119–20.
27. Thomson, "Submarine Warfare," 45.
28. "Klaxon," *The Story of Our Submarines*, 88–89.
29. Jellicoe to Fisher, letter, dated 18 September 1916; Arthur J. Marder, ed. *Fear God and Dread Nought: The Correspondence of Admiral of the Fleet Lord Fisher of Kilverstone*, vol. 3, *Restoration, Abdication, and Last Years, 1914–1920* (London: Jonathan Cape, 1959), 372.
30. Werner Rahn, "Die Seeschlacht vor dem Skagerrak," in *Skaggerakschlact: Vorgeschichte, Ereignis, Verarbeitung*, ed. Michael Epkenhans, Jorg Hillmann, and Frank Nagler (Munich: R. Oldenbourg, 2009), 192.
31. Theodor Plivier, *The Kaiser's Coolies*, trans. William F. Clarke (London: Faber, 1932), 250.
32. "Naval Operations—19 August 16," ONI 7016, dated 13 October 1916, ONI Naval Attachés' Reports December 1916, 7, USNWC Historical Collection.

33. Vice Admiral Kurt Assmann, "Factors Governing U-boats Operation in World War I" (Synopsis T.S.D./F.D.S/X263/49File "Spindler and 1917/18 U-boat Campaign"), Lieutenant Commander Walters Papers, NHB.

Chapter 6. The Baltic in Summer

1. R. D. Layman, *Before the Aircraft Carrier: The Development of Aviation Vessels 1849–1922* (London: Conway, 1989), 23 and 97–98.
2. White, *Survival through War*, 64.
3. "Finding E18," *HMS E18 Families Group*, http://www.hmse18.0rg/finding-e18/4583519154; for background on the search, see also Lorna Edwards, "Submarine Quest Ends in the Depths of the Baltic Sea," *The Age*, 20 March 2010, http://www.theage.com.au/victoria/submarine-quest-ends-in-the-depths-of-the-baltic-sea-20100319-qm8w.html.
4. Rudolph Firle and Heinich Rollman, *Der Krieg zur See: Der Krieg in der Ostsee*, vol. 3, *Von Anfang 1916 Bis Zum Kriegsende* (Berlin: Mittler, 1964), 32–33.
5. Graf, *Russian Navy in War and Revolution*, 86.
6. Rear Admiral N. B. Pavlovich, *The Fleet in the First World War*, trans. C. M. Rao (New Delhi: Amerind, 1979), 195–97.
7. George Nekrasov, *North of Gallipoli: The Black Sea Fleet at War 1914–1917* (Boulder, CO: East European Monographs, 1992), 96–97. Pavlovich, in the Soviet-era *Fleet in the First World War*, studiedly avoids using Kolchak's name, referring to him simply as "Chief of the Mine Division." Kolchak has recently received rehabilitation in a romantic film called *The Admiral*.
8. Beatty to his wife, letter, dated 23 April 1917, BTY 17/40/13–14, Beatty Papers, NMM. This comments on a later report that Kolchak was being transferred to the Baltic.
9. See Firle and Rollman, *Der Krieg zur See: Ostsee*, 3:34–35; and Pavlovich, *Fleet in the First World War*, 198–200.
10. The best English language account is Michael B. Barrett, *Operation Albion: The German Conquest of the Baltic Islands* (Bloomington: Indiana University Press, 2008), 35–37.
11. Firle and Rollman, *Der Krieg zur See: Ostsee*, 3:71.
12. Nekrasov, *Expendable Glory*, 67. This incident is not mentioned in Pavlovich, *Fleet in the First World War*.
13. Neumann, *German Air Force*, 68–69.
14. Commander Francis Cromie to Commodore S. S. Hall, letter, dated 10 October 1917, in Lambert, *Submarine Service*, 336.
15. For the *C* boats' epic journey, see Michael Wilson, *Baltic Assignment: British Submariners in Russia 1914–1919* (London: Leo Cooper, 1985), 147–57.
16. Petrov, "Crisis of the Naval Command in 1916," 8.
17. Petrov, 9.
18. Cited in Mawdsley, *Russian Revolution and the Baltic Fleet*, 3.
19. Tsar Nicholas to Tsarina Alexandra, letter, dated 7 September 1916, in *Letters of the Tsar to the Tsaritsa, 1914–1917*, http://www.alexanderpalace.org/letters/september16.html.
20. Graf, *Russian Navy in War and Revolution*, 97.
21. Rear Admiral S. N. Timirev, *Vospmoninaniia morskogo ofitsera: Baltiskii flot vo vremia voiny i revoliutsii, 1914–1918* (New York: American Society for Russian Naval History, 1961), 73–76. I am indebted to the late Commander

George Nekrasov for his informal translation. Timirev is not an entirely reliable witness. His wife, Anna Timireva, left him to continue an affair with Kolchak.

22. Petrov, "Crisis of the Naval Command in 1916," 10.

23. Captain Franz Wieting, "Torpedobootsfahrten in der Ostsee," in *Auf See unbesiegt: Erlebnisse im Seekrieg erzählt von Mitkämpfern*, vol. 1, ed. Eberhard von Mantey (Munich: Lehmanns, 1922), 71.

24. Clarke and Birch, "History of German Naval Warfare," vol. 1, pt. 2, 284; Firle and Rollman, *Der Krieg zur See: Ostsee*, 3:97.

25. Rear Admiral Hopman, diary, entry dated 22 November 1916, and fn 450 detailing Lieutenant Commander Firle's views in his diary on 17 November 1916. Michael Epkenhans, ed., *Das ereignisreiche Leben eines "Wilhelminers": Tagebücher, Briefe, Aufzeichnungen 1901 bis 1920* (Munich: Oldenbourg, 2004), 925.

26. Robinson, *Zeppelin in Combat*, 273.

27. Timirev, *Vospmoninaniia morskogo ofitsera*, 78–79. See also Nekrasov, *Expendable Glory*, 77.

28. Nekrasov, *Expendable Glory*, 72.

29. Graf, *Russian Navy in War and Revolution*, 112.

30. Mawdsley, *Russian Revolution and the Baltic Fleet*, 4.

Chapter 7. Little Ships, Submarines, and Aircraft

1. Robinson, *Zeppelin in Combat*, 214.

2. Captain von Trotha, memorandum, dated October 1916, cited in Gladisch, *Der Krieg zur See: Nordsee*, 6:183–84, NHB translation.

3. Admiral von Müller, diary, entry dated 31 October 1916; Walter Gorlitz, *The Kaiser and His Court: The Diaries, Notebooks and Letters of Admiral Georg Alexander von Müller Chief of the Naval Cabinet, 1914–1918*, trans. Mervyn Saul (London: MacDonald, 1961), 215.

4. William Guy Carr, *Good Hunting* (London: Hutchinson, 1940), 101.

5. Arthur J. Marder, *From the Dreadnought to Scapa Flow: The Royal Navy in the Fisher Era, 1904–1919*, vol. 3, *Jutland and After (May 1916–December 1916)*, 2nd ed. (Oxford: Oxford University Press, 1978), 306.

6. Captain (later Admiral Sir) Barry Domvile, diary, entry dated 22 October 1916, Domvile Papers, NMM.

7. Admiral Sir Reginald Bacon, *The Dover Patrol, 1915–1917*, vol. 1 (London: Hutchinson, 1919), 166.

8. See chart in Bacon, *Dover Patrol*, 1:57.

9. Henry Newbolt, *Naval Operations*, vol. 4 (London: Longmans Green, 1928), 64.

10. Reginald Pound, *Evans of the Broke: A Biography of Admiral Lord Mountevans* (London: Oxford University Press, 1963), 161.

11. Thomazi, *La Guerre Navale*, 134.

12. Thomazi, 138.

13. Thomazi, 136.

14. R. H. Gibson, *Three Years of Naval Warfare* (London: Heinemann, 1918), 118–19.

15. Lord Fisher was particularly vitriolic on the subject. See Fisher letter to George Lambert, dated 30 October 1916, in Marder, *Fear God and Dread Nought*, vol. 3, 381.

16. Domvile, diary, entry dated 2 November 1916, Domvile Papers, NMM.

17. Scheer, *Germany's High Sea Fleet*, 193.

18. C-in-C High Sea Fleet, Tactical Order 16, dated 10 May 1916, and Tactical Order 22, dated 8 November 1916, World War 1 Subject Matter, Box 8, NHB.

19. Paymaster Rear Admiral Sir Hamnet Share, *Under Great Bear and Southern Cross: Forty Years Ashore and Afloat* (London: Jarrolds, 1932), 218.

20. Best, diary, entry dated 28 November 1916, Best Papers, Liddle Collection.

21. Sturdee became a substantive admiral in 1917 but remained junior to Beatty and Madden in the fleet.

22. Fregattenkapitan Karl Nerger, *S.M.S. Wolf*, trans. Beate Lauterbach and Michael Zehnpfennig, ed. Paul Freedman (Birkenhead: GTO Printers, 2000), 10–13.

23. Commodore (T) to Secretary of Admiralty, letter, dated 26 November 1916, TNA ADM 137/2085; Bacon, *Dover Patrol*, 2:329.

24. Commodore (T) to Secretary of Admiralty, letter, dated 26 November 1916, TNA ADM 137/2085.

25. Bacon, *Dover Patrol*, 2:329.

26. Commander Taprell Dorling (writing as "Taffrail"), *Endless Story: Being an Account of the Work of the Destroyers, Flotilla-Leaders, Torpedo-Boats and Patrol Boats in the Great War* (London: Hodder & Stoughton, 1931), 242.

27. Domvile, diary, entry dated 30 October 1916, Domvile Papers, NMM.

28. Tyrwhitt to Keyes, letter, dated 29 December 1916, in Halpern, *Keyes Papers*, 1:376.

29. Ian Buxton, *Big Gun Monitors: Design, Construction and Operations* (Barnsley: Seaforth, 2008), 60.

Chapter 8. Crisis at Sea

1. Von Müller, diary, entry dated 13 April 1917; Gorlitz, *Kaiser and His Court*, 257.

2. Naval Staff, Admiralty, *Naval Staff Monographs (Historical)*, vol. 18, *Home Waters*, pt. 8, *December 1916 to April 1917*, 187.

3. Jellicoe to Admiral Sir Frederick Hamilton, letter, dated 20 January 1916, in Patterson, *Jellicoe Papers*, 1:201.

4. Rear Admiral (later Admiral Sir) Morgan Singer, "Contemporary Account of Work 1914–1917," 7, Singer Papers, Liddle Collection.

5. Joshua Levine, "The Hunt for the Notorious U-boat UB-29," *Smithsonian Magazine*, May 2018, https://www.smithsonianmag.com/history/hunt-notorious-uboat-ub29–180968733/.

6. Friedman, *Naval Weapons of World War I*, 391–92.

7. Nicholas Black, *The British Naval Staff in the First World War* (Woodbridge: Boydell, 2009), 177–78.

8. The website uboat.net lists the successes and other details of the U-boats. See "Ships Hit by UC 17," uboat.net, http://uboat.net/wwi/boats/successes/uc17.html.

9. Dittmar and Colledge, *British Warships 1914–1919*, 155.

10. Cited in Elizabeth Greenhalgh, *Victory through Coalition: Britain and France during the First World War* (Cambridge: Cambridge University Press, 2005), 117.

11. TNA ADM 116/1341 (1914–1916), and 116/1342 (1916–1918). Another set of the *Instructions* (1918 editions) is available at ADM 137/4055; Ranft, *Beatty Papers*,

1:456–506, has extensive extracts from copies of the *Instructions* retained in Beatty's personal Papers (BTY/7/3/4, NMM).

12. Stevens, *In All Respects Ready*, 232–33.

13. Lieutenant Commander (later Admiral Sir) Harold Burrough, "Memoirs," 13. Burrough Papers, Liddle Collection.

14. Commodore Second Light Cruiser Squadron, letter C39, dated 20 January 1917, TNA ADM 137/2139.

15. See "Notes on tactical exercises carried out on 24 February 1917," BTY/7/2/8 Beatty Papers, NMM. See also the extract in Ranft, *Beatty Papers*, 1:403–6.

16. Carr, *Good Hunting*, 114.

17. Lieutenant J. H. Bowen, "A North Sea Incident of Jan. 1917," Bowen Papers, IWM.

18. Hamilton, diary, entry dated 21–23 January 1917, Hamilton Papers, NMM.

19. Hamilton, diary, entry dated 21–23 January 1917.

20. Kevin Whitmee-Haddock and Anna Whitmee-Haddock, "Schooldays in Southwold and Reydon during World War One," Reydon Village Website, April 2014, http://reydon.onesuffolk.net/home/village-history/schooldays-in-southwold-and-reydon-during-world-war-one/.

Chapter 9. Spring in the North Sea

1. Hopman, diary, entry dated 14 March 1917, in Epkenhans, *Das ereignisreiche Leben*, 964.

2. Stumpf, diary, entry dated 6 March 1917, in Horn, *Private War of Seaman Stumpf*, 302.

3. J. Lee Thompson, *Northcliffe: Press Baron in Politics 1865–1922* (London: John Murray, 2000), 269. For a local account, see "Topic: Destroyer Bombardment of Margate and Boradstairs, 25 February 1917," discussion board at http://www.kenthistoryforum.co.uk/index.php?topic=18162.0.

4. Gladisch, *Der Krieg zur See: Nordsee*, 6:400, NHB translation.

5. Sub Lieutenant (later Commander) C. H. Drage, diary, entry dated 12 April 1917, Drage Papers, Liddle Collection.

6. Best, diary, entry dated 18 March, Best Papers, Liddle Collection.

7. Best, diary, entry dated 18 March.

8. Brown and Meehan, *Scapa Flow*, 117.

9. For online reports, see "Final Resting Place of the HMS E5 Discovered," *Royal Navy Submarine Museum*, https://www.submarine-museum.co.uk/component/content/article/1-latest-news/533-final-resting-place-of-hms-e5-discovered; and "E5," *RN Subs: Website of the Barrow Submariners Association*, http://rnsubs.co.uk/boats/subs/e-class/e5.html.

10. A. Temple Patterson, *Tyrwhitt of the Harwich Force: The Life of Admiral of the Fleet Sir Reginald Tyrwhitt* (London: MacDonald, 1973), 181.

11. Bacon, *Dover Patrol*, 2:348.

12. Naval Staff, Admiralty, *Naval Staff Monographs (Historical)*, vol. 18, *Home Waters*, pt. 8, 278.

13. Bacon, *Dover Patrol*, 2:351.

14. Commodore (T), "Proposals for Attack on Zeebrugge," dated 7 May 1917, TNA ADM 137/2088.

15. Buxton, *Big Gun Monitors*, 62–63, has the best technical description and illustrations.

16. Richmond to Keyes, letter, dated 17 May 1917, in Halpern, *Keyes Papers*, 1:397.
17. Gladisch, *Der Krieg zur See: Nordsee*, 6:416, NHB translation.
18. Admiralty. letter M 05321/17, dated 2 May 1917, in S. W. Roskill, ed., *Documents Relating to the Naval Air Service*, vol. 1, *1908–1918* (London: Navy Records Society, 1969), 479.
19. Gladisch, *Der Krieg zur See: Nordsee*, 6:427, NHB translation.
20. Black, *British Naval Staff*, 173–84, has a good analysis. For an assessment that deserves more attention than this 1933 study has often received, see also Naval Staff, Admiralty, *Naval Staff Monographs (Historical)*, vol. 18, *Home Waters*, pt. 8, 361–85. TNA ADM 137/1392 has selected original documents.
21. Newbolt, *Naval Operations*, vol. 5, 20.
22. Naval Staff, Admiralty, *Naval Staff Monographs (Historical)*, vol. 18, *Home Waters*, pt. 8, 369. The meeting may have been 15 April. See Beatty to Lady Beatty, letter, BTY/17/40/8, Beatty Papers, NMM.
23. Naval Staff, Admiralty, *Naval Staff Monographs (Historical)*, vol. 19, *Home Waters*, pt. 9, 159.

Chapter 10. Enter the Americans

1. David F. Trask, *Captains and Cabinets: Anglo-American Naval Relations, 1917–1918* (Columbia: University of Missouri Press, 1972), 52–59.
2. William Sowden Sims, *The Victory at Sea* (New York: Page Doubleday, 1920), 45.
3. Trask, *Captains and Cabinets*, 77.
4. Jellicoe to Taussig, letter, dated 1 May 1917, in William N. Still Jr., ed., *The Queenstown Patrol, 1917: The Diary of Commander Joseph Knefler Taussig, U.S. Navy* (Newport, RI: Naval War College Press, 1996), 19.
5. Taussig, diary, entry dated 4 June 1917, in Still, 47.
6. Admiral C. J. Moore USN, Oral History, vol. 1, 163, USNWC Historical Collection.
7. Admiral Sir Lewis Bayly, *Pull Together!* (London: Harrap, 1939), 222.
8. Hamilton, diary, entry dated 14 August 1917, Hamilton Papers, NMM.
9. Norman Friedman, *U.S. Destroyers: An Illustrated Design History* (Annapolis, MD: Naval Institute Press, 1982), 39–41.
10. Robinson, *Zeppelin in Combat*, 255–62.
11. Robinson, 283–84.
12. The mounting was removed after the war.
13. Commodore (T), report of action, dated 11 May 1917, TNA ADM 137/2082.
14. Günther Lütjens would later go down with his flagship, *Bismarck*, in May 1941.
15. Thomazi, *La Guerre Navale*, 179.
16. Nor, as far as can be ascertained, in the ADM 137 series.
17. Buxton, *Big Gun Monitors*, 236–39, has an excellent explanation of the development of shore bombardment.
18. Not mentioned in Gladisch, *Der Krieg zur See: Nordsee*.
19. "Report of Examination of Survivors of 'S.20,' sunk on 5 June 1917," TNA ADM 137/2082.
20. Hamilton, diary, entry dated 5 June 1917, Hamilton Papers, NMM.
21. Commodore (T), memorandum to Chief Censor 0048, dated 13 June 1917. TNA ADM 137/2082.
22. Admiralty, letter 92/17, dated 15 July 1917, TNA ADM 137/2082.
23. Karau, *Wielding the Dagger*, 148.

24. Andrew A. Wiest, *Passchendaele and the Royal Navy* (Westport, CT: Greenwood, 1995), 122–40, details the plans for this operation.

25. Karau, *Wielding the Dagger*, 167.

26. Walter Gladisch, *Der Krieg zur See 1914–1918: Der Krieg in der Nordsee*, vol. 7, *Vom Sommer 1917 bis zum Kriegsende 1918* (Hamburg: Mittler, 2006), 156.

27. Gröner, *German Warships 1815–1945*, 161.

28. Karau, *Wielding the Dagger*, 159–62.

29. "Plan IV: Chart Showing Proposed Scheme of the Great Landing 1917," in Naval Staff, Admiralty, *Naval Staff Monographs (Historical)*, vol. 6, *The Dover Command: Vol. 1*, 122 inset.

30. Karau, *Wielding the Dagger*, 169.

31. Friedman, *British Destroyers*, 154–55; see also Edgar J. March, *British Destroyers: A History of Development 1892–1953* (London, Seeley Service, 1966), 194, and 206–7.

32. "Taffrail," *Endless Story*, 374.

33. Best, diary, entries dated June–December 1917. Best Papers, Liddle Collection. The other cruisers were *Galatea*, *Inconstant*, *Phaeton*, *Blanche*, and *Bellona*.

34. Clarke and Birch, "History of German Naval Warfare," vol. 1, pt. 2, 560.

35. See Plan 11 in Naval Staff, Admiralty, *Naval Staff Monographs (Historical)*, vol. 19, *Home Waters*, pt. 9, inset to 178.

36. Captain R. F. Nichols, "I Was in Them Both," 5, Nichols Papers, Liddle Collection. (The "both" refers to Nichols being the executive officer of HMS *Royal Oak* when she was sunk in Scapa Flow in 1939.)

37. D. K. Brown, *The Grand Fleet: Warship Design and Development 1906–1922* (Scaforth: Barnsley, 2010), 168–69.

38. Naval Staff, Admiralty, *Naval Staff Monographs (Historical)*, vol. 19, *Home Waters*, pt. 9, 176.

39. Beatty to his wife, letter, dated 22 May 1917, in Ranft, *Beatty Papers*, 1:432.

40. Beatty to his wife, letter, dated 3 October 1917, in Ranft, *Beatty Papers*, 1:451.

41. Admiral of the Fleet Lord Chatfield, *The Navy and Defence* (London: William Heinemann, 1942), 163.

42. See Naval Staff, Admiralty, *The Navy List* (classified limited distribution versions), October 1916, 395m–395n; and October 1918, 887–88.

43. Beesly, *Room 40*, 274, could not locate the extensive correspondence between Beatty and Hall. But note the discussion between the C-in-C and the DNI in December 1917 that demonstrates Beatty's understanding of signals intelligence. See Ranft, *Beatty Papers*, 1:454–56.

44. Beesly, *Room 40*, 26–27.

Chapter 11. The Baltic in 1917

1. White, *Survival through War and Revolution*, 61–62.

2. Norman E. Saul, *Sailors in Revolt: The Russian Baltic Fleet in 1917* (Lawrence: Regents Press of Kansas, 1978), 56–57.

3. Gregorian dates will be given throughout.

4. Nekrasov, *Expendable Glory*, 80–81.

5. Saul, *Sailors in Revolt*, 77.

6. D. G. Kirby, "A Navy in Revolution: The Russian Baltic Fleet in 1917," in *Motivating Soldiers: Morale or Mutiny*, ed. Peter Karsten (New York, Garland, 1998), 349.

7. Cited in Mawdsley, *Russian Revolution and the Baltic Fleet*, 86.

8. Saul, *Sailors in Revolt*, 88.

9. Hopman to his wife, letter, dated 29 March 1917, in Epkenhans, *Das ereignisreiche Leben*, 968.

10. Hopman, diary, entry dated 23 March 1917, in Epkenhans, *Das ereignisreiche Leben,* 968.

11. Graf, *Russian Navy in War and Revolution*, 145.

12. The wreck was reportedly discovered by Swedish divers in 2003, although details are scanty. See "Swedish Divers Discover Hull of Russian Submarine Which Disappeared without Trace in 1917," in *The Submariners News Service*, ed. Melvin C. Pennymore, http://www.angelfire.com/va/688/v017/.

13. Pavlovich, *Fleet in the First World War*, 219.

14. Robinson, *Zeppelin in Combat*, 273.

15. Nekrasov, *Expendable Glory*, 84–85.

16. Mawdsley, *Russian Revolution and the Baltic Fleet*, 91. See also, Ivo Jurvee, "Birth of Russian SIGINT during World War 1 on the Baltic Sea," *Intelligence and National Security* 32, no. 3 (2017): 307–8.

17. Wilson, *Baltic Assignment*, 188.

18. Clarke and Birch, "History of German Naval Warfare," 1, pt. 2, 476.

19. Hopman to Grand Admiral von Tirpitz, letter, dated 4 October 1917, in Epkenhans, *Das ereignisreiche Leben*, 1029.

20. Barrett, *Operation Albion*, 33–55, explains the difficulties in organizing command and control.

21. Korvettenkapitan Bruno Gluer, "Transport und Landung zur Eroberung der baltischen Inseln," in *Auf See unbesiegt*, vol. 2, ed. Eberhard von Mantey (Munich: Lehmanns, 1922), 252–55.

22. Commander F. S. Cromie to Commodore (Submarines), letter, dated 10 October 1917, in Lambert, *Submarine Service*, 335.

23. Vice-Admiral Erhardt Schmidt, "The Conquest of the Baltic Islands" (official dispatch), dated 24 October 1917. Admiralty Naval Intelligence Division Translation, OU 6042, 1919, 4.

24. Ruge, *SM Torpedo Boat B. 111*, 59.

25. Firle and Rollman, *Der Krieg zur See: Ostsee*, 3:209.

26. For *Bayern*'s travails, see Oberleutnant Peter Lorenz, "Ostlandfahrt!," in von Mantey, *Auf See unbesiegt*, 2:235–42.

27. Nekrasov, *Expendable Glory*, 99.

28. Firle and Rollman, *Der Krieg zur See: Ostsee*, 3:257.

29. Wilson, *Baltic Assignment*, 192–95.

30. Nekrasov, *Expendable Glory*, 108.

31. Ruge, *SM Torpedo Boat B. 111*, 66.

32. Clarke and Birch, *The History of German Naval Warfare*, vol. 2, 502.

33. Barrett, *Operation Albion*, 223–26, analyzes the debates within the Russian command.

34. Lionel Dawson, *The Sound of the Guns: Being an Account of the Wars and Service of Admiral Sir Walter Cowan (1871–1956)* (London: Pen-in-Hand, 1949), 163.

35. Clarke and Birch, "History of German Naval Warfare," 1, pt. 2, 503.

36. Firle and Rollman, *Der Krieg zur See: Ostsee*, 3:293. See also Barrett, *Operation Albion*, 220.

37. Hopman to his wife, letter, dated 26 October 1917, in Epkenhans, *Das ereignisreiche Leben*, 1034.

38. Gary Staff, *Battle for the Baltic Islands 1917: Triumph of the Imperial German Navy* (Barnsley: Pen & Sword, 2008), 146.

39. Hopman to his wife, letter, dated 3 November 1917, in Epkenhans, *Das ereignisreiche Leben*, 1037.

40. Wilson, *Baltic Assignment*, 200.

Chapter 12. Twists and Turns

1. Von Müller, diary, entry dated 15 July 1917, in Gorlitz, *Kaiser and His Court*, 285.

2. Von Müller, diary, entry dated 19 October 1917, in Gorlitz, *Kaiser and His Court*, 307.

3. The total could be eleven—*UC 21*'s fate remains unknown. See Grant, *U-Boat Intelligence*, 185–86; and Dwight R. Messimer, *Verschollen: World War I U-Boat Losses* (Annapolis, MD: Naval Institute Press, 2002), 258.

4. Best, diary, entry dated 12 September 1917, Best Papers, Liddle Collection.

5. Horn, *Private War of Seaman Stumpf*, 354–55; Daniel Horn, *The German Naval Mutinies of World War I* (New Brunswick, NJ: Rutgers, 1969), 138–68.

6. Wolfgang Semmroth, "Urteile der Marinejustiz als 'Waffe gegen die Linkssozialisten,'" in *Die Flotte Schläft im Hafen Ein: Kriegsalltag 1914–1918 in Matrosen-Tagebüchern*, ed. Stephan Huck, Gorch Pieken, and Matthias Rogg (Wilhelmshaven: Deutsches Marinemuseum, 2015), 83.

7. Wolz, *From Imperial Splendour to Internment*, 156.

8. Scheer, *Germany's High Sea Fleet*, 289, 290.

9. Best, diary, entry dated 30 December 1917, Best Papers, Liddle Collection.

10. Tennant, diary, entry dated 16 August 1917, Tennant Papers, NMM. For action report see TNA ADM 137/2084.

11. Gladisch, *Der Krieg zur See: Nordsee*, 7:65.

12. Best, diary, entry dated 25 October 1917, Best Papers, Liddle Collection.

13. Charles à Court Repington, diary, entry of [?] September 1917, cited in Patterson, *Tyrwhitt of the Harwich Force*, 193.

14. Marder, *From the Dreadnought to Scapa Flow*, vol. 4, *1917: Year of Crisis*, 242–45.

15. See the comments by Admiral Sir William James to Professor Marder, in Marder, 4:295n3.

16. Beesly, *Room 40*, 278.

17. "Report of Action with German Cruisers, October 17, 1917," *Admiralty Technical History: Scandinavian and East Coast Convoy Systems 1917–1918*, CB 1515(8), Admiralty Technical History Section, July 1919, 34.

18. Gladisch, *Der Krieg zur See: Nordsee*, 7:86.

19. Beatty to his wife, letter, dated 18 October 1917, in Ranft, *Beatty Papers*, 1:453.

20. See "Loss of HMS *Mary Rose* and HMS *Strongbow*," TNA ADM 137/3723.

21. "Operation Order *AG* dated 28 October 1917," TNA ADM 137/1990.

22. Newbolt, *Naval Operations*, 5:164n2, claims nine trawlers sunk. Rear Admiral Sixth Light Cruiser Squadron, report, dated 4 November 1917, names ten, in "Miscellaneous Operations in the North Sea," TN/2/8, Napier Papers, IWM.

23. See the orders for the delayed Operation *FM* and the substituted *FO* and *FP*, TNA ADM 137/1990.

24. Captain E. A. Nicholson, letter, dated 20 December 1931, TN/2/8, Napier Papers, IWM.
25. Midshipman (later Captain) E. S. Nurse RAN, diary, entry dated 16 November 1917. I am indebted to Vice Admiral Peter Jones for this reference from the text in his possession.
26. Vice Admiral Light Cruiser Force to C-in-C Grand Fleet, "Action 17 November 1917," Minute 0845, dated 16 December 1917, TN/2/8, Napier Papers, IWM. Full details of the action are available in TNA ADM137/584, which contains the reports; ADM 137/585 signals and radio messages; and ADM 137/586 has logs and track charts.
27. Cowan to Keyes, letter, dated 23 November 1917, in Halpern, *Keyes Papers*, 1:419.
28. "Action between British and German Light Forces (17th November 1917)," *Grand Fleet Gunnery and Torpedo Memoranda on Naval Actions 1914–1918*, 55.
29. Admiral of the Fleet the Earl of Cork and Orrery, *My Naval Life 1886–1941* (London: Hutchinson, 1942), 115.
30. Best, diary, entry dated 16–19 November 1917, Best Papers, Liddle Collection.
31. Best, diary, entry dated 16–19 November 1917.
32. "Action between British and German Light Forces (17th November 1917)," *Grand Fleet Gunnery and Torpedo Memoranda*, 61.
33. E. S. Nurse, diary, entry dated 17 November 1917. Text in possession of Vice Admiral Peter Jones.
34. See "Personalities—No. 1 Book," folios 63–64, TNA ADM 137/4164; and "Personalities—No. 4 Book," no. 10, TNA ADM 137/4167.
35. For the aftermath, see "Heligoland Bight Operation, 17 November 1917—Reports," TNA ADM 137/584.
36. Captain John Creswell to Professor Marder, letter, dated 8 May 1966, in Marder, *From the Dreadnought to Scapa Flow*, 4:309. Napier's explanation is contained in Vice Admiral Light Cruiser Force to C-in-C Grand Fleet, "Action 17 November 1917," Minute 0845, dated 22 December 1917, TN/2/8, Napier Papers, IWM.
37. Beatty to Napier, letter, undated [but with pencil note "21 Nov 1917"], TN/2/8, Napier Papers, IWM.
38. "Jellicoe's account of the circumstances leading up to his dismissal from the post of First Sea Lord," in Patterson, *Jellicoe Papers*, 2:242–23.
39. Ruge, *SM Torpedo Boat B. 111*, 55–56.
40. Gladisch, *Der Krieg zur See: Nordsee*, 7:137.
41. "Notes on Visit of Director of Intelligence Division," dated 19 December 1917, in Ranft, *Beatty Papers*, 1:454–55.
42. Hamilton, diary, entry dated 10 January 1918, Hamilton Papers, NMM.
43. Domvile, diary, entry dated 25 December 1917, Domvile Papers, NMM.
44. Buxton, *Big Gun Monitors*, 152–53.
45. Commodore Dunkirk, letter, dated 10 March 1917, TNA ADM 137/2099.
46. Evans, *Keeping the Seas*, 195.
47. Buxton, *Big Gun Monitors*, 152.
48. Robert M. Grant, *U-Boat Hunters: Code Breakers, Divers and the Defeat of the U-Boats, 1914–1918* (Penzance: Periscope, 2003), 56–57.
49. Captain R. W. Blacklock, memoirs, Blacklock Papers, Liddle Collection.
50. Keyes to Beatty Letter dated 5 December 1917, in Halpern, *Keyes Papers*, 1:422–23.

51. "Movements of the Grand Fleet, 1914–1918," Ca 210, NHB.
52. Rear Admiral Sims to Captain Pringle, letter, dated 31 July 1917; Michael Simpson, *Anglo-American Naval Relations 1917-1919* (London: Scolar Press for the Navy Records Society, 1991), 330–31.
53. Admiral Henry A. Wiley, *An Admiral from Texas* (New York: Doubleday, Doran & Co., 1934), 188.
54. Clarke, "Contented Sailor," 32, Clarke A.W/14, Liddle Collection.
55. Jerry W. Jones, *U.S. Battleship Operations in World War I* (Annapolis, MD: Naval Institute Press, 1987), 86–88.
56. Wilson, Oral History, 115, USNWC Historical Collection; Nichols, "United States Battle Squadron joins the Grand Fleet," 2, Nichols Memoirs, Liddle Collection.
57. Vice Admiral John L. McRae, Reminiscences, vol. 2, 91, USNWC Historical Collection.
58. Freeman, "Getting Together," *Stories of the Ships*, 259–67.

Chapter 13. 1918 Opens in the North Sea

1. Black, *British Naval Staff*, 213.
2. Black, 215–20.
3. Marder, *From the Dreadnought to Scapa Flow*, vol. 5, *1918–1919: Victory and Aftermath*,131–37.
4. Staff, *German Battlecruisers*, 319–22.
5. See the lists of reports of German shipbuilding for 1917 and 1918 in TNA ADM 137/1988.
6. The total for September to December was 32, or 8.5 a month. See Grant, *U-Boat Intelligence*, 185–87.
7. Admiralty Letter M 76/18 dated 14 January 1918, TN/1/1, Napier Papers, IWM.
8. "Taffrail," *Endless Story*, 355–69, describes these incidents.
9. Lieutenant Commander Ralph Seymour, letter, dated 29 January 1918, in Lady Seymour, *Commander Ralph Seymour, R.N.* (Glasgow: University Press, 1926), 99.
10. Best, Diary dated 25 January 1918, Best Papers, Liddle Collection.
11. 2LCS Operation Order dated 6 March 1918. AWM30 6/8; Naval Staff History, Directorate of Naval Warfare, *British Mining Operations 1939–1945: Vol. 1* (London: Ministry of Defence, 1973), 25.
12. Rear Admiral Eberhard Wolfram, "Dummy Mines," *Marine Rundschau* (January 1934), ONI translation, 1, WMN/Belknap, Belknap Papers, Ms. Coll, 103, USNWC Historical Collection.
13. For minelaying operations in the Heligoland Bight in 1918, see TNA ADM 137/840.
14. Jones, *Australia's Argonauts*, 129–42. The original reports are in TNA ADM237/2135.
15. "Klaxon," *The Story of Our Submarines*, 209.
16. Jones, *United States Battleship Operations*, 43.
17. Commander Sixth Battle Squadron, letter, dated 13 March 1918, AWM36 30/8. See also Jones, *United States Battleship Operations*, 46.
18. Keyes, *Naval Memoirs*, 2:153.
19. Karau, *Wielding the Dagger*, 188.
20. Keyes, *Naval Memoirs*, 2:171.

21. Tyrwhitt to Keyes, letter, dated 20 January 1918, in Halpern, *Keyes Papers*, 1:448.

22. Keyes to Beatty, letter, dated 18 [?] January 1918, in Halpern, 1:444–45. Although the date is given as 18 January, from internal evidence the date is more likely 28 January.

23. Gladisch, *Der Krieg zur See: Nordsee*, 7:167.

24. Keyes, *Naval Memoirs*, 2:174–75. See also TNA ADM 137/3464, and TNA ADM 137/1566.

25. Keyes, *Naval Memoirs*, 2:174.

26. Naval Staff, Admiralty, *Naval Staff Monographs (Historical)*, vol. 6, *The Dover Command: Vol. 1*, 104.

27. Ruge, *SM Torpedo Boat B. 111*, 67. For his earlier recollections, see Oberleutnant F. Ruge, "Vorstoss de Flottille Heinecke in die Strasse Dover-Calais, 14–15, Februar 1918," in Mantey, *Auf See unbesiegt*, 2:177–85.

28. Thomazi, *La Guerre Navale*, 190–91.

29. Karau, *Wielding the Dagger*, 192–93. See also Keyes to Beatty, letter dated 19 February 1918, in Halpern, *Keyes Papers*, 1:458.

30. Keyes, *Naval Memoirs*, 2:175–81.

31. Stevens, *In All Respects Ready*, 338.

32. Thomazi, *La Guerre Navale*, 192.

33. Keyes, *Naval Memoirs*, 2:198.

34. Paul Kemp, *The Admiralty Regrets: British Warship Losses of the 20th Century* (Stroud: Sutton, 1999), 67.

35. Michael H. Clemmesen, "Preparing Fireworks on the French Coast: British Crisis Measures for a German Break-through to the Channel Coast February–October 1918," paper presented to the Commission for International Military History October 2013, http://www.clemmesen.org/cvpublications.php.

36. Records of Interrogation, TNA ADM137/2085.

37. Stephen Prince, *The Blocking of Zeebrugge: Operation Z-O 1918* (Oxford, UK: Osprey, 2010), 33.

38. Keyes, *Naval Memoirs*, 2:256.

39. Karau, *Wielding the Dagger*, 205.

40. Bernard Deneckere, *Above Ypres: The German Air Force in Flanders 1914–1918* (Brighton: Firestep Press, 2013), 148–49.

41. Karau, *Wielding the Dagger*, 213.

42. Domvile, diary, entry dated 20 April 1918, Domvile Papers, NMM.

43. Rear Admiral (T), memorandum 0026, dated 29 April 1918, TNA ADM137/2079.

44. Gladisch, *Der Krieg zur See: Nordsee*, 7:258–60.

45. Rear Admiral (T), report 409/0059, dated 22 April 1918, TNA ADM137/2085.

46. See correspondence in TNA ADM137/2085.

47. Wolfram, "Dummy Mines," *Marine Rundschau*, January 1934, ONI translation, 3.

48. Keyes, *Naval Memoirs*, 2:302.

49. Cunningham, *A Sailor's Odyssey*, 94.

50. Keyes to Beatty, letter, dated 16 June 1918, in Halpern, *Keyes Papers*, 1:501.

51. See Keyes, letter, dated 28 May 1918, in Keyes, *Naval Memoirs*, vol. 2, app. 4, 406–8. See also Roskill, *Documents Relating to the Naval Air Service*, 1:663–67, and 1:672–75.

52. Karau, *Wielding the Dagger*, 219.
53. Beesly, *Room 40*, 284.
54. Robinson, *Zeppelin in Combat*, 336.
55. Hugo von Waldeyer-Hartz, *Admiral von Hipper* (London: Rich & Cowan, 1933), 242.
56. Staff, *German Battlecruisers*, 102–6.
57. This was presumably the cause of Professor Marder's misapprehension. See Marder, *From the Dreadnought to Scapa Flow*, 5:153.
58. Beesly, *Room 40*, 288.
59. "Klaxon," *The Story of Our Submarines*, 98.
60. Staff, *German Battlecruisers*, 106.
61. Paul G. Halpern, *A Naval History of World War I* (Annapolis, MD: Naval Institute Press, 1994), 420.
62. Jones, *U.S. Battleship Operations*, 50–51.

Chapter 14. End Game in the North Sea

1. Scheer, *Germany's High Sea Fleet*, 323.
2. Michael Epkenhans, ed., *Mein lieber Schatz! Brief von Admiral Reinhard Scheer an seine Ehefrau August bis November 1918* (Bochum: Dieter Winkler, 2006), 34–35.
3. Staff, *German Battlecruisers*, 99.
4. Von Waldeyer-Hartz, *Admiral von Hipper*, 246.
5. Staff, *German Battlecruisers*, 189.
6. Staff, 246.
7. Jones, *U.S. Battleship Operations*, 104–5.
8. Surgeon Commander J. K. Raymond, "Influenza on Board a Battleship," *Journal of the Royal Naval Medical Service* 5 (1919): 86.
9. Surgeon Captain Robert Hill, "Influenza in the Grand Fleet," *Journal of the Royal Naval Medical Service* 5 (1919): 147.
10. Tennant, diary, entry dated July 1918, Tennant Papers, NMM.
11. Cunningham, *A Sailor's Odyssey*, 97.
12. Staff, *German Battlecruisers*, 191; Von Waldeyer-Hartz, *Admiral von Hipper*, 231–32.
13. Frieder Bauer, and Jörg Vögele, "Die 'Spanische Grippe' in der deutschen Armee 1918: Perspektive der Ärtze und Generäle," *Medizinhistorisches Journal* 48, no. 2 (2013): 117–52.
14. "Taffrail," *Endless Story*, 387.
15. Naval Staff History, Directorate of Naval Warfare, *British Mining Operations 1939–1945*, 1:27.
16. "Taffrail," *Endless Story*, 370–80.
17. Captain R. W. Blacklock, memoirs, 80–81, Blacklock Papers, Liddle Collection.
18. Gladisch, *Der Krieg zur See: Nordsee*, 7:409.
19. Karau, *Wielding the Dagger*, 223.
20. Operation orders are available in TNA ADM 137/1984.
21. Captain R. R. Belknap, "The Northern Mine Barrage," 26 January 1919 (?), Belknap Papers, USNWC Historical Collection.
22. Stevens, *In All Respects Ready*, 350.
23. Mine Squadron One, "Combined Mining Report," dated 26 October 1918, Belknap Papers, USNWC Historical Collection.

24. Naval Staff History, Directorate of Naval Warfare, *British Mining Operations 1939–1945*, 1:32.

25. Domvile, diary, entry dated 1 August 1918, Domvile Papers, NMM.

26. Robinson, *Zeppelin in Combat*, 338. This corrects H. A. Jones, *The War in the Air: Being the Story of the Part Played in the Great War by the Royal Air Force*, vol. 6 (Oxford, UK: Clarendon Press, 1934), 356–57.

27. Operation *F3*, TNA ADM 137/2132.

28. See RA(T) Report of Proceedings. TNA ADM 137/877.

29. Stevens, *In All Respects Ready*, 261–65.

30. Domvile, diary, dated 14 June 1918, Domvile Papers, NMM.

31. Robinson, *Zeppelin in Combat*, 338; Bell-Davies, *Sailor in the Air*, 177–79; Jones, *War in the Air*, 6:364–67; Operation *F7*, TNA ADM 137/877.

32. Robinson, *Zeppelin in Combat*, 341.

33. Herwig, *Luxury Fleet*, 222.

34. Scheer, *Germany's High Sea Fleet*, 337.

35. Tomazi, *La Guerre Navale*, 218.

36. Karau, *Wielding the Dagger*, 230.

37. Tennant, diary, entry dated October 1918, Tennant Papers, NMM.

38. Hamilton, diary, entry dated 4 October 1918, Hamilton Papers, NMM.

39. Buxton, *Big Gun Monitors*, 68.

40. Tobias R. Philbin, *Admiral von Hipper: The Inconvenient Hero* (Amsterdam: Gruner, 1982), 166.

41. Clarke and Birch, "History of German Naval Warfare," 1, pt. 2, 20.

42. Blacklock, memoirs, 81, Blacklock Papers, Liddle Collection.

43. Lord Strathclyde (Commander T. D. Galbraith), interview, dated August 1976, 20, Liddle Collection.

44. Chatfield, *Navy and Defence*, 177.

Bibliography

Books

Abbott, Patrick. *The British Airship at War, 1914–1918*. Lavenham: Terence Dalton, 1989.

Andrew, Christopher. *Defend the Realm: The Authorized History of MI5*. London: AllenLane, 2009.

Anonymous. *Onward HMS New Zealand*. Devonport: Swiss & Co., 1919.

Aselius, Gunnar. *The Rise and Fall of the Soviet Navy in the Baltic 1921–1941*. London: Routledge, 2004.

Ashmore, Vice Admiral L. H. *Forgotten Flotilla: British Submarines in Russia 1914–1919*. Portsmouth, UK: Manuscript Press, 2001.

Aspinall-Oglander, Brigadier C. F. *Roger Keyes*. London: Hogarth Press, 1951.

Bacon, Admiral Sir Reginald. *The Dover Patrol, 1915–1917*. 2 vols. London: Hutchinson, 1919.

Barrett, Michael B. *Operation Albion: The German Conquest of the Baltic Islands*. Bloomingdale: Indiana University Press, 2008.

Bayly, Admiral Sir Lewis. *Pull Together!* London: Harrap, 1939.

Beatty, Charles. *Our Admiral: A Biography of Admiral of the Fleet Earl Beatty 1871–1936*. London: W. H. Allen, 1980.

Beckett, Ian F. W., ed. *1917: Beyond the Western Front*. Boston: Brill Leiden, 2008.

Beesly, Patrick. *Room 40: British Naval Intelligence 1914–1918*. New York: Harcourt Brace Jovanovich, 1982.

Bell, Christopher M. *Churchill and Sea Power*. Oxford: Oxford University Press, 2012.

Bell Davies, Vice Admiral Richard. *Sailor in the Air: The Memoirs of the World's First Carrier Pilot*. Barnsley: Seaforth, 2008.

Benbow, Tim, ed. *British Naval Aviation: The First 100 Years*. Farnham, UK: Ashgate, 2011.

Bird, Keith W. *Eric Raeder: Admiral of the Third Reich*. Annapolis, MD: Naval Institute Press, 2006.

Black, Nicholas. *The British Naval Staff in the First World War*. Woodbridge: Boydell, 2009.

Bonatz, Heinz. *Die Deutsch Marine-Funkaufklärung 1914–1945*. Darmstadt: Wehr und Wissen, 1969.

Brodhurst, Robin. *Churchill's Anchor: Admiral of the Fleet Sir Dudley Pound GCB, OM, GCVO*. Barnsley: Pen & Sword, 2000.

Brooks, John. *Dreadnought Gunnery and the Battle of Jutland.* London: Frank Cass, 2005.

Brown, David K. *The Grand Fleet: Warship Design and Development 1906–1922.* London: Chatham, 1999.

Brown, Malcolm, and Patricia Meehan. *Scapa Flow: The Reminiscences of Men and Women Who Served in Scapa Flow in the Two World Wars.* London: Allen Lane, 1968.

Brownrigg, Rear Admiral Sir Douglas. *Indiscretions of the Naval Censor.* London: Cassell, 1920.

Busch, Fritz Otto, and Georg Gunther von Forstner, eds. *Unsere Marine im Weltkrieg.* Berlin: Brunnen-Verlag, 1934.

Buxton, Ian. *Big Gun Monitors: Design, Construction and Operations.* Barnsley: Seaforth, 2008.

Bywater, Hector. *Cruisers in Battle: Naval Light Cavalry under Fire 1914–18.* London: Constable, 1939.

Campbell, N. J. M. *Battlecruisers: The Design and Development of British and German Battlecruisers of the First World War Era.* London: Conway, 1978.

Campbell, Vice Admiral Gordon. *Number Thirteen.* London: Hodder & Stoughton, 1932.

Carew, Anthony. *The Lower Deck of the Royal Navy 1900–39: The Invergordon Mutiny in Perspective.* Manchester: Manchester University Press, 1981.

Carr, William Guy. *By Guess and by God.* London: Hutchinson, 1930.

——. *Brass Hats and Bell-Bottomed Trousers: Unforgettable and Splendid Feats of the Harwich Patrol.* London: Hutchinson, 1939.

——. *Good Hunting.* London: Hutchinson, 1940.

Chalmers, W. S. *The Life and Letters of David Earl Beatty.* London: Hodder & Stoughton, 1951.

——. *Max Horton and the Western Approaches.* London: Hodder & Stoughton, 1954.

——. *Full Circle: The Biography of Admiral Sir Bertram Ramsay.* London: Hodder & Stoughton, 1959.

Chatfield, Admiral of the Fleet Lord. *The Navy and Defence.* London: Heinemann, 1942.

Clarke, W. F., and F. Birch. "A Contribution to the History of German Naval Warfare 1914–1918." Compiled within NID 1919–1922, Ca9182/I, held by Naval Historical Branch (NHB).

Colvin, Admiral Sir Ragnar. *Memoirs of Admiral Sir Ragnar Colvin 1882–1954.* Durley, UK: Wintershill, 1992.

Cork and Orrery, Admiral of the Fleet the Earl of. *My Naval Life 1886–1941.* London: Hutchinson, 1942.

Cunningham, Viscount. *A Sailor's Odyssey.* London: Hutchinson, 1951.

Cunninghame-Graham, Admiral Sir Angus. *Random Naval Recollections.* Dumbartonshire, UK: Privately published, 1979.

Davison, Robert L. *The Challenges of Command: The Royal Navy's Executive Branch Officers, 1880–1919.* Farnham, UK: Ashgate, 2011.

Dawson, Captain Lionel. *Flotillas: A Hard Lying Story.* London: Rich & Cowan, 1929.

——. *Sound of the Guns: Being an Account of the Wars and Service of Admiral Sir Walter Cowan.* Oxford: Pen-in-Hand, 1949.

Day, Vice Admiral Sir Archibald. *The Admiralty Hydrographic Service 1795–1919.* London: HMSO, 1967.

De Chair, Admiral Sir Dudley. *The Sea Is Strong.* London: Harrap, 1961.

Deneckere, Bernard. *Above Ypres: The German Air Force in Flanders 1914–1918.* Brighton, UK: Firestep Press, 2013.

Dittmar, F. J., and J. J. Colledge. *British Warships 1914–1919.* London: Ian Allan, 1972.

Domvile, Admiral Sir Barry. *By and Large.* London: Hutchinson, 1939.

Dreyer, Admiral Sir Frederic. *The Sea Heritage: A Study of Maritime Warfare.* London: Museum Press, 1955.

Epkenhans, Michael, ed. *Das ereignisreiche Leben eines "Wilhelminers": Tagebücher, Briefe, Auzfeichnungen 1901 bis 1920.* München: R. Oldenbourg Verlag, 2004.

———. *Mein Lieber Schatz! Briefe von Admiral Reinhard Scheer an seine Ehefrau August bis November 1918.* Bochum: Winkler, 2006.

———. *Tirpitz: Architect of the German High Seas Fleet.* Washington, DC: Potomac, 2008.

Epkenhans, Michael, and Gunther P. Gross. *The Danish Straits and German Naval Power 1905–1918.* Potsdam: MGFA, 2010.

Epkenhans, Michael, Jörg Hillmann, and Frank Nägler, eds. *Skaggerakschlacht: Vorgeschichte, Ereignis, Verarbeitung.* München: R. Oldenbourg Verlag, 2009.

"Etienne" (Stephen King-Hall). *A Naval Lieutenant 1914–1918.* London: Methuen, 1919.

Firle, Rudolph, and Rollman, Heinrich. *Der Krieg zur See: Der Krieg in Der Ostsee.* Vols. 1–3. Berlin: Mittler, 1922–64. British Admiralty Naval Historical Branch (NHB). Translations available at the NHB for vols. 1 and 2.

Freeman, Lewis R. *Stories of the Ships.* London: John Murray, 1919.

Fremantle, Admiral Sir Sidney. *My Naval Career 1880–1928.* London: Hutchinson, 1949.

Frewen, Oswald. *Sailor's Soliloquy.* Edited by G. P. Griggs. London: Hutchinson, 1961.

Friedman, Norman. *U.S. Destroyers: An Illustrated Design History.* Annapolis, MD: Naval Institute Press, 1982.

———. *British Carrier Aviation: The Evolution of the Ships and their Aircraft.* Annapolis, MD: Naval Institute Press, 1988.

———. *Naval Firepower: Battleship Guns and Gunnery in the Dreadnought Era.* Barnsley: Seaforth, 2008.

———. *British Destroyers: From Earliest Days to the Second World War.* Annapolis, MD: Naval Institute Press, 2009.

———. *Network-Centric Warfare: How Navies Learned to Fight Smarter through Three World Wars.* Annapolis, MD: Naval Institute Press, 2009.

———. *British Cruisers: Two World Wars and After.* Annapolis, MD: Naval Institute Press, 2010.

———. *Naval Weapons of World War One.* Barnsley, UK: Seaforth, 2011.

———. *Fighting the Great War at Sea: Strategy, Tactics and Technology* Annapolis, MD: Naval Institute Press, 2014.

Gemzell, Carl-Axel. *Organization, Conflict and Innovation: A Study of German Naval Strategic Planning, 1888–1940.* Lund: Esselte Studium, 1973.

Gibson, R. H. *Three Years of Naval Warfare.* London: Heinemann, 1918.

Gladisch, Admiral Walter. *Der Krieg zur See 1914–1918: Der Krieg in der Nordsee.* Vol. 7, *Vom Sommer 1917 bis zum Kriegsende 1918.* Hamburg: E. S. Mittler, 2006.

Goodenough, Admiral Sir William. *A Rough Record*. London: Hutchinson, 1943.

Gordon, Andrew. *The Rules of the Game: Jutland and British Naval Command*. London: John Murray, 1996.

Gorlitz, Walter, ed. *The Kaiser and His Court: The Diaries, Notebooks and Letters of Admiral Georg Alexander von Müller, Chief of the Naval Cabinet, 1914–1918*. London: Macdonald, 1961.

Graf, H. *The Russian Navy in War and Revolution 1914 up to 1918*. 1923; reprint, Honolulu: University Press of the Pacific, 2002.

Granier, Gerhard. *Magnus von Levetzow: Seeoffizier, Monarchist und Webereiter Hitlers*. Boppard am Rhein: Boldt, 1982.

Grant, Robert M. *U-Boats Destroyed*. London: Putnam, 1964.

———. *U-Boat Intelligence*. London: Putnam, 1969.

———. *U-Boat Hunters: Code Breakers, Divers and the Defeat of the U-Boats, 1914–1918*. Penzance, UK: Periscope, 2003.

Greenhalgh, Elizabeth. *Victory through Coalition: Britain and France during the First World War*. Cambridge: Cambridge University Press, 2005.

Greger, Rene. *The Russian Fleet 1914–1917*. Translated by Jill Gearing. London: Ian Allan, 1972.

Grimes, Shawn T. *Strategy and War Planning in the British Navy, 1887–1918*. Woodbridge, UK: Boydell Press, 2012.

Gröner, Erich. *German Warships 1815–1945*. Vol. 1, *Major Surface Vessels*. Revised and expanded edition by Dieter Jung and Martin Maass. Annapolis, MD: Naval Institute Press, 1990.

———. *German Warships 1815–1945*. Revised and expanded by Dieter Jung and Martin Maass. Vol. 2, *U-Boats and Mine Warfare Vessels*. Annapolis, MD: Naval Institute Press, 1991.

Groos, Captain Otto, and Admiral Walter Gladisch. *Der Krieg zur See: Der Krieg in Der Nordsee*. Berlin: Mittler, 1920–1965. British Admiralty Naval Historical Branch (NHB) translations (except vol. 7) are available at the NHB.

Hackforth-Jones, Gilbert. *Sixteen Bells: Stories of the Royal Navy in Peace and War*. London: Hodder & Stoughton, 1946.

Hackmann, Willem. *Seek and Strike: Sonar, Anti-Submarine Warfare and the Royal Navy 1914–1954*. London: HMSO, 1984.

Halpern, Paul G. *The Keyes Papers: Selections from the Private and Official Correspondence of Admiral of the Fleet Baron Keyes of Zeebrugge*. Vol. 1, *1914–1918*. London: Navy Records Society, 1972.

———. *A Naval History of World War I*. Annapolis, MD: Naval Institute Press, 1994.

Hamilton, C. I. *The Making of the Modern Admiralty: British Naval Policy-Making, 1805–1927*. Cambridge: Cambridge University Press, 2011.

Hayward, Victor. *HMS Tiger at Bay: A Sailor's Memoir 1914–18*. London: William Kimber, 1977.

Herwig, Holger. *The German Naval Officer Corps: A Political and Social History*. Oxford: Oxford University Press, 1973.

———. *Luxury Fleet; The Imperial German Navy 1888–1918*. London: Allen & Unwin, 1980.

Hezlet, Vice Admiral Sir Arthur. *The Submarine and Sea Power*. London: Peter Davies, 1967.

———. *The Aircraft and Sea Power*. London: Peter Davies, 1971.

———. *The Electron and Sea Power*. London: Peter Davies, 1975.

Hobbs, David. *The Royal Navy's Air Service in the Great War.* Barnsley, UK: Seaforth, 2017.

Hopman, Admiral. *Das Logbuch eines deutschen Seeoffiziers.* Berlin: August Scherl, 1924.

———. *Das Kriegstagebuch eines deutschen Seeoffiziers.* Berlin: August Scherl, 1925.

Horn, Daniel, ed. *The Private War of Seaman Stumpf: The Unique Diaries of a Young German in the Great War.* London: Leslie Frewin, 1969.

———. *The German Naval Mutinies of World War I.* New Brunswick, NJ: Rutgers University Press, 1969.

Hough, Richard. *The Big Battleship: The Curious Career of HMS Agincourt.* London: Michael Joseph, 1966.

Huck, Stephan, Gorch Pieken, and Matthias Rogg, eds. *Die Flotte Schläft im Hafen Ein: Kriegsalltag 1914–1918 in Matrosen-Tagebüchern.* Wilhelmshaven: Deutsches Marinemuseum, 2015.

James, Admiral Sir William. *The Sky Was Always Blue.* London: Methuen, 1951.

———. *The Eyes of the Navy: A Biographical Study of Admiral Sir Reginald Hall.* London: Methuen, 1955.

———. *A Great Seaman: The Life of Admiral of the Fleet Sir Henry Oliver.* London: Witherby, 1956.

Jameson, Rear Admiral Sir William. *The Fleet that Jack Built: Nine Men Who Made a Modern Navy.* London: Hart-Davis, 1962.

———. *The Most Formidable Thing.* London: Hart-Davis, 1965.

Jeffery, Keith. *MI6: The History of the Secret Intelligence Service, 1909–1949.* London: Bloomsbury, 2010.

Jellicoe, Admiral of the Fleet Viscount. *The Grand Fleet 1914–16: Its Creation, Development and Work.* London: Cassell, 1919.

———. *The Crisis of the Naval War.* London: Cassell, 1920.

———. *The Submarine Peril.* London: Cassell, 1934.

Jentzsch, Christian, and Jann M. Witt. *Der Seekrieg 1914–1918: Die Kaiserliche Marine im Erstern Weltkrieg.* Darmstadt: WBG, 2016.

Jones, Basil. *And so to Battle: A Sailor's Story.* Battle, UK: Privately published, 1979.

Jones, H. A. *The War in the Air: Being the Story of the Part Played in the Great War by the Royal Air Force.* Vols. 4–6, Oxford: Clarendon, 1931–1937.

Jones, Jerry W. *U.S. Battleship Operations in World War I.* Annapolis, MD: Naval Institute Press, 1987.

Jones, Peter. *Australia's Argonauts: The Remarkable Story of the First Class to Enter the Royal Australian Naval College.* West Geelong: Echo Books, 2016.

Jones, T. M. *Watchdogs of the Deep: Life in a Submarine during the Great War* Sydney: Angus & Robertson, 1935.

Karau, Mark D. *"Wielding the Dagger": The Marinekorps Flandern and the German War Effort, 1914–1918.* Westport, CT: Praeger, 2003.

Kemp, Paul. *The Admiralty Regrets: British Warship Losses of the 20th Century.* Stroud: Sutton, 1999.

Keyes, Roger. *The Naval Memoirs of Admiral of the Fleet Sir Roger Keyes* Vol. 2, *Scapa Flow to the Dover Straits 1916–1918.* London: Thornton Butterworth, 1935.

Kilduff, Peter. *Germany's First Air Force 1914–1918.* London: Arms & Armour, 1991.

King-Hall, Admiral Sir Herbert. *Naval Memories and Traditions.* London: Hutchinson, 1926.

King-Hall, Lady L. *Sea Saga*. London: Gollancz, 1935.

King-Hall, Stephen. *My Naval Life 1906–1929*. London: Faber & Faber, 1952.

"Klaxon" (Lieutenant Commander J. G. Bower). *The Story of Our Submarines*. London: William Blackwood, 1919.

Lambert, Nicholas A. *The Submarine Service 1900–1918*. Aldershot, UK: Navy Records Society (Ashgate), 2001.

Langmaid, Kenneth. *The Approaches are Mined!* London: Jarrolds, 1965.

Lavery, Brian. *Able Seamen: The Lower Deck of the Royal Navy 1850–1939*. London: Conway, 2011.

Le Bailly, Vice Admiral Sir Louis. *From Fisher to the Falklands*. London: Institute of Marine Engineers, 1991.

Liddle, Peter H. *The Sailor's War 1914–1918*. Poole: Blandford, 1985.

Longmore, Air Chief Marshal Sir Arthur. *From Sea to Sky 1910–1945*. London: Geoffrey Bles, 1946.

Mackay, Ruddock F. *Fisher of Kilverstone*. Oxford: Clarendon, 1973.

Mantey, Eberhard von, ed. *Auf See unbesiegt: Erlebnisse im Seekrieg erzählt von Mitkämpfern*. Vols. 1–2. Munich: Lehmanns, 1922.

Marder, Arthur J. *Fear God and Dread Nought: The Correspondence of Admiral of the Fleet Lord Fisher of Kilverstone*. Vol. 3, *Restoration, Abdication, and Last Years 1914–1920*. London: Jonathan Cape, 1959.

———. *From the Dreadnought to Scapa Flow: The Royal Navy in the Fisher Era*, 2nd ed., 5 vols. London: Oxford University Press, 1978, 1969, 1970.

Mawdsley, Evan. *The Russian Revolution and the Baltic Fleet* London: Macmillan, 1978.

Maxwell, Gordon S. *The Naval Front*. London: Black, 1920.

McArtney, Innes. *Jutland 1916: The Archaeology of a Naval Battlefield*. London: Bloomsbury, 2016.

McKee, Christopher. *Sober Men and True: Sailor Lives in the Royal Navy 1900–1945*. Cambridge, MA: Harvard University Press, 2002.

Messimer, Dwight R. *Verschollen: World War I U-Boat Losses*. Annapolis, MD: Naval Institute Press, 2002.

Millett, Allan R., and Williamson Murray. *Military Effectiveness*. Vol. 1, *The First World War*. Boston: Unwin Hyman, 1988.

Monsarrat, Nicholas. *The Cruel Sea*. London: Cassell, 1951.

Moore, Major W. Geoffrey. *Early Bird*. London: Putnam, 1963.

Mountevans, Admiral Lord. *Adventurous Life*. London: Hutchinson, 1946.

Muir, Surgeon Rear Admiral J. R. *Years of Endurance*. London: Philip Allan, 1936.

Munro, Captain D. J. *Scapa Flow: A Naval Retrospect*. London: Sampson Low, 1932.

Nekrasov, George M. *North of Gallipoli: The Black Sea Fleet at War 1914–1917*. New York: Columbia University Press, 1992.

———. *Expendable Glory: Russian Battleship in the Baltic, 1915–1917*. New York: Columbia University Press, 2004.

Nerger, Karl. *S.M.S. Wolf*. Translated by Beate Lauterbach and Michael Zehnpfennig. Ed. Paul Freedman. Birkenhead, UK: GTO Printers, 2000.

Neumann, Major Georg Paul. *The German Air Force I Knew, 1914–1918: Memoirs of the Imperial German Air Force in the Great War*. Translated by J. E. Gurdon. Edited by Bob Carruthers. Barnsley, UK: Pen & Sword Aviation, 2014.

Offer, Avner. *The First World War: An Agrarian Interpretation*. Oxford: Oxford University Press, 1989.

O'Hara, Vincent, David W. Dickson, and Richard Worth, eds. *To Crown the Waves: The Great Navies of the First World War*. Annapolis, MD: Naval Institute Press, 2013.

O'Hara, Vincent, and Leonard R. Heinz. *Clash of Fleets: Naval Battles of the Great War, 1914–18*. Annapolis, MD: Naval Institute Press, 2017.

Oram, H. P. K. *Ready for Sea*. London: Seeley Service, 1974.

Pack, S. W. C. *Cunningham the Commander*. London: Batsford, 1974.

Parkes, Oscar. *British Battleships*. London: Seeley Service, 1960.

Patterson, A. Temple. *The Jellicoe Papers: Selections from the Private and Official Correspondence of Admiral of the Fleet Earl Jellicoe of Scapa*. Vol. 1, *1893–1916*. Vol. 2, *1916–1935*. London: Navy Records Society, 1966, 1968.

——. *Jellicoe: A Biography*. London: Macmillan, 1969.

——. *Tyrwhitt of the Harwich Force: The Life of Admiral of the Fleet Sir Reginald Tyrwhitt*. London: MacDonald, 1973.

Pavlovich, N. B. *The Fleet in the First World War*. Vol. 1, *Operations of the Russian Fleet*. Translated by C. M. Rao. New Delhi: Amerind, 1979.

Pelly, Admiral Sir Henry. *300,000 Sea Miles*. London: Chatto & Windus, 1938.

Persius, L. *Der Seekrieg*. Charlottenburg: Wettlübine, 1919.

Philbin, Tobias R. *Admiral von Hipper: The Inconvenient Hero*. Amsterdam: Gruner, 1982.

Plivier, Theodor. *The Kaiser's Coolies*. Translated by William F. Clarke. London: Faber, 1932.

Plunkett, Lieutenant the Hon. R. *The Modern Officer of the Watch*. Fourth ed. Portsmouth: Griffin & Co., 1910.

Polmar, Norman, and Jurrien Noot. *Submarines of the Russian and Soviet Navies, 1718–1990*. Annapolis, MD: Naval Institute Press, 1991.

Prince, Stephen. *The Blocking of Zeebrugge: Operation Z-O 1918*. Oxford, UK: Osprey, 2010.

Raeder, Erich. *Grand Admiral*. New York: Da Capo, 2001.

Ramsay, David. *"Blinker" Hall Spymaster: The Man Who Brought America into World War I*. Stroud, UK: Spellmount, 2008.

Ranft, B. McL. *The Beatty Papers: Selections from the Private and Official Correspondence of Admiral of the Fleet Earl Beatty*. Vol. 1, *1902–1918*. Aldershot, UK: Scolar Press for Navy Records Society, 1989.

Raskolnikov, F. F. *Kronstadt and Petrograd in 1917*. Translated by Brian Pearce. London: New Park, 1982.

Rippon, P. M. *The Evolution of Engineering in the Royal Navy*. Vol. 1, *1827–1939*. Tunbridge Wells, UK: Spellmount, 1988.

Robinson, Douglas H. *The Zeppelin in Combat: A History of the German Naval Airship Division, 1912–1918*. Atglen, PA: Schiffer, 1994.

Roskill, Stephen. *Documents Relating to the Naval Air Service*. Vol. 1, *1908–1918*. London: Navy Records Society, 1969.

——. *Hankey: Man of Secrets*. Vol. 1, *1877–1918*. London: Collins, 1970.

——. *Churchill and the Admirals*. London: Collins, 1977.

——. *Admiral of the Fleet Earl Beatty: The Last Naval Hero: An Intimate Biography*. London: Collins, 1980.

Ruge, Vice Admiral Friedrich. *SM Torpedo Boat B. 110*. Warship Profile 27. Windsor: Profile Publications, 1972.

——. *Scapa Flow 1919: The End of the German Fleet*. London: Ian Allan, 1973.

Saul, Norman E. *Sailors in Revolt: The Russian Baltic Fleet in 1917.* Lawrence: University Press of Kansas, 1978.

Scheer, Admiral. *Germany's High Sea Fleet in the World War.* London: Cassell, 1920.

Schofield, Vice Admiral B. B. *Navigation and Direction: The Story of HMS Dryad.* Havant, UK: Kenneth Mason, 1977.

Schoultz, Commodore G. von. *With the British Battle Fleet: War Recollections of a Russian Naval Officer.* Translated by Arthur Chambers. London: Hutchinson, 1925.

Seymour, Lady. *Commander Ralph Seymour, R.N.* Glasgow: University Press, 1926.

Share, Rear Admiral Sir Hamnet. *Under Great Bear and Southern Cross: Forty Years Afloat and Ashore.* London: Jarrolds, 1932.

Simpson, Rear Admiral G. W. G. *Periscope View: A Professional Autobiography* London: Macmillan, 1972.

Simpson, Michael. *Anglo-American Naval Relations 1917–1919.* London: Scolar Press for the Navy Records Society, 1991.

Sims, Rear Admiral William S. *Victory at Sea.* London: Murray, 1920.

Smith, Michael. *Six: A History of Britain's Secret Intelligence Service.* Part 1, *Murder and Mayhem 1909–1939.* London: Dialogue, 2010.

Spindler, Rear Admiral Arno. *Der Krieg zur See: Der Handelskrieg mit U-Booten.* 5 vols. Berlin: Mittler, 1932–1966. British Admiralty Naval Historical Branch (NHB), translation for vols. 1–3 available at the NHB.

Staff, Gary. *German Battleships 1914–18 (1).* Oxford, UK: Osprey, 2010.

———. *German Battleships 1914–18 (2).* Oxford, UK: Osprey, 2010.

———. *Battle on the Seven Seas: German Cruiser Battles 1914–1918.* Barnsley, UK: Pen & Sword Maritime, 2011.

———. *German Battlecruisers of World War One: Their Design, Construction and Operations.* Barnsley, UK: Seaforth: 2014.

Stevens, David. *In All Respects Ready: Australia's Navy in World War One.* Melbourne: Oxford University Press, 2014.

Still, William N., Jr., ed. *The Queenstown Patrol, 1917: The Diary of Commander Joseph Knefler Taussig, U.S. Navy.* Newport, RI: Naval War College Press, 1996.

"Taffrail" (Commander Taprell Dorling). *H.M.S. "Anonymous."* London: Herbert Jenkins, 1920.

———. *Endless Story: Being an Account of the Work of the Destroyers, Flotilla-Leaders, Torpedo-Boats and Patrol Boats in the Great War.* London: Hodder & Stoughton, 1931.

———. *Swept Channels.* London: Hodder & Stoughton, 1935.

Taylor, John C. *German Warships of World War I.* London: Ian Allan, 1969.

Thomazi, A. *La Guerre Navale dans La Zone des Armees du Nord.* Paris: Payot, 1924.

Thompson, J. Lee. *Northcliffe: Press Baron in Politics 1865–1922.* London: John Murray, 2000.

Thompson, Julian. *The Imperial War Museum Book of The War at Sea 1914–1918.* London: Sidgwick & Jackson, 2005.

Tirpitz, Grand Admiral Alfred von. *My Memoirs.* London: Hurst & Blackett, 1919.

Tracy, Nicholas. *Sea Power and the Control of Trade: Belligerent Rights from the Russian War to the Beira Patrol, 1854–1970.* Aldershot, UK: Ashgate for the Navy Records Society, 2005.

Trask, David F. *Captains and Cabinets: Anglo-American Naval Relations, 1917–1918*. Columbia: University of Missouri Press, 1972.

Tupper, Admiral Sir Reginald. *Reminiscences*. London: Jarrolds, 1929.

Tweedie, Admiral Sir Hugh. *The Story of a Naval Life*. London: Rich & Cowan, 1939.

Usborne, Vice Admiral C. V. *Blast and Counterblast: A Naval Impression of the War*. London: Murray, 1935.

Waldeyer-Hartz, Captain H. von. *Admiral von Hipper*. London: Rich & Cowan, 1933.

Watts, A. J. *The Imperial Russian Navy*. London: Arms & Armour, 1990.

Weir, Gary E. *Building the Kaiser's Navy: The Imperial Naval Office and German Industry in the von Tirpitz Era, 1880–1919*. Annapolis, MD: Naval Institute Press, 1992.

Weizsacker, Ernst von. *Memoirs of Ernst von Weizsacker*. Translated by John Andrews. London: Gollancz, 1951.

Wells, Captain John. *The Royal Navy: An Illustrated Social History, 1870–1982*. Stroud, UK: Sutton, 1994.

Wester Wemyss, Lady. *The Life and Letters of Lord Wester Wemyss*. London: Eyre & Spottiswoode, 1935.

White, D. Fedotoff. *Survival through War and Revolution in Russia*. London: Oxford University Press, 1939.

Wiest, Andrew A. *Passchendaele and the Royal Navy*. Westport, CT: Greenwood, 1995.

Wiley, Admiral Henry A. *An Admiral from Texas*. New York: Doubleday, Doran & Co., 1934.

Wilson, Michael. *Baltic Assignment: British Submariners in Russia, 1914–1919*. London: Leo Cooper, 1985.

Wingate, John. *HMS Dreadnought: Battleship 1906–1920*. Profile Warship 1. Windsor, UK: Profile, 1970.

Winkler, Jonathan Reed. *Nexus: Strategic Communications and American Security in World War I*. Cambridge, MA: Harvard University Press, 2008.

Winton, John. *Jellicoe*. London: Michael Joseph, 1981.

Wolters, Timothy S. *Information at Sea: Shipboard Command and Control in the U.S. Navy, from Mobile Bay to Okinawa*. Baltimore: Johns Hopkins University Press, 2013.

Wolz, Nicholas. *From Imperial Splendour to Internment: The German Navy in the First World War*. Translated by Geoffrey Brooks. Barnsley, UK: Seaforth, 2015.

Woodward, David. *The Collapse of Power: Mutiny in the High Seas Fleet*. London: Arthur Barker, 1973.

Woollard, Commander C. L. A. *With the Harwich Naval Forces 1914–1918*. Antwerp: Private printing, 1931.

Young, Desmond. *Rutland of Jutland*. London: Cassell, 1963.

Articles, Chapters, and Papers

Beesly, Patrick. "Cryptoanalysis and Its Influence on the War at Sea 1914–1918." Fifth Naval History Symposium, Annapolis, MD, 1981.

Bird, Keith W. "The Origins and Role of German Naval History in the Inter-War Period, 1918–1939." *Naval War College Review* 32, no. 2 (March–April 1979).

Demchak, Tony E. "Rebuilding the Russian Fleet: The Duma and Naval Rearmament, 1907–1914." *The Journal of Slavic Military Studies* 26, no. 1 (2013).

Goldrick, James. "John R. Jellicoe: Technology's Victim (1859–1935)." In *The Great Admirals: Command at Sea, 1587–1945*, edited by Jack Sweetman. Annapolis, MD: Naval Institute Press, 1997.

——. "Coal and the Advent of the First World War at Sea." *War in History* 21, no. 3 (2014).

Grove, Eric, ed. "The Autobiography of Chief Gunner Alexander Grant: HMS *Lion* at the Battle of Jutland, 1916." In *The Naval Miscellany* 7, edited by Susan Rose. Aldershot, UK: Navy Records Society (Ashgate), 2008.

Grove, Eric. "Seamen or Airmen? The Early Days of British Naval Flying." In *British Naval Aviation: The First 100 Years*, edited by Tim Benbow. Farnham, UK: Ashgate, 2011.

Halvorsen, Peter. "The Royal Navy and Mine Warfare, 1868–1914." *Journal of Strategic Studies* 27, no. 4 (2004).

Hammant, Thomas R. "Russian and Soviet Cryptology I—Some Communications Intelligence in Tsarist Russia." *Cryptologia* 24, no. 3 (July 2000).

Herrick, Claire E. J. "Casualty Care during the First World War: The Experience of the Royal Navy." *War in History* 7, no. 2 (2000).

Hiley, Nicholas. "The Strategic Origins of Room 40." *Intelligence and National Security* 2, no. 2 (1987).

Hines, Jason. "Sins of Omission and Commission: A Reassessment of the Role of Intelligence in the Battle of Jutland." *Journal of Military History* 72, no. 4 (October 2008).

Kennedy, Greg. "Intelligence and the Blockade, 1914–1917: A Study in Administration, Friction and Command." *Intelligence and National Security* 22, no. 5 (October 2007).

——. "Strategy and Power: The Royal Navy, the Foreign Office and the Blockade, 1914–1917 *Defence Studies* 8, no. 2 (2008).

Lambert, Nicholas A. "'Our Bloody Ships' or 'Our Bloody System'? Jutland and the Loss of the Battle Cruisers, 1916." *Journal of Military History* 62, no. 1 (January 1998).

——. "Strategic Command and Control for Maneuver Warfare: Creation of the Royal Navy's 'War Room' System, 1905–1915." *Journal of Military History* 69, no. 2 (April 2005).

——. "Transformation and Technology in the Fisher Era: The Impact of the Communications Revolution." *Journal of Strategic Studies* 27, no. 2 (2004).

Martin, Christopher. "The Declaration of London: a matter of operational capability." *Historical Research* 82, no. 218 (2009).

Morley, S. "The Royal Navy of Lieutenant Commander W. E. V. Woods, RN." *99 Years of Navy*. London: Cpg, 1995.

"Onlooker" (Captain A. W. Clarke). "The Fleet Air Arm–Another Fiftieth Anniversary." *Naval Review* 52, no. 4 (October 1964).

——. "H.M. Navigation School 1903–1968." *Naval Review* 56, no. 3 (July 1968).

Pitcairn-Jones, Commander L. J. "Navigation in War of 1914–1918." Royal Naval Staff College 1939 Session (Naval Historical Branch).

Rodger, N. A. M. "The Royal Navy in the Era of the World Wars: Was It Fit for Purpose?" *Mariner's Mirror* 97, no. 1 (2011).

"R. P. D." (Admiral Sir Reginald Plunkett-Ernle-Erle-Drax). "D. B. II." Obituary in *Naval Review* 24, no. 2 (May 1936).

"Sea Gee" (Rear Admiral C. G. Brodie). "Some Early Submariners I & II." *Naval Review* 62, no. 4 (November 1963): 483; 64, no. 1 (January 1965).

"S. D. S." (Captain S. D. Spicer). "The Fuel of the Future?" *Naval Review* 23, no. 2 (May 1935).

Smith, Canfield F. "Essen, Nikolai Ottovich." In *The Modern Encyclopedia of Russian and Soviet History*, edited by Joseph L. Wieczynski. Vol. 10, *Do to Es*, 239–41. Gulf Breeze, FL: Academic International Press, 1979.

Stevenson, Gene C. "Russian 'Lake' Type Submarines and the Baltic War 1914–1916." In *Warship 1990*, edited by Robert Gardiner. London: Conway, 1990.

Sumida, Jon Tetsuro. "British Naval Operational Logistics, 1914–1918." *Journal of Military History* 57, no. 3 (July 1993).

———. "Challenging Parkinson's Law." *Naval History* 8 (November–December 1994).

———. "Expectation, Adaptation and Resignation: British Battle Fleet Tactical Planning, August 1914–April 1916." *Naval War College Review* 60, no. 3 (Summer 2007).

———. "Forging the Trident: British Naval Industrial Logistics, 1914–1918." In *Feeding Mars: Logistics in Western Warfare from the Middle Ages to the Present*, edited by John A. Lynn. Boulder, CO: Westview Press 1993.

———. "Geography, Technology and British Naval Strategy in the Dreadnought Era." *Naval War College Review* 59, no. 3 (Summer 2006).

———. "A Matter of Timing: The Royal Navy and the Tactics of Decisive Battle, 1912–1916." *Journal of Military History* 67 (January 2003).

Thomson, Commander G. P. "Submarine Warfare." *Minutes of Proceedings of the Royal Artillery Institution* 48, no. 2 (1921).

Vinogradov, Sergei E. "Battleship Development in Russia from 1905 to 1917." Part I. *Warship International* 35, no. 3 (1998).

Weir, Gary E. "Reinhard Scheer: Intuition under Fire, 1863–1928." In *The Great Admirals: Command at Sea, 1587–1945*, edited by Jack Sweetman. Naval Institute, Annapolis, MD, 1997.

Yankovich, V. "The Origins of Communications Intelligence." Translated by Thomas R. Hammant. *Cryptologia* 8, no. 3 (July 1984).

Unpublished Theses

Brown, W. M. "The Royal Navy's Fuel Supplies 1898–1939; The Transition from Coal to Oil." PhD dissertation, King's College, London, 2003.

Dunley, Richard. "The Offensive Mining Service: Mine Warfare and Strategic Development in the Royal Navy 1900–1914." PhD dissertation, King's College, London, 2013.

Farquharson-Roberts, Surgeon Rear Admiral Michael. "To the Nadir and Back: The Executive Branch of the Royal Navy 1918–1939." PhD dissertation, University of Exeter, UK, 2011.

Randel, J. C. "Information for Economic Warfare: British Intelligence and the Blockade, 1914–1918." PhD dissertation, University of North Carolina, Chapel Hill, 1993.

Romans, Elinor. "Selection and Early Career Education of Officers in the Royal Navy, c. 1902–1939." PhD thesis, University of Exeter, UK, 2012.

———. "The Supply of Scapa Flow in World War One." MA thesis, University of Exeter, UK, 2005.

Official Documents

Naval Staff, Admiralty. *Naval Staff Monographs (Historical)*:

    Vol. 6, *The Dover Command: Vol. 1.*

    Vol. 7, *Monograph 19, Tenth Cruiser Squadron—1.*

    Vol. 17, *Home Waters, Part 7, From June 1916 to November 1916.*

    Vol. 18, *Home Waters, Part 8, From December 1916 to April 1917.*

    Vol. 19, *Home Waters, Part 9, From May 1917 to July 1917.*

    The Economic Blockade 1914–1919 (CB 1554).

    Grand Fleet Gunnery and Torpedo Memoranda on Naval Actions 1914–1918, April 1922 (OU 5444).

    The History of British Minefields.

    History of British Minesweeping in the War (CB 1553).

    The Naval Staff of the Admiralty. Its Work and Development (CB 3013).

    Operations off the East Coast of Britain 1914–1918 (OU 6354(40)).

    Progress in Naval Gunnery 1914 to 1918 (CB 902).

    Review of German Cruiser Warfare 1914–1918 (OU 6337(40)).

    Reports on Zeebrugge and Ostend Operations 22–23 April 1918 and Ostend Operations July 1918 (OU 6170), July 1918.

    Translation of Vice-Admiral Schmidt's Despatch (The Conquest of the Baltic Islands):Translation from the Original Text, Berlin 1917 (OU 6042), November 1919.

——. *Technical Histories* (CB 1515 series):

    Submarine v Submarine CB 1515(1).

    Aircraft v Submarine: Submarine Campaign 1918 CB 1515(4).

    The Anti-Submarine Division of the Naval Staff December 1916–November 1918 CB 1515(7).

    Scandinavian and East Coast Convoy Systems 1917–1918 CB 1515(8).

    Defensive Armament of Merchant Ships CB 1515(13).

    The Atlantic Convoy System 1917–1918 CB 1515(14).

    The Development of the Gyro-Compass Prior to and during the War CB 1515(20).

    Fire Control in H.M. Ships CB 1515(23).

    Ammunition for Naval Guns CB 1515(29).

    Control of Mercantile Movements Part 1 CB 1515(30).

    Anti-Submarine Development and Experiments Prior to December 1916 CB 1515(40).

——. *Admiralty Weekly Orders* (Naval Historical Branch).

——. *Baltic Pilot* HMSO, London.

——. *The Manual of Seamanship* HMSO, London, 1915 (Vol. 1) and 1909 (Vol. 2).

——. *Narrative of the Battle of Jutland* HMSO, London, 1924.

——. *The Navy List* HMSO, London.

——. *North Sea Pilot* HMSO, London.

Naval Staff, Director of Naval Construction. *Notes on Damage to Warships: 1914–1919* (Naval Historical Branch).

Personal Manuscript Collections
British/Australian

Ashbourne, Vice Admiral Lord. Memoirs (Liddle Collection)

Backhouse, Admiral of the Fleet Sir Roger. Papers (Naval Historical Branch)

Bagot, Commander A. G. D. Journal (Liddle Collection)

Beamish, Rear Admiral Percy Tufton. Papers (Churchill College Archives)

Beatty, Admiral of the Fleet Earl. Papers (National Maritime Museum)

Best, Admiral Sir Matthew. Diary (Liddle Collection)

Bethell, Admiral Sir Alexander. Papers (Liddell Hart Centre)

Bethell, Lieutenant Maurice. Papers (Liddell Hart Centre)

Blacklock, Captain R. W. Interview, Memoirs & Papers (Liddle Collection)

Blagrove, Rear Admiral H. E. C. Letters (Imperial War Museum)

Buckley, Rear Admiral F. A. Diary (National Maritime Museum)

Burrough, Admiral Sir Harold. Papers (Liddle Collection)

Cardew, Lieutenant J. StE. Journal (RN Museum Library)

Childers, Lieutenant Erskine. Diary (Imperial War Museum)

Clarke, Captain A. W. Journal & Diary (Liddle Collection)

Clarke, William. Papers (Churchill College Archives)

Crooke, Admiral Sir Henry. Diary (Churchill College Archives)

Daniel, Admiral Sir Charles. Diary (Churchill College Archives)

Denniston, Alfred. Papers (Churchill College Archives)

De Winton, Captain F. S. W. Memoirs (Liddell Hart Centre)

Dewar, Vice Admiral K. G. B. Papers (National Maritime Museum)

Domvile, Admiral Sir Barry. Diary (National Maritime Museum)

Downes, Commander A. B. Journals (RN Museum Library)

Drage, Commander C. H. Diary (Imperial War Museum and Liddle Collection)

Dreyer, Admiral Sir Frederic. Journals (Churchill College Archives)

Duff, Admiral Sir Alexander. Diary (National Maritime Museum and
    Mr. Simon Harley)

Duke, Captain M. V. Papers (Liddell Hart Centre)

Farquhar, Captain Malcolm. Papers (RN Museum Library)

Fell, Captain W. R. Memoir Letter (Liddle Collection)

Fletcher, Chief Petty Officer Edwin. Diaries (RN Museum Library)

Goldsmith, Vice Admiral Lennon. Letters (Churchill College Archives)

Grenfell, Captain F. H. Diary (Imperial War Museum and Liddle Collection)

Haddy, Eng. Rear Admiral Frederick. Letters (RN Museum Library)

Haldane, T. G. N. Diary (Churchill College Archives)

Hamilton, Admiral Sir Frederick. Papers (National Maritime Museum)

Hamilton, Admiral Sir Louis. Diary (National Maritime Museum)

Harper, Lieutenant Commander G. C. Diary (Churchill College Archives)

Howson, Captain John. Papers (Liddell Hart Centre)

Humphreys, Commander L. A. Papers (Liddell Hart Centre)

Jerram, Admiral Sir Martyn. Papers (National Maritime Museum)

Kennedy, Admiral Francis. Papers (Liddell Hart Centre)

King-Harman, Captain R. D. Letters (Imperial War Museum)

Leslie, Shane. Papers (Churchill College Archives)

MacGregor, Lieutenant Commander Donald. Letters (RN Museum Library)

MacLiesh, Commander Fraser. Diaries (Churchill College Archives)

Madden, Admiral of the Fleet Sir Charles. Grand Fleet War Diary (National Maritime Museum)
Napier, Admiral Sir Trevelyan. Papers (Imperial War Museum)
Nichols, Captain R. F. Memoirs (Liddle Collection)
Noble, Admiral Sir Percy. Papers (Liddell Hart Centre)
Nurse, Midshipman E. S. Diary (Vice Admiral Peter Jones)
Oliver, Admiral of the Fleet Sir Henry. Memoirs (National Maritime Museum)
Owen, Commander B. W. L. Journal (Imperial War Museum)
Pakenham, Admiral Sir William. Papers (National Maritime Museum)
Perry, Allan Cecil. Memoirs (Liddle Collection)
Plunkett-Ernle-Erle-Drax, Admiral Sir Reginald. Papers (Churchill College Archives)
Ramsay, Admiral Sir Bertram. Diary (Churchill College Archives)
Richmond, Admiral Sir Herbert. Papers (National Maritime Museum)
Shearer, G. Papers (RN Museum Library)
Shearer, W. Papers (RN Museum Library)
Singer, Admiral Sir Morgan. Papers (Liddle Collection)
Somerville, Admiral of the Fleet Sir James. Diaries (Churchill College Archives)
Strathclyde, Lord. Interview (Liddle Collection)
Sturdee, Admiral of the Fleet Sir Doveton. Papers (Churchill College Archives)
Tennant, Admiral Sir William. Diaries (National Maritime Museum)
Tomkinson, Vice Admiral Wilfred. Diaries (Churchill College Archives)
Voysey, Sub Lieutenant T. A. Journals (RN Museum Library)
Walters, Commander J. D. Memoirs (Liddell Hart Centre)
Ward-Smith, Paymaster Captain Guy. Papers (RN Museum Library)
Whittaker, Lieutenant J. K. Diary (National Maritime Museum)

United States
Belknap, Rear Admiral Reginald. Papers (U.S. Naval War College [USNWC] Historical Collection)
Dolan, James H. Diary (USNWC)
Erle, Norman P. Letters (USNWC)
Hewitt, Admiral H. Kent. Reminiscences (USNWC))
Hill, Admiral Harry W. Reminiscences (USNWC)
McRea, Vice Admiral John L. Reminiscences (USNWC)
Moore, Vice Admiral C. J. Reminiscences (USNWC)
Sims, Admiral William S. Letters (USNWC)
Taussig, Vice Admiral Joseph K. Diary (USNWC)

Index

Acworth, Bernard, 76

Admiralstab, 9, 55, 85, 92, 95–96, 105; criticism of Grasshof's performance, 218; decision against fleet deployment in Baltic, 200–201; dismissive toward American capacity to contribute to Allied effort, 129–30; fleet stand-down, 122; on neutrals entering the war, 129–30; permit of return of Sixth Half-Flotilla to Flanders, 218; prize warfare, 109; response to Scheer's sortie plan, 146–47; Scheer criticism of influence on kaiser, 252; Scheer replacing von Holtzendorff as head of, 270; Scheer's criticism of, 109; six month promise, 129–30; transfer of units to Dover Command, 147; unrestricted campaign argument of, 129–30

Admiralty: admonitions for speed reduction, 36; American repairs, agreement to, 162; analysis of operations, 248; assessments and studies, 42, 132, 254–56, 265; aviation, aircraft, and airships, 83, 109, 154; Bacon, support for, 63, 127; Baltic flotilla reinforcement alternatives, 98–99; Baltic Project debate in, 11; Beatty battle cruisers' transfer to Scapa Flow, agreement to, 124; Beatty's problem with, 157–58; boxing competition, support for, 19; claims of German ships sunk in Dover raid, 118; communication issues, 131; control of naval war, 5; controlled sailing procedures, 136; convoy issue, 131, 134–35, 136–37, 156–59, 278; criticism of, 131, 153, 278, 282; cruiser operations cancellation, 111;

defensive policies, 68, 263; deployment policies, 80–81; direction finding reports of, 254; Dover Command, 118, 147; English Channel operations, 68, 113–14; Flanders Coast, 152–53, 271; German shipbuilding, estimates of, 231; Grand Fleet and, 57–58, 157–58, 218, 280; Harwich Force, 7, 111, 113, 147; Heligoland Bight, 211, 262; incident concealment attempts, 36; information access restrictions, 34, 68; Jellicoe command, 123, 124; Keyes, backing of, 238; Mayo, discussions with, 225–26; mine warfare, 51, 139, 158, 166, 174, 278–79; Napier, criticism of, 218; naval aviation, 158, 165; Northcliffe and, 145; Northern Barrage, 263–64; offensive approach, enthusiasm for, 162, 225–26; Operation ZO plans, 239–41, 249–50; operational planning failures of, 208–11; personnel for, 5, 124; public criticisms of, 206, 218, 221; reorganization of, 131, 157; requisition of trawlers, 135–36; signal intelligence access, 43–44, 70, 73, 78, 131, 165; strategy and command, crises of, 199–203, 204; survivors, policy on, 170; transatlantic traffic protection, 260; Tyrwhitt's criticism of Bacon to, 127; U-boat campaign, 123, 223, 231; USN policy and, 225–26; Wemyss as First Sea Lord, 230

Albrecht, Conrad, 145, 241

Alexander-Sinclair, Edwyn, 217

Allen, C. H., 255

antisubmarine warfare, 130–37; convoys and, 156–57; doctrinal and tactical

323

About the Author

James Goldrick is a retired two-star rear admiral in the Royal Australian Navy who held several seagoing commands and later led the Australian Force Academy, Australia's Border Protection Command, and the Australian Defence College. He lives in Canberra, Australia.

The **Naval Institute Press** is the book-publishing arm of the U.S. Naval Institute, a private, nonprofit, membership society for sea service professionals and others who share an interest in naval and maritime affairs. Established in 1873 at the U.S. Naval Academy in Annapolis, Maryland, where its offices remain today, the Naval Institute has members worldwide.

Members of the Naval Institute support the education programs of the society and receive the influential monthly magazine *Proceedings* or the colorful bimonthly magazine *Naval History* and discounts on fine nautical prints and on ship and aircraft photos. They also have access to the transcripts of the Institute's Oral History Program and get discounted admission to any of the Institute-sponsored seminars offered around the country.

The Naval Institute's book-publishing program, begun in 1898 with basic guides to naval practices, has broadened its scope to include books of more general interest. Now the Naval Institute Press publishes about seventy titles each year, ranging from how-to books on boating and navigation to battle histories, biographies, ship and aircraft guides, and novels. Institute members receive significant discounts on the Press' more than eight hundred books in print.

Full-time students are eligible for special half-price membership rates. Life memberships are also available.

For a free catalog describing Naval Institute Press books currently available, and for further information about joining the U.S. Naval Institute, please write to:

Member Services
U.S. Naval Institute
291 Wood Road
Annapolis, MD 21402-5034
Telephone: (800) 233-8764
Fax: (410) 571-1703
Web address: www.usni.org